DATE DUE

LIBERATION THEOLOGIES
A Research Guide

Ronald G. Musto

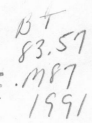
GARLAND PUBLISHING, INC. • NEW YORK & LONDON
1991

Library of Congress Cataloging-in-Publication Data

Musto, Ronald G.
　　Liberation theologies : a research guide / Ronald G. Musto.
　　　　p.　cm. — (Garland reference library of social science ; vol.
507)
　　Includes bibliographical references and indexes.
　　ISBN 0-8240-3624-7 (alk. paper)
　　1. Liberation theology—Bibliography. 2. Feminist theology—
Bibliography. I. Title. II. Series: Garland reference library of
social science ; v. 507.
Z7809.M87　1991
[BT83.57]
016.23'0046—dc20　　　　　　　　　　　　　　　　　　90-29156
　　　　　　　　　　　　　　　　　　　　　　　　　　　　　　CIP

Printed on acid-free, 250-year-life paper
Manufactured in the United States of America

To Richard and Gloria

CONTENTS

*   *
   *

PREFACE

As I write these words, the United States launches an unprecedented air and ground war upon the people of Iraq and enters its third major war in my lifetime, after countless interventions around the world. I write as the hopes and the liberating energies of the 1990s, born amid the silences and darkness of the 1980s, in the desert of hope that that decade of self and waste created, lie newborn, ready to declare a new age. Yet, it seems that the Herods of the world are always quick to discover rivals to their sterile power.

The revolutions of Eastern Europe, which overthrew decades of totalitarian rule and empty materialist dreams through nonviolence and human solidarity, have been caught in a web of empty promises of consumption and by newly reawakened nationalist, racist, and anti-Semitic demons. They – and we – are told by a steady stream of propaganda that it was not the people who took history into their own hands and became the subjects of their fate, but that these momentous changes have been the work of a few tired and cynical men at the top.

As North Americans eagerly dreamt of the benefits to the poor, the homeless, those dying of

AIDS and the reawakened diseases of the nineteenth century through the "peace dividend"; as artists and activists envisioned a society reborn from the sterility of the 1980s, a few frightened rulers and their minions plot to steal the new-born child of hope from its cradle and dash it to death in the deserts of the Middle East in a new slaughter of the innocents.

In Latin America, a decade of nonviolent struggle brought about through the patient work of conscientization in base Christian communities has brought the end to dictatorship and the national security state. Yet the Northern Nero now tells the people that their experiment with localization and self-help has been a failure and promises them that, despite their own desires, a new international "order" will reestablish the development models of the 1970s that saw unprecedented impoverishment and disparities of wealth and individual power. In the Philippines the revolution brought about by "people power" has been coopted by the very ruling class responsible for the inhuman impoverishment and now increasing oppression of that people.

While Europeans celebrate their new unity and wealth, and North Americans spend billions a month to war over oil in the desert, millions of Africans once more face certain starvation, civil war, and racial hatred.

In the Roman Catholic Church, women, gays and lesbians, and laity of every class, race, and profession are being silenced. Reforms set into motion by Vatican II are slowed or reversed and progressive church leaders humiliated, while bishops squabble over public-relations campaigns and fulminate against young women deciding the fate of their own bodies, their own lives. Meanwhile, the infant mortality rate of many U.S. communities equals that of the poorest of the Third World. While millions prepare to kill in war or to starve in famine, the pope and bishops remain silent and prefer to work out statements in committee or to press the hands of heads of state.

Why then a book on Liberation Theology at this time? Have not the events of the past year proven the naivete of such "utopian" schemes, does not the collapse of Marxism signal the end of peoples' struggles? Does not the real business of earning and keeping, winning and killing, negate any faint message of liberation that theologians, campesinos or lesbians proclaim? No. They have not and do not. For now, more than ever, especially here in North America, faced with economic depression, war, and growing disease, Jesus' message of liberation to the oppressed is needed: "for he has anointed me to bring the good news to the afflicted. He has sent me to proclaim liberty to captives, sight to the blind, to let the oppressed go free, to proclaim a year of favour from the Lord" (Luke 4:18).

*

Completing this book has been a very difficult and challenging process for me. I am trained as a historian of religious reform and of dissenting movements in the Middle Ages and Renaissance and am thus prepared for the diversity of view and the active interchange between religious, social, political, and economic forces involved in liberation theologies. I also approach the work of liberation from my perspective as a person of peace and historian of nonviolence. Yet, as a white male, I found many of the insights of Third-World theologians, people of color, and feminists challenging and unsettling. Reflection on the the anger, alienation, and immediacy of these writers' marginalization found a ready and sympathetic ear and heart in this "white ethnic," pacifist, "Catholic intellectual," non-academic and married "partner" who has consciously chosen a life of mutuality, to remain in New York City as an independent writer in the 1980s, in a racially and economically integrated community, to speak for nonviolence and a history of peace and unspoken and forgotten peoples. All these have given me some insights into marginalizations of a certain type.

The fact that I have seen "peace history" ignored or reviled by the academic establishment has fueled my own "hermeneutic suspicion" about the links between knowledge, discourse and class, race, power and gender. It has, I hope, opened me to the many forceful and valid insights of the theologians surveyed in the following pages concerning objectification, marginalization, and the need for conscientization and liberation that must come from the people themselves and not from institutions or intellectuals who would seek to expropriate their force and value.

*

The original impetus for this book came at the suggestion of Paula Ladenburg, my editor at Garland Publishing. I accepted the challenge of this project with alacrity and a great deal of naivete, for I then did not realize the immensity of the task that lay before me, nor the profundity of the theological thought that I must encounter, understand, and imperfectly encapsulate here. I thank her for that initial suggestion, continued support, and for her long patience awaiting the completion of this project through the many distractions of my life as an independent writer, partner in a small publishing company, and active member of a New York City community. My thanks are also due to Rita Quintas and to Garland's production staff for their close reading of my text. I express my gratitude to the staffs of the Columbia and Fordham University libraries, and especially to Betty Bolden of Union Theological Seminary in New York, for making their collections accessible to me. I would also like to thank John Eagleson of both Orbis Books, and then of Meyer Stone, for originally opening to me the vision of liberation theology, to Meyer Stone Books, and to René Turcott and Robert Gormley of Orbis Books for making much material – both published and in production – available to me.

Eileen Gardiner, my dear companion, has displayed remarkable patience and discretion in the midst of several book projects of her own as I distracted her with countless discussions of the theologians and theologies I have encountered in the course of this project. For those qualities, for her keen editorial sense, and for her valuable insights during our discussions of the many remarkable books and people I have encountered here I offer my continued thanks and love.

New York City
January 16, 1991

INTRODUCTION

The following is a comprehensive scholarly bibliography of published materials on the varieties of liberation theology, mostly in book form, available in English. It is intended as an introductory survey to this vast and quickly expanding field for the teacher and student of contemporary theology, of biblical hermeneutics, and to the interrelationship of politics and religion around the world. It will also serve as a comprehensive bibliography for the specialist who seeks an up-to-date research guide to such materials. The author also hopes that his approach – to define as liberation theologies many of the most important, if disparate, forms of contemporary religious thought – will highlight the basic similarities of approach, sources, and aspiration of these theologies in order to help facilitate the search for common ground and solidarity so important in the quest for integral liberation that all these movements seek. The author, who has studied long and written on the history of peacemaking in the Roman Catholic tradition, approaches his field from a broad perspective and as an outgrowth of newly reemphasized Judeo-Christian definitions of peace: as the ongoing work of justice in the world.

The materials presented here are books, predominantly from the last two decades, since about 1970, when a clearly definable liberation theology first began to emerge from Latin America. While the focus has been on the primary texts and proponents of liberation theology, at times it has been necessary to include both deep historical background and important reflections contained in articles in the scholarly or popular press, most of these in published collections. In some very few occasions an article has been included as an exception, such as review or bibliographical articles on the literature or because, quite simply, there exists no other literature on a particular topic. While this may have posed problems for some areas of study, such as feminist theology, where many of the most important works originally appeared in article form, the explosion of reprints and collections in the late 1980s has made a great deal of this material available in book form. For materials previous to that, and for these almost countless journal materials, this author has benefited greatly from already published bibliographies, which are presented at the beginning of each chapter under the heading "Bibliographies." In using these, I have tried to be as exclusive as possible: that is, I have attempted not to duplicate materials that have already appeared in published annotated bibliographies. I have, however, repeated entries in some exceptional cases, as when a book is a classic in its field and of immense influence, or when I feel that my own comments might help the overall context of a chapter. In either case I have made a cross-reference to the bibliography or bibliographies in which it first appeared.

WHAT IS LIBERATION THEOLOGY?

One might begin a definition of liberation theology with a quotation from one of the works of the Boffs[1] or from Phillip Berryman[2] and thus reflect the efforts and controverted position of important liberation theologians and their allies. Yet perhaps more useful, because closer to the roots of the movement and obviously in accord with the spirit of Vatican II, which gave birth to this theology, is the following brief statement in "Justice in the World." This comes from the 1971 Synod of Bishops, presided over by Pope Paul VI and bearing the stamp of both the pope and the majority of the world's Roman Catholic prelates.

A Word of Hope

The power of the Spirit, who raised Christ from the dead, is continuously at work in the world. Through the generous sons and daughters of the Church likewise, the People of God is present in the midst of the poor and of those who suffer oppression and persecution; it lives in its own flesh and its own heart the Passion of Christ and bears witness to his resurrection.

The entire creation has been groaning till now in an act of giving birth, as it waits for the glory of the children of God to be

revealed (cf. Rom. 8:22). Let Christians therefore be convinced that they will yet find the
fruits of their own nature and effort cleansed
of all impurities in the new earth which God
is now preparing for them, and in which
there will be the kingdom of justice and love,
a kingdom which will be fully perfected
when the Lord will come himself.

Hope in the coming kingdom is already
beginning to take root in the hearts of men
[sic]. The radical transformation of the world
in the Paschal Mystery of the Lord gives full
meaning to the efforts of men, and in
particular of the young, to lessen injustice,
violence and hatred and to advance all
together in justice, freedom, brotherhood
and love.

At the same time as it proclaims the
Gospel of the Lord, its Redeemer and
Saviour, the Church calls on all, especially
the poor, the oppressed and the afflicted, to
cooperate with God to bring about liberation
from every sin and to build a world which
will reach the fulness of creation only when
it becomes the work of man for man.[3]

One should not be surprised to find that most of
the key elements of liberation theology – which
continue to be faithfully propounded by the Boffs
and reflected by a writer like Berryman – are here in
concise nutshell. Let us therefore take a moment to
expand out the text and to emphasize key elements:

- the work of liberation is initiated and guided by the Spirit, not by human agency or motivation
- the People of God, a key concept of liberation theology in its discussion of the Church, is the human agency of such change: that is, change is brought about by the people, who *are* the church
- the People of God are the sons and *daughters* of the Church, men and women equal
- they are found especially among the poor and the oppressed
- as the People of God, men and women cooperate with God in the act of creation, of giving birth to a new heaven *and* earth
- while the kingdom will be perfected only with the coming of the Lord himself, it is a kingdom of justice and love that must be built through human efforts, and thus *in* this world
- the transformation of the world will take place both in human hearts and it will be *radical*. While the synod did not mean "radical" in the sense of a specific political program or ideology, it clearly stated that the transformation will be the work of human agency, especially of the young
- it will *specifically* lessen injustice, violence, and hatred
- it will advance *all together* in justice, freedom, brotherhood and love. It will thus be *societal* rather than individualistic, external in its form and effect, rather than internal and only "spiritual"
- it is a work of proclamation: that is, a prophetic task that speaks out the truth by proclaiming the Gospel

• it is based on the liberation theme of Christ's mission in Luke 3:18: "The spirit of the Lord is on me,/ for he has anointed me/ to bring the good news to the afflicted./ He has sent me to proclaim liberty to captives,/ sight to the blind,/ to let the oppressed go free,/ to proclaim a year of favour from the Lord.

• in fact, this Synodal passage is nothing more than an official church explication of this radical Gospel text

• such liberation is the work of these people themselves to define and then to overcome oppression

• the aim is liberation from *every* sin, both individual and internal, and social, structural, political, and economic

• such liberation is based on the Gospels

• it is essentially a religious task: it is work done in cooperation with God, not with political structures, economic systems or ideologies, not through force or blood, but "with God"

• its aim is to "build a world which will reach the fullness of creation" that is, will strive for the creation of the kingdom of God, here on earth, but in the full realization that God's kingdom is not of the world

• finally, it stresses that the true work of liberation is not through some miraculous deliverance from above, or some escape into internal piety and spiritual liberation, but will come only when it becomes "the work of man for man," the human work of liberation on behalf of fellow men and women, not in heaven, but on earth.

While the Synod of Bishops could have had only an inkling of the tremendous vitality of the theological movement to which they were about to give birth, liberation theology has, with few exceptions, lived up remarkably well to their prescription. In contrast to many of the academic theologies of the First World, liberation theology is born out of the actual experience of the people: not its professional theologians or academics but from the lives of the poor in the Third World, from the oppressed gays and women of the First, from the poor and blacks living on the fringes of prosperity in comfortable North America, from the deeply spiritual thinkers of the creation theology movement who see an intimate link between inner spirituality and the pressing needs for a new global environmental activism and nonviolent reverence for life.

In addition, this is a theology born out of the *historical* traditions of both the First and Third Worlds. (In Latin America, where liberation theology was first recognized as a distinct way of speaking about God) certain facts were decisive elements in the context of doing theology. They include long colonial dependency, economic development that favored small elites, and the emergence of the 1970s' "national security state" that attempted to protect these elites from the growing political upheaval spurred by the Cuban Revolution. Yet even a small sampling of the historical works that bear immediate relevance to liberation theology assembled in chapters 1 and 2 bear witness to the fact that liberation theology can find its roots equally in the missionary founders of Latin America as in the liberating books of the Bible. While defined and limited by their times and by their age's understanding of God, nature and society, these traditions of nurturing indigenous traditions, of offering protection and hope against the exploitation of colonial powers, and of speaking out forcefully against injustice with a clear vision of the just society are deeply embedded in the religious culture of Latin America.

On the other hand, just a cursory glance through the notes and bibliographies of the leading liberation theologians of the Third World will reveal a great erudition based not on faddish ideology or superficial synthesis of current academic research with politics but on a learned and very profound *theological* understanding of human existence that is based on Christian tradition and a close study of the Bible.

In Latin America, for example, liberation theology is the intellectual and theological expression of the deeply religious experience of poverty and oppression of the mass of the people, yet it owes much of its intellectual structure and discipline to the philosophies and theologies of twentieth-century Europe, where many of the leading liberation theologians were educated. The works of these theologians owe much to the thought of Bultmann, Metz, Moltmann, Chenu, Congar, Barthe, Heideggar, Rahner, Ladriere, Maritain, Teilhard de Chardin; as well as to the methodology of Marx and to the structuralist insights of Deridda, Foucault, or Bataille. On the whole, however, it is fair to say that we are dealing with works of *theology* that deal first with the Bible, the spiritual state of the world and its individuals, the role of God and humanity in salvation, and the entire spiritual apparatus and structure of the church, including its sacramental, liturgical, pastoral, and ecclesiological aspects and therefore with all the classic categories of traditional theology.

Thus liberation theology is not a new theology, but a new *way* of doing theology. It seeks not to displace the objects of theology, the categories just enumerated, but the subjects of that theology: that is, its principal agents are not professors in comfortable seminaries in North America or Europe, but the poor and oppressed all around the world. The role of the liberation theologian, professional, rigorously trained, yet sensitized to the revelation given the people themselves, is to help the People of God form their own theology, their own understanding of God, and to then take these insights and express them in forms that traditional theologians and members of the churches can understand. In this way theological reflection can truly appreciate the truths that God has spoken to the poor and marginalized.

Liberation theology also grows from the realization, felt most strongly in Europe at the end of World War II, that a new age had dawned that had forever divorced the world of spirit from any one political system, from any "Constantinian" sense of triumphalism – a unity of the church with the powers of the world that had brought theologians to face the reality that at best the church is "a ministry in service to the majority"[4] of the world's *un*believers.

We would, however, be offering only one part of the development of liberation theologies were we to restrict ourselves to its first impulses in Latin America. By the time a recognizable theology of liberation had appeared in Latin America in the early 1970s, there had already emerged a revolutionary form of liberation theology in both the United States and in Africa. As a result of the black consciousness and Civil Rights movements of the 1950s and 1960s in the United States and South Africa, a clearly defined black theology had offered its first essays on the spiritual meaning of the black struggle, white racism and the possibilities for reconciliation or radical transformation within their societies. While often equated with the black power movement in the United States, black theology was just that, a *theology* of liberation that reflected on politics and society but that remained essentially *theology*, a way of talking about the God of the poor and oppressed and the path to freedom.

At the same time many European theologians who had given impetus to Vatican II were also developing a form of theology that spoke of the essential connections between the political and social life of the world and the spiritual mission of the church. Their theological message had immense influence upon John XXIII's and Vatican II's message of the "opening" of the church to the world and *for* the world.

Other factors that came together in the late 1960s and early 1970s to form the theology of liberation presented below were the women's movement in the United States and Europe, the gay rights movement, and the emerging movements for democratization in the Third World, especially in the Christian communities of the Pacific Rim and in India during the late 1970s. In all three cases – if one will excuse a broad generalization – theological reflection came *after* the original social and economic insights of oppression faced by women, gays and lesbians, by the Asian poor and oppressed, and by Native and Hispanic Americans. In all these cases, however, it is important to stress that these theologies were not born of academic abstraction but were theological responses to very real contexts and situations of oppression, marginalization, and awakening consciousness for liberation.

Thus in every case the liberation theologies presented here are serious, truly religious attempts to come to terms with oppression, explore its theological meaning, value and burden, and to evolve religious ways of explaining how God can permit oppression, present the opportunity for the oppressed to realize their conditions of oppression and sin, and finally offer the theological underpinnings of hope, and faith, and love needed to overcome oppression and to convert oppressors so that the kingdom of God can be built.

THE SCOPE OF THIS WORK

This book will, therefore, include not only the classic and more recent texts of Latin American liberation theology but also works on the historical roots of this vital theology. These include the Hebrew and Christian biblical origins of liberation and studies that focus on the role of Jesus as a prophet of liberation and on his mission to raise up the marginalized and the oppressed. This will be the focus of Chapter 1.

Since contemporary liberation theologians are also currently examining the on-going tradition of liberation, Chapter 2 presents materials from the Christian tradition of the Middle Ages and early modern Europe, focusing a good deal of attention on the mendicant missionaries in Latin America during the Conquest and Colonial periods best exemplified by Bartolomé de Las Casas.

Because liberation theology is fully within the orthodox Christian tradition, Chapter 3 treats the papal, episcopal, and conciliar foundations of the theology and praxis of liberation, foundations that are stressed again and again by practicing liberation theologians. In fact, one of the key elements of liberation theology is its authors' attempt to deepen and broaden the specifically theological basis and message of these papal, conciliar and synodal letters, to examine the biblical foundations of these revolutionary documents, and to meditate profoundly on their meaning in the lives of the majority of Christians around them. The bibliography also therefore presents materials on the most important practical element of the theology: the base Christian communities that have grown all over the world.

While liberation theology is at root a Third-World theology, flowing from the praxis of Latin America, Asia and Africa, it has begun to reach out to the liberation traditions and aspirations of the First World. Chapter 4 therefore presents materials on liberation theology's impact on European thought and action. This chapter presents important European reflections on liberation theology from both sympathetic and critical schools of thought. These include Political theology, which, according to at least a few theologians, should be the inclusive category that *includes* liberation theology. In this chapter I have also chosen to present some material already covered in my annotated bibliography on peacemaking in the Catholic tradition.[5] This is a section on Danilo Dolci and his attempts to raise the consciousness and standard of living of the poor and marginalized in western Sicily. It has been, as far as I know, the only documented European program that has attempted to do what liberation theology and European Political theology claim to want to do: lead the people themselves to become the subjects of their own history and to apply the principles of the Christian tradition of social justice and non-violence to real praxis. Where Dolci differs from the liberation theologian may perhaps be clear from the entries; yet his example is too compelling to omit here.

Chapters 5 to 7 contain the heart of any discussion of liberation theology: the "Third World" theologies of Africa, Asia and Latin America. Consistent themes that emerge throughout these chapters are a deep adherence to the Gospels, the essentially theological nature of the inquiry, and yet the profound impact of the social, economic and political contexts of the Third World in doing theology. Poverty, oppression, racism, and sexism lie at the heart of any understanding of God and creation here. At the same time, these theologians are neither naive nor provincial when it comes to either their situations or the intellectual means for liberation. The books listed here are the work of highly trained and very aware professionals who have studied their own religious traditions and those of the European and North American theological schools. These are also theologians in constant communication with one another, through regional, national, international and intercontinental conferences, collections of essays, journals and teaching positions. Careful study of each and every one of these forms of liberation theology will leave the comfortable North American reader humbled by his or her own political naivete, economic self-absorption and intellectual self-satisfaction.

The collection contains materials that may surprise many North Americans: books on the various forms of liberation theology that increasingly affect Americans: not only black theology and the immediate impact of Latin American religious thought on such groups as the

Sanctuary Movement and the United Farm Workers, but also such diverse areas as the U.S. Bishops' recent pronouncements on economic and social justice, on the embattled creation spirituality movement, and on gay and lesbian liberation theology. In all these areas of religious thought one central insight is quickly coming to the fore: that the way in which North America produces, spends, defends, and thinks about its physical and spiritual life is in profound crisis – some theologians might even say in a profound state of sinfulness – and that while the insights of liberation theology cannot be imported wholesale or exploited like so many Third-World commodities, they can at least point the way toward a new way of life for us. This path is born more from a way of doing theology than from any specific theological categories or statements: for North America to regain a sense of human value in its increasingly exploitive way of life – and death – it must open itself to the insights of its own poor, exploited and marginalized minorities; it must realize that God has spoken first and most importantly to these about wealth, power, justice, and the meaning of the good life and true humanity. And after it has listened, and learned, it must make those changes of life, those conversions, that are the true point of theologies of liberation: the liberation of both oppressed and oppressors.

Finally, in Chapter 9, the bibliography includes important materials on feminist theology. In its attempts to raise consciousness, redefine structures, empower individuals from *all* forms of oppression, and realign our thinking about the sacred and the profane away from patriarchy, hierarchy and authority and toward more ancient realizations of the liberating power of spirit, equality and compassion, feminist theology may perhaps be the most inclusive of all the liberation theologies. As many of its proponents affirm, the dichotomies and alienations of the woman's life is truly the most ontologically human situation of oppression. Successfully addressing these most basic human situations may, in fact, be the final path to a total human liberation. It is for this reason that feminist theology has been the last word here.

CRITERIA FOR SELECTION

Throughout, this book attempts to focus on *theological*, though not necessarily academic, works. While certain materials included on political, social and economic structures are essential for understanding the role of praxis in this theology, primary focus is on the reflections of liberation theologians on God and creation and humanity's relation to both, to itself, to the larger history of creation and salvation and to the structures of community and worship embodied in the churches. Such an approach is not overly exclusive, nor does it avoid the political, social, economic, liturgical and sexual issues at the core of the controversy over liberation theology. For such criteria – almost by definition – include the works of Gutiérrez, Boff, Starhawk, Tutu, Sobrino, Segundo, Dussel, Cardenal, Comblin, Fox, Ruether, Russell, Cone, Daly and scores of the most important theological thinkers today.

The scope of this material is so far-flung that the reader may be tempted to ask whether I consider that there is any theology that is *not* a liberation theology. While there is certainly a huge amount of work that has been done that merits this name, and some see liberation theologies as the most important theological movement since the Protestant Reformation, it remains a theology of the margins. While it has certainly gained much attention and has influenced thinking within the bastions of First World theological seminaries to a greater or lesser degree, the observation made by Nelle Morton (see **1256**) bears considerable weight: while we may describe all these theologies as "women's," or "black," or "Asian," or "Latin American" theology; when we speak of the theology made by white males, we still tend to name it simply "Theology." Thus, while the contents of each chapter may appear fairly straightforward from the Table of Contents or the brief survey just completed, it may be useful to distinguish certain themes and directions that define a theology *of liberation*.

My first major criterion was, of course, that such works have as a central concern the emancipation of individuals from stereotype, from objectification and from social and economic oppression and marginalization of many kinds, but that, *as theology* they are also concerned with the unique place of salvation that combines this material liberation with the spiritual in a profound unity: liberation from earthly oppression as an essential element of the kingdom preached by the Judeo-Christian tradition.

A second essential aspect of a theology of liberation is that it be *of* and not *on*, that it be *by* and not *about* a group, context, or way of life. Thus I have not, for example, chosen to include all works on gays and religious traditions, or all works by women theologians, or even in many cases books *on* women, or gays, or blacks, or Latin Americans, or Native Americans. This is because many theological works seek to discuss the *problem* of homosexuality, or of women's claims for equality within the church or for full recognition of their spiritual and material equality in society at large, or to analyze the mythologies or religious practices of Native Americans. While such works might even be sympathetic, they continue to objectify the group they discuss; and to discuss them from the point of view of the sympathetic, or not, dominant group. Returning to our original definition, liberation theology, on the other hand, both reflects the aspirations of the People of God and is their own handiwork.

The third, relatively subjective, criterion distinguishes works of a theology of liberation from the disciplines that inform and support them: thus works of feminist theory may or may not also be of theology, and these in turn may or may not also be a feminist theology; works on Latin American economy may be about poverty and oppression there, and may thus be of essential background for understanding the context of liberation theology or of essential background for a theologian writing a work of liberation. Such a work, however, may also be a major contribution to liberation theology. Enrique Dussel's books of sociology, history and ethics come to mind immediately in this context.

Ultimately, of course, I had to rely upon my own informed judgments in very many cases as to which works were, indeed, liberation theology according to the criteria that I have set forth. Thus some readers will be surprised to find certain works included and others excluded.

For the most part my criteria for including a particular work within a chapter or subheading were fairly straightforward: U.S. black theology, Asian liberation theology, the works of Bartolomé de Las Casas, papal and conciliar documents as foundations for liberation theology, Vatican reactions and condemnations were all easy to identify as works, or condemnations, of liberation theology and to place them within a chapter. Difficulty arose, however, when many of the works crossed over areas of theology: black theology and African theology, or black women's theology are examples. In most cases a simple cross-reference addressed the situation of a book being relevant to more than one area of liberation theology. Only in the first chapter, "The Biblical Roots of Liberation Theology" did this approach pose difficulties. Here a distinction had to be made between liberation themes and texts in the Bible and various forms of interpretation stemming from liberation perspectives. I realize that *prima facie* this may appear epistemologically naive, but I have tried to focus

here on liberation themes as they derive from the
Bible itself, to highlight those biblical texts used as
sources for liberation theologians, and to present
those works of biblical scholarship that see the life
of Israel and then of Jesus as essentially liberation
histories.

In a very real sense, of course, all liberation
theology, in fact all real Judeo-Christian theology
worth the name, is an interpretation of the Bible.
Beyond that truth, however, my criteria for
inclusion are those hermeneutic tools that open the
Bible for us as a source of the major liberation
themes.   If this seems somewhat obtuse and
artificial, let me illustrate my point using a set of
examples drawn from various forms of feminist
theology.

Works on the Goddess, the pre-patriarchal, pre-
Judeo-Christian worship of the Earth Mother, both
historically and in the present, obviously belong to
the chapter on feminist theology and not with that
on Biblical roots. On the other hand, works on the
politics of Jesus, his life and dealings with the
women who formed his inner circle and their
religious significance for liberation themes
obviously belong in this first chapter, as would
liberation interpretations of individual books of the
Bible, such as Ephesians or Exodus. Yet a third
category, such as feminist interpretation of the
Bible, may fall in between. There are, for example
works of biblical interpretation done by well-known
liberation theologians that are not essentially works
of liberation theology. An example might be
Tolbert's *Sowing the Gospel*.[6] On the other hand,

books dealing with a feminist interpretation of the infancy narratives would seem to call for inclusion here.

An argument could also be made to include lesbian theology under feminist thought in Chapter 9, instead of under gay/lesbian theology in Chapter 8. I felt, however, that the issues of oppression and liberation for gays, especially in the reactionary atmosphere of the 1980s in the United States, warranted their inclusion under North American liberation. Here I have also made the distinction between works that discuss the history of Judeo-Christian religious and ethical attitudes towards homosexuality and the gay/lesbian in the church, which I have not included according to the criterion outlined above, and specifically gay/lesbian *theology*, which I have.

My selection is again the result of sorting through many ambiguities and nuances, but the criterion has been a theology of gayness and lesbianism that focuses on the divine in human nature, that acknowledges and attempts to free the bipolarity of human sexuality in its creative and religious sense as born from the practical experience of gays and lesbians in our culture, and then that attempts to convert these insights for both gay and lesbian liberation to the liberation of us all.

The chart on page xxxviii and its caption may, I hope, prove useful in distinguishing the works that I have chosen to include in my definition of liberation theologies and those fields and works that I considered important, or less important, as background.

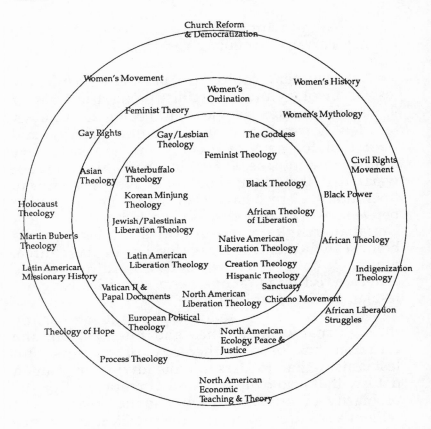

LIBERATION THEOLOGIES AND THEIR SOURCES
A CHART OF READINGS

The distance from the center of the circles indicates the degree of concentration of titles in the following bibliography, based on the immediate bearings of these topics to a true theology of liberation. Topics overlapping circles indicate that in the bibliography I have included certain books of relevance to this topic but have felt that other titles, or topics, are not as central.

The ultimate direction of this argument is, of course, an admission that in so vibrant and cross-fertilizing an area as liberation theology neat categories, while useful to the bibliographer and editor, confound the truth that all true theology, and all true liberation, enlightens and liberates us all. Many of my categorizations may not therefore do justice to the topic or the work; I am simply asking the reader's indulgence in advance for my imperfect judgments.

THE ENTRIES

The entries are arranged here by subject according to chapter, then by subheading within each broad, usually geographical, field, then alphabetically by author and title. All entries are numbered consecutively, while cross references are noted in parentheses in bold face, as for example, **(625)**. Entries in the index are likewise keyed to entry, and not page, number.

Simply browsing through these already existing works is a humbling one for the non-theologian, for, perhaps more so than in many fields in the Humanities, certainly better than in history, theologians are equipped with excellent research and bibliographical tools, both printed and electronic. Such a wealth of data has been both a blessing and a potential pitfall for an "outsider," since it indicated both a richness of materials and warning that any attempt to master *all* of these materials might indeed be fruitless to all but the few mature scholars well versed in the field. Nonetheless, having accepted this challenge, I have attempted to be as complete as possible, within the scope of the project.

As I have noted above, this bibliography is designed to give the English-speaking reader an introduction to, and a mastery of, the materials readily available. We are fortunate that so much on Latin American liberation theology has been translated into English through Orbis Books of Maryknoll, Meyer-Stone, and now other major presses, and so many other forms of liberation theologies: feminist, creation, and black are basically already available in English through presses like Crossroad/Continuum, Harper & Row, Seabury, Westminster, Fortress and Abingdon. Simply presenting *these* materials would be both a comprehensive survey and a solid introduction. In addition, journals, such as *Concilium,* which is devoted to the works of Vatican II, have published many volumes of collected essays as special issues around the central themes of liberation theology. Other journals of note include *Signs* for feminist theory, *Radical Religion, Exchange,* and others, which are listed here.

The statements of important political and theological opponents of liberation theology have also been included. Such materials will help explain the importance and the continued controversy of this vital Judeo-Christian tradition. One important area of research has not been included: unpublished dissertations specifically on liberation theology. Even a hasty glance through *Dissertation Abstracts,* now happily in electronic form, or through the catalog of Union Theological Seminary in New York City will reveal a growing flood of such dissertations. In general, one can say that they tend to focus on one aspect of liberation theology: the formal links between mostly Latin American – but sometimes African or Asian – liberation theologians and their intellectual fore-bearers among the academic theologians of Europe. Such an approach, while useful, tends to implicitly interpret liberation theologies in a way very different from what their major proponents see them to be: not as reflections of praxis, and the praxis of a suffering oppressed majority at that; but as a stage in the intellectual history of Europe, with an emphasis on orthodoxy as a measure of success or failure (closeness to European models), benefit or danger (amount of Marxist influence).

CRITICISM AND OUTLOOK

This last form of analysis, whether positive or negative, betrays an important North American concern: the impact of liberation theology upon economic and social structures in the Third World and here at home. Despite the materialist obsessions of many of liberation theology's critics who see it as an essentially economic and political form of discourse, one must stress at the outset that the primary "economics" in these works remains the economics of salvation in the classic theological sense. Yet many critics in the First World, especially those of North America with links to the U.S. administrations of the 1980s, have tended to focus on liberation theology's Latin American form, and on that form's supposed Marxism.

Liberation theologians, especially in Latin America, have, in fact, made Marxism an important, while not central, element of their theological discourse. This derives from several factors: the realities of poverty and oppression, linked with the right-wing military dictatorships of Latin America during the 1970s, the popularity of Marxist theory in historical and sociological analysis in Latin American intellectual circles, and the very real hopes that the Marxist revolution in Cuba in the 1960s seemed to offer for Latin America's impoverished peoples.

Any theologian writing in Latin America who was at all aware of his or her context therefore would feel it necessary to make some recognition of Marxism: whether to condemn it (as many on the right did), to study and use its influential analytic tools (as many in Latin America, Europe, and North America have done), or to embrace the Marxist revolution and equate it with the mission of the church (as some, very few, did).

Many of the most important liberation theologians seem to fall into the second category, using Marxist forms of analysis as only *one* methodological tool for describing structures of oppression and alienation, of marginalization and domination. The very fact that we use these terms, in fact, highlights the problem, because Marx and his school originated our discussions of these very categories. In fact, in calling into question the obvious references to Marxian class and economic analysis, one may as well call into question the very foundations of modern sociology, history, or economics for borrowing or criticizing Marxist methodologies and categories. Marx, like Max Weber, Freud, or Einstein (as much as this might still discomfort some high Catholic church officials and U.S. conservatives) is part of the modern psyche and intellectual vocabulary. To deny his importance would be the equivalent of denying the discovery of nuclear fission.

Yet, as an attorney recently told me with some surprise after studying Gutiérrez' *A Theology of Liberation*, a careful reading reveals far less Marx than Jesus, far more strict, and classic, theology than attempts to analyze social or economic problems. Despite this, however, the late 1970s and 1980s saw a steady stream of condemnations of "Marxist" liberation theologians from U.S. neoconservative intellectuals; a constant reiteration of the tragic story of Camilo Torres, the guerilla priest killed with revolutionaries in Colombia in 1966, tracts that seem to claim that this priest's hasty political pamphlets and diary were the root and core of liberation theology; or that the polemical statements about Christianity by Nicaragua's former minister of Defense, Tomas Borges, were to be seriously considered the soul of liberation theology.

Perhaps not coincidentally, the 1980 document prepared by the Santa Fe Group, neoconservative think-tankers, stressed that one of the best ways to counter the growing religious influence of Latin America's liberation theologians on political and economic life was to press a consistent campaign to discredit them through several clearly defined means. These included the maligning and belittling of the concerns of the theologians, attacking the motives and qualifications of the theologians themselves, and finally incessantly associating them with Marxist political and intellectual influences and thus with the Soviet bloc. A look at many of the materials, and their consistent themes, presented in Chapter 8 under the section, "The Northern Reactionaries," will bear this out.[7]

In this warfare the "neocons" had a straunch and important ally. Pope John Paul II and his chief agent, Joseph Cardinal Ratzinger, head of the revived Holy Office of the Inquisition, have relentlessly pursued what they also considered the Marxist taint of any liberation theology not controlled, or sanctioned, by the Vatican. Using a "Polish" model of church government that defines the "People of God" as the loyal troops who form their battalions behind the leadership of the pope in his declared wars against godless communist regimes, the Vatican has forced confrontation, humiliation, and occasionally (admittedly) some clarification of the lives and intellectual positions of liberation theologians. Yet, despite the onslaughts of the 1980s, liberation theology has survived, matured and spread.

*

Times, and political winds, change. In fact, the disappearance of communist regimes and ideological influence from most parts of the traditionally Judeo-Christian world over the past two years, far from comforting the opponents of liberation theology, will probably clear the air of the specters of fear and ideological stereotype; it will also allow a less passionate examination of the true meaning of liberation theology. For the demise of communism, despite the *a priori* conclusions of conservative North American and European circles, does not mean the decline of liberation theology.

The reasons for this are several. One is that at its heart liberation theology appeals to an other world: not an otherworldly appeal, but to a world beyond the grasp of political systems, consumer or command societies, or their mass media. The creators and audience of liberation theology are the solitary reader and the thought and action of small groups of individuals. In keeping with the truest meaning of the Gospels these have come together to discuss a biblical passage or to address themselves, in the light of a biblical text, to some small, very local problem and condition that would appear dull and unimportant to the electronic world of the multinational corporations who define what "discourse" is in the late twentieth century. They will, instead, take up the issue of a drainage ditch, or an unfair landlord or farm manager far from the centers of power and influence, completely unknown and ignored by the world of print or voice or image that spell power and influence.

Hence, while its reach seems minimal, while the attention of the First World wavers as soon as a major thinker has returned from Rome exonerated or humbled, the power of liberation theology is immense and its scope incomprehensibly broad because it is based on the long-term and the *real*, not the flickering electronic image that grasps, sways, and disappears almost instantaneously.

This continuing influence is, in fact, one of the primary motivations for compiling this volume, for while much has been written and recorded on Third World theologies, the influence of liberation theology on our own North American culture and society is only now beginning to be felt and will have immense and widespread impact in the years and decades ahead. This will be due both to the rising influence of the "minorities" within the United States who will soon constitute the majority of U.S. citizens, and because North American churchpeople and churches are becoming increasingly aware that the problems of North American society and the continued relevance of their religions will be greatly affected by the currents emerging from Third World theologies.

This historian might draw a concluding analogy, in fact, to the influence exerted by the "marginal" religions of the late Roman Empire – those of the remote Eastern provinces especially – on the fossilized religious life of the center. As the official state cults and their tired rituals and meaningless doctrines failed to attract attention or adherents, the spiritual yearnings of the people were satisfied increasingly by those religions of the marginalized themselves, among them Mithraism, the cult of Isis and Osiris, Judaism and, last of all, that most radical and naive cult: Christianity itself.

NOTES

1. In particular the helpful book, by Leonardo Boff and Clodovis Boff, *Introducing Liberation Theology* (Maryknoll, NY: Orbis Books, 1988). See **425**.
2. *Liberation Theology. The Essential Facts About the Revolutonary Movement in Latin America and Beyond* (New York: Random House; Oak Park, IL: Meyer Stone, 1987). See **421**.
3. From David J. O'Brien and Thomas A. Shannon, *Renewing the Earth. Catholic Documents on Peace, Justice and Liberation* (New York: Doubleday, 1977), p. 408. See **105**.
4. Ibid., p. 40.
5. Ronald G. Musto, *The Peace Tradition in the Catholic Church. An Annotated Bibliography* (New York: Garland Publishing, 1987), pp. 364-77.
6. Mary Ann Tolbert, *Sowing the Gospel. Mark's World in Literary-Historical Perspective.* Minneapolis, MN: Fortress Press, 1989.
7. See entries **765-797** below.

Liberation Theologies

Chapter 1: *The Biblical Roots of Liberation Theology*

The Sources

1   Bloom, Harold. *The Book of J.* David Rosenberg, trans. New York: Grove Weidenfeld, 1990.

   Argues that the author of the oldest biblical texts, parts of Genesis, Exodus and Numbers, all written c.950 BCE, was a woman, "J," and that her portrayal of Yahweh is that of a childish male. Beautiful prose and poetry translations that will long be as controversial as the contention that their author reflects the deep wisdom and sensibility of the female who understood both creation *and* liberation.

2   Carmody, Denise Lardner. *Biblical Woman. Contemporary Reflections on Scriptural Texts.* New York: Crossroad, 1988.

   Discusses a collection of texts from both Old and New Testament with the proposition that a study of these texts can be a liberating experience. The book situates texts both historically and contextually and suggests modern implications. In the Old Testament it deals with legal status, the family, women's role in Israelite society, the biblical image of the ideal woman, and the feminine aspect of wisdom. In the New Testament it treats such themes as women as disciples of Jesus and a reinterpretation of many key texts long seen through patriarchal eyes.

3   Cohn-Sherbok, Dan. *On Earth As It Is in Heaven. Jews,
         Christians, and Liberation Theology.* Maryknoll,
         NY: Orbis Books, 1987.

         Examines the Jewish prophetic tradition with a
         close eye toward demonstrating the common heritage
         of the Judeo-Christian theology of liberation.

4   Croatto, José Severino. *Exodus. A Hermeneutics of
         Freedom.* Salvator Attanasio, trans. Maryknoll,
         NY: Orbis Books, 1981.

         His purpose is to add epistemological considera-
         tions to the theology of liberation: how was the
         kerygma of liberation treated in the Bible? Croatto
         finds that an emphasis on captivity is an essential
         antidote to the triumphalism that reemerges in an
         emphasis on liberation, even though liberation is the
         key to a new theology. Such a theology, however,
         must be one of process: the struggle from captivity,
         rather than one of achieved liberty. Chapters deal
         with hermeneutics, Exodus, the Prophets, Genesis as a
         liberation text, and the prophetic in Jesus and in Paul.

5   Dawes, Gilbert. *Let My People Go. A Study Old and
         New; and The Exodus. A Bible Study.* Detroit, MI:
         CFS National Office, 1980.

         Dawes is a Methodist minister who analyzes
         Moses, Leviticus, and Jesus in terms of modern class
         struggle, giving special emphasis to the cause of
         liberation in the U.S. today.

6   Gottwald, Norman K., ed. *The Bible and Liberation.
         Political and Social Hermeneutics.* Maryknoll, NY:
         Orbis Books, 1983.

This is an exhaustive collection of essays by biblical scholars of the "social scientific" and materialist schools. Includes studies of social class, the role of women, political structures, and the Bible in political, theological, and Marxist interpretations. Contributors include Gottwald, Carlos Mesters, Phyllis Bird, Carol Meyers, E. Schüssler Fiorenza, Arthur McGovern, Juan Luis Segundo, Alfredo Fierro, Sergio Rostagno, and David Lochhead, among others.

7   —. *Tribes of Yahweh. A Sociology of the Religion of Liberation Israel, 1250-1050 B.C.E.* Maryknoll, NY: Orbis Books, 1979.

Essential reading on how religion was formed by, and lived in, the daily life of a people. Exhaustive analysis of the literary and historical sources, and the socioeconomic and political structures of Israel from a structuralist point of view. Gottwald sees Yahwism as a new system of social egalitarianism that brings the themes of liberation to the forefront. A good example of the cultural materialist school, and excellent background.

8   Lochhead, David M. *The Liberation of the Bible.* Saint Louis, MO: World Student Christian Federation of America, 1979.

A popularizing introduction to the hermeneutics of a materialist interpretation. The author insists that the Bible must be read with an emphasis on its context. Liberation theology is the only vigorous program that relates faith to the context of life.
Lochhead concludes that his book is not a theology of liberation but a prolegomenon to a Canadian

theology of liberation that takes into account not the
marginalization of the majority of North Americans,
but our very affluence. While we free the Bible itself
from an ideology that seeks to comfort the wealthy
and powerful, we will discover a praxis that allows
us to side with the poor and the oppressed.

9   Lohfink, Norbert. *Option for the Poor. The Basic
         Principle of Liberation Theology in the Light of the
         Bible.* Linda M. Maloney, trans. Berkeley, CA:
         BIBAL Press, 1987.

         This brief overview analyzes our understanding of
         God and the poor both in the ancient Near East and
         today. Topics include Exodus in its historical context,
         the Exodus theology of Israel's birth, and the "Poor of
         Yahweh" in the New Testament.

10   Moltmann-Wendel, Elisabeth. *The Women Around
         Jesus.* John Bowden, trans. London: SCM, 1982.

         This is a brief, but excellent, study both of the
         larger issues involved in the feminist study of the
         Bible and in a reexamination of several long-neglected
         or misinterpreted women around Jesus. The author
         states that the impetus for her work came from a
         Bible study group conducted by none other than
         Ernesto Cardenal at Solintiname, where the poet,
         liberation theologian and minister of education for
         Nicaragua actually played down the importance of
         women in the Jesus movement in response to a peasant
         woman's discovery of their power and strength.
            Moltmann-Wendel introduces her study by noting
         that such attitudes have long been with the church,
         and that much of the evidence for the role of women
         in the Jesus movement and in the early church was

deliberately destroyed in the first centuries, especially during the struggle against Gnosticism, in which
women played an important role. She then briefly
reviews the patriarchal tradition within the church
and the role of men in composing and selecting the
canon of the Bible. Much of the current struggle to
regain insight into women's role must therefore shed
this tradition and exercise a theological imagination
that will bring women back in touch with these roots.

Several examples of women who play major parts
in the biblical narrative of Jesus and his mission are
presented. Each is a fascinating study in itself, rich
in thoughtful reflection and information on the redis-
covered tradition of veneration that these women
enjoyed into the Middle Ages and as late as the
Baroque, especially in art. Figures include Martha
and Mary, Mary of Bethany, Mary Magdalene, the
unknown women who anointed Jesus, the group of
women at Jesus' passion in Mark, the activist mothers
in Matthew, and the figure of Joanna in Luke.

11   Pixley, George V. *God's Kingdom. A Guide for Biblical
      Study.* Donald D. Walsh, trans. Maryknoll, NY:
      Orbis Books, 1981.

A hermeneutic of the "kingdom" in the New
Testament as infused with Old Testament meanings.
In contrast to modern interpretations of the "kingdom"
as an otherworldly reality, Pixley offers a new
reading in light of the option for the poor. Topics
include cultic celebrations of Yahweh as king, the
relationship between the tribes of Israel and
Yahweh's kingdom, the "kingdom" as an ideology of
the Israelite state, as a foundation of the hieratic
society of first-century Palestine, and Jesus' inter-
nalization of God's kingdom to emphasize equality,

justice, and abundance, all of which are meanings of liberation.

In the modern world religion has often masked forms of domination. Both Catholic and Protestant churches in the U.S. have used the theology of the kingdom as an ally of imperialism. The new theology must therefore criticize theologies created for a dominating church. Only experience will tell whether the Gospel will indeed be good news for the poor and the oppressed.

12   —. *On Exodus. A Liberation Perspective.* Maryknoll, NY: Orbis Books, 1987.

Provides a new translation and a new reading of the book from the perspective of Latin American liberation theology.

13   Schaberg, Jane. *The Illegitimacy of Jesus. A Feminist Theological Interpretation of the Infancy Narratives.* San Francisco: Harper & Row, 1987.

A close reading of the birth and infancy narratives in Matthew and Luke reveals not a mythologizing of divine miraculous birth, but the reality of illegitimate birth on the margins of society, a marginalization that reveals God's true nature and intent. Only by recognizing the dignity and power of those on the margins – the world's outcasts and "sinners" – can we understand the nature of Jesus' mission and why he is the Son of God.

14   Schillebeeckx, Edward and Bas van Iersel, eds. *Jesus Christ and Human Freedom.* New York: Herder & Herder, 1974.

Freedom and liberation as essential themes of Christology in essays by Duquoc, Neuner, Lash, Schillebeeckx and others. Includes texts by Gutiérrez, Scannone and Adler.

15   Swidler, Leonard. *Biblical Affirmations of Woman.* Philadelphia: Westminster Press, 1979.

The author's goal is to search out biblical texts and traditions that bear positive images of women, as opposed to a critique of biblical texts that further the tradition of misogyny. Chapters deal with the feminine imagery of God in the biblical and post-biblical periods, positive and negative portrayals of women in the Hebrew Bible and Jewish tradition, and women in the New Testament and Christian tradition.

16   Tetlow, Elisabeth Meier, *Women and Ministry in the New Testament. Called to Serve.* 2d ed. Lanham, MD: University Press of America, 1985.

The present exclusion of women from the ministry is based on a misinterpretation of the role of women in the Jesus movement and in the first century. Tetlow uses the results of current biblical scholarship to examine the social and religious background and the meaning of ministry.

Chapters examine the status of women in Greek, Roman and Jewish societies, the biblical foundations of ministry, female ministry in the New Testament and early church. She concludes that Jesus called both men and women to the ministry and that first-century practice followed him in this. Good bibliography, mostly on ministry.

17   de Villiers, Pieter G. R. *Liberation Theology and the
        Bible.* Pretoria: University of South Africa, 1987.

        Essays by M. B. G. Motlhabi, F. E. Deist, J. H. Le
        Roux, and de Villiers on liberation theology, Marxism
        and the Bible, and readings of Isaiah and the Gospels
        from a liberation perspective.

18   Walzer, Michael. *Exodus and Revolution.* New York:
        Basic Books, 1985.

        "Revolution" here means "this-worldly redemp-
        tion, liberation, revolution." Walzer's insight into
        the revolutionary nature of Israel's deliverance from
        Egypt in Exodus derives from his experience of the
        Black civil-rights movement of the 1960s, where
        Exodus became the central religious text. The text
        has long been of great potency for liberation theology.

The Politics of the Gospels

19   Bammel, Ernst, and C. F. D. Moule, eds. *Jesus and the
        Politics of His Day.* New York: Cambridge Univer-
        sity Press, 1985.

        A collection of essays that sets out to examine the
        thesis that Jesus was somehow allied with the
        Zealot movement of armed resistance to Rome. Topics
        discussed range from Jesus' relations to the Zealots,
        his religious opposition to establishment Judaism, the
        sources for the trial of Christ, the revolt of 70 CE in
        Christian tradition, Jesus' reputation as a brigand in
        the anti-Christian polemics of the pagans, the
        question of the tribute coin, Jesus' claim to bring "no
        peace but a sword," the question of the two swords
        brought by the Apostles just before his arrest, the

political charges against Jesus, and his trial. The overriding conclusion of the collection is that Jesus was announcing a new kingdom that went beyond political aims but that inevitably brought him and his followers into conflict with the established order. Well annotated with an excellent index to biblical citations.

20   Belo, Fernando. *A Materialist Reading of the Gospel of Mark.* Maryknoll, NY: Orbis Books, 1981.

This is the fundamental text of materialist readings of the Bible. By "materialist" the author does not mean the opposite of "spiritual," but "structuralist," the socioeconomic, political and cultural background of the biblical narrative and its text. Belo was self-admittedly heavily influenced by the Parisian structuralists: Althuser, Barthes, Foucault, Bataille, and Deridda, among others.

While his work shares much of the concerns of the liberation theologians of the Third World – that theology must be based on the practical reality of people's lives – the lives he bases his work on are those of the intellectual elites of the First World. This is biblical theology from the top down, not the bottom up. Despite its insistence that it is a book for "subtle subversions and transformations," it remains a heady work of the First World that, like its European colonial antecedents, seeks to coopt and control the creations born out of the spiritual and intellectual resources of the Third World.

Belo's work has opened up discussion of the scriptures to the considerations and concerns of class, power structures, forms of control and liberation; yet it is more important as an intellectual analog to liberation theology than an essential component of the movement.

21   Cardenas Pallares, José. *A Poor Man Called Jesus. Reflections on the Gospel of Mark.* Robert R. Barr, trans. Maryknoll, NY: Orbis Books, 1986.

This careful textual analysis reveals a Jesus whose life was an option for the poor and the marginalized.

22   Cassidy, Richard J. *Jesus, Politics and Society. A Study of Luke's Gospel.* Maryknoll, NY: Orbis Books, 1983.

While Jesus and the Zealots were on opposite poles of the world of action and ideas, Jesus' teachings were still powerfully revolutionary, and he was considered dangerous to the Roman Empire. Cassidy examines Luke as a historian, Jesus' social teachings, his attitudes toward political rulers, his trial and execution, the political situation in Israel at the time, social and economic factors, and the various political factions vying for supremacy within Judaism. Well annotated, excellent bibliography.

23   —, and Philip Scharper, eds. *Political Issues in Luke-Acts.* Maryknoll, NY: Orbis Books, 1983.

Essays on politics and society as they existed in Jesus' time. This means that the secular notion of politics as divorced from religious issues bears no meaning in this context. The themes discussed therefore include Jesus' new meaning of peace, the issue of tribute to Caesar, reciprocity in the ancient world, the status of women, reconciliation and forgiveness, martyrdom, the innocence of Jesus, the blame for Jesus' execution, and an analysis of Luke's audience.

24   Donders, Joseph G. *Reflections on the Gospels.* Maryknoll, NY: Orbis Books, 1980-87.

Open-verse readings from the Gospels for the liturgical calendar, stressing Jesus and those around him as human, poor, suffering, and searching for liberation. Includes:

25   *Hope Drawing Near...C Cycle.* 1985.

26   *Jesus, Heaven and Earth...A Cycle.* 1980.

27   *The Jesus Option...S Cycle.* 1982.

28   *Liberation, The Jesus Mode...B-Cycle.* 1987.

29   Echegaray, Hugo. *The Practice of Jesus.* Matthew J. O'Connell, trans. Maryknoll, NY: Orbis Books, 1984.

Focuses on what in the fourteenth century was hotly debated as the question of the "poverty of Christ and the Apostles." The comparison is apt, for the Franciscans of the Middle Ages were as deeply committed to bringing peace and justice to the oppressed and marginalized of the world as are today's liberation theologians. Echegaray examines the life of Jesus in the Gospels and his option for the poor and attempts to analyze what poverty – material, social, and spiritual – means and how it can be applied today.

30   Esler, Philip Francis. *Community and Gospel in Luke-
       Acts. The Social and Political Motivations of Lucan
       Theology.* New York: Cambridge University Press,
       1987.

       Topics include the socio-redaction criticism of
       Luke-Acts and objections to this form of interpretation;
       an analysis of the community of Luke's audience and
       Luke's method of addressing them, the issue of the
       Jesus movement as a sectarian one in Judaism and its
       strategies, the theme of "table fellowship" as a
       breaking down the walls between Jews and Gentiles
       among the first Christians, the issue of the Law, the
       prominence of the Temple in Luke-Acts, and the
       themes of poor and rich, including Luke's theology of
       the poor, which like liberation theology stressed a
       this-worldly – as well as other-worldly – dimension
       to salvation.   Finally, the author addresses the
       themes of Rome and the political dimension in Luke-
       Acts.

31   Fierro, Alfredo Bardaji. *The Militant Gospel. An
       Analysis of Contemporary Political Theologies.*
       Maryknoll, NY: Orbis Books; London: SCM Press,
       1977.

       Fierro's work is a direct challenge to that of Belo
       (20). He reviews the several varieties of contempor-
       ary theology that have a social militancy, including,
       in Chapter 7, forms of liberation theology, from a de-
       cidedly European point of view. Extensive
       bibliography.

32   Hellwig, Monika. *Jesus, the Compassion of God. New
       Perspectives on the Tradition of Christianity.*
       Wilmington, DE: M. Glazier, 1983.

The book's purpose is to approach Christology and the preaching of Jesus from the questions raised by liberation theology and liberation movements; and soteriology is the key to her Christology. Discusses the tasks of Christology, the process of a constructive Christology, and what the believer takes Christ to be in a pluralistic world. The book also attempts to demonstrate how liberation may be understood in each of the great world religious traditions: detachment and liberation (Buddhism), law and liberation (Judaism and Islam), redemption and liberation (Marxism), nonviolence and salvation (Jesus and Gandhi).

33 Hendrickx, Herman. *Peace, Anyone? Biblical Reflections on Peace and Violence.* Quezon City, Philippines: Claretian Publications, 1988.

More than just absence of war, biblical concepts of peace are essentially those of justice and nonviolence on a personal and societal level: they seek to overcome the exploitation of the weaker by the stronger. This book focuses on the axis where peace issues merge with those of justice and thus contains important theoretical background for the theology of liberation.

34 —. *Social Justice in the Bible.* Quezon City, Philippines: Claretian Publications, 1985.

Traces the roots of social justice in Mesopotamia and Egypt, in Israelite history, and in the Hebrew Bible through the Torah, Prophets and Wisdom literature. Then traces the concept in the Gospels, Acts and James. Good background.

35   Herzog, Frederick. *Liberation Theology. Liberation in the Light of the Fourth Gospel.* New York: Seabury, 1972.

Herzog's task is to attempt a new "black theology" for the white middle class of America based on John's Gospel, for the fourth Gospel provides a key toward understanding liberation in history. This theology is an option out of the "death of God" that still preoccupies the white middle class and its church, in stark contrast to the God of liberation that gives hope to the wretched of the earth.

Liberal theology, Herzog contends, only reinforces the consumerist focus on the self, a private self that is a luxury of the leisure class. Thus liberal theology's focus continues to be religion's adjustment to things as they are. Liberation theology, on the other hand, focuses on Christ, but within time and place.

John's Gospel, Herzog finds, is the most coherent presentation of Jesus as the liberator of the oppressed. It is a gospel deeply rooted in the Jewish covenant community, *not* as is so often claimed of John, an otherworldly, mystical gospel but one of prophetic protest against the oppressive forces within religion and society. Herzog thus invites us to a new reading of John, not verse for verse, but according to the major themes of the gospel. These include an analysis of God (John 1:1-18), the Liberator (1:19-7:53), humanity (8:1-12:50), the liberation church and the counter-church (13:1-17:26), and the liberated method (18:1-21:25).

36   Horsley, Richard A. *The Liberation of Christmas. The Infancy Narratives in Social Context.* New York: Crossroad, 1989.

This is an excellent example of liberation theology from a First-World perspective, for it stems from the experience and concerns of a largely middle class, North American audience. Horsley begins with the fundamental reality of North American consumerism and waste, especially as it centers around the celebration of Christmas. While the U.S. consumes 70% of the world's resources annually, 40% of this consumption occurs during the Christmas buying season: thus nearly 30% of the world's resources are consumed on the North American celebration of "Christmas."

Horsley then places Christmas squarely in the center of a sentimentalized, yet thoroughly materialist civil religion, where the consumption and ownership of goods is *the* North American belief system. Like liberation theologians all over the world, Horsley explains that, despite the best efforts of the priests of this civil religion to distinguish economics and politics from religion, Christmas, and the religious significance that it contains, cannot be separated from economics and how we live. It is not a choice of religion or economics, he stresses, but of styles of life that revere or that destroy life and the resources of the planet and its oppressed peoples. His book is, therefore, an attempt to get back to the Biblical meaning of the Christmas and infancy narratives: to set them within a very specific socioeconomic and political context and from this analysis to draw some conclusions for our own situation both in the United States and in areas of the world where U.S. policy results in the misery and oppression of the majority of the people.

Topics include the roles of kingdoms and empires in the birth stories: what did Caesar and Herod represent in forms of tyranny and exploitation, who

were the Magi and what was their prophetic and
messianic role; who were the Jewish people, what
was the condition of their piety, and what does
Christ's birth in a stable, on the margins of society,
mean for that society; what were the forms of popular resistance to Rome, the role of women in the
infancy narratives and the Jesus movement, the challenges to patriarchy and the power of the priestly
class that they represented; who were the shepherds
and what was their sociological and theological
meaning?

Far from denuding the birth and infancy narratives of their charm and magic, Horsley recaptures
it for a society glutted on acquisition. His analyses of
the three songs of liberation sung by Mary (the
Magnificat), by Zechariah, and by Simeon reveal the
power, mystery and joy in liberation brought by
Christ's coming; since Jesus' birth was an event of
political liberation, as this close reading of the texts
makes clear.

Horsley concludes with some parallels to the
political theology of the seventeenth-century Puritans
in New England, and to the peasants of Solintiname
in Nicaragua in the 1970s and 80s. The book ends
with a review and rejection of the nineteenth century's attempt to mythologize the birth and infancy
narratives by placing them in the tradition of the
"hero birth."

37   Jervell, Jacob. *Luke and the People of God. A New Look
      at Luke-Acts*. Minneapolis, MN: Augsburg Press,
      1972.

      Not seen.

38   Kappen, Sebastian. *Jesus and Freedom*. Maryknoll,
        NY: Orbis Books, 1977.

        Kappen writes for a young audience in India, using
        a radical adherence to Jesus' message to critique
        contemporary Christian practice. There exists, he
        contends, a stark contrast between the practice of Jesus
        and his disciples and that of the institutional church.
        In chapters 1 and 2 he relates the biblical Jesus to the
        life of the poor in today's India; while in chapters 3
        to 9 he addresses key biblical texts that prophesy a
        "new humanity."

39   Myers, Ched. *Binding the Strong Man. A Political
        Reading of Mark's Story of Jesus*. Maryknoll, NY:
        Orbis Books, 1989.

        This book has been widely acknowledged as one
        of the most important works of biblical interpretation
        in recent years. It sets Jesus' mission firmly within
        the context of the Roman occupation of Palestine, the
        oppression of the Jewish people, and the attempts by
        some of Jesus' contemporaries to liberate their people
        by violent means. Employs a variety of critical tools
        that go beyond traditional biblical studies.

40   Niebuhr, Reinhold. *Moral Man and Immoral Society*.
        New York: Charles Scribner's, 1960.

        The classic statement of the position that the
        individual Christian's morality and the Gospel call
        to perfection has nothing to do with the morality of
        politics or the secular world, and that the Christian
        message is at heart nonpolitical. A major objection to
        any definition of theology as active and engaged
        with social justice.

41   Rensberger, David K. *Johannine Faith and Liberating
        Community.* Philadelphia: Westminster Press,
        1988.

        A refreshing shift away from interpretation of
        John as the "spiritual" Gospel to a close study of the
        Johannine community and the socio-political meaning
        of the text: the conflict with the Synagogue's
        attempts to hereticize and marginalize the nascent
        Christian movement within its midst after the
        destruction of Jerusalem in 70 CE.
        Nicodemus and the blind man are key figures to
        this interpretation: both in the obvious tension
        involved in a "Nicodemian" attempt to remain
        within an orthodox context and in the sense of the
        rich man's solidarity with the poor. Rather than
        being indifferent to the realm of "politics," John was
        fully aware of the predicament of the Pharisees and
        their collaboration with the Roman occupiers and the
        rival claim of Jesus made during his trial.
        Rensberger concludes with a study of John and the
        roots of liberation theology. John's Christology, he
        contends, is not other-worldly but clearly for the
        oppressed. The love ethic is a strong indication that
        Jesus shared the sense of alienation and struggle
        against the world's powers that marks the lives of
        the marginalized. Good bibliography.

42   Schottroff, Luise, and Wolfgang Stegemann. *Jesus and
        the Hope of the Poor.* Matthew J. O'Connell, trans.
        Maryknoll, NY: Orbis Books, 1986.

        A collection of essays by such biblical materi-
        alists as Kuno Füssel, Jürgen Keglen, Dorothee Sölle,
        and Luise Schottroff. The church's option for the poor

today occasions this rereading of the Gospels and a new understanding of Jesus' mission. A good example of how the First-World materialist school of theology derives many of the same insights as that of Third-World liberation theologians. Despite these insights, however, such theology is born out of European theology departments, not from the lives of the poor. It is academically "in solidarity" with a radical option but offers little of real substance for a First-World audience except informed sympathy. For an excellent example of how First-World theology might actually lead to liberation of First-World Christians see **36.**

43   Schottroff, Willy, and Wolfgang Stegemann, eds. *God of the Lowly. Socio-Historical Interpretations of the Bible.* Matthew J. O'Connell, trans. Maryknoll, NY: Orbis Books, 1984.

This collection of essays, largely from Europe's materialist school of biblical studies, emphasizes the context of biblical revelation: the social, economic and political setting of God's message of liberation and redemption. In this these essays parallel the efforts by liberation theologians to set their God-talk amid the realities of poverty and oppression of today's Third World, yet without the foundation in existential reality.

Topics include the historical Jesus and his followers among the outcasts of the earth: the tax collectors, prostitutes, beggars, sinners, and ill. A discussion on the historical evolution of the problem of voluntary poverty of Jesus and the disciples strikes the reader as archly academic in light of the quite involuntary poverty of the mass of the world's

population today and the real liberation theology
that has risen from it.

44   Stegemann, Wolfgang. *The Gospel and the Poor.*
        Philadelphia: Fortress Press, 1984.

        This book results from the author's interest in
        developing a "theology of the poor." It discusses the
        poor in the Gospels, the meaning of poverty and the
        poor in that context, the New Testament's confronta-
        tion with poverty, in the Jesus movement, its meaning
        for Christian discipleship within the Roman Empire
        and its social ethos, within the developing class
        structure of the Christian church, and in terms of our
        own affluence.

45   Topel, L. John. *The Way to Peace. Liberation Through
        the Bible.* Maryknoll, NY: Orbis Books, 1979.

        An introduction to the biblical roots of the Judeo-
        Christian response to oppression and injustice. Topics
        include the roots of liberation theology, just govern-
        ment, law and society, the biblical accounts of the
        origins of sin, the call to justice, the kingdom, the
        personal liberation preached by Paul, and Christian
        responsibility in light of the Sermon on the Mount.

46   Yoder, John. *The Politics of Jesus. Vicit Agnus Noster.*
        Grand Rapids, MI: W.B. Eerdmans, 1972.

        Concentrates on Jesus' peace message, but concludes
        with an interesting discussion on the role of the lamb
        in the Apocalypse and the place of suffering, sacri-
        fice, and martyrdom in Christian doctrine. Suffering,
        Yoder contends, is not noble in itself, but is the price
        that the peacemaker must be willing to pay for

following Jesus in the world. Nonviolence is thus a revolutionary position, for it rejects power relationships and even the temptation to take power to relieve oppression. The politics of Jesus are thus the rejection of self-righteousness, even of the nonviolent variety and the acceptance of the powerlessness that the poor and the oppressed live with. Good background for the political stance of liberation theology.

The Epistles and Apocalypse

47   Cassidy, Richard J. *Society and Politics in the Acts of the Apostles.* Maryknoll, NY: Orbis Books, 1987.

Based on a new reading that demonstrates how the early church can be an effective model for ethics and social action today. Chapters deal with the portrayal of Jesus and Rome in Luke, the social movement of the Apostles in Jerusalem, the politics of the Jerusalem community, the social status of Paul and his opposition from both non-Romans and the Roman authorities, and Jesus' disciples and their relationship to Roman rule.

48   Maynard-Reid, Pedrito U. *Poverty and Wealth in James.* Maryknoll, NY: Orbis Books, 1987.

The impulse for this study is the new sociological exegesis of the Bible, but one based on a study of the documents. The author examines the social stratification of the first century CE, the poor and the rich in Jewish and Christian literature, James' attitude toward the rich, the merchant class, the farmers and the poor to demonstrate that James' Epistles clearly demonstrate an option for the poor. This is a good example of the theological approach to scripture that is absorbing much of the lessons of liberation theology: that real conditions and people must be at the heart of religious talk and life.

49   Russell, Letty M. *Imitators of God. A Study Book on Ephesians.* United Methodist Church, 1984.

   Not seen.

*   *

*

Chapter 2: *The Early Tradition of Liberation*

The Early Church to the Renaissance

50   Boff, Leonardo. *Saint Francis. A Model for Human Liberation.* John W. Diercksmeier, trans. New York: Crossroad/Continuum, 1982.

Not so much a biography as a spiritual portrait of the liberated person and an extended meditation on certain basic Franciscan themes.   These include Francis as a model of gentleness and care; the preferential option for the poor; Francis' life of liberation: his emphasis on an integral of the human, both body and spirit; Francis' contribution to a church of the poor and "base" as the people of God; and Francis as the symbol of the individuated, whole person who integrates both the positive and negative, the opposites of eros and pathos, life and death, and the acceptance of life's contradictions with a tenderness and communion with nature that overturns consumerist materialism and rationality.

51   Hoornaert, Eduardo. *The Memory of the Christian People.* Robert R. Barr, trans. Maryknoll, NY: Orbis Books, 1988.

This is a history of the early church from the viewpoint of liberation theology, away from the standard "Eusebian" model, as Hoornaert calls it, of a steady triumphalist march toward Christian domination, and toward a history from below, one that can be used as a model for the base Christian communities of today.   Hoornaert draws upon what he calls the lost traditions of the Christian people, though he uses many standard texts, well-known to students of the period, including the apocrypha, the Syrian *Didache,* the *Apostolic Constitutions* and the *Shepherd of Hermas.* Among Hoornaert's heros are Tertullian, Justin Martyr, and Ignatius of Antioch.

Christian marginalization and its theology of the margin was fundamental to the first three centuries, but these factors were lost, sometimes deliberately, in a church in awe of Roman structures and rapidly converting to the successful discourses of Hellenism. In so doing the simple, ethical and political message of Christianity's Judaic roots was lost on the official level, while the very many valuable aspects of late ancient paganism: a concern for health, family, land, peace were swept under the rug of an increasingly legalistic religion.

A valuable and original approach well founded on the sources and secondary materials.

52   Kee, Alistair. *Constantine Versus Christ. The Triumph of Ideology.* London: SCM, 1982.

This is an examination of Constantine and his rule from the viewpoint of Political theology and in an attempt to close the divide between the secular and the religious in our contemporary, as well as in our historical, analyses. Topics include the religion of Constantine, his religious policy, and his ideology, all in an attempt to explain the roots of Christianity's current marriage to political ideologies.

53   Lesbaupin, Ivo. *Blessed Are the Persecuted. Christianity in the Roman Empire, A.D. 64-313.* Robert R. Barr, trans. Maryknoll, NY: Orbis Books, 1987.

This is an interpretation of martyrdom and persecution from the perspective of liberation theology. The author surveys the persecutions of Christians by the Roman Empire, the causes, and Roman legislation. He then treats Christian organization designed to sustain these persecutions on structural, physical and spiritual levels. The most important chapters of the book deal with a theology of persecution and a reading of Revelations for a contemporary audience, designed to offer hope amid persecution.

54   Rowland, Christopher. *Radical Christianity. A Reading of Recovery.* Maryknoll, NY: Orbis Books, 1988.

Examines Christianity's "foundation documents" in the New Testament in the light of liberation theology. Themes range from the hidden messiah, the prophetic and protest traditions to Christian apocalyptism. Christianity has always demonstrated its ability to call for and bring about radical transformations in social and political systems. This book illustrates this through Western history from its biblical roots in Jewish messianism and Christian expectations of the Kingdom, through the Apocalypse, medieval apocalyptism, including Joachim of Fiore and the Spiritual Franciscans, the Protestants, including Thomas Münzer and Winstanley, and concluding with Brazil, Nicaragua, and South Africa. Interesting survey. Good, unannotated, bibliography.

55 Troeltsch, Ernst. *The Social Teaching of the Christian Churches.* Olive Wyon, trans. New York: Harper & Row, 1960.

An historical survey of the development of Christian ethics, stemming from the same tradition as Niebuhr's (40), that saw Christian ethics as essentially quietist. Cogently argued and researched, this is an excellent and fundamental work in the quietist tradition that has influenced so many Catholics and Christians throughout the world.

The Colonial Period

56 Bataillon, Marcel. *Erasme et l'Espagne.* Paris: Droz, 1937.

Traces Erasmus' influence on the Spanish Humanists, discusses translations of his works, and follows his persecution and condemnation by Spanish ecclesiastics of the Counter Reformation. Useful for tracing his influence through the Humanists and the court of Cardinal Ximénez to the missionary orders, including the Franciscans and Dominicans whom the crown sent out to evangelize and protect the native Americans.

57 Dussel, Enrique. *A History of the Church in Latin America: Colonialism to Liberation 1492-1979.* 3d ed. Alan Neely, trans. Grand Rapids, MI: W.B. Eerdmans, 1981.

The best historical background for the development of Catholic peacemaking and liberation in Latin America. But Dussel's book is more than this. It is a theology of liberation written through history, with careful attention to historical fact and accuracy, for only through the "praxis" of history can the church fully appreciate the meaning of liberation.

The book's four parts include a hermeneutical introduction on the theology of domination and liberation; Latin American culture, and relations between church and culture; Christendom in the West Indies from 1492 to 1808, which covers both chronological narrative and thematic analysis of evangelization; the neocolonial period from 1808 to 1962 examined from historical, structuralist-institutional, social, cultural, and theological viewpoints; and finally a survey of the church and Latin American liberation from 1962 to 1979, including a description of recent events: the national security state, violence, bourgeois elites and the masses, the church's evolution in councils and in praxis, and the theological significance of these events.

Dussel's work is often difficult for the nontheologian, all the more so since liberation theology depends so much on drawing its data from the living world of Catholic practice and application to real social and political conditions. The reader is thus often faced with interpretive schematizations of the events narrated that compel reevaluation of accepted methods of viewing Latin America and its history. Nonetheless, the result is well worth the effort. Dussel's historical processes are dialogues between world views that have not yet ended, not Marxist dialectical confrontations between classes or economic systems that must end in the victory of one or the other. His analysis of pre-Columbian cultures pinpoints the truly devastating effect of the Spanish conquest and lays the groundwork for understanding all further European efforts either to conquer or convert and protect the native Americans. He also reminds the reader of the limitations of the Spanish culture that came to dominate the region: its authoritarianism; its feudal concepts of land, work, and personal relations; and the cultural shock inflicted on the native Americans by Spanish technology, society, and theological universe.

Along with Dussel's analyses comes a continuous narrative of Catholic efforts at liberation from the time of Antonio de Montesinos through the career of Bartolomé de Las Casas (65 to 81), the Franciscans, Dominicans and Augustinians, the New Laws and the New Law bishops, reform church councils that attempted to redress the atrocities of the conquistadors and emphasize the Christian nature of the conversion process. Dussel claims that Las Casas and these other clerics are the true fountainhead of liberation theology: their efforts to protect the native Americans and to restore to them their human dignity is based directly on the Gospels and the Old Testament books of liberation and prophetic protest.

Dussel's major theme for the neocolonial period is the struggle between the church and the colonial aristocracy over the survival of the feudal *patronato*, the system under which the native Americans had been subjected to a feudal serfdom worse than slavery. In this light Dussel cites the efforts of the Jesuits and the other missionary orders. Despite the decadence of the Bourbon period (1700-1808) and its legacy of deserted missions, accommodation, and an ensuing anticlericalism, Dussel stresses that an active lay spirituality survived and made new strides in the nineteenth and twentieth centuries. While this was not always in keeping with strict Tridentine orthodoxy, it did lay the groundwork for the activist approach of Latin America's peoples and gave rise to liberation theology as understood today.

58   — . *History and Theology of Liberation. A Latin American Perspective.* John Drury, trans. Maryknoll, NY: Orbis Books, 1976.

Essentially a distillation of much of his *History of the Church* but with the emphasis on the larger theological schema rather than on historical narrative.

59   Goodpasture, H. McKennie, ed. *Cross and Sword. An Eyewitness Account of Christianity in Latin America.* Maryknoll, NY: Orbis Books, 1989.

Documents range from Columbus to the 1980s. Pages 14-27 include selections from Las Casas, Motolinía, Pedro de Gant (Peter of Ghent), and de Sahagun. Other chapters include texts on the Jesuit *reduciones* and on base ecclesial communities in Nicaragua today. Useful introductory materials.

60   Hanke, Lewis. *The Spanish Struggle for Justice in the Conquest of America.* Philadelphia: University of Pennsylvania Press, 1949.

Two factors inherent in the Spanish colonial system helped establish a basis for the struggle for peace and justice in the New World. Spanish legal formality thoroughly saturated every aspect of Spanish European and colonial life far beyond the legal fiction of the *requerimiento* used as a pretext for aggressive wars of conquest. A widespread freedom of speech was also encouraged by the Spanish monarchy, within the bounds of religious orthodoxy, and open discussion and movement of news from America was a vital aspect of Spanish policy.

There were, therefore, elements of Spanish culture that worked in favor of Bartolomé de Las Casas and the other missionary workers for peace and justice in the New World. From Montesinos on a series of denunciations of Spanish colonial leadership was not only voiced heroically in America, but also faithfully transmitted and reported to the Spanish court. This made possible the commissions of inquiry that followed up charges made in the letters and writings of the missionaries. The open and often heated debates that these reports produced resulted in the Laws of Burgos, the New Laws, the appointment of the New Law bishops to implement royal reform decrees, and the termination of many of the most onerous of the Spanish colonial oppressions.

Hanke details the workings of an entire "Indian lobby" at the Hapsburg court that did much to persuade Charles V, and Philip II later, to check the greed and brutality of the colonial aristocracy. Perhaps the most dramatic example of this combination of legalism and free speech was the Valladolid debate between Las Casas and Juan Ginés de Sepúlveda in 1550/51 over the basic human rights and nature of the Americans. The debate was decided in Las Casas' favor and resulted in the Royal Council's openly questioning the justice of wars against the native Americans and, ironically, the banning of Sepúlveda's views in Spain. A basic work in the area.

61   Latourette, Kenneth Scott. *Three Centuries of Advances, A.D. 1500-A.D. 1800.* New York: Harper & Row, 1939. Vol. 3 of *History of the Expansion of Christianity.* 7 vols. New York: Harper & Row, 1937-1945. Reprint, Grand Rapids, MI: Zondervan, 1976.

This remains the best single work on missionary activities in the early modern period. This volume surveys the general movement of missionary activity and details the lives of many of the most important missionaries and peacemakers in the Americas and what is now the Third World. These include Bartolomé de Las Casas (**65 - 81**), the Jesuits and the Flemish Franciscans in Mexico and California, Luis Cancer de Barbastro in Florida, Alfonso Sandoval and Pedro Claver in Colombia, Francis Xavier in the Orient, Robert de Nobili in India, and Diego de Herrera and Domingo de Salazar in the Philippines. Very useful reference material.

62   Muldoon, James. *Popes, Lawyers and Infidels. The Church and the Non-Christian World 1250-1550.* Philadelphia: University of Pennsylvania Press, 1979.

Pages 8-24 review Las Casas' attack on the legal fiction of the *requerimiento* that underpined the entire Spanish conquest as a just war.

63   Neill, Stephen. *A History of Christian Missions.* Baltimore: Penguin Books, 1964.

Pages 140-449 trace the early modern missions of the Catholic church, among others, from Nicholas V's *Romanus pontifex* in 1454, through the bulls of demarcation of Alexander VI and the activities of the missionary orders in the New and Third Worlds. Surveys the lives of Francis Xavier and the Japan missionaries and martyrs and traces the progress of the Jesuit and Ursuline missions in Canada. Neill sets the Latin American missions in the context of Spanish genocide, the *encomienda* system, and the missionary peacemakers who campaigned to stop them. These include Antonio de Montesinos, Bartolomé de Las Casas, and Bishop Zumárraga of Mexico. Neill also traces the reaction against the creation of an indigenous clergy under Gregory XIII and in a series of councils in the New World through the sixteenth century.

By the time of Francesco Ingoli's tenure over the Propaganda, however, the church had again begun to move away from the political domination of the colonial powers and to insist on peaceful persuasion as the chief means of conversion. Later chapters provide useful background material for Catholic missions into the twentieth century. The researcher needs to remember that these missions were, almost without exception, nonviolent attempts to spread Christianity and to protect non-Europeans from the exploitation of their colonial masters. Good background for the foundations of liberation theology as a fundamentally Christian response. At times, especially on pages 140-240, his account seems to rely heavily on Latourette. See **61**.

64   Santa Ana, Julio de, ed. *Separation Without Hope?* Maryknoll, NY: Orbis Books, 1980.

The subtitle reads, "Essays on the Relation Between the Church and the Poor During the Industrial Revolution and the Western Colonial Expansion." Contributors include André Biéler, John Kent, Julio Barreiro, Sam M. Kobia, among others. Much of the thrust of this collection focuses on the negative impact of Christianity as a force of Western imperialism or on the churches as bulwarks of the established order.

Bartolomé de Las Casas

65   Fernandez, Manuel Gimenez. "Fray Bartolomé de Las Casas: A Biographical Sketch." See 67, pp. 67-125.

A useful survey of his life and the main issues and events that shaped it, with careful attention to chronology. Fernandez reminds us of Las Casas' connection with Adrian of Utrecht, Cardinal Ximénez de Cisneros, and others of Erasmus' circle at the Spanish court. He thus sets Las Casas' work for peace and justice in the New World within the context of Spanish court politics and the rivalries of the various religious orders conducting missions in America. The article also discusses papal efforts to defend native Americans.

66   Friede, Juan. "Las Casas and Indigenism in the Sixteenth Century." See 67, pp. 127-234.

Friede summarizes much of his theory that the actions of Las Casas and other defenders of the native Americans stemmed as much from economic self-interest as from any morality. Las Casas' efforts grew out of the need to organize the new colonies both politically and economically and to protect the work force put at the friars' disposal by their "reforms."

67   Friede, Juan and Benjamin Keen, eds. *Bartolomé de Las Casas in History.* DeKalb, IL: Northern Illinois University Press, 1971.

An excellent collection of essays by prominent scholars of the Spanish conquest and early colonial period. Includes 65, 66, 73, and 80.

68   Hanke, Lewis. *All Mankind Is One*. DeKalb, IL: Northern Illinois University Press, 1974.

Studies the debate between Las Casas and Juan Ginés de Sepúlveda, a Jesuit theologian and opponent of Erasmus, held in the presence of the royal Spanish court at the palace at Valladolid in 1550/51. The debate centered on Sepúlveda's adherence to the Aristotelian view that all barbarians, i.e. non-Europeans, were naturally inferior and thus just objects for conquest and enslavement, being less truly human than "civilized" peoples. Las Casas' arguments for the God-given equality of all peoples and against the injustice of the Spanish conquest won the day and resulted in important reforms of the colonial administration. This book is of fundamental importance for the study of Las Casas and other colonial forbearers of liberation theology. An excellent bibliography.

69   —. *Aristotle and the American Indians*. London: Hollis & Carter, 1959.

Focuses on the Valladolid debate of 1550/51 between Bartolomé de Las Casas and Juan Ginés de Sepúlveda. Hanke traces the sources of Sepúlveda's theory and contrasts them to the words and actions of many Catholic missionaries in the New World, such as Juan de Zumárraga and Motolinía, whose strong condemnations of Spanish exploitation implicitly bore a rebuttal of Aristotle's theory and helped develop the traditions that have led to liberation theology.

70   —. *Bartolomé de Las Casas*. The Hague: Nijhoff, 1951.

This is still the best single volume available for an introduction to Las Casas. Hanke divides his study into three parts: Las Casas' struggle for justice during the Spanish conquest; his achievement as a political theorist and historian, analyzing his writings and their impact; and Las Casas as an anthropologist, that is, his attempts to understand the culture of the native Americans and to translate the message of Christianity into a form they could accept and adopt.

71   —. *Bartolomé de Las Casas, Bookman, Scholar and Propagandist.* Philadelphia: University of Pennsylvania Press, 1952.

On his work as a historian and apologist for the native Americans.

72   —. *Spanish Struggle.*

See 60, passim.

73   Keen, Benjamin. "Approaches to Las Casas, 1535-1970." See **67**, pp. 3-63.

On historiography. Las Casas himself was a major source of the "Black Legend" of Spanish atrocity and injustice in the New World. His accounts made vivid reading and effective propaganda against the Catholic Monarchy when used by Protestant reformers and later Dutch rebels and English competitors. At the same time, these external attacks helped reduce Las Casas' popularity in Spain, as he began to be seen as a turncoat. In the Enlightenment, however, he again became a hero of humanity against the forces of violence and injustice. In revolutionary Europe sentiment for him was so strong that a movement was launched to have him canonized, while he became the nemesis of conservatives and reactionaries. Keen sums up American opinion and then warns that there is a real danger of a "White Legend" growing up around Las Casas and his associates that over-stresses their efforts for peace and justice and leads us to ignore the grim reality behind the "Black Legend."

74   Las Casas, Bartolomé de. *Apologetic History.* In Lewis Hanke, trans. and ed. *All The Peoples of the World Are Men.* Minneapolis, MN: University of Minnesota, 1970.

Hanke's title refers to the debate within Spain as to whether the native Americans were even human beings. He traces Las Casas' evolving notions of universal kinship and human rights, first in defense of the native Americans and, later, in defense of the freedom of black slaves. Hanke concludes that Las Casas' message is in exactly the same spirit as that of John XXIII's *Pacem in Terris.* See **104.**

75   —. *A Collection of His Writings.* George Sanderlin, ed. New York: Knopf, 1971.

Not seen.

76   —. *The Devastation of the Indies. A Brief Account.* Herma Briffault, trans. New York: Seabury Press, 1974.

Here is the chief source of the "Black Legend," the history of Spanish genocide in the New World. While historians may question Las Casas' statistics of the number of native Americans actually killed by the Spanish, his record of war, massacre, atrocity, abuses of basic human rights, torture, and enslavement are more vivid than anything until the Holocaust. The book caused a sensation and immediate royal investigations into the conduct of their colonial empire in the New World. It has been used as a weapon against the Spanish and Catholic treatment of native Americans ever since. Las Casas' goal was quite different, however: to awaken the consciences of his compatriots to the grim reality behind their new-found wealth and empire. In this regard it looks forward to such contemporary works as Penny Lernoux's *Cry of the People*. See **389**.

77 —. *History of the Indies*. Andrée Collard, trans. and ed. New York: Harper & Row, 1971.

Las Casas was among the first generation of New World colonists, and his first-hand sources go back to the voyages of Columbus, which he also recalled. His work is thus a fundamental source for the period of discovery and conquest. More than this, however, it is Las Casas' narrative of the struggle of the missionary peacemakers, including himself at center stage, for peace and justice in America. Much of what we know of this struggle comes from Las Casas, but his account seems reliable on most points. A good English edition.

78 —. *In Defense of the Indians*. Stafford Poole, C. M., trans. and ed. DeKalb, IL: Northern Illinois University Press, 1974.

Las Casas' examination of native American culture, its importance and its dignity, and its right to be protected against the depredations of the Spanish conquerors.

79   —. *Las Casas as a Bishop. A New Interpretation.* Helen Rand Parish, trans. and ed. Washington, DC: Library of Congress, 1980.

This is an edition and a facsimile of a newly discovered autograph letter of Las Casas (Kraus MS 139), written to Charles V in 1543. It contains the newly appointed bishop's "program" for his work on nonviolent conversion among the native Americans of Chiapas. Las Casas' proposals include nonviolence, strengthening the ecclesiastical arm and protectorate over the Indians, and the promotion of a new type of colonization: by small farmers who will live in peace side by side with the native population. The letter also demonstrates Las Casas' attempt to use the penitential system of the confessional to force restitution to the natives. An excellent edition that confirms Las Casas' hopes of liberating the Amerindians from the grasp of the conquistadors.

80   Losada, Angel. "The Controversy between Sepúlveda and Las Casas in the Junta of Valladolid." See **67**, pp. 279-307.

Among the issues debated were Sepúlveda's contention that Aristotle and the Old Testament had stressed the difference between Jew and Gentile, Greek and barbarian. Traces Las Casas' successful rebuttals.

81   Wagner, Henry Raup, and Helen Rand Parish. *The Life and Writings of Bartolomé de Las Casas.* Albuquerque, NM: University of New Mexico Press, 1967.

A new biography based on extensive reexamination of the primary documents. Contains a "Narrative and Critical Catalogue" of La Casas' works.

Individual Mission Areas

82   Burrus, Ernest J., ed. and trans. *The Writings of Alonso de la Vera Cruz. The Original Texts with English Translation.* 5 vols. Rome and St. Louis, MO: Jesuit Historical Institute, 1968-1976.

De la Vera Cruz was a lawyer at Salamanca who left Spain in 1536 to join the Augustinian mission in Mexico. He quickly became a strong defender of native American rights against the conquistadors, emphasizing their God-given human rights and allying with Las Casas to fight for justice. While Vera Cruz was far more moderate in his defense than Las Casas, between 1562 and 1573 he was able to use his position at the Spanish court to protect the rights of both American and Philippine peoples.

Burrus is an acknowledged expert on Vera Cruz and on the entire issue of the role of the missionaries in fostering peace and justice during the colonial period. Here he presents the results of his exhaustive editing and translation project in five volumes of facing Latin (and some Spanish) with English translation. Vol. 1 contains Sermons and Letters, 2 the *Defense of the Indians. Their Rights,* 3 a facsimile of the tract with index, 4 *Defense of the Indians. Their Privileges,* and 5 Letters and Reports. Vera Cruz' theological arguments on behalf of the indigenous populations went hand in hand with Las Casas' Humanist, historical approach. His work, while infused with his Scholastic philosophical and

theological categories and forms of discourse, looks
forward to the liberation theologians of the twentieth century.   Each volume contains an excellent
bibliography.

83   Caraman, Philip. *The Lost Paradise. The Jesuit Republic
        in South America.* New York: Seabury Press, 1976.

The historical background to the film, *The
Mission,* and a fascinating account of the Jesuit
attempt in what is now modern Paraguay to save
their native American converts from the depredations
of conquistadors and slave traders.   After failing at
attempts at itinerant missions, the Jesuits accepted a
commission from Philip II to convert the native
Americans by nonviolent means, without exploitation.
They proceeded to set up a colonial state, a series of
reduciones complete with secular and religious institutions: church, schools, hospitals, courts, and –
eventually – a strong military force that kept
aggressors at bay in a series of bloody battles.   They
combined this with journeys to the colonial capitals
to preach against the injustices of the Spanish regime
or to liberate prisoners from Brazilian slave traders.
      Ultimately, however, the Jesuit experiment was a
failure.   Their paternalistic control provided the
Americans with little skill in self-government or
ability to resist colonial exploitation.   "Liberation"
was an independence defined and maintained from
the top down and thus unsuccessful.   In the end the
reduciones melted away into the forests.   This is fascinating adventure reading combined with sobering
lessons in the nature of political and cultural
liberation.

84   Deck, Allan F. *Francisco Javier Alegre. A Study in
        Mexican Literary Criticism.* Rome: Jesuit Historical
        Institute, 1977.

        Alegre was one of the expatriate Mexican Jesuits
        who carried on a running criticism of Latin American
        tyranny from the salons of Enlightenment Europe. His
        works helped build the foundations for the political
        liberation of the region. While Deck does not deal
        explicitly with Alegre's criticisms of Spanish colo-
        nial rule and his enlightened Humanism, he does
        provide some biographical and intellectual back-
        ground and a thorough and useful bibliography.

85   Ennis, Arthur, O.S.A. *Fray Alonso de la Vera Cruz,
        O.S.A. (1507-1584). A Study of His Life and
        Contribution to the Religious and Intellectual Affairs
        of Early Mexico.* Louvain: Augustiniana, 1957.

        A good introduction, largely supplanted by Burrus
        (see **82**).

86   Fogel, Daniel. *Junipero Serra. The Vatican and
        Enslavement Theology.* San Francisco: ISM Press,
        1988.

        This is a work that sets history in the service of
        polemic. At issue is the impending canonization of
        Serra at the instigation of John Paul II. John Paul's
        assertion that Serra, and his fellow missionaries,
        defended Indian rights against the depredations of
        their fellow Spanish, and his use as an exemplar of
        tradition and obedience, is enough for Fogel to realize
        that Serra must, indeed, be of the same camp as the
        current Vatican reactionaries.

The book then traces the development of Christology in early Christianity, the Spanish crusade ideal, and the politics of sanctification. Fogel then reviews Serra's missionary life, the native Americans of California, and the impact of European colonization.

We next segue to John Paul II's attack on liberation theology and the "counter-reformation" elsewhere (120) dealt with in far greater detail. Since Serra has been befriended by John Paul II, he is obviously guilty by association. The Franciscan missionary is finally made the enemy of gay and lesbian liberation, women's theology, and liberation theology. A sketchy bibliography.

87   Geiger, Maynard, O.F.M. *Franciscan Missionaries in Hispanic California 1769-1848. A Biographical Dictionary.* San Marino, CA: Huntington Library, 1969.

The Spanish missionaries in California were adventurous heroes committed to nonviolent conversion. Their lives gripped the popular imagination of New Spain and provided a counterbalance to the tales of the conquistadors. Geiger's book provides a useful reference guide to the lives of many of these adventurers.

88   Kennedy, J. H. *Jesuit and Savage in New France.* New Haven: Yale University Press, 1950.

The Jesuit mission in Canada was a marriage of the order's thorough grounding in Christian humanism and its members' willingness to acculturate to the languages, customs, and poverty of the Americans. Despite this intellectual preparation, however, the

Canadian mission was still an act of martyrdom, both in the conditions imposed on these Europeans and in their physical deaths, which the Jesuits saw as an imitation of Christ. For the Jesuits the New World offered the opportunity to return to the first centuries of the church, to opt for the poverty and suffering of the first age, among a people morally and intellectually equal to the Europeans but untouched by the centuries of religious decline. A study of the Jesuits' early history in the Americas will remind the reader that recent martyrdoms in Central America are not unique or new for the order.

89   McNaspy, C. J., S.J. *Conquistador without Sword. The Life of Roque Gonzalez, S.J.* Chicago: Loyola University Press, 1984.

On the most important founder of the Jesuit *reduciones* in Paraguay.

90   —. and Jose Maria Blanch, S.J. *Lost Cities of Paraguay.* Chicago: Loyola University Press, 1982.

A history of the Jesuit *reduciones* of Paraguay.

91   Phelan, John Leddy. *The Millennial Kingdom of the Franciscans in the New World.* Berkeley and Los Angeles: University of California Press; London: Cambridge University Press, 1956; revised, 1970.

Focuses on the life and often contradictory thought of Geronimo de Mendietta, O.F.M. (1525-1604), a Spanish missionary in Mexico. Mendietta's life is as interesting for his theories as for the missions that grew out of them. Through Mendietta's own *Historia eclesiatica indiana (Ecclesiastical History of the Indies)* and his biography by Juan de Torquemada, O.F.M. it emerges that Mendietta saw the Spanish Empire as the universal millennial kingdom of the last days that would bring all the peoples of the world to Christianity. While much of his historical thought derived directly from the apocalyptic Joachimism of Cardinal Ximénez de Cisneros and his Franciscan circle, Mendietta agreed with Sepúlveda and other just-war theorists in seeing war as a valid means of bringing this universal monarchy about. He saw the Spanish conquest in the light of the Old Testament wars of the Israelites and Cortes as a new Moses.

If the time of Cortes was the Golden Age of the New World, one of unspoiled purity that was close to the life of the primitive church, Mendietta's own age was closer to the apocalyptic time of troubles that preceded the coming of the New Jerusalem. His own Franciscan Order had pointed the way to the restoration of the primitive church, and the native Americans were the true children of this age in their poverty, simplicity, and humility. Yet the Franciscans had therefore to protect them from the moral pollution and greed of their European overlords. In order to guarantee their "evangelical liberty" the Franciscans would therefore have to reeducate the native Americans to form their own commonwealth. Mendietta thus opposed any policy that would force the Hispanization of indigenous peoples and stressed that existing social and cultural structures that did not clash with Christianity must be retained.

While he was therefore very much a man of his times in accepting the role of force in the conquest of the New World, he looked forward to some aspects of liberation theology in stressing that the Hispanization of Latin America did not equal its Christianization, and that, in fact, it might be the very opposite. He thus, paradoxically, opposed all efforts to force them to conform to Spanish institutions, including the *encomienda*.

Phelan's work is remarkable both for its early appreciation of the role of Joachimite prophesy in the religious thought of the time and in his discernment of a theology of liberation at work in colonial Latin America.

92   Ricard, Robert. *The Spiritual Conquest of Mexico. An Essay on the Apostolate and Evangelizing Methods of the Mendicant Orders in New Spain, 1523-1572.* Berkeley and Los Angeles: University of California Press, 1966.

While the special emphasis of the mendicants – Franciscans, Dominicans, Hieronymites, and Augustinians – in converting the New World may have differed somewhat from order to order, their basic outlook was essentially the same: the creation of a safe refuge for both body and soul from exploitation and brutality, education to create a native elite, instruction in new trades and crafts, a religious cycle and liturgy that would build on the remnants of pre-Columbian practice and world view. The mendicants hoped that these methods of nonviolent persuasion would attract the Americans to the Christian life with a deep-rooted appreciation for its truths. While paternalistic, their theological outlook contains many of the elements of today's liberation theology.

93   Ronan, Charles E. *Francisco Javier Clavijero, S.J. (1731-1787), Figure of the Mexican Enlightenment.* Rome: Institutum Historicum; Chicago: Loyola University Press, 1977.

Clavijero was another of the Mexican emigré intellectuals who carried on a campaign against the political and cultural tyranny of late colonial Latin America. His *Ancient History of Mexico* picks up where Las Casas left off, combining a deep understanding of pre-Columbian civilization with criticism of the Spanish conquest. His ultimate goal was to show native American culture and individual status as the equal of the European and so press for full human rights in the New World.

* *
*

Chapter 3: *Popes and Councils. The Role of Rome in Liberation*

Vatican II and Papal Encyclicals

94   Abbott, Walter M. and Joseph Gallagher, eds. *Documents of Vatican II.* New York: Guild, America, and Association Presses, 1966.

The best collection for Vatican II available in English. Presents all the texts for the entire council, including *Gaudium et Spes* (The Pastoral Constitution on the Church in the Modern World, 99), with comments by respected theologians and scholars, among them Lawrence Cardinal Shehan, Avery Dulles, S.J., Donald R. Campion, S.J., R. A. F. MacKenzie, S.J., John Courtney Murray, S.J., Robert McAfee Brown, and Jaroslav Pelikan.

95   Alberigo, Giuseppe, Jean-Pierre Jossua and Joseph A. Komonchak, eds. *The Reception of Vatican II.* Matthew J. O'Connell, trans. Washington, DC: Catholic University, 1987.

An engaging collection of essays by Poltmeyer, Vaucelles, Galilea (on Latin American liberation theology), Gutiérrez (on the church and the poor), among others. Themes include the reception of the council among local churches, faith and history, preaching the Gospels, ecumenism, peace and war. Problem areas not yet implemented or resolved that the contributors address include collegiality, reform of canon law, clerical reform, and the liturgy as a communal expression. In chapter 16 (pp. 325-48) Daniele Menozzi reviews the "Opposition to the Council

(1966-1984)" and focuses on the conservative opponents of the council's tactic of following the letter of the wording included in the final documents as a concession to them that is outside the spirit of the council; while groups like communion and liberation seek confirmation in texts for positions developed independently of the council. In Chapter 17 Avery Dulles, S.J. reviews the gains consolidated by the Extraordinary Synod of 1985.

96   Dorr, Donal. *Option for the Poor. A Hundred Years of Vatican Social Teaching.* Maryknoll, NY: Orbis Books, 1983.

A survey of the church's teaching on social justice, poverty and oppression.

97   Flannery, Austin, ed. *Vatican Council II. The Conciliar and Post Conciliar Documents.* Northport, NY: Costello Publishing; Wilmington, DE: Scholarly Resources, 1975

English translations with some annotation. An appendix gives post-conciliar documents. Index.

98   —. *Vatican Council II. More Postconciliar Documents.* Grand Rapids, MI: W.B. Eerdmans, 1982.

These are grouped around the headings of Liturgy, Ecumenism, Religious Life, Ministry, Current Problems, and the Synod of Bishops. The last presents "Justice in the World" on pp. 695-710.

99   *Gaudium et Spes* (The Pastoral Constitution on the Church in the Modern World). See **94**, pp. 183-316; **105**, pp. 178-284.

Essential reading. This document defined the Catholic church and its relationship to the world in the late twentieth century and set off a revolution that is still being fought, and resisted, around the world. Its essential question is how the church may be of service to a world that has changed profoundly since the triumphalist First Vatican Council (pars. 2-3) and that it no longer seeks to control but to serve and to learn from. It thus overturns centuries of thinking that saw the Catholic church as the only vehicle of salvation, the only avenue for legitimate change, and its clergy and hierarchy the only agents of truth. In these elements it thrust responsibility upon the laity to "scrutinize the signs of the times" and to change the world according to gospel precepts and so gave the doctrinal underpinning for many elements associated with liberation theology.

Its major themes are "personalism" (pars. 12-22), the priority of the human being as the measure for all human institutions and, at the same time, an essentially social being; the implementation of justice in the world, the removal of obstacles to economic equality; and development (29-32).

The tone of the Constitution is a startling departure from the dualisms and fears of the nineteenth-century church and one whose themes were to become major concerns for all later liberation theology. It insists that we cannot ignore the salvation of the world while focusing on our own individual salvations, and that while progress is not the kingdom of God, it remains an essential concern of that kingdom (par. 39). It discusses the "people of God" as the true agents of change (11), Christian faith as liberation, both from sin (13) and from ignorance in the world (60-61); it stresses an integralism that joins both body and spirit as legitimate concerns for all Christians

(14) and offers an "incarnationist" theology for this integralism (40-45, 58).

Among its economic themes it stresses that human dignity lies not in technology but in human interaction (23), that human society and nature is communitarian (24), that economic inequalities must be resolved (63), and it reiterates the Catholic doctrine of the common purpose of all created goods (66), even while acknowledging the proper limits of private ownership (71-73). The Constitution also firmly rejects the church's connection to all forms of "Christendoms," that is the association of Christianity with any particular form of government or political system (76), and thus marks the end of the Constantinian age that is an essential element to the ecclesiology of liberation theology.

100   Gremillion, Joseph, ed. *The Gospel of Peace and Justice: Catholic Social Teaching Since Pope John.* Maryknoll, NY: Orbis Books, 1976.

Documents include *Gaudium et Spes* (**99**), *Mater et Magistra* (**103**), *Pacem in Terris* (**104**), *Populorum Progressio* (**107**), and the Medellin documents, among others.

101   Gudorf, Christine E. *Catholic Social Teaching on Liberation Themes.* Lanham, MD: University Press of America, 1981.

This is an excellent review of the topic. Part 1 surveys papal social teaching in the last century from Pius XI to Paul VI. Part 2 examines the theological methods in papal teaching and deals with the similarities and differences between liberation theology and current church teaching. Part 3 surveys thought on private property, 4 on Marxism, and 5 on women.

A good bibliography, especially for its rather complete index of papal documents on these topics.

102   Henriot, Peter J., Edward P. De Berri, and Michael J. Schultheis. *Catholic Social Teaching. Our Best Kept Secret.* Maryknoll, NY: Orbis Books, 1988.

This is a useful introduction to the tradition of Catholic social thought, primarily aimed at the student. It contains excellent outlines of the major social encyclicals of Leo XIII, John XXIII, Paul VI, John Paul II, the U.S. and Latin American bishops.

103   John XXIII, Pope. *Mater et Magistra* (Christianity and Social Progress). See **105**, pp. 44-116.

This papal encyclical was issued on May 15, 1961 to commemorate and to update the social encyclicals *Rerum Novarum* of Leo XIII and Pius XI's *Quadragesimo Anno* of 1931 and in an attempt to offer some guidance and prophetic insight into the damage caused by the unbridled economic systems of communism on the one hand and liberal capitalism on the other. It was met with wide enthusiasm, since it signalled the end of the church's isolation from the modern world; in fact, it announced the church's embrace of the world, its various currents and problems, and called on the church to take on a new role of service, not of authoritarian rule.

Several themes important for the development of liberation theology emerge from the letter: the social use of property, new norms for the use of private property that insure distribution, the role of the state as a positive force in economic life if it acts on behalf of social justice, the rights of workers, the concept of "subsidiarity" (that the state should not assume to

itself what individuals acting individually and col-
lectively can accomplish), new standards of economic
justice and equality. These norms strike a careful balance between "development" in a technological sense
and social progress that enhances human dignity.

The encyclical takes bold aim at the waste and
over-consumption of the industrial world in the face
of the needs of the Third World for simple subsistence
and insists on the obligation to justice and humanity
(par. 161). It condemns neocolonial forms of exploitation by the elites of these countries and their allies in
the North (169-74), and stresses the Christian duty to
contribute to civil institutions and to remove obstacles
to human dignity. In this light, it emphasizes that
individual humans are the foundation, cause and end
of all human institutions (218) and stresses the
importance of the lay apostolate: the primary role of
the laity in informing society with Christian values
and bringing about change (233-35). The laity, in fact,
is enjoined to "observe, judge, and act" in accordance
with circumstances and moral teachings (236). On the
ecclesiological level, the pope emphasizes that both
laity and clergy are ontologically equal: both are
living members of the body of Christ (258-59).

104   —. *Pacem in Terris.* See **105**, pp. 117-70.

While primarily devoted to the themes of peace
as international order, the pope breaks new ground in
moving away from the church's "theology of war"
and the just-war tradition and toward a theology of
peace based on the Gospels and on the Christian
tradition of active nonviolence and peacemaking.
Thus peace becomes a work of justice as the individual is called upon to judge and to act. An essential
document for all later liberation theologians

105 O'Brien, David J., and Thomas A. Shannon, eds. *Renewing the Earth. Catholic Documents on Peace, Justice and Liberation.* Garden City, NY: Doubleday, 1977.

Extremely useful collection of documents that are the ecclesiatical keystones for liberation theology, from John XXIII's *Mater et Magistra* to Vatican II, the social encyclicals of Paul VI, Medellin, and statements by U.S. Catholic bishops. Includes good editions of *Mater et Magistra* (Christianity and Social Progress) on pages 44-116 (**103**), *Gaudium et Spes* (the Pastoral Constitution) on pages 171-284 (**99**), *Populorum Progressio* (On the Development of Peoples) on pages 307-46 (**107**), *Octagesima Adveniens* (Letter on the Eightieth Anniversary of Rerum Novarum) on pages 347-83 (**106**), *Justice in the World*, the declaration by the 1971 Synod of Bishops on pp. 384-408 (**108**).

106 Paul VI, Pope. *Octagesima Adveniens.* (A Call to Action; Letter on on Eightieth Anniversary of *Rerum Novarum*).

This was issued on May 14, 1971, on the eightieth anniversary of *Rerum Novarum.* Its essential theme is social justice (par. 1). Christian communities, the pope declares, must analyze their own situations and shed Gospel light on them (4). In this process the church acts as servant, at the service of all who seek justice (5).

The letter then reviews the changes in the modern world (pars. 7-17): new conditions of production, fairness of exchange, divisions of wealth, increased consumption, and the need of shared responsibility, urbanization, problems of youth and women (grouped together in par. 13), and of workers, discrimination and emigration.

The pope's "call to action" then takes up the challenges (18-21): creating employment, caring for the environment (nearly twenty years before most other world leaders), distinguishing between true human liberty and that offered by competing ideologies, whether Marxist or liberal capitalist (26). While there is nothing inherently wrong with analyzing Marxist or capitalist thought for aids in analysis, the Christian must use discernment in borrowing methodologies (31-6). Bureaucratic socialism, technocratic capitalism and authoritarian democracy all offer false utopian visions and reveal the ambiguity of human "progress."

True human progress must make way for greater justice, it must change attitudes and structures, "liberation," it declares, "starts with interior freedom" (45). Nevertheless, this is the start, not the end of human life: involvement in politics is a Christian duty, and Christians should try to make political choices consistent with the Gospels (46). Ultimately, the "call to action" is to the laity to *act* after personal conversion and the realization that we all bear guilt for injustices (48) in our consumption habits, our life choices, our politics and our own drives. The pope concludes with a praiseworthy example: those worker priests who take on the life of the poor and oppressed to transform the Gospel into true justice.

107　　—. *Populorum Progressio* (On the Development of Peoples, March 26, 1967). See **105**, pp. 307-46.

Condemned by the *Wall Street Journal*, which called its message "warmed-over Marxism," this papal encyclical is the starting point of Latin American and other Third-World liberation theologies. Paul is careful to stress that the encyclical falls firmly within the Catholic tradition on social teaching but has been written to meet the realities of the increasing imbalance between the world's wealthy and destitute. Building on *Gaudium et Spes* (see **99**), he declares that the church has been founded to establish the kingdom of heaven here on earth and to "scrutinize the signs of the time." It thus has a prophetic and a critical role, not one of lordship or domination. In fact, its truest social role is to press for integral development.

Several themes of the encyclical look forward to those of liberation theology, including the existence of oppressive social structures that insure the oppression and destitution of the many (21), the role of justice in giving the poor their due, even if this involves expropriation of immorally held private property (23-24), a new definition of "development" away from technological projects and toward the distribution of income and social planning (34) whose aim is an integral humanism. The pope calls on the wealthy, both nationally and individually, to turn superfluous wealth to the service of the poor and to turn the wealth of nations being spent on armaments and luxuries to the aid of the poor (49-51).

Peace is inextricably bound to social justice and the economic progress of all peoples, especially those of the developing world. "In fact, development is the new name for peace" (76-80). One cannot condemn violent revolution while not simultaneously condemning the violence of repressive injustice. Finally, the pope stresses that it is the role of the laity to implement change (81).

108   Synod of Bishops. *Justice in the World.* See **105**, pp. 384-408.

    As Paul VI's pontificate progressed, many contradictory elements of the modern papacy came more and more to the fore. While the pope held rigidly to nineteenth-century definitions of clerical celibacy, birth control, and abortion; he took to heart, and in fact deepened, the most progressive calls of John XXIII and Vatican II, including the call for peace and justice and sweeping ecclesiatical changes, including the notion of collegiality – the shared responsibility for leading the church by the pope and the bishops. The 1971 Synod of Bishops is the outcome of many of these progressive trends so encouraged by Paul VI.

    While the media latched on to the insistence on a celibate priesthood announced at the Synod, little attention was given its almost radical endorsement of justice for the Third World. Molded and inspired by the pope and the new majority of Third World bishops in attendance, its document, "Justice in the World," overflows with the seeds of a barely emerging liberation theology.

    After declaring that it is the duty of the church to scrutinize the "signs of the times," the bishops cast their gaze on the serious injustice, domination and oppression that characterize most of the world. Their aim therefore is to reject fatalism and to seek the furthering of justice (Introduction). Liberation is clearly the theme of the letter. The bishops declare that "action on behalf of justice and participation in the transformation of the world fully appear to us as a constitutive dimension of the preaching of the Gospel or, in other words, of the Church's mission for the redemption of the human race and its liberation from every oppressive situation" (p. 391).

The past twenty-five years have given rise to a great irony: despite the linkage of the world through communications and commerce, there has been a rise of oppression and of the "marginal" person. Ecological damage done by both capitalist and socialist systems has risen to a crisis, and gross imbalances between the haves and have-nots widen. In order to foster true development, we must remove the structures that stand in the way of the conversion of hearts and of overcoming marginalization. We must face the plight of migrants, refugees, the persecuted, those deprived of human and religious rights, victims of torture, political prisoners, and we must respect the "right to life" and rights to education and media access.

In Part 2 the prelates focus on the biblical message of liberation, of a God revealed as the "liberator of the oppressed and the defender of the poor" (p. 397). For its part, therefore, "the Church has the right, indeed the duty, to proclaim justice on the social, national and international level, and to denounce instances of injustice when the fundamental rights of man [sic] and his [sic] salvation demand it" (p. 399). Yet the pope and bishops are clear that the church's role is not to act of itself and not to offer concrete solutions but to defend the fundamental dignity of the human person.

Part 3 therefore contains the call to action for Christians. Nonviolence is stressed as *the* Christian form of action. Yet for all its talk of external action, the Synod also turns an eye inward: to ecclesiastical structures. Justice and human rights must be respected within the church as well, it declares. The role of women must be expanded, while authority must be shared in the spirit of collegiality.

In the end the church must educate for justice (p. 401). The family and the community level are the

keys to this education. The use of the liturgy, the
sacraments, of catechesis are all endorsed as valid
methods to teach justice and to "discover the teaching
of the prophets." Collegiality and ecumenism are
both endorsed, as are international bodies, such as the
U.N. and its commissions on human rights, economics,
development, ecology and nutrition.

The letter concludes on an optimistic note,
recognizing the role of the spirit in motivating all
Christians and members of the "People of God" (p.
408). Its imagery is positive and feminine, almost
mystical, in its sense of renewal: "The entire creation
has been groaning till now in an act of giving birth, as
it waits for the glory of the children of God to be
revealed" (cf. Rom. 8:22) (p. 408). The document concludes with what is a full statement of the theology
of liberation: "At the same time as it proclaims the
Gospel of the Lord, its Redeemer and Saviour, the
Church calls on all, especially the poor, the
oppressed and the afflicted, to cooperate with God to
bring about liberation from every sin and to build a
world which will reach the fulness of creation only
when it becomes the work of man [sic] for man [sic]"
(p. 408).

109   Vorgrimler, Herbert, ed. *Commentary on the Docu-
       ments of Vatican II.* Vol. 5: *Pastoral Constitution on
       the Church in the Modern World.* New York:
       Herder & Herder, 1969.

An excellent companion to the documents of the
council, including both detailed discussions of the
political aspects of the council and of the doctrinal
issues involved in each.

110 Walsh, Michael, and Brian Davies, eds. *Proclaiming Justice and Peace. Documents from John XXIII to John Paul II.* Mystic, CT: Twenty-Third Publications, 1984.

Good editions of *Mater et Magistra* (pp. 1-44), *Pacem in Terris* (45-76), *Gaudium et Spes* (77-140), *Populorum Progressio* (141-64), *Octagesima Adveniens* (165-87), *Justice in the World* (188-203), *Evangelii Nuntiandi* (204-42), *Redemptoris Hominis* (243-61), *Dives in Misericordia* (262-70), and *Laborem Exercens* (271-311).

John Paul II and Liberation Theology

111 Baldwin, Louis. *The Pope and the Mavericks.* Buffalo, NY: Prometheus Books, 1988.

This is a journalistic and quippy, if unsympathetic, view of John Paul II. It examines the personality and background of Karol Wojtyla and his later dealings to silence Küng, Schillebeeckx, Curran, Gutiérrez, Boff, and Hunthausen, highlighting the role of Cardinal Ratzinger as a papal tactician. Baldwin treats the liberation theologians on pages 81-96. Fairly well researched for so popular a treatment. Penny Lernoux's analysis of the papal "Restoration" is far broader and more compelling. See **120.**

112   Commission Iustitia et Pax. *The Social Teaching of John Paul II.* Roger Hickel, S.J., ed. Vatican City: Pontifical Commission Iustitia et Pax, 1979-.

This multi-volume booklet series examines the pope's thought on many areas. Volume 4 discusses the "theme of liberation" and notes how infrequently the pope had used the term at Puebla or in Poland.

113   Eagleson, John and Philip Scharper, eds. *Puebla and Beyond.* John Drury, transl. Maryknoll, NY: Orbis Books, 1980.

The best treatment of the council of Puebla, Mexico in 1979, which conservatives in the church had intended to mark the end of Medellin's influence and of liberation theology. The council was attended by important clerics and laity from around the world, including such Latin American bishops as Oscar Romero and Helder Camara. Press attention focused on the debates between conservatives and radicals within and outside the council, especially since Pope John Paul II attended the meetings and confirmed its conclusions. To the surprise of conservatives, the pope actually endorsed the thrust of the church's new "option for the poor" and for nonviolent change in Latin America, while he also applied its theory to liberation struggles in other parts of the world. As the result of a church council, the final document is now part of the official teaching of the Catholic church throughout the world.

The edition presents the entire final document, the pope's major addresses, and commentaries by leading theologians and observers of the Latin American scene. The editors were largely responsible for bringing the works of Latin America's liberation theologians to a North American audience.

114   John Paul II. *John Paul II in Mexico. His Collected Speeches.* New York: Collins, 1979.

The trip to Puebla, complete with color glossies. This looks like the coffee-table version of the Daughters of St. Paul edition. See **116**.

115   —. *On Social Concern.* Sollicitude Rei Socialis. *Encyclical Letter, December 30, 1987.* Washington, DC: U.S. Catholic Conference, 1987.

The "Res Socialis" is the great bugaboo of the nineteenth-century papacy before Leo XIII and the master achievement of the twentieth-century papacy: the Social Question. Thus the "Res Socialis" is the human condition in the modern world and the church's role in fostering social and economic justice as it attempts to make God's kingdom a reality. "On Social Concern" may therefore be far too tame an English translation for the theme of this encyclical, which embodies most of the progressive social thinking of the popes of the last hundred years and expands upon these declarations in unambiguous terms.

The pope recognizes both the problems of the late twentieth century and endorses the church's role in trying to guide Christians to face them. He also frankly acknowledges that these problems have become worse as a result of both the excesses of liberal capitalism the authoritarian planning of socialist countries, which destroys all initiative, and through the mistakes of the Third World itself. To the categories of oppression, marginalization and poverty the pope also adds his concern for the Fourth

World: the discarded marginalized of the First and Second worlds whose misery stands out in even starker contrast to the the affluence around them.

Yet even this bold statement of the church's social mission reflects the contradictions and ambiguities of this "Restoration" pope. John Paul wholeheartedly endorses the tradition of *Populorum Progressio,* yet he does so in terms that seem to water down the "option for the poor" to replace it with an "option or love of preference for the poor" (par. 42) that then becomes the "love of preference for the poor." While he speaks of "liberation" his endorsement of liberation theology is qualified by the criticisms of his papacy bound up in Cardinal Ratzinger's inquisitions and in the papal "Instruction" (46). While he calls on lay Christians, both men and women, to act in accord with the Gospels, it is clear that the "magisterium" will define what this accordance will be from on high. Little mention or praise is given to those Christians who have acted in base Christian communities.

After the difficult task of individual conversion away from sin, and the "structures of sin" that sinful individuals create on a global scale, comes the awareness of the need for solidarity, which is the Christian virtue of sharing the misery and the struggle of the marginalized and oppressed, a determination to commit oneself to the common good. Neither ideology nor the idolatry that competing political blocs espouse can bring this about. He stresses that nonviolence is the most potent force that the world has to bring about change and that Christians are bound to act, albeit nonviolently, to confront sinful structures that are corrupt or inefficient. Drawing on a long tradition of Catholic thought on property, the pope emphasizes that the goods of creation are meant for all, that private property is limited by the principle of social use, the "social mortgage."

The pope concludes his letter with a call to integral development and full liberation: the development of the entire human being – both spirit and flesh – that guarantees or restores human dignity in the fulness of rights and duties. True peace, which is the justice and dignity of all people, must be won on a global scale, the scale that makes us all truly co-creators.

On the whole the papal letter is a clear victory for the progress of liberation and liberation theology in the church.

116   —. *Speeches.* Daughters of St. Paul, compilers and eds. Boston: St. Paul Editions, 1979-80.

These have been collected and translated from the pages of *Osservatore Romano,* the Vatican house organ. They include volumes on Puebla and Poland (1979), Africa (1980), Brazil and Africa (1980), and the Far East (1981). Much useful material for the student of his thought.

117   —, and others. *Reflections on Puebla.* London: Catholic Institute for International Relations, 1980.

Essays by Julian Filochowski on Karol Wojtyla the man, Jon Sobrino on the significance of Puebla, Francis McDonagh on Puebla's influence on Great Britain, and by John Paul II on evangelization and liberation, drawn from *Osservatore Romano,* in which he endorses Puebla's view of liberation.

118 Johnson, Paul. *Pope John Paul II and the Catholic Restoration*. London: Weidenfeld and Nicolson, 1982.

"Restoration" is used here in a positive sense: Johnson highly favors the Vatican's attempts to turn back many of the trends in the church since Vatican II, yet he does so with ever the slightest trace of dry ambiguity so that his conservatism does not come across nearly as engagé as it truly is.

Chapter 8, "The Shadow of Heresy," pp. 146-65, begins with a disparagingly offhand treatment of the work and importance of Congar, Danielou, de Lubac, Rahner and other major thinkers of Vatican II and turns into an apologetic for John Paul II's silencing of Küng, Schillebeeckx, and the Dutch bishops.

Chapter 5, pp. 85-104, "The Temptation to Violence," is a sleight of hand attack on liberation theology, Medellin and Puebla. As Johnson notes (pp. 89-90), "Latin American Catholic radicalism expresses itself in a variety of ways, but above all, in the institutional structure of the *comunidades de base* (basic Christian communities) and the philosophical system of 'liberation theology'." Johnson then proceeds to spell out the essentially hidden and political agenda of liberation theology and sees its origin in Germany "like most new theological ideas." Metz, Rahner, Moltmann and Pannenberg, not the experience of the Latin American people, are responsible for the thought of the Latin America "theolibs." Elegantly distasteful.

119 Küng, Hans, and Leonard Swidler, eds. *The Church in Anguish. Has the Vatican Betrayed Vatican II?* San Francisco: Harper & Row, 1987.

A more scholarly approach to the papal "Restoration" than either Baldwin (**111**) or Lernoux (**120**) with essays written by most of the major victims and participants. Part I analyzes Karol Wojtyla and Cardinal Ratzinger. Part II then examines their victims: Küng, Pohier, Schillebeeckx, the Boffs, Curran, and religious and lay women. Part III looks at the American scene; while a fine essay by Norbert Greinacher looks at the motives and aims of the antagonists and defamers of liberation theology (pp. 144-62). Rosemary Radford Ruether examines the themes of John Paul II and the alienation of women (pp. 279-83).

The volume also contains essays by Charles Curran, Eugene C. Kennedy, Andrew Greeley, the Boffs, Bernard Häring, and Robert McAfee Brown.

120 Lernoux, Penny. *People of God. The Struggle for World Catholicism*. New York: Viking Books, 1989.

This is a startling and eye-opening account of the "Restoration" currently being imposed upon the Catholic church worldwide. Lernoux's book is a detailed narrative of the attempts of John Paul II, Cardinal Joseph Ratzinger and an entrenched Curia to roll back the reforms of Vatican II, most especially in the realms of episcopal collegiality and the role of the laity in forming both praxis and doctrine in the modern church.

According to Lernoux, who writes in a style that is both journalistic and engaged, John Paul II had warned those who elected him in 1978 that "you do not know the kind of man I am." Lernoux expounds, at great length and detail, John Paul's deep devotion, personal charm, love of justice and peace, his commitment to the poor and his heart-felt condemnations of both communism and capitalism for their alienating structures. Yet Lernoux analyzes the model for all of John Paul's activities and attitudes: the political and spiritual world of the church in Poland.

For John Paul II the entire world, and the Catholic church set aside from it, matches the Polish model: a church that must stress unity and obedience to the hierarchy as it fights a godless world and political system on behalf of the powerless, all of whom are faithful servants of the church, at least in public discourse. Once given this unquestioning obedience, the church can then champion all the causes dear to the heart of John Paul and the modern church, but only with the clear recognition that the pope is the absolute monarch and leader of world Catholicism.

John Paul's campaign thus collides directly with the thrust and meaning of Vatican II and with progressive church people in the laity and hierarchy all over the world. The pope's world is Eurocentric, it opposes all the ecumenism and multi-culturalism that Vatican II opened, it ignores the role of the laity in formulating church teaching and of the bishops as equal partners in evangelization, and it both fears and resents the modern world, its secularism, materialism, yet also its pluralism. Thus the pope's model is that of the triumphalist, pre-Vatican II church of Pius XII and its successful battles against "modernism" and other forms of progressive thought and action.

In order to achieve his plans for "Restoration" the pope has employed various procedural and bureaucratic tools to stem the tide of change that Lernoux sees as inevitable. These include the revived power of the Inquisition (Congregation of the Faith) under Joseph Ratzinger, the division of once powerful archdioceses headed by church progressives such as Cardinal Arns in Sao Paolo in Brazil, disciplinary actions against such American progressives as Raymond Hunthausen of Seattle, the appointment of conservative bishops when vacancies occur, the support of far-right and quasi-fascist "Catholic lay" groups, including the secretive Opus Dei. These not only provide a wealthy and influential support group for the Catholic right's numerous publications attacking the reforms of Vatican II but also a fifth-column within the dioceses of the most progressive bishops that keeps up both internal criticism and supplies a reactionary Curia with a constant stream of letters impugning the orthodoxy and pastoral rectitude of progressive church leaders. The Vatican also entered into political alliances of convenience with the U.S. Reagan administration to further its authoritarian purposes in Central America and to gain support for its defiance of Communist authorities in Poland.

On the doctrinal level the pope's chief targets have been the proponents of liberation theology, and here Lernoux's crisp and succinct writing offers good introductions to the major confrontations between the pope's men and the major liberation theologians, including Boff and Gutiérrez. Concluding sections deal with the situation in Central America, most especially Nicaragua.

121   Quade, Quentin L., ed. *The Pope and Revolution. John Paul II Confronts Liberation Theology*. Washington, DC: Ethics and Public Policy Center, 1982.

Essays by Gutiérrez, Vree, Novak, James Schall, with writings and speeches by John Paul II. The book resembles an FBI firing range: we hang up the targets at a safe distance and then turn on the big guns. The book's tone can be summed up as follows: "throughout Christian history, some Christians have sought to use religion for earthly ends...." With premises like these the conclusions are foregone: liberation theology is one such movement. Luckily, however, our current chief pastor has seen through the leftist priests of Latin America. The church may not become directly involved in the world. The laity's job is to act, not theologize, and the clergy's is to teach, not to become involved.

"When the clouds have cleared, this central fact should be apparent: liberation theology and its cousins are not religion but politics, a series of programs for the economic and political redemption of society" (p. 11).

122   Ratzinger, Joseph. *Church, Ecumenism and Politics. New Essays in Ecclesiology.* New York: Crossroad, 1988.

Essays on the nature of the church, its structure, the ecumenical scene, and the relationship of the church to the world. The essays may be new but the ideas contained in them are those of the medieval papacy. As in his inquisition against liberation theology, Ratzinger sets up his answers as if they are questions and his foregone conclusions as if they were categories of intellectual discourse. His dichotomy, "liberation vs. Redemption," is an example. Rather than inquiring how or whether "Redemption" takes on a fuller meaning in liberation theology – both a spiritual and a physical unity – Ratzinger begins his discourse with the type of dichotomies that liberation theology seeks to dissolve: thus refusing to encounter even its intellectual position with good will or intellectual honesty.

In another dichotomy of the "church" and the "people of God" we find the same attempt to present conclusions as the criteria for discussion. The church, Ratzinger decrees, is not the people of God but the mystical body: it is an organization not of equals, as the "emotionalism" of the phrase "people of God" connotes, but of members of a body with a clearly defined head. Who, or more appropriately, what, is that head? Ratzinger clearly indicates his preferences: the hierarchy is no simple administrative body but a special sacramental order of being – ontological supermen if you will; and papal primacy is the core of the hierarchical church.

As in the rest of Ratzinger's current corpus, liberation theology is condemned by insinuation and by the establishment of new categories, in this case by equation with "Marxist-inspired forms."

123   —. *Instruction on Certain Aspects of the "Theology of Liberation."* Rome: Sacred Congregation for the Doctrine of the Faith; Washington, DC: U.S. Catholic Conference, 1984.

Assumes immediately a sharp distinction between liberation from sin, which he asserts to be purely spiritual, and liberation from "servitude of an earthly and temporal kind." Ratzinger thus condemns a priori what he has set out to examine, since the unity of spiritual and temporal sin lies at the heart of liberation theology. One cannot speak of physical oppression, political tyranny, or economic exploitation without defining them as sins against God and humanity, the liberation theologians contend, yet Ratzinger would stress the pre-Vatican II assumption that one can be saved from sin individually and internally while one ignores the injustices and calamities of the world around.

Ratzinger does, however, then go on to examine the origins of liberation theology in the praxis of Latin America and the Third World, to review its biblical foundations, and the "voice of the magisterium," that is the church's own pronouncements, on the process of liberation as found in *Mater et Magistra, Pacem in Terris, Populorum Progressio,* and *Evangelii Nuntiando.*

Ratzinger then goes to what he considers the heart of the problem, the confusion among good-intentioned clergy and laity to adopt "Marxist" analysis to further the process of liberation. While many currents exist within Marxism, its "pure" form emphasizes "class-struggle," and this is not compatible with Christianity. One must avoid treating Marxism as if it were a scientific analysis of reality and not simply a sympathetic language. Ratzinger rejects what he considers the fundamentally violent interpretation of class-struggle and implies that this colors all of liberation theology, although he is careful to note that it is explicit only in "certain of the writings." He then goes on to stress that this identification is incompatible with Vatican II.

What also seems to disturb Ratzinger is what he sees as a sinister perversion of Christian doctrine into a "real system" complete with a rival "church of the poor," a rival liturgy of struggle, that rejects the true sacramental nature of the Eucharist, a questioning of the hierarchical structure of the church, and a "radical politicization of faith's affirmations," which is bad a priori.

Pure liberation theologians, he asserts, stress that whoever disagrees with them are members of the oppressor class. These people hold church social teaching in disdain, attempt a political re-reading of scripture, and make the kingdom of God an earthly goal. Even the assertions of complete faith in Christian creeds and doctrines espoused by the liberation theologians are mere shams, and the Jesus of struggle that they preach denies the Incarnate Word, "God made Lord and Christ." True liberation is baptism, not "the political liberation of a people."

In conclusion Ratzinger asserts that he is not for earthly oppression and calls on all clergy to dialogue with the "Magisterium of the Church," to reject "blind" violence, to seek for the roots of injustice in the hearts of men, and to reject the temptation to seek solutions in structural change. He also dismisses base Christian communities as misinformed and ignorant (if only because they are composed of the laity, a lower form of existence), if "generous," sessions in which these false doctrines are spread

By his stress on what he begins by saying are "certain aspects" of liberation theology – Marxism, class-division, violence, un-Christian Christologies – Ratzinger raises so many red herrings that the reader who is not also familiar with the basic texts of liberation theology will come away believing that these "certain aspects" are the root and heart of the theology. In fact, it is not entirely clear if this is not what the cardinal has in mind, or whether he himself has not fully understood the texts and intent of these works.

124   — . *Instruction on Christian Freedom and Religion.*
         March 22, 1986. Vatican City: Congregation for
         the Doctrine of the Faith, 1986; reprinted in
         Liberation Theology and the Vatican Document, vol.
         3. *Perspectives from the Third World.* Quezon City,
         Philippines: Claretian Publications, 1988.

While bearing the signatures of Cardinal
Ratzinger and Alberto Bovone, titular archbishop of
Caesarea in "Numidia," the letter is apparently the
work of John Paul II himself. It begins by declaring
its inextricable link to the 1984 "Instruction" and by
noting that both documents are to be read together as
part of the papal Magisterium.

Liberation is defined primarily as liberation from
sin, which is defined primarily as spiritual, inner
and individual. The key text for the pope's doctrine
of liberation is found in paragraph 4: "the truth shall
set you free" (John 8:32); and this encapsulates the
papal position. For who, but the pope, and the
Magisterium, declares the truth? And what other
path to freedom than strict adherence to the dictates
of Rome? Here we seem to have turned back not only
from the liberation theology of Latin America but
from most of the Western tradition since the close of
the Middle Ages. And this, in fact, is the very truth
of the document so constructed by the pope and
cardinal.

The Renaissance, Martin Luther, the Enlightenment and the evil French Revolution are all to be
regretted, though in slightly ambiguous terms, for
bringing us "false freedom" (par. 6-13) and only new
forms of oppression, the danger of total annihilation
and new inequalities (14-16). Modern freedom is ambiguous at best (17-19). Instead, the pope preaches,
freedom is not technological but is liberation from sin

and evil. Modern progress will bring freedom only if tied to spiritual liberation (24).

Chapter 2 emphasizes that freedom is only relative: that "man" is not free in relationship to God. In this and in the subsequent sections the pope seems intent on returning the discussion of liberation back to the parameters of medieval scholasticism as he repeats for his modern audience medieval definitions of sin, alienation, idolatry and disorder.

Chapter 3 then tackles the question of liberation and Christian freedom. After reviewing the Old Testament (44-49), the pope declares that the Jewish people were saved from Egypt to become "a kingdom of priests and a holy nation" (44). In the New Testament we have Jesus' proclamation of his mission, a standard foundation of liberation theology, reduced by the pope to the mission that "the poor have the good news preached to them" (50), again asserting the priestly nature of the Judeo-Christian tradition. "The heart of the Christian experience of freedom," we are told, "is in justification by the grace received through faith and the church's sacraments" (52), very "Lutheran" sounding for one who condemns the Reformation.

Freedom and liberation, as the pope seems to define them, are the deliverance from the world into the authoritarian bosom of priests. Human struggle is the fight against the slavery of sin (53). Love is the key to all human relationships. What the pope then concludes from this – in terms Oscar Romero was slain for having renounced – is that the rich are bound to do their duty of charity toward the poor (56). The chapter concludes with a note on Christian eschatology that clearly distinguishes what it considers illusory earthly hopes for a better life with the kingdom of the afterlife.

Thus the document attempts to use many of the standard liberation theology texts and the language of papal social encyclicals to bring the terms of discussion back to the level of pre-Vatican II: a spirituality that is divorced from the "world" and a piety that expresses itself solely on individualistic, inner terms.

Chapter 5 discusses the "liberating" mission of the church through a series of vague sections on the church's social and economic concerns, but then launches off into a series of defensive attacks on vague enemies who infringe on the church's teachings. Medellin's "option for the poor" is watered down to "a love of preference for the poor," which might as easily be understood as an intellectual and sentimental position of sympathy, not any real option (66). In fact, without exaggeration, this lies at the thrust of the pope's thought. The poor are to be pitied and helped, not taught or encouraged to organize and to help themselves. They are to be the objects of charity, not the subjects of their own destiny (66-67). Another aspect of this new "love of preference" is a "detachment from riches," not an actual rejection of them; and in fact Jesus taught the "sort of poverty, made up of detachment, trust in God, sobriety and a readiness to share." Thus the pope and Cardinal Ratzinger, the former student of St. Bonaventure, do for liberation theology what earlier popes with Bonaventure's help did to the social message of St. Francis and his strict followers: they have so internalized and spiritualized it as to make it socially meaningless to the masses of the *real* poor. The chapter concludes with an endorsement of base Christian communities, provided they remain under the control of the Magisterium, the hierarchy and the order of the church and sacraments, thus making them more parish auxiliaries than true communities of believers.

Chapter 5 reviews very superficially the social teachings of the church over the last century, rejecting class struggle, violence and any notion of "revolution," stressing that reform is the only way. Violence in the just revolution, being a venerable church teaching, is admitted as a last resort. As in *Sollicitude Rei Socialis*, the pope concludes with a rapture on the Virgin Mary; yet here he transforms the Magnificat, Mary's song of the humble turning the mighty from their thrones, and a favorite text of the liberation theologians and base communities, into a paean on Mariology, and of Mary as the "patient servant." His ultimate conclusion is that the "sensus fidei," the consensus of the faithful, must be turned away from the illusion of earthly change to a contemplation of Mary.

Thus the pope has attempted to coopt the images, texts, and areas of discourse of liberation theology to turn the social agenda of the church back to the era before Vatican II: to a world tightly controlled by the man at the top, to a humble flock of charitable rich and passive poor, to a church that dictates from on high and listens to no ignorance, wisdom, or independent thought from "below."

125 —. and Vittorio Messori. *The Ratzinger Report. An Exclusive Interview on the State of the Church.* Salvator Attanasio and Graham Harrison, trans. San Francisco: Ignatius Press, 1985.

Essential reading into the mind of the grand inquisitor. Ratzinger expounds his – and he would claim the magisterium's – views on a wide variety of issues. These include the continued existence of

heresy, the misinterpretation of Vatican II, the
nature of the papal "Restoration" under John Paul II,
the distortion of the meaning of the church by modern
innovators; the supremacy of Rome in all things
Catholic, the shattering of the traditional bonds of
theology, catechesis, exegesis, Christology; the need
to reaffirm the authority of the Father; the drift
from liberalism to permissiveness; the natural subor-
dination of women and the role model of Fatima; a
reaffirmation of the anticorporal, ascetic nature of
pre-Vatican II Catholic spirituality and of the body-
spirit split that liberation theologians have rejected;
the call for a restoration of some of the pre-conciliar
liturgy; the necessity of reviving Catholic teaching on
the devil, hell and purgatory, the angels and the
whole host of spiritual weapons long held dear by
ecclesial supremacists; a turn away from "modern"
Christianity; a call for an adherence to his *Instruction on Certain Aspects;* a rejection of class struggle as
a valid foundation for theology; and the centrality of
European models of Christendom throughout the
world.

126   Schall, James V., S.J. *The Church, the State and Society
       in the Thought of John Paul II.* Chicago, IL:
       Franciscan Herald Press, 1982.

A volume in *The John Paul Synthesis. A Trinity
College Symposium.* This is a deeply sympathetic
analysis. Schall's sources are almost exclusively
primary: the letters, speeches and encyclicals of the
pope, as is appropriate. But let the uninitiated be-
ware. His bibliography of secondary works is
another matter: Catholicism from an Anglican
drawing room, addressing the problems that the
modern church, including this pope, have tackled

with enthusiasm with decades-old works on "society" by such noted intellectual conservatives from our grandparents' generation as C. S. Lewis, Hilaire Belloc, Malcolm Muggeridge, Dorothy Sayers, and such modern conservatives as Michael Novak and the American Enterprise Institute.   Barely a word is spake on the problem and importance of liberation theology.

127   Williams, George Huntston. *The Law of Nations and the Book of Nature.* Collegeville, MN: St. John's University, 1984.

This is a series of three essays on John Paul II's Christian humanism, including a reflection on the pope's *Instruction* on liberation theology and his alternative to the Latin American model.

* *
*

Chapter 4: *Liberating the First World. Liberation Theologies in Europe*

Theological Foundations

128 Burnham, Frederic B., Charles S. McCoy and M. Douglas Meeks, eds. *Love. The Foundation of Hope. The Theology of Jürgen Moltmann and Elisabeth Moltmann Wendel.* San Francisco: Harper & Row, 1988.

This collection of essays offers an excellent introduction to the thought of these two ground-breaking theologians, whose thought and lives have been profoundly influenced by their experience as young Germans in World War II. Moltmann's work was born out of the despair of war service and defeat. In a prison camp he was moved to begin to think about answers and discovered the self-sacrificing love of Christ and a way of hope. His "theology of love" thus became a means of transporting the emptiness of the self into a positive force that would transform society. Elisabeth Moltmann-Wendel grew from a similar experience of despair and powerlessness over the destruction of her world. Her feminist theology has emerged as a means of empowering women's, and men's, personal and societal lives to recognize the divinity in us all.

The organization of this book is a masterful guide, from the personal dynamics of the theology of love to a realization of its key role in liberating and rebuilding society. It includes essays by Moltmann, Moltmann-Wendel, Meeks, José Míguez Bonino, Letty M. Russell, and Susan B. Thistlewaite. Míguez Bonino demonstrates how the personal love of

individuals for one another sets the tone of the
household and family, which in turn is the model of
love that binds together the base Christian community. Like the early church, these "households"
based on love thus become models of societal justice.
Russell then emphasizes that communities empowered
by love are the hope for the future as they overcome
a Christianity and society in which the partnership
taught by Christ has been overcome by Caesar and
his patriarchy. The communal characteristics of love
are therefore justice, liberation, and authority that
are based on covenant, not compulsion. Thistlewaite
adds a new dimension to this process by stressing that
black women must first love themselves in a profound
way that goes beyond self-acceptance. The love that
these individuals then give in community is the
foundation of hope for a new, just society.

129   Metz, Johann Baptist. *The Emergent Church. The
      Future of Christianity in a Postbourgeois World.*
      Peter Mann. trans. New York: Crossroad, 1981.

Metz was a leading figure at Vatican II and is
considered by most to be one of the most influential
European theologians on the development of
liberation theology. This book is a series of lectures
around the themes of Christianity's need to free itself
from "bourgeois" religion. By this he means that in
the relatively prosperous industrial democracies religion does not claim our lives but is itself the creature
of our materialistic middle-class values. This is the
phenomenon that he calls "bourgeois unapproach-
ability." Our religion therefore must once again
become a creation of the Gospels, not of the Western
bourgeoisie. Metz insists that the only way to save
our valid "middle class" freedoms is to realize our

solidarity with the poor, the miserable and the oppressed and to overcome the political and moral challenges of our age. We therefore cannot continue a Christianity isolated from the prophetic calls to justice and liberation and must instead undergo a conversion of our hearts and lives.

Catholicism itself, Metz insists, must move beyond a paternalistic, authoritarian model to a church inspired by the "base community," that is, a church made up of, and responsible to, ourselves, not to a remote hierarchy. At the same time, change cannot come from above but must come from the people as the Third World errupts into our historical and social situation.

There are several obstacles to this process of becoming a "base community" church, Metz contends. These include Pope John Paul II, the hierarchical structure of the church, and progressive bourgeois theology, which seeks to fit religion to the conditions of our time and place.

130　　—. *Faith in History and Society. Toward a Practical Fundamental Theology.* David Smith, trans. New York: Seabury Press, 1980.

This is an extended analysis of the basis for a new political theology that first attempts to clear the air from the misconception that Christianity has never had a political theology and to chart a middle way between the extreme "privatization" of religion and its strict secularization. Metz' concept of "privatization," the turning of Christianity's piety, sacramental life, theological reflection and ethics away from the life of community and society and toward the dynamics of an inner salvation, has been of tremendous influence on later forms of liberation theol-

ogy. His notion of a political theology as a critique
of middle-class religion, a political theology that
seeks to uphold the values and structures of our
present society, has also been fundamental. Metz
stresses that Christianity needs to return to a faith in
history and society through an emphasis on praxis.

The major elements of this fundamental theology
therefore include the freedom of Jesus Christ, the
memory of suffering, the dialectics of progress,
redemption and emancipation. Thus the realities of
suffering and liberation must once again become
fundamental to Christian thought. Metz insists that
a return to "narrative" and memory, an insistence that
theology is talking about real events, real suffering,
and real people – and the solidarity that this
implies – is basic to our faith.

131   —. *Theology of the World.* William Glen-Doepel, trans.
London: Burns & Oates; New York: Herder &
Herder, 1969.

This is a collection of essays written between 1961
and 1967 around the theme of the secular responsibility of the believer. Part 1 examines how the
Christian views the world and how the believer in
the historical Jesus and the Jesus event lives in
today's world. Part 2 examines the eschatological
view, how we as Christians and Westerners are
fascinated by the new to the diminution of tradition.
Any competent theology, Metz argues, must face this
fact and must discover how to fit an other-world
eschaton to the social gospel to create an eschatology
that is demanded by our biblical faith.

This faith must contain a creative and militant
eschatology that eschews false distinctions between
the sacred and the profane. In this light Metz calls

for a new asceticism that does not turn a hateful eye
away from the world but that springs from a hope for
the world in its elimination of egotism and individualism. Thus asceticism also becomes part of a mysticism that is realigned with social activism.

132   —, as ed. *Christianity and the Bourgeois. Concilium*
       125. New York: Seabury Press, 1979.

       Essays by Baum, Schüssler Fiorenza, Castillo,
       Metz, Waskow, Schiffers and others on the meaning
       of "bourgeois," on bourgeois religion, on its cultural
       history in early Christianity, and in Judaism and
       Christianity, the U.S. and Europe today.

133   — and Jean Pierre Jossua, eds. *Christianity and
       Socialism. Concilium* 105. New York: Seabury
       Press, 1977.

       Essays by Ruggieri, Baum, Muru, Warnien, Garcia-
       Gomet, Weiler, Füssel, Traber, Lesbaupin, Ellacuria
       and others on Christianity and socialism in Europe,
       Africa, and Latin America.

134   Moltmann, Jürgen. *The Crucified God. The Cross of
       Christ as the Foundation and Criticism of Theology.*
       R. A. Wilson and John Bowden, trans. New York:
       Harper & Row, 1974.

       A deeply focused examination of the meaning of
       the cross and of Christocentric theology that grows
       out of Moltmann's experience of the disaster and
       despair of Germany after World War II. He exam-
       ines all aspects of the cross as a symbol and sacrament
       of our time and condition that will liberate us and our
       religion from the lies and vanity of our situation and

from the struggle for power and from the fear that dominates our lives.

The Christology of the Cross is essentially that of the human abandoned by God. While Moltmann has been criticized for abandoning his "theology of hope" in favor of this view, he emphasizes that it is essentially the same theology: one cannot have the cross without the resurrection, and vice-versa.

Moltmann examines two forms of liberation: the psychological one that follows Freud's analysis and categories; and the political, which attempts, as did Freud on the personal level, to free us from the ideologies of political religions that have always been part of Western tradition from Greco-Roman and Judaic time on. Moltmann calls for a rejection of the Constantinian tradition of Christian political thought and calls on the church to take a critical stance toward power. In so doing Christians will be able to free themselves from a series of vicious political cycles: of poverty, of force, of racial and cultural alienation, of the industrial pollution of nature, of senselessness and godforsakenness.

He rejects both capitalist and Marxist forms of salvation, but insists that socialism is impossible without democracy and vice-versa. Elite dictatorships and technocracies do not work in establishing social justice, since both forms ignore the fact that liberation cannot succeed without an understanding and the participation of the particular and the historical.

Moltmann's forms of liberation thus look forward to, and help form, the various forms of liberation theology today.

135   —. *The Gospel of Liberation.* H. Wayne Pipkin, trans. Waco, TX: Word Books, 1973.

Not seen.

136   —. *The Power of the Powerless. The Word of Liberation for Today.* Margaret Kohl, trans. San Francisco: Harper & Row, 1983.

This is a collection of sermons on biblical texts in the Old and New Testament relating to the history of the powerless and the hope and power that faith in God and community bring. Neither anger nor resignation are answers for the oppressed, but action in the light of faith and hope is. Texts range from Genesis, the Prophets, and the Gospels, many of them key for liberation theology. The book concludes with essays on solidarity, the birth of hope, Easter as a protest against death, Pentecost as a feast of sharing, liberation and acceptance for the handicapped, and the ministry of the church.

Ultimately Moltmann calls for a church that will be the subject of its own history, and a liberating and a prophetic community.

137   —. *Theology of Hope. On the Ground and the Implications of a Christian Eschatology.* James W. Leitch, trans. New York: Harper & Row; London: SCM, 1967.

This is the reverse side of the theology of the cross and sees the world through an eschatological hope. After an introductory meditation on hope the book discusses eschatology and revelation, promise and history, resurrection and the future Jesus Christ, eschatology and history, and the "exodus church," the concrete form of eschatological hope, the church as a community of salvation. These are topics that were to become major themes of liberation theology.

138   —. and others. *Communities of Faith and Radical Discipleship*. G. McLeod Bryan, ed. Macon, GA: Mercer University Press, 1986.

Not seen.

139   Pannenberg, Wolfhart. *Theology and the Kingdom of God*. Philadelphia: Westminster Press, 1969.

A collection of four essays on the theology of the kingdom of God, the kingdom of God and the church, the kingdom of God as the foundation of ethics, and a study of the ministry of Jesus according to the theology of "appearance," the immanence of the kingdom in the here and now as revealed in the life and words of Jesus. Includes a lengthy portrait of Pannenberg by Richard John Neuhaus.

Pannenberg stresses that the church is not the kingdom, and that the kingdom demands an involvement with the world in the here and now, as the world is also part of the kingdom. The church, on the other hand, exists to serve the kingdom: to allow humans to build the kingdom and not to throw itself up as a substitute for it. A fundamental thinker for an emerging political theology.

140   Schillebeeckx, Edward. *God Among Us. The Gospel Proclaimed*. New York: Crossroad, 1983.

A series of biblical reflections on the way to freedom, a Christocentric spirituality, and the unity of inner spirituality and a life in the world.

141   Verkuyl, Johannes. *Break Down the Walls. A Christian Cry for Racial Justice*. Leis B. Smedes, trans. Grand Rapids, MI: W.B. Eerdmans, 1973.

Not seen.

142   —. *The Message of Liberation in Our Age.* Dale Cooper, trans. Grand Rapids, MI: W.B. Eerdmans, 1970.

Liberation, far from being tied solely to Third-World concerns, is a universal theme. Verkuyl, a Dutch theologian, discusses liberation in the context of the Bible, in our own age, as liberation from sin, the "powers of this age," and from death. He then focuses on Christ as liberator, the role of mission in proclaiming the message of the liberator, and the themes of liberation in contemporary religion and ideology. Final chapters deal with the role of the church in God's plan for liberation and the process of changing the church to meet this role.

Political Theology and Liberation

143   Ambler, Rex, and David Haslam, eds. *Agenda for Prophets. Towards a Political Theology for Britain.* London: Bowerdean Press, 1980.

This collection of essays seeks to promote a "British theology" that will take the insights of Third-World theologies, especially as applied to liberation situations in the U.S., for an "engagement of Christian thought with Christian praxis [to] create a new vision of kingdom." /This view must, almost of necessity, be that of the left, since the tradition of religious thought on politics has almost exclusively been from the right. It must also be a theology from the prophetic tradition to inspire action for badly needed social change. /
Essays are grouped around the themes of action, history, perspective and styles. Míguez Bonino gives

"a view from Latin America" on pp. 102-9. In the words of Johann Baptist Metz, this is also an attempt to "deprivatize theology."

144   Casalis, Georges. *Correct Ideas Don't Fall from the Skies. Elements for an Inductive Theology.* Jeanne Marie Lyons and Michael John, trans. Maryknoll, NY: Orbis Books, 1984.

A series of essays that insist that all theory must derive from praxis (inductive) rather than from the traditional methods of theology that attempt to apply maxims to real life (deductive). His aim is not to debate the validity of revolutionary militancy but to reflect on its spiritual consequences. The theologian and theology in general cannot be neutral toward politics. Casalis relates how life under Hitler, the French wars in Vietnam and in Algeria brought home to him the modern choice: suicide in the face of overwhelming injustice and complicity or conversion of life.

Themes include the awareness of the role and function of the dominant theology, the rediscovery and rereading of scripture, a reshaping of hermeneutics, reshaping our identities in relation to that of Jesus of Nazareth, the political interpretation of events and personal life.

Casalis' outlook is frankly leftist, aimed against "capitalist domination, exploitation, oppression, and alienation." Only revolution will overcome these structures to bring economic justice (collectivity of means of production), a grass-roots political constitution to society, and the liberation of creativity to form a new human being. No hope remains in European capitalism.

One wonders how Casalis might respond to recent changes and revelations on the appeal among peoples of the alternative systems and "correct" ideas and what theological deductions he might draw. A stark contrast to the people-based theologies of Latin America that attempt to eschew any ideology.

145   Forrester, Duncan. *Theology and Politics.* Oxford and New York: Basil Blackwell, 1988.

"Political theology" is not an invention of twentieth-century European elites but has been with the Western tradition since antiquity and has always played a key role in Christianity, though its almost universal support of existing structures and power have given it a transparency that has only now begun to be analyzed.

This is an excellent introduction to political theology and its ties to other liberation theologies traced through certain key themes. Chapter 1 surveys historical forms of political theology in the ancient world; chapter 2 deals with the church-state dichotomy of the private and political since the Reformation and Enlightenment; chapter 3 with the "promise of liberation theology," which contains a succinct comparison between the Latin American theology and European political theology; 4 treats the political exegesis of the Bible and its critics; 5 the question of a political Christ in Marxism, popular piety, and the imitation of Christ; 6 the church, theology and the poor, including a discussion of a new ecclesiology based on the base Christian communities and the "bourgeois captivity" of the Northern churches. The concluding chapter treats the responsibilities of political theology and various forms of political theology, including the Eusebian, church, and prophetic theologies.

146 Garaudy, Roger. *The Alternative Future. A Vision of Christian Marxism.* Leonard Mayhew, trans. New York: Simon & Schuster, 1974.

An optimistic prophesy that 1970s youth will opt for a future neither capitalist nor Stalinist and that the Christian image will inform and infuse the new form of social and economic life that emerges: a socialism of self-management.

147 Kee, Alistair. *Marx and the Failure of Liberation Theology.* London: SCM; Philadelphia: Trinity Press International, 1990.

Not seen.

148 —. *A Reader in Political Theology.* Philadelphia, PA: Westminster Press, 1974.

A collection of readings from the varieties of European and North American thought that sees the varieties of liberation as a form of political theology.

149 —. *The Scope of Political Theology.* London: SCM, 1978.

Not seen.

150 —. *Seeds of Liberation. Spiritual Dimensions to Political Struggle.* London: SCM, 1973.

Essays and interviews with and by Kee, Daniel Berrigan, Colin Winter, Jim Forest, Basil Moore, Mary Condren, Viv Broughton and Thomas Cullinan on social and political signs, a new community of spirit and resistance, keeping sanity in the face of the beast, on materialism, the sacramental life, liberation and resistance for both men and women.

151   Lakeland, Paul. *Freedom in Christ. An Introduction to Political Theology.* 2d ed. New York: Fordham University Press, 1986.

Surveys political theology in the Old and New Testament and their worlds, in Christian history and in today's "real" world.   Chapter 7, "A Political Theology," discusses freedom from ideology, indignation, people as subjects or objects of their history, the cross, and base communities.   Chapter 8, "Political theology and the Vatican," sees liberation theology as a form of political theology, along with German political theology, black theology, and feminist theology.

152   McDonagh, Enda. *Church and Politics. From Theology to a Case History of Zimbabwe.* Notre Dame, IN: University of Notre Dame Press, 1980.

McDonagh writes about the explicit meeting of theology and the new realities of the Third World and its revolutionary situation, yet her reflections are, ultimately and openly, about the situation in Ireland and the condition of the marginalized of the First World as well.   See also **227**.

153   Petulla, Joseph M. *Christian Political Theology. A Marxian Guide.* Maryknoll, NY: Orbis Books, 1972.

This is an attempt to use Marxist analytic tools to examine the political implications of the faith. Despite the author's obvious slant, he critiques elements of both Marxist and liberal capitalist systems. Petulla surveys the roots of political theology, Marx' criticism of religion, the thought of Bloch, Moltmann, and Metz. He then examines the Marxist theory of alienation from Marx through Castro and Guevara, liberation in Marxist theory, ethical praxis in the early church, and the contemporary relevance of Marx, Engels, Lenin, and Mao. Remarkable, recent events have made the foundation of this theory – the appeal of Marxism among peoples – a praxis of fantasy as Marx, Lenin and Mao seem to slide into oblivion.

154   Sölle, Dorothee. *Political Theology.* John Shelley, trans. Philadelphia: Fortress Press, 1974.

The author traces a growth from the existentialism of Bultmann to the engagement of freeing the gospel kerygma from ideological fixations, from the "death of God" to the "God of the oppressed." John Shelley provides an excellent introduction to both Sölle's work and the tradition of political theology. Key themes include a new interest in the Jesus of history and the ministry of liberation, a new understanding of sin and of forgiveness that steps beyond

the individualistic piety of the enlightenment church
to the liberation of all: the oppressed, the poor, those
who mourn.

155   Stockwood, Mervyn. *The Cross and the Sickle.* London:
       Sheldon Press, 1978.

The bishop of Southwark, a London working-class
district just opposite the affluence of the City's stock
exchange, reflects on the relationship of Marxism and
Christianity. His book is born out of the experience
of his parishioners' poverty and alienation and his
despair over Christianity's failure. His conclusions
are a form of liberation theology for the First World:
the Bible is not about inner tranquillity and pastoral
care but about society. The Old Testament prophets
and Jesus' preaching of the kingdom are its main
focus. The church is the instrument of the kingdom,
not the kingdom itself, and in this Christianity can
offer an alternative to Marxist vision.

Reflections of Liberation

156   Anderson, Gerald H., and Thomas F. Stransky, eds.
       Liberation Theologies in North America and Europe.
       Mission Trends 4. New York: Paulist Press, 1979.

This collection of essays includes an introductory
section by McAfee Brown, Herzog, Richard A.
McCormick, S.J., Jim Wallis, Moltmann, Paul VI and
others.

157   Baltazar, Eulalio. *Liberation Theology and Teilhard de
       Chardin.* Chambersberg, PA: ANIMA Books, 1989.

Not seen.

158   Caudron, Marc, ed. *Faith and Society. Acta Congressus Internationalis Theologica Lovaniensis 1976.* Paris: Duculot, 1978.

        Essays on God and society, man-woman relations, the theology of liberation (pp. 157-207), and the community phenomenon. The European theologians who examine liberation theology include Ponthot, van Nieuwenhove, De Graeve, Asveld, and Borrat.

159   Chapman, G. Clarke, Jr. *Bonhoeffer and Liberation Theology.* St. Louis, MO: Chapman, 1980.

        Not seen.

160   Clark, David B. *Basic Communities. Towards an Alternative Society.* London: SPCK, n.d.

        An excellent account of the movement in the U.K. Attempts to demonstrate their importance for both the church and the wider world.

161   Dickinson, Richard D. N. *To Set at Liberty the Oppressed. Towards an Understanding of Christian Responsibilities for Development/Liberation.* Geneva: World Council of Churches, 1975.

        The Protestant response to the Catholic encyclicals, bishops' synods and theology of the Vatican II era.

162   Elliott, C. *Is There a Liberation Theology for the U.K.?* York: University of York, 1985.

        Not seen.

163   Gatti, Vincenzo. *Rich Church – Poor Church.*
       Maryknoll, NY: Orbis Books, 1974.

       Not seen.

164   Greinacher, Norbert, and Alois Müller, eds. *The Poor
       and the Church. Concilium* 104. New York:
       Seabury, 1977.

       Essays by Gutiérrez, Bockmann, Michel Mollat (on
       the historical development of the notion of the poor
       and poverty in Christian thought), Marie Dominique
       Chenu (on Vatican II and the church of the poor),
       Lukács, Post, Muñoz, Ives Congar, Conzemius and
       others on the church and the poor in the Bible, in
       history, in Latin America, and in Europe. An excel-
       lent survey that brings together some of the best
       theologians and historians of Europe and Latin
       America.

165   Jossua, Jean-Pierre, and Johann-Baptist Metz, eds.
       Doing Theology in New Places. Concilium 115. New
       York: Seabury Press, 1979.

       Essays on new contexts and cultural factors in
       theology. Includes essays by Schüssler Fiorenza
       ("Towards a Liberating and Liberated Theology.
       Women Theologians and Feminism in the U.S.A.," on
       pp. 22-32) and by Alfredo Fierro Bardaji and Fumio
       Tabuchi (on Kim Chi Ha).

166   Lane, Dermot A., ed. *Liberation Theology. An Irish Dialogue.* Dublin: Gill and Macmillan, 1977; published in the U.S. as *Ireland, Liberation and Theology.* Maryknoll, NY: Orbis Books, 1978.

Essays by Enda McDonagh, Francisco Claver, and Garrett FitzGerald, including McDonagh's "An Irish Theology of Liberation?" pp. 87-102. The authors examine the possibility of developing an Irish theology of liberation that will address the issues of dependency, marginalization, alienation, poverty, religious hatred and violence in both the north and south, among both Catholics and Protestants. The situations in Latin America and the Philippines are used not as rigid models but as keys to the application of theology and religious values to social and economic problems. McDonagh stresses that an Irish liberation theology must grow out of the Irish experience and must enable the Irish once again to become subjects, not objects, of their history. Irish economics, history, sexuality and spirituality are all areas that must be addressed by a revived theology.

167   Laurentin, René. *Liberation, Development and Salvation.* Maryknoll, NY: Orbis Books, 1972.

Not seen.

168   Metz, Johann-Baptist, and Edward Schillebeeckx, eds. *The Teaching Authority of Believers. Concilium* 180. Edinburgh: T. & T. Clark, 1985.

Essays by Vorgrimler, Schillebeeckx, Waldenfel, Schüssler Fiorenza, Sobrino, and others on the legacy of Vatican II, new structures in the church, the change from "sensus fidei" (now reasserted by John Paul II) to "consensus fidelium," the people claiming authority and power, the people of God in Latin America, and the role of the people in defining Christian faith.

169   —. *Martyrdom Today. Concilium* 163. Edinburgh: T. & T. Clark; New York: Seabury Press, 1983.

Essays by Baumeister, Rahner, Boff, Sobrino, Claver, McDonagh, Hernandez Pico, Barth, Casaldáliga, Tutu, Herzberg, Cone, Casalis and Daniel Berrigan on martyrdom in history, in ecclesiology and in theology. Their discussion of the world today includes Latin America, the Philippines, Ireland, South Africa, the Holocaust, Bonhoeffer, Martin Luther King, and the Plowshares in the U.S. An essential theme of liberation theology.

170   Metz, René, and John Schlick, eds. *Liberation Theology and the Message of Salvation*. Papers of the Fourth Cerdic Colloquium. Strasbourg, May 10-12, 1973. David G. Gelzer, trans. Pittsburgh, PA: Pickwick Press, 1978.

Essays by Merle, Valadier and Duquoc on ideologies of liberation; by van Lunen-Chenu, Guichard, Casalis, and Wieser on women's liberation, class struggle, conscientization, and the church as a sign of liberation and salvation.

The colloquium came to several conclusions: that there are fundamental differences in approach among liberation theologians, largely grouped as inductive and deductive approaches; that the class struggle, despite church pronouncements and the condemnations of conservative critics, is a reality that liberation theology must come to grips with; and that liberation, however it is used by theologians, is not the same as salvation.

171   O'Halloran, James, SVD. *Living Cells. Developing Small Christian Communities.* Maryknoll, NY: Orbis Books, 1984.

Written with a European audience in mind, this is less a "how to" than a "point of reference." Replaces the term "base Christian community" with "small" Christian community to emphasize the fact that the church grows outward from such groups and that they are not at the bottom of any hierarchical structure. In another sense the author hopes to demonstrate that the "base" need not necessarily mean only the economically poor but that this form of church can be translated to every Christian church and continent.

Topics include the origin and growth of small Christian communities; their nature; how to organize such a community, the youth apostolate, and new models for an emerging church. Good, if brief, annotated bibliography on basic communities.

172   Paoli, Arturo. *Freedom to Be Free.* Charles Underhill, trans. Maryknoll, NY: Orbis Books, 1973.

Life's true theme is the journey toward freedom; and the constant theme of the Bible is liberation. Truth is the integralism of the person and the world; while freedom means freedom *within* the church. Ultimately it is difficult to determine whether Paoli's liberation and integralism looks forward to key elements of liberation theology or whether it is a throw back to an earlier twentieth-century Catholic Action form.

173 ——. *Gather Together in My Name: Reflections on Christianity and Community.* Robert R. Barr, trans. Maryknoll, NY: Orbis Books, 1987.

Paoli's pastoral, discursive, extremely personalist form of theology is difficult to assess, especially in the context of liberation theology's very social and economic themes. Nevertheless, this Italian theologian's thrust *is* liberation, although he comes from the same personalist, rather than structuralist, framework that seems to motivate Pope John Paul II. Paoli's work seeks to lead the reader on a journey from alienation toward a realization of self and from self to community. This community is both personal and sacramental: reconciliation and communion have both sacramental and societal aspects. Thus poverty can have positive value when taken in this personalist sense: a Franciscan adoption of the inner and outer poverty that allows the Christian to live in solidarity with the poor and the oppressed.

Beyond this, however, Paoli stresses that the poor must build their own church, and that the hierarchical church must listen to the poor and become the church of the poor. While left-leaning analyses tend to verge on ideology, they are preferable to capitalist-inspired analyses, he contends. In any case, building community is always a revolutionary activity, Paoli reminds us; and a thorough examination of the roots of Christian piety and their honest application will demonstrate their liberating and revolutionary potential, both in the church and in society.

174   Pohier, Jacques, and Dietmar Mieth, eds. *The Dignity of the Despised of the Earth. Concilium* 130. New York: Seabury Press, 1979.

Essays by Bianchi, Sobrino, Eckert, Pietri, Blumenkranz, Dussel, Proaño, Claver, Dhavamony, and McDonagh on "those without dignity" in the Old and New Testaments, Palestinian Christianity, the early church of the second and third centuries, relations between Jews and Christians in the Middle Ages, the "savage" and "other" in the era of discovery, the wretched in Latin America, in India and among women, ethnics, and immigrant populations in the First World today.

175   Preiswerk, Matias. *Educating in the Living Word. A Theoretical Framework for Christian Education.* Robert R. Barr, trans. Maryknoll, NY: Orbis Books, 1987.

The subtitle reads, "A Theoretical Framework for Christian Education." That education takes full account of the socio-economic conditions of those being educated, their requirements and desires. A handbook for an education that liberates, this surveys the various types of educational settings, the various descriptions – philosophical, political, pastoral, pedagogical – and the principal models. It then proceeds to discuss the hermeneutic analysis in the Hebrew Bible, Jesus as teacher, how to define a liberative Christian education, and the church's mission in theology, conscientization, and methodology.

176   Winter, Derek. *Hope in Captivity. The Prophetic Church in Latin America.* London: Epworth, 1977.

This is an attempt to write a liberation theology for a British audience based on the experiences of the author in returning to Brazil, where he had been a missionary, and realizing that he had missed the most important element of his mission: learning from the experience and inspiration of the people themselves.

177   Wolterstorff, Nicholas. *Until Justice and Peace Embrace.* Grand Rapids, MI: Eerdmans, 1983.

The Kuyper Lectures delivered at the Free University of Amsterdam in 1981. Topics include the impact of Christianity upon the world and vice-versa, its place in the modern world system, the choice of liberation in the modern church and the tasks ahead of it: justice, the reconciliation of rich and poor and nations based on the true meaning of *shalom,* as a fullness and harmony.

178   Wren, Brian A. *Education for Justice. Pedagogical Principles.* London: SCM; Maryknoll, NY: Orbis Books, 1977.

Like Paolo Freire's education for liberation in the Third World, this is an education for the First World and focuses on local redevelopment, women's rights, and justice in international affairs. The goal of such education is to explain the meaning of social justice. Topics covered include the act of knowing, education as dialog, justice as rational thought and in Christian faith, justice, power and conflict, the marks of cultural oppression, the awakening of justice, learning the realities of power, taking political stands, and the question, "is justice possible?"

European Praxis: Danilo Dolci

179   Ammann, Walter. *Danilo Dolci.* Bern: Benteli, 1972.

Even before Vatican II set into motion changes that would recognize the laity as equals to the hierarchy in spreading Christ's kingdom. Danilo Dolci was implementing the council's hidden seeds of liberation by working among the poor and uneducated of western Sicily and attempting to conscienticize their lives and have them create cooperatives and political action groups to overcome their oppression. He was also confronting a reactionary hierarchy bent on turning back any reforms that would make the people the subjects of their own history.

This is a review of his life, with special focus on his nonviolent activities.   Nicely illustrated with photos. Topics include Dolci, Sicilian life and culture, economy, history, including the Mafia. Briefly traces his career, highlighting the Partinico trial, his contest with the Mafia, and his debt to Gandhi.   An excellent chronology up to July 1972.

180   Dolci, Danilo, *Creature of Creatures. Selected Poems.* Justin Vitiello, trans. Saratoga, CA: Anma Libri, 1980.

Dolci's poems on the life of Sicily's peasants, their exploitation, the need for nonviolent change.   A good introduction to Dolci's life and career.

181   —. *For the Young.* Antonia Cowan, trans. London: Macgibbon & Kee, 1967.

Answers letters from children who have written supporting his efforts. The letters come from all over

Europe and the United States. Their constant theme is the "waste" of Sicilian lives. The points are often made through simple dialogs.

182 —. *The Man Who Plays Alone.* New York: Pantheon, 1968.

Two pieces of peasant wisdom typify the problem: in western Sicily *chi cammina solo, si trova sempre bene* (the man who walks alone always feels at ease) and *chi gioca solo non perde mai* (the man who plays alone never loses). Dolci's own recollections of his struggle to raise the consciousness of the Sicilian peasants to overcome their sense of isolated self-interest and to struggle nonviolently for basic human rights. The alienation of the Sicilian poor is expressed in hostility to any loyalty other than to self and to the closed circle of the family. The opposition of the church hierarchy to his efforts is not merely personal but official policy.

183 —. *A New World in the Making.* R. Munroe, trans. New York: Monthly Review Press, 1965.

An attempt to go beyond the moral laws of the past to find new answers for a new age, a new ethical system for a new united world. Studies efforts in the Soviet Union, Yugoslavia, Senegal, and Ghana to familiarize the West with different approaches.

184 —. *The Outlaws of Partinico.* R. Munroe, trans. New York: Orion Press, 1963.

Dolci's account of the conditions around Partinico in western Sicily, its poverty, violence and alienation. Focuses on Dolci's group and their struggle against violence and examines the life of violence in the region. The book's heart is a portrait of these "outlaws," the fishermen and the poor peasants, their living conditions, lack of education, social life and values, and their sense of exploitation.

Part V of the book turns the term "outlaw" on its head by describing the "strike in reverse" by Dolci and the region's unemployed to begin work on a damaged section of road. They did so without government permission but in accordance with Article IV of the Italian Constitution guaranteeing the right to work to all citizens. Follows their nonviolent action, arrest, and trial, and Dolci's apologia for nonviolent civil disobedience. While he and his group were found guilty, the judge passed light sentences in view of "the high moral value of Dolci's action." The book concludes with some notes from Dolci's Study Centers.

185   —. *Poverty in Sicily.* Harmondsworth: Penguin Books, 1966.

The findings of a series of surveys among the poor and unemployed in and around Palermo in western Sicily. Responses to the question, "Do you think it is God's will that you are unemployed?" show an almost pagan belief in the unbridgeable gap between God and the world of humans. God takes care of himself and leaves us to do the same. He is not concerned with "social" issues. As one informant remarked, "In my opinion God's got nothing to do with unemployment." A vitally important insight into the forms of informed action that both shaped and were set in motion by Vatican II and the forms of traditional spirituality that liberation theology seeks to replace.

186   —. *Report from Palermo.* P. D. Cummins, trans. New York: Orion Press, 1959.

In his introduction to this volume Aldous Huxley calls Dolci, "one of these modern Franciscans with-a-degree" who have attempted to apply modern sociological and other professional skills to the problems of exploitation, poverty and violence in a new age, but in the same spirit as the medieval saint.

This book is a study of the unemployed in the province of Palermo. It relies on first-hand accounts collected through questionnaires on such areas as education, trade, means of support without work, self-assessment of the situation, religious beliefs, social and political views, opinions on corruption, and ideas for action. Dolci prints the responses verbatim.

187   —. *Sicilian Lives.* New York: Pantheon, 1982.

Accounts of the individuals who make up the "problem" and solution of poverty and liberation in rural Sicily.

188   —. *To Feed the Hungry.* Harmondsworth: Penguin Books, 1966.

Not seen.

189   —. *Waste. An Eye-Witness Report on Some Aspects of Waste in Western Sicily.* R. Munroe, trans. New York: Monthly Review Press, 1964.

This documents "waste" in all its forms: superstition, water pollution and waste, violence and murder, soil erosion, abject poverty and ignorance, waste of natural resources, of human labor and construction, poor housing, depopulation, infant mortality and more. The book is compellingly illustrated with photos, maps, and charts.

190   Hope, Marjorie, and James Young. *The Struggle for Humanity.* Maryknoll, NY: Orbis Books, 1979.

Pages 73-107 treat Dolci's life and struggle for nonviolent change in Sicily, based on interviews and first-hand observations by the authors.

191   Mangione, Jerre. *A Passion for Sicilians. The World Around Danilo Dolci.* New York: William Morrow, 1968.

An excellent book. Dolci mentions God frequently in his early writings but not in his later ones. Has he given up belief? What is the nature of his nonviolence? What are his hopes for revolution and political change? Who is the man behind the legend? Mangione sets out to find some answers.

He first gives an interesting account of Dolci in the U.S. on a speaking tour and the hostility shown him by some Italo-Americans for the bleak picture he draws of Sicily and of Italian corruption. Mangione then travels to Italy where he encounters a marked hostility or bored disinterest in the man from many of Italy's most brilliant writers, thinkers and activists, who find that Dolci has outlived his usefulness. Even some of his former closest friends have now turned against him. Why?

Mangione travels to western Sicily, finds even Sicilians living in the region ignorant of his efforts, finds intense opposition to the man even within his own organization. Much of the hostility stems from Dolci's trust in native Sicilians on his staff, for his "nonprofessional" staff and methods, for the lack of drama in his work at present. Many are bewildered over his commitment: is it religious, political, naive? Dolci does seem to have trouble as an organizer and in keeping the loyalty of his associates.

Most of Mangione's book is in the form of a journal, and this does recount several of Dolci's group actions in Sicily and in Rome. This is important reading for any First-World analyst or activist who seeks to apply the lessons of the Third World and liberation theology to situations close to home.

192   McNeish, James. *Fire Under the Ashes. The Life of Danilo Dolci.* London: Holder & Stoughton, 1965.

The best and most complete biography of Dolci available in English.

193   Melville, Harcourt. *Portraits of Destiny.* New York: Sheed & Ward, 1966.

Dolci is covered on pages 48-97. Focuses on his life, work in Sicily, the Centro Studi, his personality. A good, brief introduction.

194   Peachment, Brian. *The Defiant Ones: Dramatic Studies of Modern Social Reformers.* Oxford: Religious Education Press, 1969.

Discusses Dolci.

195 Waller, Ross D. *Danilo Dolci.* Manchester: Manchester Library and Philosophical Society. *Memoirs and Proceedings*, vol. 102, 1959-1960.

Not seen.

* *
*

Chapter 5: *African Theology*

Bibliographies

196   Parratt, John. *African Theology. A Bibliography.* Zomba: University of Malawi, 1983.

A brief typescript, arranged alphabetically by author, with approximately 300 books and articles.

Introduction

197   Abraham, K. C., ed. *Third World Theologies. Commonalities and Divergences.* Maryknoll, NY: Orbis Books, 1990.

Essays by Bingemer, Carvalho, Battung, Míguez Bonino, Oduyoye, Balasuriya, Torres, James Cone, Tamez, Chikane, Pablo Richard and others on the liberation, contextual and integralist themes that unite all these forms of theology.

198   African Independent Churches. *Speaking for Ourselves.* Braamfontein: Institute for Contextual Theology, 1985.

Chapter 4 contains an outline of an independent African theology.

199   Amirtham, Samuel, and John S. Pobee. *Theology by the*
        People. Reflections on Doing Theology in
        Community. Geneva: World Council of Churches,
        1986.

        This is a collection of essays by Dussel, Kudadjie,
        Ian Fraser, Kwok Pui Lan, Elsa Tamez and others
        that describes and analyzes a theology born out of the
        people of God themselves: their concerns and their
        reception of the Spirit as equal ministers of God's
        word. Thus base Christian communities, Minjung the-
        ology, black, African, feminist, and other forms of
        liberation theology are at base "theology by the
        people."

200   Appiah-Kubi, Kofi and Sergio Torres, eds. *African*
        Theology en Route. Papers from the Pan-African
        Conference of Third-World Theologians, December
        17-23, 1977, Accra, Ghana. Maryknoll, NY: Orbis
        Books, 1979.

        Essays on current trends in African religion, its
        theological sources in the Bible, African beliefs and
        black African arts. Part 3 presents essays on libera-
        tion currents, including women, the church and
        politics, liberation theology, and black American per-
        spectives by Rose Zoé-Obianga, Constance Barratang
        Thetele, Kodwe E. Ankrah, Desmond Tutu, Allan
        Boesak, James Cone, and G. Wilmour.

201   Baëta, Christian G. *Theology As Liberation. Four*
        Contemporary Third World Programmes. Accra:
        Academy of Arts and Sciences, 1983.

        Not seen.

202 Bakole Wa Ilunga. *Paths of Liberation. A Third World Spirituality.* Matthew J. O'Connell, trans. Maryknoll, NY: Orbis Books, 1984.

Spiritual salvation goes hand-in-hand with Zaire's gradual process of economic and social liberation.

203 Baltazar, Eulalio. *The Dark Center. A Process Theology of Blackness.* New York: Paulist Press, 1973.

Not seen.

204 Banana, Canaan. *The Gospel According to the Ghetto.* Rev. ed. Gwelo, Zimbabwe: Mambo Press, 1981.

Not seen.

205 —. *The Theology of Promise. The Dynamics of Self-Reliance.* Harare: College Press, 1982.

This is a call for post-independence Zimbabwe to live up to its socialist ideals and to establish justice in lines with the call of Christianity. At the same time, it is a call on the church to truly become a church of the people. With a preface by Prime Minister Mugabe, this book begs the question: are we forming a new Constantinian alliance?

206 Bavarel, Michel. *New Communities, New Ministries. The Church Resurgent in Africa, Asia and Latin America.* Francis Martin, trans. Maryknoll, NY: Orbis Books, 1983.

This is a process of learning from the Third World, the end of our old notions of missionary religion, and a realization that the poor and marginalized can be, and are becoming, the subjects of their own history, their own theology. This book is a series of descriptions of newly emerging praxis in Africa, Latin America, and Asia. It includes descriptions of beliefs in the Peruvian Andes, lay pastors in Kinshasa, base communities in El Salvador, and Egyptian nuns ministering to the ragpickers of Cairo.

207   Becken, H.-J., ed. *Relevant Theology for Africa.* Durban: Lutheran Publishing House, 1973.

       Not seen.

208   Bengu, Sibusiso. *Mirror or Model? The Church in an Unjust World.* New York: Lutheran World Ministries, 1984.

       Not seen.

209   Buthelezi, Manas. *Towards an African Theology.* Stuttgart: E. Klett, 1974.

       An English summary of his thought.

210   Dickson, Kwesi A. *Theology in Africa.* London: Darton, Longman & Todd; Maryknoll, NY: Orbis Books, 1984.

       All aspects of its theological development and variety: African religion, colonial factors, theology's remoteness from current realities, biblical continuity, the theology of the cross, and theology in seminaries, congregations and communities. The focus throughout is on developing black theology. Good bibliography.

211   Donders, Joseph G. *Non-Bourgeois Theology. An African Experience of Jesus.* Maryknoll, NY: Orbis Books, 1985.

A collection of mostly previously published essays on religious life among Africa's Christians. Topics include the nature of God, liturgy, the clergy among the people, mythology, the role of forgiveness and reconciliation, pain and suffering, prayer, politics and religion, and the role of the people of God.

212   Éla, Jean-Marc. *African Cry.* Robert R. Barr, trans. Maryknoll, NY: Orbis Books, 1986.

Beginning with the actual heart of the liturgical and sacramental life: the rite of the Eucharist, Éla focuses in on the essential problem of Christianity in Africa: does it address the deepest urgings for salvation of the African people, or is it a hostile import, a relic of colonialism that seeks to maintain a *spiritual* bondage after political bondage has passed? Africans, the author argues, must seek out their own brand of Christianity by returning to the biblical roots of this religion and taking new meaning from the essential liberation texts: Exodus and the Gospels. The church in Africa must reject its indifference to the socio-economic and political realities of the continent, and must reveal a God who deeply cares for the sufferings of his people, as they exist. An important text of African liberation theology.

213   —. *My Faith as an African*. John Pairman Brown and
        Susan Perry, trans. Maryknoll, NY: Orbis Books,
        1988; London: Geoffrey Chapman, 1989.

        This is a book that takes its life from the reality
        of African rural poverty in the midst of a world, and
        national, economy of plenty. On a theological level
        Éla also begins from African roots: the inheritance of
        African religion, and the role the Christ figure can
        play in bringing meaning to these deeply religious
        myths and practices. Having come from the grass
        roots up, the author then asks whether God can be
        indifferent to the suffering of the African people, and
        so calls for a new activist Christianity that will both
        address the material needs of God's children and
        reveal God in terms that African culture will
        approve.

214   Fabella, Virginia, M.M., and Mercy Amba Oduyoye,
        eds. *With Passion and Compassion. Third World
        Women Doing Theology*. Maryknoll, NY: Orbis
        Books, 1988.

        Essays by Rosemary Edet and Bette Ekeya,
        Dorothy Ramodibe, Thérèse Souga, Louise Tappa,
        Elizabeth Amoah, and Teresa Okure.
        Particularly African conditions are the state of
        oppression left in the post-colonial period, the oppres-
        sive structures of African social and economic life, and
        the oppressive cultural burden that African women
        must contend with.
        There are also strengths in the African religious
        tradition that make Christian faith viable. The role
        of women as prophetesses and priestesses has always
        been strong and equal to that of men. A revival of
        Mariology to confirm the feminine nature of God and

the role of women is important. African religion itself is highly receptive to the notion of a suffering and then victorious Christ who brings health and plenty. Such directions have the full support of biblical texts and of Jesus' own ministry.

215 Ferm, Deane William. *Profiles in Liberation. Thirty-Six Portraits of Third World Theologians.* Mystic, CT: Twenty-Third Publications, 1988.

Theologians from Africa, Asia and Latin America are discussed, including their lives, work and thought. Bibliographies of books and articles, as well as photographs, are provided for each. An excellent introduction. African theologians include Appiah-Kubi, Boesak, Buthelezi, Dickson, Fashole-Luke, Mbiti, Milongo, Mveng, Nyamiti, Oduyoye, Shorter, and Tutu.

216 —. *Third World Liberation Theologies. An Introductory Survey.* Maryknoll, NY: Orbis Books, 1986.

Discusses the various forms of liberation theologies, their resemblances and differences, studies, and criticisms of this theology.

217 —. *Third World Liberation Theologies. A Reader.* Maryknoll, NY: Orbis Books, 1986.

Selections from a host of liberation theologians, including Mbiti, Oduyoye, Tutu, Boesak, Widjaja, and others.

218   Fraser, Ian. *The Fire Runs*. London: SCM, 1975.

         Not seen.

219   Frostin, Per. *Liberation Theology in Tanzania and South Africa. A First-World Interpretation*. Lund, Sweden: Lund University Press, 1988.

         Frostin hopes to interpret for Western audiences two types of African liberation theology: in Tanzania and in South Africa; the one in a socialist state, the second among the oppressed and marginalized. Frostin's emphasis is on the relationship between God and humanity, the analysis of social conflict, including the use of Marxist analysis, and the challenge of "modernity." Frostin stresses the importance of textual analysis as a means of removing our own Western hermeneutic blinders, the "holistic" nature of these theologies of liberation, which see salvation of the soul, of the person, the community and society as one. Good bibliography.

220   Hadjor, Kofi Buenor, and Brian A. Wren, eds. *Christian Faith and Third World Liberation*. London: Third World Communications, 1985.

         Not seen.

221   Healy, Joseph G., M.M. *A Fifth Gospel. The Experience of Black Christian Values*. Maryknoll, NY: Orbis Books, 1981.

         An excellent introduction to base Christian communities in Africa.

222   Katjavivi, Peter, Per Frostin and Kaire Mbuende, eds.
        Church and Liberation in Namibia. London and
        Westminster, MA: Pluto Press, 1989.

        A collection of essays on all aspects of the
        church's role in the struggle for independence in
        Namibia, including the role of liberation theology.
        The book includes a collection of relevant documents
        and a brief bibliography on black and liberation
        theologies.

223   Kijanga, Peter A. S. *Ujamaa and the Role of the Church
        in Tanzania.* Arusha: Evangelical Lutheran
        Church in Tanzania, 1978.

        On the relationship between Christianity and
        politics, socialism and the need for change in
        Tanzania.

224   Magesa, Laurenti. *The Church and Liberation in Africa.*
        Eldoret, Kenya: Gaba, 1976.

        The church and liberation theology in Latin
        America are paradigmatic for the African today.
        The message of liberation theology – that oppression,
        injustice, and poverty are not God-given – has power-
        ful implications for African nations and peoples
        engaged in liberation struggles. Magesa examines the
        place of religion in overcoming Africa's wounds and
        divisions, new liberating ecclesial structures, the role
        of violence and nonviolence, and the demands of
        liberation.   Contains essays by S. Mkude, D. M.
        Mwasaru, and M. Giblin.

225   —. *Liberation Theology in Africa.* Kampala: Gaba
        Publications, 1976.

        Not seen.

226   Mbiti, John S., ed. *African and Asian Contributions to
        Contemporary Theology. Report.* Céligny: Ecu-
        menical Institute, 1977.

        Essays and commentary by Mbiti, Philip A.
        Potter, C. Duraising, Kofi Appiah-Kubi, John Pobee,
        Gerald H. Anderson, John Ramadhani and T. K.
        Thomas on methods, Christology, the church and
        community and theologies in dialog.

227   McDonagh, Enda. *Church and Politics. From Theology
        to a Case History of Zimbabwe.* Notre Dame, IN:
        University of Notre Dame Press, 1980.

        McDonagh writes about the explicit meeting of
        theology and the new realities of the Third World
        and its revolutionary situation; yet her reflections
        are, ultimately and openly, about the situation in
        Ireland and the condition of the marginalized of the
        First World as well.
        Topics in Part 1 include Christian faith and social
        justice, politics and violence in Christian perspective,
        prayer and politics. Part 2 surveys the transition
        from colonial Rhodesia to independent Zimbabwe, the
        liberation of a people and the role of armed struggle
        in that liberation, and the Catholic theory of just
        revolution.
        The author then draws some conclusions for both
        Third and First Worlds: that while revolutionary
        violence may be justified, the just society that it
        proclaimed has not yet been achieved; that non-

violence must be the revolutionary means toward a just society, that the churches must become intimately involved in this process, and that a new ecclesiology of the church as a just society for its own people must be formulated. See also **152**.

228 Mofokeng, Takatso A. *The Crucified Among the Crossbearers. Towards a Black Christology.* Kampen: J.H. Kok, 1983.

Chapter 1 discusses the emergence of black theology out of the black consciousness movement and its eventual focus on Exodus as central to the black experience. Chapter 2 examines the Christology of Jon Sobrino and its roots in liberation theology, in which text and context are intimately related. The author then goes on to clarify how a historical Christology lends itself to a radical theology of praxis in South Africa. Chapter 3 discusses Karl Barth's theology as stemming from his praxis of crisis and powerlessness and its implications for the oppressed. After an examination of the differences in Sobrino's and Barth's hermeneutics, the author then makes an attempt to frame a black Christology of liberation, which is based on reconciliation with everything in their world: land, history, culture and value systems. An emphasis of Christ's suffering love offers the key to changing an oppressed people into the subjects of their own history.

229 Muzorewa, Gwinyai H. *The Origins and Development of African Theology.* Maryknoll, NY: Orbis Books, 1985.

Part 1 discusses the sources, in African traditional religion, the coming of Christianity to Africa in the nineteenth and twentieth centuries, the African Independent Church movement, African nationalism, and in the All-Africa Council of Churches. Part 2 discusses the varieties of theology in sub-Saharan Africa, including traditional religions, African theology and black theology in South Africa.

230 Mwoleka, Christopher and Joseph Healey, eds. *Ujamaa and Christian Communities.* Eldoret, Kenya: Gaba Publications, 1976.

"Ujamaa" means "familyhood." This is a theology, officially sanctioned by the government of Tanzania, that calls for a change of life-style: to self determination, life organized around base Christian communities, and a life meant to be lived in community. It is also a theology that is fully aware of the call of Vatican II for the laity to play an active role in transforming the world and bringing about full human liberation, to overcoming our old dichotomies, and to making the church an agent for the world and the clergy servants and educators of the community.

231 Nyamiti, Charles. *African Theology. Its Nature, Problems and Methods.* Kampala: Gaba, 1974.

Not seen.

232 —. *The Scope of African Theology.* Kampala: Gaba, 1973.

Not seen.

233 Parratt, John, ed. *A Reader in African Christian Theology.* London: SPCK, 1987.

This collection of essays discusses theological methods, aspects of doctrine, the church and the world, and current issues in African theology. Contributors include Harry Sawyer, Pobee, T. Tshibangu, Tutu, Charles Nyamati, Kofi Appiah-Kubi, Dickson, Buthelezi, Marc Ntetem, Julius Nyerere, Boesak, and Parratt. Each reading is followed by a series of study suggestions.

234   Perrin Jassy, Marie-France. *Basic Community in the African Churches.* Jeanne-Marie Lyons, trans. Maryknoll, NY: Orbis Books, 1973.

The base Christian community in Africa set against the context of the church in North Mara, Tanzania and the Luo people. Examines the sociological, historical background in African religion and Christianity, and the doctrines and organization of the African church.

235   Pero, Albert and Ambrose Moyo, eds. *Theology and the Black Experience. The Lutheran Heritage Interpreted by African and African-American Theologians.* Minneapolis, MN: Augsburg, 1988.

Articles on many of the key tenets of Lutheranism and their relation to the black experience of religion in both Africa and the United States. Includes articles by Richard J. Perry, Simon Maimela, Judah Kiwovele, John S. Pobee, Pero, Cheryl A. Stewart, Vivian V. Msomi and others.

236   Pobee, J. S. *Toward An African Theology.* Nashville,
       TN: Abingdon Press, 1979.

       African identity has been destroyed both by
       colonialism and by a Christianity that sees God and
       "man" in the white image. Africa therefore needs an
       African theology.

237   Setiloane, Gabriel. *African Theology. An Introduction.*
       Johannesburg: Skotaville, 1986.

       A booklet that attempts a brief introduction.
       Chapters treat the sources of knowledge in African
       tradition, "genesis," community, personhood, the
       human family, the nature of God, a definition of
       African theology, its claims and forms of expression.

238   Shorter, Aylward. *African Christian Spirituality.*
       Maryknoll, NY: Orbis Books, 1980.

       See Evans (686), item 440.

239   — . *African Christian Theology. Adaptation or
       Incarnation?* Maryknoll, NY: Orbis Books; London:
       Geoffrey Chapman, 1975

       A general survey of Christianity in Africa. Good
       background for African theology. See Evans (686),
       item 439.

240   Upkong, Justin. *African Theologies Now. A Profile.*
       Eldoret, Kenya: Gaba, 1984.

       Not seen.

241   Wan-Tatah, Fon Victor. *Emancipation in African Theology.* New York: Peter Lang, 1989.

The subtitle reads, "An Inquiry on the Relevance of Latin American liberation theology to Africa."

242   Witvliet, Theo. *A Place in the Sun. An Introduction to Liberation Theology in the Third World.* John Bowden, trans. Maryknoll, NY: Orbis Books, 1985.

Attempts to refocus attention on liberation theology away from its roots in Latin America to demonstrate that it is a world-wide phenomenon that is giving voice to the poor and marginalized of all cultures and continents. Surveys the roots of the theology in modern conditions of socio-political and economic domination, imperialism, racism, and the quest for liberation. Examines Africa, Asia, Latin America, the Caribbean, and North America. An excellent brief introduction with a useful bibliography.

243   Young, Josiah U. *Black and African Theologies. Siblings or Distant Cousins?* Maryknoll, NY: Orbis Books, 1986.

Focuses on the disagreements between African-American and African theologians, and focuses on several leading figures: James and Cecil Cone, Major Jones, J. Deotis Roberts in the U.S.; and John Mbiti, Harry Sawyer and John Pobee in South Africa to discuss the historical background in both North America and Africa; black theologies of liberation and notions of God. Christology, African cultural categories, and relation to black feminism, Marxism and the Third World; African theology as one of indigenization; and differences between black and

African theologians. A final chapter attempts to answer whether they are siblings or distant cousins and finds that the universal themes of enpowerment, context and liberation makes them siblings. Extensive bibliography arranged by topic.

South Africa

244 Biko, Steve. *I Write What I Like. A Selection of His Writings.* Aelred Stubbs, C.R., ed. London: Bowerdean, 1978; rev. ed., San Francisco: Harper & Row, 1986.

Biko was the founder of the black Consciousness movement, and his death at the hands of South African police in 1977 became a symbol not only of the lengths to which white South Africa would go to preserve its position but also of the martyrdoms faced by thousands of black South Africans every day in order to maintain their humanity and achieve freedom. Essays on black consciousness, black spirituality, the role of the churches and the need to change them in order to pave the way to liberation, the conditions of black South Africans, and strategies for liberation.

245 Boesak, Allan Aubrey. *Black and Reformed. Apartheid, Liberation and the Calvinist Tradition.* Leonard Sweetman, ed. Maryknoll, NY: Orbis Books, 1984.

This is a collection of sermons, speeches, and essays on the place of a leader trained in the Calvinist traditions of the South African church that has justified apartheid on theological grounds. Boesak's work traces his, and his nation's, gradual shift from the inheritance of oppression to the new assumption of liberation.

246   —. *Black Theology, Black Power.* London and Oxford: Mowbrays, 1978.

A study of black theology and black power that sees both as integral parts of liberation theology, and all the theologies of liberation around the world as essentially one. It is also a book that stresses the unique situation of South Africa and the need of South African blacks to formulate their own theology and solutions, for whites to let go of their liberal innocence of "helping" the blacks in a remote situation and to instead work for liberation within their own contexts.

Themes include the coming of the black messiah in a black theology of liberation based on the Bible and Gospels of the poor; the necessity of facing the need for blacks to assume or take power themselves and to become their own subjects, which includes a critique of Martin Luther King's apparent willingness to concede to the white powers that be; and then detailed discussion of black theology and black power, on ideology and theology, and the quest for a black ethic.

247   —. *Comfort and Protest.* Philadelphia: Westminster Press, 1987.

Not seen.

248   —. *Coming in Out of the Wilderness. A Comparative Interpretation of the Ethics of Martin Luther King, Jr. and Malcolm X.* Kampen: KOK, 1976.

Reflects the influence, and the interdependence of, the North American and African black theological movements. Models of both nonviolence and more agressive empowerment are examined.

249 — . *Farewell to Innocence. A Socio-Ethical Study on Black Theology and Black Power.* Maryknoll, NY: Orbis Books, 1977.

What is the meaning and relationship of North American black theology and black power, or secondarily of Latin American liberation theology, to the South African and African situations? Boesak here carefully analyzes these movements through a reading of the works of Cone (838-844), King (865-877), Roberts (896-902), and others.

250 — . *The Finger of God. Sermons on Faith and Responsibility.* Peter Randall, trans. Maryknoll, NY: Orbis Books, 1979.

This collection brings Christian faith to bear on the responsibility of all people to bring about a society that is just and compassionate to all.

251 — . *If This Is Treason, I Am Guilty.* Grand Rapids, MI: W.B. Eerdmans, 1987.

Boesak, then president of the 709 million-member World Alliance of Reformed Churches, delivers a series of sermons of "holy rage" on racism in the reformed tradition, the church and politics, a Christian response to the new South African constitution, Jesus as the life of the world and a model for the fight against greed, exploitation, violence and the bringer of the good news for the weak, for peace and justice, and for action to overcome despair.

252   —. *Walking on Thorns. The Call to Christian Obedience.*
       Geneva: World Council of Churches; Grand
       Rapids, MI: W.B. Eerdmans, 1984.

       Seven sermons and one letter growing out of the
       actual situation of oppression and Christian response
       in South Africa. Topics discussed include prophesy,
       the risk of division that such prophesy brings, faith
       in the struggle, God's presence amid suffering, all
       based on the biblical insights of Exodus, the psalms,
       and Jesus' prophetic mission.

253   — and Charles Villa-Vicencio, eds. *A Call for an End
       to Unjust Rule.* Edinburgh: Saint Andrew Press,
       1986.

       The European edition of *When Prayer Makes News.*

254   —. *When Prayer Makes News.* Philadelphia:
       Westminster Press, 1986.

       Prayer makes news in South Africa when it is
       said by blacks, in public and in church, on behalf of
       their own suffering and oppressed brethren. Then it is
       considered a subversive activity. Yet prayer is
       effective in seeking justice and overthrowing tyrants.
       Essays by Boesak and Villa-Vicencio, Alan Brews,
       Lionel Louw, Shun Govender, Albert Nolan, O.P., de
       Gruchy, William R. Domeris, and Gabriel Setiloane.

255   Bosch, David J. "Currents and Crosscurrents in South
       African Black Theology." See **918**, pp. 220-37.

       Briefly traces the development of black theology
       in South Africa and then sums up the major elements
       of the theology: overcoming the slave mentality,

eliminating white tokenism and the patronizing of white liberals. At the same time black theology calls for love of the white enemy, ecumenism, and a shift beyond the inner, pietistic elements of Christianity and toward an emphasis on the whole person.

256 Chikane, Frank. *No Life of My Own. An Autobiography.* Maryknoll, NY: Orbis Books, 1989.

Chikane has long been a major leader of the church opposition to apartheid and was the chief inspiration behind the Kairos Document (see **269**). This is an example of "narrative theology" in the form of autobiography. It is also a confession of faith in the tradition of the apologists and martyrs. Themes of this autobiography include the life of the Christian in South Africa, the secondary status of the black growing up in a "white man's country," the discovery of an African spirituality at the grass roots, finding the God of liberation, his detention and torture at the hands of South African security forces, Christian social action, and new forms of theology.

257 De Gruchy, John W. *Bonhoeffer and South Africa. Theology in Dialogue.* Grand Rapids, MI: W.B. Eerdmans, 1984.

Examines Bonhoeffer's role in drawing the line between church, culture, and society and demonstrates its great importance for the Calvinist Afrikaaner church, the relevance of Bonhoeffer and his witness for conscience and civil disobedience in South Africa, among the privileged and comfortable, as well as among the oppressed today. De Gruchy is an important student of this German theologian; and he places him in the context of a theologian for the oppressed and their right to resist unjust authority. Examines loyalty to Jesus as a major liberating action. Includes the Barmen Declaration as an appendix. Bonhoeffer's theology of the cross is also of major importance.

258 —. *The Church Struggle in South Africa.* 2d ed. Grand Rapids, MI: W.B. Eerdmans, 1986.

Examines the historical origins among the black and white churches; the place of apartheid in the various churches; the conflict over racism; the black renaissance, protest, black consciousness and theology; the role of Soweto and white evangelical liberation. His final chapter deals with the meaning of the kingdom of God in South Africa. Good bibliography.

259 —. *Cry Justice! Prayers, Meditations, and Readings from South Africa.* Maryknoll, NY: Orbis Books, 1986.

A collection of readings from scripture, literature, history and current events brought to bear on the religious meaning of apartheid and the struggle for liberation.

260 —. *Doing Christian Theology in the Context of South Africa. Or God Talk Under Devil's Peak.* Cape Town: University of Cape Town, 1986.

Human life cannot be understood without reference to God, and our talk about God without reference to very real human conditions.

261 —. *Theology and Ministry in Context and Crisis. A South African Perspective.* London: Collins; Grand Rapids, MI: W.B. Eerdmans, 1987.

This is an examination of Christian ministry in the context of liberation theology and the praxis of a suffering and oppressed people. Discusses the theological and practical aspects of ministry and the life of the minister, the prophetic role of the minister and its biblical basis, and the context of suffering and oppression in South Africa today. De Gruchy also pays close attention to the role of the people themselves as the source of theology, as the people of God, and the theological significance of pastoral work, liturgy and the hope that grows from community.

262 — and Charles Villa-Vicencio, eds. *Apartheid Is a Heresy.* Grand Rapids, MI: W.B. Eerdmans, 1983.

This book celebrates the World Alliance of Reformed Churches condemnation of apartheid as a heresy from Christian faith at the 1982 meeting at Ottawa. Essays by Boesak, Chris Loff, David Bosch, Tutu, Simon Maimela, Villa-Vicencio, De Gruchy, Willem Vorster, Douglas Bax. Also presents documents from the South African churches. Examines apartheid as heresy in the sense of unorthodoxy, in current anthropological thought, in its ecclesiological sense, and on biblical grounds.

263 Donders, Joseph G. *Non-Bourgeois Theology. An African Experience of Jesus.* Maryknoll, NY: Orbis Books, 1985.

A survey of current African theological movements for a North American audience.

264   Dubb, Alice A. and A. G. Schutte, eds. *Black Religion in South Africa*. Johannesburg: Witwatersand University, 1974.

Not seen.

265   Du Boulay, Shirley. *Tutu. Voice of the Voiceless*. Grand Rapids, MI: W.B. Eerdmans, 1988.

A biography based on Tutu's writings, letters, interviews, newspaper reports, speeches, and the work of other South African religious leaders. Includes a brief bibliography.

266   Goba, Bonganjalo. *An Agenda for Black Theology in South Africa. Hermeneutics for Social Change*. Johannesburg: Skotaville, 1988.

Not seen.

267   Hope, Marjorie, and James Young. *The South African Churches in a Revolutionary Situation*. Maryknoll, NY: Orbis Books, 1983.

Examines the role of all the South African churches today and devotes a good deal of attention to the Catholic church there. Catholicism entered South Africa as a minority religion, pushed off to the margins. This, and its linguistic and anthropological methods of evangelization, brought it success among the oppressed blacks and gave root to the creation of an indigenous leadership. Not part of the ruling establishment that created apartheid, it thus has an easier time colliding with it.

The Catholic church thus maintained school integration after the Bantu Education Act of 1953 prohibited it, and it continued its policy after the Group Areas Act of 1960. Catholic bishops' condemnations of apartheid first appeared in 1948 and were repeated in 1952, 1957, and 1960, when the hierarchy urged the Catholic laity to obey God's law above human law. On the parish level, however, Catholics have been more hesitant to break with their neighbors; but strong leadership, especially that of Archbishop Denis Hurley of Durban, has begun to change attitudes. In 1976 the bishops' announcement that they would integrate the Catholic schools despite the law saw lay and government opposition collapse. Catholics polled were 85% in favor of integration.

Within the church itself, however, things have been slower to change, as few blacks have won high positions. In 1977, however, the bishops vowed to speed up this process.

Another of the church's most significant acts has been to urge the provision of a conscientious objector status for the military. This would, in effect, allow the young Catholic to refuse the military service that defends apartheid. The church has, significantly, thus put itself behind a nonviolent revolution among South African whites. Questions remain, however: what has the church's effect been among blacks? Can nonviolence, a word looked on with scorn in South Africa today, win the race against apartheid's increasing oppression, and against the counterviolence of the oppressed?

268   Hopkins, Dwight N. *Black Theology USA and South Africa. Politics, Culture, and Liberation.* Maryknoll, NY: Orbis Books, 1990.

Traces the roots of black theology in the black power and black consciousness movements and makes an essential link between black culture and black theology in both the U.S. and South Africa as essentially deriving from the biblical messages of liberation. At the core of Hopkins' liberation theology is a "holistic humanity" – the insight that salvation and liberation are one: that freedom from slavery and oppression is also a liberation from sin and that one must involve the other, that the inner person cannot be removed from the outer, that culture, politics, and religion are all aspects of a single world, creation, and revelation.

This is an excellent work, based on exhaustive reading, analysis, and interviews with the leading black theologians on both sides of the Atlantic. Part 1 deals with the historical contexts of black theology in both the U.S. and South Africa, including the civil rights and black power movements, and civil disobedience and black consciousness movements in South Africa. Part 2 surveys black theology in the U.S., including the thought of Cleage, Cone, Deotis Roberts, William Jones, Wilmour, Long, Cecil Cone, and Harding on politics, culture, and theology. Part 3 examines black theology in South Africa, including a survey of the work of the black consciousness movement, of Buthelezi, Boesak, Maimela, Chikane, Goba, Mosala, Mofokeng, and Tutu. Part 4 discusses the dialog between the two forms, both through printed influence, and in direct dialog among the leading thinkers. It then goes on to draw some implications for the future. Extensive and excellent bibliography.

269   Kairos Theologians. *The Kairos Document. Challenge to the Church.* Stony Point, NY: Theology Global Context, 1985; Grand Rapids, MI: W.B. Eerdmans, 1986.

The text of the document. In the words of its preface, the document "is a Christian, biblical, and theological comment on the political crisis in South Africa today." It emerged from the people of Soweto and South Africa themselves in the midst of pre-revolutionary crisis. It includes a critique of state theology: the national security reading of Romans 13:1-7, a critique of church theology, that is, from the white, European, colonial churches that have underpinned apartheid, including their ideas of reconciliation, justice and nonviolence; and the progress toward a prophetic theology based on the liberation texts of the Bible and the reality of oppression in South Africa. The document concludes with a call to action.

270   Kameeta, Zephania. *Why, O Lord? Psalms and Sermons from Namibia.* Geneva: World Council of Churches; Philadelphia: Fortress Press, 1986.

Meditations and prayers on apartheid, oppression and liberation in the form of reworked psalms from this Lutheran minister. Apartheid has long enjoyed the bolster of South African churches' strict adherence to Romans 13: the obedience to secular authority stressed in Reform churches. Now, however, religion is being confronted by the need to address oppression. Texts include a song of questioning God over the present state of injustice, the role of the mission as an act of liberation and cooperation with ongoing creation, and a black theology of liberation as a potent and threatening combination. Other texts include an examination of the Magnificat (Luke 1:46-55), a Christmas meditation on Isaiah 9:2-6, and Zechariah's prophesy in Luke 1:68-79.

271   Kleinschmidt, H. *White Liberation. A Collection of Essays*. Johannesburg: Ravan Press, 1972.

Essays by Clive Nettleton, J. Metz Rollins, Jr., Larry C. Coppard and Barbara J. Steinwachs, by John Krige and Rick Turner. The central theme of the collection is that now that blacks have decided to take liberation into their own hands, with their own organizations, whites must now turn toward themselves and uproot their own structures of oppression. Includes discussions of the role of religion in this liberation.

272   Kretzschmar, Louise. *The Voice of Black Theology in South Africa*. Johannesburg: Ravan Press, 1986.

Chapters include discussion on the rise of South African black theology from both African, European and American roots, the Africanization of Christianity, the African Independent Churches, the relationship between black theology and black consciousness movements, black liberation and black theology and white theological responses to both apartheid and black theology. Good bibliography, containing many articles on the topic.

273   Logan, Willis H., ed. *The Kairos Covenant. Standing With South African Christians.* Oak Park, IL: Meyer Stone Books, 1988.

Part 1 includes the text of the Kairos Document, along with a collection of essays on the meaning and importance of the document and the covenant that has grown out of it.
Part 2 is a series of essays on each section of the document. Writers include Frank Chikane, Karen Bloomquist, Sheila Briggs, Malusi Mpumlwana, Cornel West, Albert Pero, and Harold Washington. Each section of essays concludes with a Bible study by Thomas Hoyt, Jr. The book concludes with the Kairos Covenant by U.S. Christians, discussion guides, and a listing of anti-apartheid organizations in the U.S. See also **269**.

274   Mayson, Cedric. *A Certain Sound. The Struggle for Liberation in Southern Africa.* Maryknoll, NY: Orbis Books, 1985.

An autobiographical reflection on the role of the Christian minister in speaking up and acting against injustice and oppression.

275   Motlhabi, M. *Essays on Black Theology.* Johannesburg: University Christian Movement, 1972.

This is the original version of Basil Moore, ed. *Black Theology. The South African Voice,* 1973. See **276**.

276   Moore, Basil. *Black Theology. The South African Voice.* London: C. Hurst, 1974.

Includes essays by Adam Small, Manas Buthelezi, Steve Biko, James Cone, Nyameko Pityana, Sabelo Ntwasa, Mokgethi Motlhabi, Ananias Mpunzi (on "Black Theology as Liberation Theology," pp. 130-40). Topics include defining a black theology, African vs. black theology, black consciousness, black theology and black liberation, African Christianity, the church in black theology, training ministers, and the theological ground for an ethic of hope.

277   —. *The Challenge of Black Theology in South Africa.* Atlanta, GA: John Knox Press, 1974.

The U.S. edition of the preceding.

278   Mosala, Itumeleng J. *Biblical Hermeneutics and Black Theology in South Africa.* Grand Rapids, MI: W.B. Eerdmans, 1989.

Part 1 discusses the use of the Bible in black theology and the varying hermeneutics of oppressors and exploiters and social-scientific approaches to the Bible. Part 2 discusses the experience of blacks in South Africa as the starting point of a new exegesis. Part 3 is devoted to "materialist" readings of Micah and Luke 1 and 2; and the black hermeneutical appropriation of praxis in Luke 1 and 2.

279   —. and Buti Tlhagale, eds. *Hammering Swords into Plowshares. Essays in Honor of Archbishop Mpilo Desmond Tutu.* Trenton, NJ: Africa World Press; Grand Rapids, MI: W.B. Eerdmans, 1987.

This is a collection of essays by over two dozen leading South African theologians who seek to spell out clearly the nonviolence of this fighter for black liberation against his maligners. Themes addressed include personal tributes, theological tributes, African theology, prophetic theology, the struggle in South Africa, and black theology in South Africa.

280 —. *The Unquestionable Right to Be Free. Essays in Black Theology*. Johannesburg: Skotaville; Maryknoll, NY: Orbis Books, 1986.

A collection of essays by black South African theologians on the relationship of African theology to U.S. black theology, to liberation theology, feminist theology and on the need to find a common ground for all struggling for liberation.

281 Motlhabi, Mokgothi, ed. *Essays on Black Theology*. Johannesburg: UCM, 1972.

Not seen.

282 Nolan, Albert, O.P. *God in South Africa. The Challenge of the Gospel*. Cape Town: D. Philip; Grand Rapids, MI: W.B. Eerdmans, 1988.

Nolan is a noted theologian in South Africa and a major force behind the drafting of the Kairos Document (see **269**). Religion is central to South African life; and preaching the Gospel in South Africa has never been neutral. When the church therefore legitimizes change, that change becomes possible. This book is an attempt to preach a gospel of liberation to spur that change. Topics include the nature of the Gospel, sin in the Bible, a crucified people, unmasking apartheid, sin and guilt in South Africa, salvation in the Bible, signs of hope, the struggle for liberation, the good news of salvation, the challenge to, and the role of, the church.

283 — . *Jesus Before Christianity. The Gospel of Liberation* London: Darton, Longman & Todd, 1977; Maryknoll, NY: Orbis Books, 1978.

Jesus as the prophet for the poor and the outcast. Chapters include new perspectives on Jesus, prophesy in John the Baptist, the poor and oppressed in Jesus' time, Jesus' work of healing and forgiveness, the kingdom of God, solidarity, prestige and power, and politics and religion. Nolan also examines the cleansing of the Temple, the temptation to violence, the role of suffering and death, and the trial of Jesus. Faith in Jesus is a revelation of what God means to us and who our God is. Nolan insists that we must deduce all that we know about God from Jesus and not vice-versa.

284 — . *The Service of the Poor and Spiritual Growth.* London: Catholic Institute for International Relations, 1985.

Not seen.

285 — . *Taking Sides.* London: Catholic Truth Society, 1985.

Not seen.

286 — and R. Broderick. *To Nourish Our Faith. Theology of Liberation for Southern Africa.* Santa Barbara, CA: Cornerstone, 1987.

Not seen.

287   Paton, Alan. *Apartheid and the Archbishop.* New York:
       Charles Scribner's, 1973.

       The subtitle reads *The Life and Times of Geoffrey
       Clayton, Archbishop of Cape Town.* Paton is probably
       South Africa's best-known novelist; and his fiction
       has long dealt with the full humanity of both black
       and white Africans.

288   Regehr, Ernie. *Perceptions of Apartheid. The Churches
       and Political Change in South Africa.* Scottsdale,
       PA: Herald Press; Kitchener, ONT: Between the
       Lines, 1979.

       Outlines events and attitudes of the churches
       toward South African society and the state, with
       some attention to the Catholic church. While the
       church is not as actively opposed to injustice as in
       Latin America, it did begin to voice its protests as
       early as the 1950s, and in response to black pressures
       it began to speak out against bannings, restrictions,
       pass laws, and eventually for the nonviolent over-
       throw of the apartheid system itself. Despite this,
       the church still has much progress to make in a very
       short time. In a church overwhelmingly black, blacks
       still represent only a small minority of the church
       hierarchy.

289   Tutu, Desmond B. *Crying in the Wilderness.* Grand
       Rapids, MI: W.B. Eerdmans, 1982.

       Tutu is the Nobel Peace Prize winner for 1986, the
       archbishop of Cape Town and hence primate of the
       Anglican church of South Africa. He is and has been
       for two decades a leading voice in the nonviolent
       struggle against apartheid and a champion for Nelson

Mandela and the other prisoners of conscience in South Africa. This is a collection of his writings. Part 1 focuses on the emerging church, on Jesus, the church and the world, politics and religion, the theology of liberation. Part 2 discusses the struggle for justice in South Africa; Part 3 individuals and current events; Part 4 the certainty of freedom; and Part 5 the challenge of the 1980s.

290 —. *Hope and Suffering. Sermons and Speeches.* Grand Rapids, MI: W.B. Eerdmans; Johannesburg: Skotaville; London: Collins, 1983.

Essays on several themes. Part 1 discusses South Africa and the seamless garment of politics and religion; Part 2 liberation as a biblical theme; Part 3 current concerns; and Part 4 the divine intention for South Africa and all its people.

291 —. *The Nobel Peace Prize Lecture.* New York: Anson Phelps Stokes Institute, 1986.

The themes of oppression and liberation through nonviolence in South Africa.

292 —. *The Words of Desmond Tutu.* Naomi Tutu, compiler. New York: Newmarket Press, 1989.

Tutu's writings on a variety of topics, including faith and responsibility, apartheid, violence and nonviolence, the family, the community both black and white, and his hopes for a new South Africa. Also included is the text of his Nobel Peace Prize acceptance speech.

293   Villa-Vicencio, Charles. *On Reading Karl Barth in South Africa.* Grand Rapids, MI: W.B. Eerdmans, 1988.

    Not seen.

294   —. *Theology and Violence. The South African Debate.* Grand Rapids, MI: W.B. Eerdmans, 1988.

    Essays by Cuthbertson, Durand and Smit, Boesak and others on the issue of violence in South Africa history; by Tutu, Tlhagale and Mpumlwana on the present context; whether violence is seen as terrorism or legitimate counter-force; and by Bax, Mosala, Mosothoane, Dwane, De Gruchy on the traditions of violence and nonviolence from the Old Testament prophets to the early church and the Anabaptists. Essays by Petersen, Nolan and Armour, Villa-Vicencio, Ackerman, Duncan and Law, Lund, and Winkler also address the contemporary debate, including the various religious traditions' attitudes toward armed revolution. Paul Germond's presents "Liberation Theology: Theology in the Service of Justice" (pp. 215-32). A concluding essay by Frank Chikane seems to dismiss the entire validity of the book by dismissing the entire debate: violence is the condition in which South African blacks unwillingly find themselves; there is no other choice but to resort to it.

295   —. *Trapped in Apartheid. A Socio-Theological History of the English-Speaking Churches in South Africa.* Maryknoll, NY: Orbis Books, 1989.

    Even those supposedly "anti-apartheid" churches must face up to their own histories and practices of elitism, racism, and paternalism if they are to become truly liberating vehicles. Good background.

296   — , ed. *Between Christ and Caesar. Classic and Contemporary Texts on Church and State.* Cape Town: David Philip; Grand Rapids, MI: W.B. Eerdmans, 1986.

A collection of readings with the editor's introductions. Part 1 covers the classical period from the early church through the medieval, Reformation and radical Protestant texts. Part 2 treats the contemporary world from the crisis of the Third Reich, the Barmen Declaration, Barth, Bonhoeffer, Vatican II, Medellin, the U.S. black church, the African church, and the eastern Orthodox church under persecution and in cooperation. Part 3 highlights South Africa from 1914 to the present. Included are statements by the South African Council of Churches, Boesak, Tutu, the Kairos Document, and the South African Catholic bishops. An excellent collection from the viewpoint of South African liberation theology.

297   — and John W. De Gruchy, eds. *Resistance and Hope. South African Essays in Honor of Beyers Naudé.* Grand Rapids, MI: W.B. Eerdmans, 1985.

Not seen.

298   *Voices From the Third World.*

Not seen.

299 Walshe, Peter. *Church vs. State in South Africa.*
Maryknoll, NY: Orbis Books, 1983.

Despite its open condemnations of apartheid in
1957, 1960, and 1962, the Catholic church has a long,
slow way to go in living up to its words. Only in 1973
were its own seminaries integrated, and Archbishop
Denis Hurley has had to face the criticism of his own
colleagues, clergy, and laity for his opposition to
apartheid. Despite this, Hurley has called on fellow
Catholics to join him in a nonviolent revolution to
overthrow the South African system. This and other
pressures, including the Soweto Massacre, have
spurred the hierarchy to admit its own failure to
pursue peace and justice actively enough and to commit itself to the poor and the oppressed, to ally with
the black consciousness movement, and to call for true
conversion. Despite these moves, however, time continues to run out in South Africa.

300 Wallis, Jim, Joyce Hollyday and others. "The Church
Confronts Apartheid." *Sojourners* 17, 8 (1988)
Special Issue. Reissued, Maryknoll, NY: Orbis
Books, 1990.

A collection of essays and interviews by and with
Wallis, Hollyday, Boesak, Tutu, Chikane, Villa-
Vicencio, among others.

301 West, Martin. *Bishops and Prophets in a Black City.*
African Independent Churches in Soweto,
Johannesburg. Cape Town: David Philip, 1975.

An analysis and survey of the nearly 3,000
independent black churches and their role on the
prophetic mission to call for justice and decry the op-

pression of their people. Describes many of the
beliefs and practices of the churches as well.

302 Wink, Walter. *Violence and Nonviolence in South
Africa. Jesus' Third Way.* Philadelphia: New
Society Publishers and Fellowship of Reconcilia-
tion, 1988.

On first encounter this seems like the worst
scenario of "liberation" theology: a North American,
white, middle-class academic preaching to the people
of South Africa to refrain from violence as a means of
overcoming their oppression. Wink frankly admits
the dangers of his endeavor, and with those caveats
his analysis of both violence and nonviolence from
ethical, theological and pragmatic approaches is
deep and thought-provoking.

Wink clearly holds that neither structural nor
spiritual change alone in South Africa will bring
about any real change: the approach must be integral.
Nor are the extreme opposites of passive obedience
and violent revolution likely to bring about any
change. Wink makes it very clear that neither is
Jesus' way; instead he offers Jesus' "third way," of
nonviolent, militant revolution.

* *
*

Chapter 6: *Liberation and Deep Ecumenism. Liberation Theology in Asia*

Bibliographies

303   Suh, Chang Won. *A Formulation of Minjung Theology. Toward a Socio-Historical Theology of Asia*. Seoul: Nathan Publishing, 1990, pp. 253-82.

An excellent and up-to-date collection of works of minjung theology, arranged by books and articles, most of which have been published in South Korea; as well as other influential books of liberation theology.

General

304   Abraham, K. C., ed. *Third World Theologies. Commonalities and Divergences*. Maryknoll, NY: Orbis Books, 1990.

See **197**.

305   Amirtham, Samuel, and John S. Pobee. *Theology by the People. Reflections on Doing Theology in Community*. Geneva: World Council of Churches, 1986.

See **199**.

306   Anderson, Gerald H., ed. *Asian Voices in Christian Theology*. Maryknoll, NY: Orbis Books, 1976.

Essays by M. M. Thomas, Lynn A. de Silva, U. Kyaw Than, Kosuke Koyama, Choang-seng Song and others on theology in India, Sri Lanka, Burma,

147

Thailand, Indonesia, the Philippines, Taiwan, Korea and Japan. Includes a briefly annotated bibliography of books and articles arranged by country.

307   Balasuriya, Tissa. *The Eucharist and Human Liberation.* Maryknoll, NY: Orbis Books, 1979.

At the heart of liberation theology is the insight that internal spirituality cannot be divorced from the spirit of the world and that sacramental salvation is meaningless unless society, and the world itself as God's creation, are also saved. Balasuriya here focuses on the meaning of the Eucharist in a liberation setting: that the sacrament of nourishment and salvation, of participation in divinity's healing and grace, must have real meaning in a world where abundance and dire poverty, fullness and starvation vie in stark contrast. To "break bread" must have a real social, economic and political meaning if its sacramental meaning is to be real.

308   —. *Jesus Christ and Human Liberation.* London: SCM, 1977; Maryknoll, NY: Orbis Books, 1979.

Not seen.

309   —. *Planetary Theology.* Maryknoll, NY: Orbis Books; London: SCM, 1984.

This is a response to what Balasuriya sees as a planetary system of injustice brought about by the new economic and political unities of the world that enforce the prosperity of the few in the North against the misery of the majority in the South. It is a "world system of unjust relationships" that traditional theology, with its emphasis on individualistic piety, dominated by capitalist and bourgeois concerns, not only fails to address but in many cases actively condones as "Christian."

Many of Balasuriya's criticisms are reminiscent of Matthew Fox's work (see **930-932**). Christianity's past has, the author notes, been culturally bound, tied to its European origins, church-centered, male-dominated, and age-dominated, that is tied to the values of aged male scholars and ecclesiatical hierarchs. In addition it is a pro-capitalist, anti-communist, and reactionary theology that revels in theory and flees relevance to the social and economic plight of most of the planet's peoples.

Balasuriya therefore calls for a theology that is both contextual and global: that grows out of the experience and concerns of the people it addresses and that, at the same time, seeks to stress the unity of all humanity. In this desire it seeks a link to the liberation theologies of the world, whether Latin American, black, feminist, Asian, or European political.

A planetary theology would seek to build a new earth as it seeks a new heaven that hopes in the promise of the Cosmic Christ, emphasizes radical conversion, not only of individuals but also of structures – especially church structures – and insists on the necessity of struggle and liberation. In this process much of the old church thinking in ecclesiology, sacramental life and liturgy, and in forming a new spirituality of justice become key.

310   Bavarel, Michel. *New Communities, New Ministries.*
       The Church Resurgent in Africa, Asia and Latin
       America. Francis Martin, trans. Maryknoll, NY:
       Orbis Books, 1983.

       See **206.**

311   Chung, Hyun Kyung. *Struggle to Be the Sun Again.*
       Introducing Asian Women's Theology. Maryknoll,
       NY: Orbis Books, 1990.

       The author attempts to find the elements of a
       theology that is born from the experience of, and
       speaks to the souls, of Asian women. Themes include
       the historical and social background of women's the-
       ology in Asia, the meaning of Jesus and Mary for
       women in Asia, a new Asian woman's spirituality and
       women's theology.

312   Commission on Theological Concerns of the Christian
       Conference of Asia, ed. *Minjung Theology: People*
       as the Subjects of History. Maryknoll, NY: Orbis
       Books, 1983.

       A collection of essays on "minjung" theology,
       which is the Korean word for "people's." It is a
       theology, like liberation theology, born out of the
       concern of the people's praxis. Examines the histor-
       ical, biblical, and contemporary roots of the theology.

313   Elwood, Douglas J., ed. *Asian Christian Theology.*
       Emerging Themes. Rev. ed. of *What Asian Chris-*
       tians Are Thinking. Philadelphia: Westminster
       Press, 1980.

Essays by Charles C. West, Kosuke Koyama, Shoki Cole, Jung Young Lee, Carlos H. Abesamis, S.J., Samuel Rayan, S.J., Masao Takenaka, Choan-seng Song, Lynn de Silva, Aloysius Pieris, S.J., Sebastian Kappen, S.J. and others on forming a Christian theology for Asia, varying understandings of humanity and nature in the West and East, the role of theology in Christian mission, a theology of pluralism, the theology and development of liberation. Part 7 presents various theological statements of the Asian churches and other Christian groups. Contains a useful bibliography of bibliographies and of journals on Asian Christianity.

314   —. *Faith Encounters Ideology. Christian Discernment and Social Change.* Quezon City, Philippines: New Day, 1985.

Not seen.

315   —. *What Asian Christians Are Thinking.* Quezon City, Philippines: New Day Publishers, 1976.

First edition of *Asian Christian Theology.* See above **313**.

316   England, John C., ed. *Living Theology in Asia.* Maryknoll, NY: Orbis Books, 1982.

A collection of readings, with introductions, on the theologies of South Korea, Japan, China, the Philippines, Southeast Asia, Indonesia, Sri Lanka, and India. Authors include Kim Chi Ha, Takenaka Masao, Raymond Fung, Francisco Claver, Koson Srisang, H. Marianne Kartoppo, Aloysius Pieris, and Samuel Amirtham, among others.

317   Fabella, Virginia, M.M., ed. *Asia's Struggle for Full Humanity.* Maryknoll, NY: Orbis Books, 1980.

Essays by Fabella, Balasuriya, Eunice Santanade Velez, Samuel Rayan, Aloysius Pieris, Lynn de Silva, Sebastian Kappen, Rose Zoé Obianga, James Cone, Sergio Torres and others on the development of a liberation theology for Asia; "living in," that is developing theology from the experience of sharing the life of the poor; on social, political and economic realities in Asia; on developing Christian theology against the background of Buddhism and other Asian religions; and developing an Asian women's theology.

318   —, and Mercy Amba Oduyoye, eds. *With Passion and Compassion. Third World Women Doing Theology.* Maryknoll, NY: Orbis Books, 1988, pp. 69-121.

Essays by Aruna Gnanadason, Mary John Mananzan, Christine Tse, Yong Ting Jin and Virginia Fabella.

The Asian situation, like that of Africa, combines the legacy of colonialism with structures of oppression inherited from Asia's traditional religions: Islam, Buddhism, Confucianism, and Hinduism, in which the role and life of women are decidedly secondary. In such cases Christianity, not in its current ecclesiastical structures, but in a true reading of the Jesus community of the Bible, can be a liberation agent. Asia, the traditional home of deep and important spiritualities, can also nurture an emerging Christian woman's spirituality that has compassion and liberation as its hallmarks: the women's role of birthing, divorced from natalism and the idolization of motherhood, is the chief model in the quest for wholeness that the four major Asian religions vaunt but rarely put into practice when women are concerned. See also **214**.

319   —, and Sun Ai Lee Park. *We Dare to Dream. Doing Theology as Asian Women.* Maryknoll, NY: Orbis Books, 1989.

Not seen.

320   Ferm, Deane William. *Profiles in Liberation. Thirty-Six Portraits of Third World Theologians.* Mystic, CT: Twenty-Third Publications, 1988.

Theologians from Africa, Asia and Latin America are discussed, including their lives, work and thought. Bibliographies of books and articles, as well as photographs, are provided for each. An excellent introduction. Asian theologians include Abesamis, Byung-Mu, Balasuriya, Koyama, Osthathios, Pieris, Rayan, and Choan-Seng Song. See also **215**.

321   —. *Third World Liberation Theologies. An Introductory Survey.* Maryknoll, NY: Orbis Books, 1986.

Discusses the various forms of liberation theologies, their resemblances and differences, studies, and criticisms of this theology. See also **216**.

322   —. *Third World Liberation Theologies. A Reader.* Maryknoll, NY: Orbis Books, 1986.

Selections from a host of liberation theologians, including Koyaa, Balasuriya, Ryan, Yong-Bok and others. See also **217**.

323   Habito, Ruben. *Total Liberation. Zen Spirituality and the Social Dimension.* Maryknoll, NY: Orbis Books, 1989

This is a cal for both Zen spirituality and Christian pietism to come together and then to refocus energies away from an inner salvation through separation and toward a salvation that comes about by participating in the divine activity of saving the world.

324   Hongi, Anton G. *Trends in Present Asian Theology.* Special Issue *Exchange* (Leiden) 32-33 (1982).

Not seen.

325   Mbiti, John S., ed. *African and Asian Contributions to Contemporary Theology. Report.* Céligny: Ecumenical Institute, 1977.

See **226.**

326   Míguez Bonino, José. *An Emerging Theology in World Perspective. Commentary on Korean Minjung Theology.* Mystic, CT: Twenty-Third Publications, 1988.

An interesting example of how liberation theologies have self-consciously cross-polinated their insights and how, at root level, the problems that they address are the same all over the world.

327   Moon, Cyris Hee-Suk. *A Korean Minjung Theology. An Old Testament Perspective.* Maryknoll, NY: Orbis Books, 1986.

A sociological interpretation of the Old Testament that sees the history of the Korean poor and oppressed foreshadowed in the story of the Hebrews' liberation in Exodus. Includes an introduction to minjung (people's) theology, the Hebrews in Exodus, the Hebrews of pre-monarchical Canaan, the rise of rulers and victims in Solomon's Israel, and the role of the prophets in protesting injustice and oppression. Moon then examines the parallels in Korean minjung theology and examines the nature of a life that is both prophetic and liberating in today's Korea.

The Indian Subcontinent

328   Amaladoss, M., T. K. John, and G. Gispert-Sauch, eds. *Theologizing in India.* Bangalore: Theological Publications in India, 1981.

Collected essays to ask the what, where, when, and whence of an Indian theology. Contributors include Peter Fernando, Ignatius Puthiadam, S.J., S. Kappen, Sara Grant, Felix Wilfred, and others.

329   Arokiasamy, S., S.J., and G. Gispert-Sauch, S.J., eds. *Liberation in Asia. Theological Perspectives.* Jesuit Theological Forum Reflections 1. Delhi: Vidyajyoti Faculty of Theology; Gujarat: Gujarat Sahitya Prakash, 1987.

This book is a response to the Vatican's *Instruction on Certain Aspects* and the *Instruction on Christian Freedom and Liberation* (123-124) and includes essays by Samuel Rayan, Aloysius Pieris, T. K. John, Errol D'Lima, Marianne Katoppo, George V. Lobo, and others. Topics in Part 1 include liberation

theology in Asia, its relationship to Marxism, the
issue of social class and class struggle, sinful structures, and the Gandhian praxis of liberation. Part 2
includes commentaries and reflections on the
Instructions. In all, the book is a well positioned defense of emerging Asian liberation theology and an
acceptance of the Vatican's measured endorsement.

330   Boyd, Robin H. S. *An Introduction to Indian Christian
        Theology.* Madras: Christian Literature Society,
        1975.

        This is a very useful and informed survey of the
        varieties of Christian encounters with Indian reli-
        gions: from refutations, to coexistence, to the formula-
        tion of a new Indian theology that will synthesize
        Christian revelation with Indian praxis. The work
        focuses on individual thinkers and follows their
        thought on all aspects of theology. Good
        bibliography.

331   Jesudasan, Ignatius. *A Gandhian Theology of Liberation.*
        Maryknoll, NY: Orbis Books, 1984.

        Gandhian nonviolence as the path toward libera-
        tion from oppressions both physical and spiritual.

332   Mookenthottam, Antony, M.S.F.S. *Towards a Theology
        in the Indian Context.* Bangalore: Asian Trading
        Corporation, 1980.

        Topics include a brief review of Indian theology,
        of the Vedas and Upanishads, Jainism, Buddhism,
        the Bhagavadgita, and the view of reality and truth
        in the western Bible. The author then discusses the

possibilities of a pluridimensional approach toward an Indian theology.

333   Pieris, Aloysius, S.J. *An Asian Theology of Liberation.* Maryknoll, NY: Orbis Books, 1988.

Part 1 examines the impact of Vatican II in calling for an end to the dichotomies in Christian religious life between spirituality, contemplation, action, in the world and liturgy, calling for a more integralist view of life and creation, and a deeper understanding of Western spirituality and its relatedness and relevance to Asian spiritual and religious forms. It then focuses on questions of Jesus' life of poverty and his option for the poor, the questions of ideology as an enemy of, and then a substitute for, religion and its relationship to the world of action.

Part 2 then highlights aspects of Asia's non-Semitic religions, the issues of inculturation, Asian attitudes toward poverty and the poor, models of inculturation from the Mediterranean, northern Europe, which will not work for Asia, and finally of Christian monasticism, which Pieris claims is a working alternative.

Part 3 then outlines the elements of an Asian theology of liberation: the forms of speaking about God in language, in metaphysics and cosmology, in socio-economic discourse, and the role Asian religions have to play in the development of Asian Christianity. In conclusion Pieris returns to the theme of the poor and their essential role in defining and becoming the liberated person.

Also contains a bibliography of Pieris' articles that have appeared in English since 1968.

334   Prabhakar, M. E., ed. *Towards a Dalit Theology.*
           Delhi: ISPCK, 1988.

Essays by Saral K. Chatterji, Sundar Clarke, K. Wilson, M. Azariah, M. John, Swarnalata Devi, and others on a theology for the "untouchables." *Dalit,* in both its Sanskrit and Hebrew roots, means "broken" or "downtrodden." This is thus an attempt to create a theology for, and out of, the experience of the marginalized of Indian society both as a response to liberation theology and to the fact that many Christian dalits have converted to either Islam or Hinduism in the 1980s.

Thus a dalit theology seeks to foster liberation both within Indian society and within church structures that have adopted the rigid casteism of India. One of its chief targets is therefore the ideology of caste *(varnashrama dharma)* and the creation of a group of people as objects. Instead, a dalit theology would focus on making people their own subjects, first by fostering their own theologizing that stems from their own experience, whether they be the economically poor, or women and widows within their own classes. This is not without a process of struggle and alienation from the predominant brahim culture, however.

Like other liberation theologies, dalit theology also focuses on inner conversion: to lead to the dalits' own consciousness of their worthiness and to dispel the Hindu and Jain notion of their present state being a result of sins in a previous life. It thus focuses on social sins against them and on reintegrating the divorce between a spiritual and physical reality. Above all, dalit theology means "doing theology" among and with the dalits themselves: a theology born out of praxis.

East Asia

335   Katoppo, Marianne. *Compassionate and Free. An Asian Woman's Theology.* Maryknoll, NY: Orbis Books, 1979.

Woman as other, women's liberation, women in Asian theology, from an Indonesian perspective.

336   Koyama, Kosuke. *Mount Fugi and Mount Sinai.* London: SCM, 1984; Maryknoll, NY: Orbis Books, 1985.

This is a theological reflection on idolatry, especially in Japanese society, born out of the devastation of World War II, which saw both Hiroshima and the turning of Tokyo into a desert, like Sinai, through months of U.S. bombing. It is an attempt to find a theology that will focus on the God of creation with the insights of the Old Testament and, as with Jürgen Moltmann, the theology of the Cross to save us from despair. Reflections focus on four texts: Jeremiah 4:26, Psalm 121:2, Exodus 20:7, and Hosea 11:8.

337   —. *Waterbuffalo Theology.* Maryknoll, NY: Orbis Books, 1974.

The term derives from the author's own ministry among the people of Thailand and the intimate connection between the Thai people and the water buffalo in their agrarian lives. It is a symbol for the author to discard all abstractions when doing theology, and to focus instead on the concrete realities and to fit theology to people's experience. Topics include the interpretations of history and the world for the Asian reality, rooting the Gospel in both its Western traditions and new surroundings, an understanding of Buddhist life in Thailand, and attempting to interpret Christianity for an Asian life. Koyama calls for a multi-denominational approach to Asian Christianity in order to have religion more faithfully reflect local tradition and situations.

338   Lak, Yeow Choo. *Doing Theology and People's Movements in Asia.* Singapore: Association for Theological Education in South East Asia, 1986; reprint (revised) ed., 1987.

Essays by Carlos Abesamis, S.J., John C. England, Staoshi Hirata, Eto Naozumi, Masao Takenaka and others on women's liberation and women's theology, Christian ties with peoples' movements, theologizing through storytelling and through the experience of people's movements, and new forms of biblical interpretation that derive from the experience of the world's peoples. John C. England provides "People Movements as Source for Asian Theologians: A Bibliographical Survey," arranged by topic and author, on pages 182-200.

339   Lee, Jung Young, ed. *An Emerging Theology in World Perspective. Commentary on Korean Minjung Theology.* Mystic, CT: Twenty-Third Publications, 1988.

"Minjung" is the Korean theology of the poor, oppressed, and destitute. Essays by José Míguez Bonino, Robert McAfee Brown, John B. Cobb, Harvey Cox, Kwesi A. Dickson, Kosuke Koyame, George Ogle, J. Deotis Roberts, Letty M. Russell, and C. S. Song attempt to meet minjung from various other liberating perspectives.

340   *Liberation Theology and the Vatican Document.* Vol. 3:
       Perspectives From the Third World. Quezon City,
       Philippines: Claretian Publications, 1988.

       The book is divided into two parts: six essays on
       liberation theology by leading theologians around the
       world, and a reprint of the Vatican document:
       Instruction on Christian Freedom and Liberation (see
       also **123-124**), which is the final version of the
       Vatican statement. The essays range from analyses of
       how liberation theology has been articulated in the
       reality of the Third World to reviews of the
       Instruction and its success or failure in explaining
       liberation theology and in aiding the process of
       opting for the poor.

341   Suh, Chang Won. *A Formulation of Minjung Theology.*
       Toward a Socio-Historical Theology of Asia. Seoul:
       Nathan Publishing, 1990.

       This is an introduction to this Third-World
       theology that is self-consciously attempting to rid
       itself of its European and North American baggage.
       Discusses the context of military oppression in South
       Korea; Korean Christians' participation in the strug-
       gle for human rights; the intellectual content of the
       theology both formally and in its historical develop-
       ment; and its new contributions to the discussion of
       God, revelation, sin, liberation, Christology, the
       Holy Spirit, the church, and eschatology.
       Final sections deal with minjung in the context of
       Asian theology, in nation building, indigenization,
       the people as subject of their own history and authors
       of their theology, and a new Asian hermeneutic.
       Contains an excellent bibliography of Korean minjung

theology, most items published in South Korea, and on Asian theology in general.

342   Trompf, Garry W. *The Gospel Is Not Western. Black Theologies from the Southwest Pacific.* Maryknoll, NY: Orbis Books, 1987.

A collection by indigenous theologians from aboriginal Australia, the Torres Straits and Melanesia.

343   Witvliet, Theo. *A Place in the Sun. An Introduction to Liberation Theology in the Third World.* John Bowden, trans. Maryknoll, NY: Orbis Books, 1985.

See **242.**

The Philippines

344   Abesamis, Carlos H. *Where Are We Going. Heaven or the New World?* Manila: Foundation Press, 1983.

Not seen.

345   Claver, Francisco F. *The Stones Will Cry Out.* Maryknoll, NY: Orbis Books, 1978.

A collection of letters from this bishop to his diocese on the conditions of oppression within the Philippines, the injustices and brutalities of their lives under tyranny. It focuses on the faith of the Philippine Christians, and the work of the basic Christian communities in bringing hope in the midst of this darkness.

346   Digan, Parig. *Churches in Contestation. Asian Christian Social Protest.* Maryknoll, NY: Orbis Books, 1984.

An excellent introduction to Christianity in Asia. Digan's account includes background on the origins and nature of Christianity there as a marginal, if not tenuous, Western cultural import. Tied to authoritarianism and colonialism, the church's passive role merged well with the lack of an Asian tradition of protest. By the late twentieth century, however, this very marginality and Christianity's base among the poor and oppressed had combined with an older Christian tradition of prophetic protest to forge a new Asian movement that began to fight against the "national security state" and its institutionalized oppression.

By the 1960s Asian bishops had begun organizing and launching programs for conscientization and social action that merged with the efforts of Vatican II and the emerging liberation theology in its option for the poor, influenced by Marx, Mao, Gandhi, and Martin Luther King. This has led to a theology that also borrows from the Asian tradition of Buddhist nonviolence but that also sees violence as inevitable under certain conditions of oppression.

Digan then goes on to offer several examples of this new Christian activism at work in South Korea and in the Philippines. In the latter, under Jaime Cardinal Sin, the church has moved from its condemnation of revolutionary violence and reluctant support of oppressive state violence to a rejection of both. It acts, however, in a race against time between the communists and national security state and in fear of either communist infiltration of its work in the basic Christian communities or of government repression of these efforts.

347   Elwood, Douglas J. *Faith Encounters Ideology. Christian
        Discernment and Social Change.* Quezon City,
        Philippines: New Day Publishers, 1985.

        Not seen.

348   Garcia, Ed. *The Filipino Quest. A Just and Lasting
        Peace.* Quezon City, Philippines: Claretian
        Publications, 1988.

        Begins with a narrative of the 1986 People's
        Power revolution that overthrew Marcos and then
        proceeds into an analysis of the religious roots of the
        revolt: liberation theology's role in shaping economic,
        social and political structures, but on a deeper level a
        liberationist reading of all these factors in the larger
        context of a people's journey toward true justice and
        peace.
        Even more interesting is Garcia's analysis of the
        processes of securing human rights in a post-revolu-
        tionary situation and his analysis of the role of older
        structures, such as police and the military, in forming
        a new society. This is a hands-on narrative and
        handbook of the path to a new vision of liberation.

349   Gaspar, Karl. *How Long? Prison Reflections from the
        Philippines.* Maryknoll, NY: Orbis Books, 1985.

        In March 1983 Gaspar, a lay theologian and
        church worker, was kidnapped by forces directed by
        Juan Ponce Enrile. He was held without charge for
        two years and repeatedly interrogated on suspicion of
        being a communist leader.
        This book is a collection of his letters that,
        together, form a diary of life in prison amid physical
        and mental deprivations, boredom, beatings and tor-

ture. Gaspar's hopes and physical condition were kept alive, however, by the quick work of friends and organizations who got wind of his disappearance and continued to pressure the government for his eventual release. A living witness against the forces bent on silencing the work of religious liberation.

350   Hunt, Chester L. "Liberation Theology in the Philip-
         pines: A Test Case," *Christianity Today* 26 (March
         5, 1982): 24-26.

A negative assessment. Sees liberation theology as Marxist, pro-violence, -class war and -revolution, and anti-Western, anti-rational, and ideological. Only one-third of the Filipino clergy are really opposed to Cardinal Sin's "critical collaboration." In fact, most of the liberation theology emerging in the Philippines is pressed on the native clergy by foreigners. Yet these discontents have failed in their attempts to stir up anti-American feeling. Conscientization is similar to the Alinsky technique of exacerbating grievances to bring on the revolution. "Liberation theology brings the frustrated Filipino intellectual and the expatriate clergy together. It combines the usual Marxist views with long-standing nationalist grievances." Written at a period when it looked as if the forces of reaction would succeed in silencing both the new theology and the voice of the people.

351   Lernoux, Penny. *People of God.* (See **120**).

Pages 47-49 discuss Pope John Paul II's displeasure with Cardinal Sin and the Filipino nonviolent revolution that seemed too popular and political for the pope's taste. When no alternative seemed avail-

able, however, the papacy gave half-hearted support
for the revolution.   The pope has since, however,
repeatedly attempted to humiliate and exclude
Cardinal Sin from the favor of the Vatican.

352   *Liberation Theology and the Vatican Document.* Vol. 2:
        A Philippine Perspective. Quezon City, Philippines:
        Claretian Publications, 1988.

A series of ten essays by Filipino pastoral
workers, theologians and bishops on the first Vatican
document. On the whole the essays attempt to read
the document positively as an endorsement of their
efforts to confront the realities of oppression and
deprivation in the Philippines and to bring about
justice in a way consistent with their Christian faith.
On the other hand, these responses also highlight
the fact that liberation theology is an import to the
Filipino reality: what the experience of Latin
America can bring to bear on their experience must
now be matched with a home-grown perspective that
is less concerned about institutional issues and dogmas
than about real-life issues informed by the preferential option for the poor.

353   Rossa, Alberto, ed. *The Theology of Liberation. Selected
        Writings from the Medellin Documents.* Manila:
        Historical Conservation Society, 1986.

These are documents selected to match the revolutionary situation in the Philippines and to show a
path of nonviolent action.

354   Socio-Political Institute. *With Raging Hope. A
        Compilation of Talks on the Church Involved in*

Social Transformation and Its Emerging Theology.
Quezon City, Philippines: Claretian, n.d.

Not seen.

355   Torre, Edicio de la. *Touching Ground, Taking Root.*
Theological and Political Reflections on the Philippine
Struggle. Quezon City, Philippines: SPI, 1986.

De la Torre, a prominent social activist in the
Philippines since the 1960s, reflects on the search for
a Filipino theology in the context of the struggle for
justice. Topics include the theological basis of reflection in peasant life, forging a theology neither
Marxist-Maoist nor bourgeois, and the birth of liberation out of prison, oppression and struggle.

The Middle East

356   Ateek, Naim. *Justice and Only Justice. A Palestinian*
Theology of Liberation. Maryknoll, NY: Orbis
Books, 1989.

Micah 6:18 lies at the heart of any meaningful
movement in the Palestinian situation: "To act justly
and to walk humbly with your God." Ateek addresses himself to his own Palestinian community and
seeks to bring about reconciliation based upon human
compassion and a striving for justice that cannot meet
hate or fear with either. Good discussion of the historical background, the biblical roots of Christian
Palestinians' work for justice and peace, the struggle
for liberation, and the prophetic imperatives of a
church that serves the oppressed and marginalized.
Discusses the historical background and current
shape of the Jewish-Palestinian (Arab and Christian)

conflict, anti-Semitism, Zionism, the birth of modern Israel; the life of Palestinians in modern Israel, voices of protest, and a Jewish theology of liberation. Ateek then focuses on the biblical roots of a Palestinian theology, its uses and abuses, its confrontation with Zionism, both Christian and Jewish; the cry for justice and compassion; the role of the peacemaker and the church's duty to make peace; the need for Palestinians and Jews to recognize the injustices committed against each other; and the threats and promises of the present situation.

357   Buber, Martin. *A Land of Two Peoples. Martin Buber on Jews and Arabs.* Paul Mendes-Flohr, ed. New York: Oxford University Press, 1983.

Martin Buber, the preeminent Jewish existentialist, the theologian of dialog, and "I and Thou," was a fervent Zionist who saw no separation between his religious and philosophical thought and the life of action embodied in Zionism. In fact, for Buber, the state of Israel was the essential embodiment of Judaism because it gave the concrete manifestation of the religious and ethical traditions of Jewish life a reality test and an unfolding measure against praxis. Key to this Zionism, however, was Buber's conviction that the life of Israel must be based on justice for all its citizens: Jewish and Palestinian.

It is this "Arab Question" that unites all the collected essays, mostly written as occasional pieces between the Balfour Declaration 1918 and his death in 1965. Throughout Buber seeks a theology of justice and liberation for both Jews and Palestinians that will bring forth the fullness of the biblical promise for Israel. A timely and well-edited collection.

358   Chakmakjian, Hagop. *In Quest of Justice and Peace in the Middle East. The Palestinian Conflict in Biblical Perspective.* New York: Vantage Books, 1980.

Not seen.

359   *Children of the Stones.* Jerusalem: Palestinian Center for the Study of Nonviolence, 1988.

Not seen.

360   Cohn-Sherbok, Dan. *On Earth As It Is in Heaven. Jews, Christians and Liberation Theology.* Maryknoll, NY: Orbis Books, 1987.

The reemergence of Hebrew Old Testament and modern Jewish ethical themes in Christian action in the Third World offers new hope for a common ground based on the thawing of theological rigidity and on a common tradition. The Jewish understanding of God's will in creation may be a bridge between these traditions.

Contents include discussions of the differences between Christianity and Judaism, how liberation theology has returned certain Christian ethical themes back into line with Judaism, and a new common ground for joint action.

361   Committee Confronting the Iron Fist, eds. *We Will Be Free in Our Own Homeland.* Jerusalem: CCIF, 1986.

The subtitle reads, *A Collection of Readings for International Day of Fast and Solidarity with Palestinian Prisoners.*

362   Ellis, Marc H. *Toward a Jewish Theology of Liberation. The Uprising and the Future.* Maryknoll, NY: Orbis Books, 1989.

The Holocaust and the state of Israel are the twin poles for all Jewish theology in the "Third Era." This is the period after the Holocaust that must inevitably replace the rabbinic age of the Diaspora and the age of the Temple of ancient Israel. Put in other terms, the memory of annihilation and the death of God is counterbalanced by new Jewish empowerment, both in Israel and in the West, especially in the U.S. While this is necessary and reflects new realities, Ellis warns, in the prophetic tradition, that Israel and world Judaism are now in danger of losing an essential component of Judaism: the religious core of its ethical life. Israel has increasingly opted for the legitimate exercise of power but has forgotten a key element of the Jewish tradition: the solidarity with the oppressed that was born from captivity in Egypt and that flourished even after its liberation. In this central reality Judaism has much to remember and to give to the rest of the world, for the vocabulary of liberation was first formed by the Jews in their historical experience.

The lessons and questions for today are thus just beginning to emerge. With the Palestinian *intifada*, or Uprising, the old categories of Holocaust theology must be expanded: Jews must face the reality that they are in danger of becoming the oppressors in their quest for security. A new theology of liberation that recognize the solidarity of all oppressed peoples must make its way back into a very sharply limited Jewish discourse, and only then will Judaism reclaim its full biblical and ethical heritage. A provocative book that raises controversial questions.

363   Elwood, Douglas J. *Faith Encounters Ideology. Christian Discernment and Social Change.* Quezon City, Philippines: New Day, 1985.

Not seen.

364   Grossman, David. *The Yellow Wind.* Haim Watzman, transl. New York: Farrar, Straus & Giroux, 1988.

A collection of vignettes on the Palestinian people and the conditions under which they live in Israel and the West Bank.

365   Ruether, Rosemary Radford, and Herman J. Ruether. *The Wrath of Jonah. The Crisis of Religious Nationalism in the Israeli-Palestinian Conflict.* San Francisco: Harper & Row, 1988.

Examines "the religious and ideological under-pinnings of Zionism, of the Christian support for Zionism, and the tragic unfolding of the Zionist project in the Israeli-Palestinian conflict." The authors approach the subject with a deep affiliation for both the Jewish and Palestinian peoples, human rights and the injustices perpetrated against both Jews and Palestinians in the twentieth century. Topics include the meaning of the Holy Land in Judaism, Christianity and Islam, historical roots of the conflict, the roots of Zionism and its alliance with Christians, Palestinian nationalism, contradictions of the Jewish state, and Christian relations to both Judaism and Zionism today. The book concludes with examinations of Jewish and Christian Holocaust theology, and a theological and ethical evaluation of the Jewish land – religious community

or secular nation – and the theology of redemption
inherent in the revived Israel.

* *
*

Chapter 7: *Latin America, Theory and Praxis*

Bibliographies

366   Dahlin, Therrin C., and others. *The Catholic Left in Latin America. A Comprehensive Bibliography.* Boston: G.K. Hall, 1981.

An excellent introduction to the materials available, including both violent and nonviolent movements for change.

367   Kirk, John M. "Religion and Politics in Revolutionary Cuba: A Bibliographical Guide" *Revista Interamericana de Bibliografia* 37, 3 (1987): 27-43.

Not seen.

368   Wagner, C. Peter. *A Catalog of the C. Peter Wagner Collection of Materials on Latin American Theology of Liberation.* Pasadena, CA: Fuller Theological Seminary, 1974.

Books and articles arranged by author and year, in all languages. A useful resource for earlier work.

Introduction and Background

369   Antoncich, Ricardo. *Christians in the Face of Injustice. A Latin American Reading of Catholic Social Teaching.* Maryknoll, NY: Orbis Books, 198??.

Readings cover such issues as economics, politics, and competing ideologies, all with a focus on church teachings and their confrontation with the realities of oppression and injustice.

370   Bamat, Thomas. "The Catholic Church and Latin American Politics." *Latin American Research Review* 18, 3 (1983): 219-26.

A review article. The church's activities throughout Latin America are the single most important development since the Cuban revolution.

371   Beeson, Trevor, and Jenny Pearce. *A Vision of Hope. The Churches and Change in Latin America.* Philadelphia: Fortress Press, 1984.

Examines the plight of Christians who have opted for the poor and the message of liberation theology in the face of repressive regimes in Latin America. Discusses the situation there, the nature of Christian mission, including some analysis of liberation theology and its chief proponents, and analyzes the situations in Cuba, Brazil, Argentina, Chile, Paraguay, Peru, Mexico, and Central America. A useful survey.   Good bibliography, arranged by topic, mostly of political issues.

372   Bigo, Pierre. *The Church and Third World Revolution.* Sr. Jeanne Marie Lyons, trans. Maryknoll, NY: Orbis Books, 1977.

Part 1 examines the themes of revolution from the viewpoint of history, including the themes of marginalization, dependency, and liberation, including a brief survey of the modern revolutions and their interpreters.

Part 2 examines the political aspects of Christian faith, including Jesus and his age, the themes of eros, power, and wealth in the Bible, forms of liberation; the church's own response to the world and its temptations; and the attitude of the church and its people to the political issues of the day.

Part 3 then examines the role of Marx and Marxist analysis in the Third World. Finally, Part 4 develops some ideas for the future based on the notion of community in special economic and political senses and the role of democracy in the world today, both in its capitalist and socialist senses. The book concludes with a study of the role of violence in the world and in the church, seeking a way to break from its vicious cycle, to build a just society, and to wean the church itself from its "violent" use of power and to become, instead, a prophetic force in the seeking of true peace based on justice.

373   Block, Walter, and Donald Shaw, eds. *Theology, Third-World Development and Economic Justice.* Vancouver: Fraser Institute, 1985.

Not seen.

374   Bruneau, Thomas C. *The Political Transformation of the Brazilian Catholic Church.* London: Cambridge University Press, 1974.

Essential background to the change in the hierarchy's stance from collaboration and Constantinian alliance, to critical support, and then to an embrace of the people, support of base Christian communities and dynamic nurturing of liberation.

375　　Cleary, Edward L., O.P. *Crisis and Change. The Church in Latin America Today.* Maryknoll, NY: Orbis Books, 1985.

Surveys the new leadership, changes from Medellin to Puebla, the new theology of liberation, base Christian communities, the emergence of the laity, the conflict between the church and the national security state, and the emergence of the leadership role of the Latin American church in world Catholicism today. A very good introduction.

376　　Comblin, José. *The Church and the National Security State.* Maryknoll, NY: Orbis Books, 1979.

This is a work of theological observation and reflection. It begins with a discussion of forms of theology, academic and liberation, European and Latin American. It then reviews the influence of Marx and the methods of modern social science on Catholic thought and goes on to outline a new "theology of revolution." Comblin then briefly traces the history of Latin America from colonialism to modern times, the creation of the national security state and the role it plays in worldwide geopolitics and as a bolster to local elites.

The doctrine of the National Security State has, in effect, become a new theology, since it underpins the elite rule of military dictatorships with supposedly Christian sanctions and goals. Comblin next discusses the role of the church as the subservient tool of the state, its growing criticism, and ensuing conflict. This conflict is expressed in new theologies, in new practice of organization and evangelization, and in new divisions between a true church of the people and the false myths and brutal force of the political ideology of the state.

377 —. *Retrieving the Human. A Christian Anthropology.* Maryknoll, NY: Orbis Books, 1990.

Rejects the Manichean duality so deeply ingrained in so much of quietistic Christian spirituality: that body and soul are two separate realities, that inner spirit is distinct and more lofty than the body and its needs. Instead, Comblin calls for a unified view of human nature, in which the soul is the life of the body, indistinct from it, and that therefore the needs of the body become indistinct from the spiritual needs of the person, and vice-versa. He examines the scriptures for textual foundations of a praxis for the theologian and church worker.

378 Dussel, Enrique. *A History of the Church in Latin America. Colonialism to Liberation, 1492-1979.* 3d ed. Alan Neely, trans. Grand Rapids, MI: W.B. Eerdmans, 1981. See **57**.

The Latin American church entered the twentieth century as truly marginal: impoverished, powerless, and cut off from European Christendom. At the same time, from the 1930s a reawakening among the laity and the survival of collegiality among the region's hierarchy insured that the church would become a strong force for change, especially after Vatican II and in the face of the national security state's brutal defense of "Western Christian Civilization" in the 1960s and 1970s.

Traces the immense impact of Vatican II, of Paul VI's *Populorum Progressio*, of CELAM (The Conference of Latin American Bishops), of the Medellin

Conference, and emerging liberation theology. Follows the events of the 1960s and 1970s in Brazil, Argentina, Peru, Paraguay, and Cuba. Then examines the examples of several individuals, including Helder Camara, Leonidas Proaño and Fr. Camilo Torres as an introduction to the problem of violence in Latin America and the quest for an appropriate "vocabulary of peace" that will match the risk and the challenge of nonviolence.

Dussel also traces the reaction to liberation in North America, in the reign of terror unleashed against the church by the national security state between 1973 and 1979 (which created more martyrs for the church than the past 500 years combined) and at the councils of Sucre and Puebla. Surprisingly, however, Puebla ended as a triumph for the "People of God," endorsed liberation theology, and put the church in Latin America clearly back in the tradition of Montesinos and Las Casas. (See Chapter 2.) The church thus declared decisively that it sought not to replace one oppressor with another, not the rule of elites over the masses, but to take up the role of teacher and prophet to lead the people themselves to their own liberation. Liberation theology thus reembraced the peaceful apocalyptic of the Catholic tradition as an understanding of the mysteries of history and a process of gradual revelation, leading the people from the womb of the present into a new age.

379   Foubert, Charles, ed. *The Church at the Crossroads. Christians in Latin America from Medellin to Puebla (1968-1978).* Rome: IDOC International, 1978.

This is a collection of essays grouped around several themes: the ten years of Latin American history from Medellin to Puebla; issues for the Puebla conference, including the growth of liberation Theology; the Latin American ecumenical movement; interviews with major participants; and documents from various theologians and prelates. The volume concludes with a bibliographic essay on recent works of liberation theology.

Contributors include Alain Touraine, Ralph Della Cava, Clodovis Boff, Ernesto Balducci, Míguez Bonino, Dussel, Atoncich, Richard, Balasuriya, Santa Ana, Helder Camara, and Johann Baptist Metz.

380   Gheerbrant, Alain. *The Rebel Church in Latin America.* Baltimore, MD: Penguin Books, 1974.

On the journey of Paul VI to Latin America in the midst of religious and political ferment; the Medellin conference; the new phenomenon of Christians entering revolutionary movements; Camilo Torres, and the prospects of a reformed, revolutionary church.

381   Goodpasture, H. McKennie. *Cross and Sword. An Eyewitness History of Christianity in Latin America.* Maryknoll, NY: Orbis Books, 1990. See **59**.

Selections from primary sources that go beyond the "important men" and let the people themselves – men and women and children, of all walks of life – speak for themselves. Excellent background for the emergence of a theology from the "grass roots up."

382   Hanks, Thomas D. *God So Loved the Third World. The Bible, the Reformation, and Liberation Theologies.* Maryknoll, NY: Orbis Books, 1983.

Uses a careful reading on the Bible to focus on the poverty and oppression of the marginalized, especially of Latin America.

383   Hanson, Eric O. *The Catholic Church in World Politics.* Princeton, NJ: Princeton University Press, 1990.

This is a comprehensive survey of Catholic politics and culture, its history, its organization and its ideology. Liberation theology and Latin America are treated as examples, but the main focus remains on Europe, North America and the U.S. conflict with the Soviet Union.

384   Kadt, Emanuel de. *Catholic Radicals in Brazil.* London: Oxford University Press, 1970.

Traces the Catholic left from the 1930s to the origin and development of the MEB.

385   Kee, Alistair. *Domination or Liberation: The Place of Religion in Social Conflict.* London: SCM Press, 1986.

Kee examines feminist, black and Latin American liberation theologies and finds that they all represent a new change in religious life: away from an alliance with power and domination and toward a new voice for the oppressed. In a final chapter he examines the rise of the religious right wing in the U.S. in the 1980s.

386   King, Paul G., and David O. Woodyard. *The Journey Toward Freedom. Economic Structures and Theological Perspectives.* Rutherford, NJ: Fairleigh Dickinson University, 1982.

Not seen.

387   Lange, Martin, and Reinhold Iblacker, eds. *Witnesses of Hope.* William E. Jerman, trans. Maryknoll, NY: Orbis Books, 1981.

Documents the sufferings of Christians under the national security state in Latin America between 1968, in the wake of the Medellin Conference, and 1980. During these years over 1,500 bishops, priests, nuns, religious lay workers, numerous Indians and poor campesinos were imprisoned, tortured, murdered, and "disappeared" precisely because of their witness as *Christians* in seeking peace and justice according to the call of Medellin and Vatican II. The editors cite many examples from around the region, ranging from Archbishop Oscar Romero (See **631-641**) and the American religious women martyred in El Salvador (See **642-647**), to the plight of the poor and oppressed in Chile, to indigenous peoples exterminated in Brazil. This often recalls the Acts of the Christian Martyrs. It should. Foreword by Karl Rahner, S.J.

388   Latorre Cabal, Hugo. *The Revolution of the Latin American Church.* Frances K. Hendricks and Beatrice Berler, trans. Norman, OK: University of Oklahoma Press, 1978.

After a brief survey of the church's role in Latin America from Alexander VI to John XXIII, the author surveys the effects of Vatican II in social, scientific, ecclesiological, and political realms.

389   Lernoux, Penny. *Cry of the People*. New York: Penguin Books, 1982.

In minute, often painful detail, this journalist and expert on Latin American political and religious affairs narrates the sufferings of the Latin American people under the national security state of the 1960s and 1970s. Her theme is the concerted U.S. policy of supporting military coups and dictatorships, and their rampages of arrest, torture, disappearances and murders against those struggling for human rights, most especially the Roman Catholic church. The church itself underwent a dramatic change from conservative bulwark of the status quo to the most dynamic force for change in the region in the period after Vatican II and Medellin, and it consequently suffered more martyrdoms than at any time since the Roman Empire.

Sometimes reading like the acts of the martyrs, sometimes like pure investigative reporting, sometimes like war correspondence, Lernoux's narrative is riveting and emotionally packed. Her research is meticulous, based on first-hand interviews, newspaper and magazine accounts, church and government documents. The book covers the rise of the new dictators, the church's response, and numerous examples of the repression that this response invited, including ones from El Salvador, Chile, Mexico, and Brazil.

It then documents the role of the U.S. in training and motivating the Latin American officer corps that has unleashed this persecution, the doctrine of the national security state, designed to protect U.S. development and regional elites, the role of U.S. multinationals, and the work of the CIA. Also examines the new ideology of "family, tradition, and property" that has been the rallying cry of oligarchs and death squads throughout the region. Lernoux also details European and U.S. funding for the repression.

The book then examines the role of the Catholic church in resisting this repression, the divisions within the church's hierarchy and between hierarchy, lower clergy, and laity in working out a new "option for the poor," and finally the U.S. role in supporting the church's progressives and reactionaries in Latin America. This work is a shocking eye-opener for any North American who is concerned with U.S. government and church policy toward Latin America, and it is still an indispensable introduction to events there.

390   —. *The People of God.* (See **120**).

Latin America has probably been the most important battle field in John Paul II's attempts to impose his "Restoration" on world Catholicism, not only because the Latin American church is now numerically the most important element of world Catholicism, but also because it is the birthplace of both liberation theology and of the base Christian communities, both of which have taken up the call of Vatican II for the church to embrace the world and to involve the laity and its experience in the deepest processes of doctrinal and practical development of the church.

While no single model for a Latin American church exists, Lernoux demonstrates how the pope and Cardinal Ratzinger, aided by a reactionary Curia, and far-right elements within Latin American society, and quasi-fascist lay groups, have attempted to disrupt the unity of such progressive churches and bishops' conferences as that in Brazil, while contributing to the division and ineffectuality of such churches as the Chilean and Peruvian. In Central America Lernoux shows clearly the workings of a papal double standard calling progressive church-people to task for political involvement in Nicaragua, for example, while aiding and abetting the political agenda of a conservative hierarchy, their support of the *contras* and links to the Reagan administration.

Lernoux narrates splendidly the political struggles of the Latin American bishops' conferences against the Curia and traces clearly the political issues – if not the theological ones – of the pope's inquisitions of leading liberation theologians Gustavo Gutiérrez and Leonardo Boff. Excellent introduction to the political and broadly ecclesiological issues involved in the fight over liberation theology.

391   Levi, Werner. *From Alms to Liberation. The Catholic Church, the Theologians, Poverty and Politics.* New York: Praeger, 1989.

Attempts to examine the question of the relationship between the church's rhetoric on issues of poverty and its willingness to foster change. Examines church theology and social thought on poverty in the nineteenth and twentieth centuries, including the role of Vatican II. Then surveys liberation theologians on the causes and remedies of poverty, including the issue of violent revolution, and compares them with those of nineteenth-century church thought.

In Part 2 Levi examines the political consequences
of this thought in the Latin American churches and
the state; and he concludes with discussions of John
Paul II, the Vatican and North American responses to
liberation theology. Bibliography.

392   Levine, Daniel H. *Religion and Politics in Latin
       America. The Catholic Church in Venezuela and
       Colombia.* Princeton: Princeton University Press,
       1981.

Religion is a vital and important factor in Latin
America today; it is not a vestige of the past. These
two countries provide case studies of the church's
influence and the forms that it takes. The work tends
to focus on the hierarchy, however, and devotes little
attention to the base Christian communities. It also
links liberation theology to Marxist and socialist
political aims.

393   —, ed. *Churches and Politics in Latin America.* Beverly
       Hills, CA: Sage Publications, 1980.

This is a collection of essays centered around the
following themes: background and general issues, the
spectrum of religion and politics, and patterns of
innovation. Contributors include Renato Poblete, S.J.,
Phillip Berryman, Robert Calvo, Katherine Anne
Gilfeather, M. M. Thomas Bruneau and Margaret E.
Crahan, among others. Issues include the impact of
Puebla, the Christian left, the role of religious
women, base Christian communities, and the influence
of Marxism.

394   —, ed. *Religion and Political Conflict in Latin America.*
        Chapel Hill, NC and London: University of
        North Carolina Press, 1986.

        Essays by Levine, Berryman, Thomas C. Bruneau,
        Mainwaring, Susan Rosales Nelson and others on
        religion, the poor and politics in Latin America, the
        rise of popular religion, the role of religion in El
        Salvador's civil war and Nicaragua's revolution, the
        base communities in Brazil, and the church's role in
        Chile, Colombia, and Bolivia.

395   Maduro, Otto. *Religion and Social Conflicts.* Maryknoll,
        NY: Orbis Books, 198?

        Introduction to the interactions of religious, social,
        and political spheres in Latin America today. Good
        background for the development and meaning of
        liberation theology.

396   Mainwaring, Scott. *The Catholic Church and Politics in
        Brazil, 1916-1985.* Stanford, CA: Stanford
        University Press, 1986.

        A narrative and interpretive history in three
        parts. Part 1 traces the church from 1916 to 1964, in
        the era of neo-Christendom, reform and the birth of
        the Catholic left. Part 2 discusses the church and the
        military regime, from 1964 to 1973. Part 3 brings the
        history up to 1985, including the growth of the
        popular church, its politics and rise and fall. This is
        a detailed, well-documented study that gives full
        attention to new currents in religious thought, in-
        cluding liberation theology, with an excellent
        bibliography.

397   —, and Alexander Wilde, eds. *The Progressive Church in Latin America.* Notre Dame, IN: University of Notre Dame Press, 1989.

Essays grouped around the themes of Central America, Brazil, and Peru by Margaret Crahan, Ana Maria Doimo, Catalina Romero, and Luis Pasara, among others. A good amount of discussion of liberation theology.

398   Marins, José, and team. *Cry of the Church. Witness and Martyrdom in the Church of Latin America Today.* Quezon City, Philippines: Claretian Publications, n.d.

Not seen.

399   Mutchler, David E. *The Church as a Political Factor in Latin America, with Particular Reference to Colombia and Chile.* New York: Praeger, 1971.

Seeks to examine the church's role in affecting political and social change, with special emphasis on these two countries. Examines the church bureaucracy, church involvement with political change on various levels from prelates, to orders, to individuals; to the church's role as a structural institution, and the detrimental effects of the church's involvement with such efforts. The author, who looks at sociological structures from a purely secular viewpoint, concludes that the church's role will become increasingly marginal.

400 Nuñez, Emilio A., and William D. Taylor. *Crisis in Latin America.* Chicago: Moody Press, 1989.

This is a view of Latin American religious life and politics from an evangelical Christian point of view. Topics include the Latin American scene and background, post-conciliar Catholicism in Latin America, the situation for evangelicals, and the place of evangelical mission in the region. While hailing the changes of Vatican II that opened the ecumenical world for both Catholics and Protestants, the authors are wary of liberation theology, citing it as a "theological-ideological system," and view base communities as a threat to evangelical efforts. The authors also look forward to what terrifies many Catholics: a split along Lutheran lines between the institutional and the "biblical" church similar to Luther's. The book is ultimately a call for theological love of North Americans toward Latin Americans through their missions.

401 Philp, Peter. *Journey With the Poor.* Blackburn, VICT: Collins Dove, 1988.

This is a narrative of travels and encounters throughout Latin America with the poor and oppressed, a record of the struggles for liberation being waged by the poor themselves. Excellent first-hand experience of the broader trends usually found in political and economic analysis.

402 Pottenger, John R. *The Political Theory of Liberation Theology. Toward a Reconvergence of Social Values and Social Justice.* Albany, NY: State University of New York Press, 1989.

This is a careful and scholarly appreciation of only one element of liberation theology: its political implications, if such can be extracted from the general way of doing theology. Pottenger recognizes the sides in the debate over liberation theology's political content; but he states that its view that religion and politics are inherently intertwined is a factor of the situation that needs careful analysis, as no political scientist or philosopher has yet grappled with the precise nature of this political theory.

The book discusses the context of liberation theology in religion and politics, its theological methodology, the tensions between Marxist analysis and Christian doctrine, its assessment of Latin American economics in the region, world and in the national security state, the ethics of the theology vis à vis reform and revolution, and its overriding social theory. The book is well indexed and contains a solid bibliography.

403 Rubenstein, Richard L., ed. *Spirit Matters. The Worldwide Impact of Religion in Contemporary Politics.* Washington, DC: Washington Institute Press, 1987.

A collection of essays on the impact of religion on politics around the world. Includes articles by Wellington W. Nyangoni on Africa; Frank K. Flinn and Rubenstein on liberation theology and Latin America.

404   —, and John K. Roth, eds. *The Politics of Latin American Liberation Theology. The Challenge to U.S. Public Policy.* Washington, DC: Washington Institute Press, 1988.

This is a collection of essays that seeks to open North American eyes to the realities behind liberation theology, its nature, and the way in which it addresses the politics and economics of Latin America. Topics include the development of the theology, its relevance to the crisis of Western culture, its place in Western theological tradition, its views on violence, its response to underdevelopment, the base Christian communities, its relationship to Marxism, dependency theory, and Latin American revolutions.

Essays also treat liberation theology's view of the U.S. and U.S.S.R., the U.S. bishops' letters on war, peace and economic justice, and human rights and U.S. security.

Contributors include Senator David Durenberger, Paul Sigmund, Marc Ellis, Frederick Sontag, Roland Robertson, Michael Fleet, Humberto Belli, John Roth, Philip Berryman, Dennis McCann, John Cooper, and others. Good bibliography of books and articles.

405   Skidmore, Thomas E., and Peter H. Smith. *Modern Latin America.* New York and Oxford: Oxford University Press, 1984.

A political and socio-economic account that traces modern structures from the colonial period and views Latin American history in terms of this neo-colonial "dependency." Good, up-to-date bibliography.

406   Smith, Brian H. *The Church and Politics in Chile.*
       Challenges to Modern Catholicism. Princeton:
       Princeton University Press, 1982.

       How can the church as a whole implement the
       aims of Vatican II? Marxist analysis seems a valu-
       able tool; yet on the whole the church in Chile is
       hesitant to take up its prophetic role unless its own
       hierarchical structures are threatened. A sociological
       approach based on extensive field research.

407   Vaughan, Benjamin N. Y. *The Expectation of the Poor.*
       The Church and the Third World. Valley Forge,
       PA: Judson Press, 1972.

       Surveys the problems with "development,"
       economic structures and faulty models, the seed for
       peaceful change, the end of old colonialism, and the
       beginnings of a neocolonial culture, the conflicts be-
       tween historical culture and tradition and pressures
       for modernization. The author then discusses the role
       of education for development, the place of ideology,
       and the place of theology, mostly from the point of
       view of World Council of Churches activities. He
       concludes with reflections on the nature of humanity
       and religious mission.

Theological Reflection

408   Abraham, K. C., ed. *Third World Theologies.*
       Commonalities and Divergences. Maryknoll, NY:
       Orbis Books, 1990.

       See **197.**

409   Adriance, Madeleine. *Opting for the Poor: Brazilian Catholicism in Transition.* Kansas City, MO: Sheed & Ward, 1986.

This book examines the church in Brazil amid the contexts of military rule and oppression. The author contends that a new church has emerged in Brazil from the grass roots of the base Christian communities despite persecution and authoritarian rule. Traces the Brazilian church's actual experience as a model for liberation theology: from its alliance to power to its preferential option for the poor, the creation of base Christian communities and its difficult struggle toward liberation. A good introductory case study.

410   Alves, Rubem A. *A Theology of Human Hope.* New York: Corpus Books, 1971.

Alves is a Protestant theologian from Brazil who uses the insights of Mannheim, Kuhn, Fanon, Marx, Moltmann, and Barth to demonstrate the exhaustion of First-World theologies, with which he is thoroughly familiar, when dealing with Third-World issues of poverty and oppression. Like Moltmann, Alves essays a new theology of hope, but unlike his European counterpart, Alves bases his hope on the experience of the marginalized in the concrete reality of Latin America. This book examines the theological theme of freedom and its similarities to and differences with political humanism, existentialism, "humanistic messianism," and the politics of liberation. Ultimately theology itself is a method of talking about freedom.

411 Amirtham, Samuel, and John S. Pobee. *Theology by the People. Reflections on Doing Theology in Community.* Geneva: World Council of Churches, 1986.

See also **199**.

412 Anderson, Gerald H., and Thomas F. Stransky, C.S.P., eds. *Mission Trends No. 3. Third World Theologies.* New York: Paulist Press; Grand Rapids, MI: W.B. Eerdmans, 1976.

Selections illustrating the varieties of new theologies that have arisen in the Third World.

413 —. *Mission Trends No. 4. Liberation Theologies.* New York: Paulist Press; Grand Rapids, MI: W.B. Eerdmans, 1979.

A good introductory collection of readings.

414 Araya, Victorio. *God of the Poor. The Mystery of God in Latin American Liberation Theology.* Robert R. Barr, trans. Maryknoll, NY: Orbis Books, 1987.

This is a work of synthesis of the major lines of thought on the nature of God and God's relationship to a suffering humanity in Latin American liberation theology, including the work of Boff, Gutiérrez and Sobrino. Excellent bibliography.

415 Arias, Esther, and Mortimer Arias. *The Cry of My People. Out of Captivity in Latin America.* New York: Friendship Press, 1980.

This is an introduction to the people of Latin America, from the viewpoint of a spiritual geography. Themes include relations to North America, the mirage of development, human rights, women's liberation, the church and the poor in liberation theology.

416   Assmann, Hugo. *Practical Theology of Liberation.* London: Search, 1975.

Topics include the political dimension of faith: the liberation of humanity in history, the theology of liberation, and the impact on theology of the struggle for liberation. The book includes discussion of the Christian contribution to liberation in Latin America. How hotly contested this issue is, and how open to various forms of interpretation, is highlighted by the contrast between the piece written by poet Ernesto Cardenal, who seems to reduce liberation to communist revolution, and Gustavo Gutiérrez, whose carefully laid out theology provides the basis for much liberation thought.

417   —. *Theology for a Nomad Church.* Paul Burns, trans. Maryknoll, NY: Orbis Books, 1975.

Assmann's nomadism is that of the radical reformer forced to flee from one area of persecution to another, much like Erasmus or the new Protestants of the Reformation. In another sense his nomadism is of the temporary nature of grace and the active work of making justice, rather than upholding laws and institutions.

His themes include the development of a relevant political theology, the birth and meaning of liberation theology, its key concepts, sources and methods, its ties to theology of revolution, political theology, and the theology of hope. It then discusses the particular context in which liberation theology arose: a revolutionary situation that cannot truly gain inspiration from other forms, the influence of Vatican II, and the concept of the people of God, among others.

The final chapters deal with the relationship between our sociological and political outlooks and true theology, and the contribution – or possibility of contribution – of individual Christians to liberation.

418   Avila, Rafael P. *Worship and Politics.* Alan Neely, trans. Maryknoll, NY: Orbis Books, 1981.

Avila seeks to make the Eucharist, and through it Jesus Christ, once more the center of the life of the church through a theological and historical critique of the church's ritual. The Eucharist today is an appendage to an empty rite that celebrates the corporate status quo of the church and its alliance with the powers that be. Avila therefore seeks to give the sacrament new life by tying it to the political struggle for liberation in the context of Vatican II.

Surveys the rise of ritual in Israel from its break with Chaldean religion, through Exodus to the Exile and the criticisms of the prophets. Then traces the passage from Jewish ritual in the life of Jesus to the Primitive Church and the history of Christianity to Vatican II. Chapter 3 then seeks out the elements for a new theology and practice of the Eucharist as the center of a liturgy of liberation and as a sacrament of the church's relationship to the world, as the objectification of history, and as the affirmation of justice in the world and community.

419   Bavarel, Michel. *New Communities, New Ministries.*
        The Church Resurgent in Africa, Asia and Latin
        America. Francis Martin, trans. Maryknoll, NY:
        Orbis Books, 1983.

        See **206**.

420   Berryman, Phillip "Latin American Liberation
        Theology." See **550**, pp. 20-83.

        A solid, and sympathetic introduction to the
subject.

421   — . *Liberation Theology. Essential Facts About the*
        Revolutionary Movement in Latin America – and
        Beyond. Oak Park: IL: Meyer Stone Books, 1987.

        For the lay North American reader, and for the
student wishing a good teaching text or review, this
is the best introduction to liberation theology available. Berryman places the theology in its historical
and structural context, laying out the political and
economic forces at work in Latin America since the
1960s that have brought about the new way of
talking about God.
        As the title indicates, Berryman's emphasis is on
the *facts* of the phenomenon, and less on the actual
theology itself. For its audience, however, this is
exactly the right balance since one of the themes of
the book, as of liberation theology itself, is how theology is born out of, and gives its critical insights to,
praxis, or action. Contains excellent background for
Latin America, the theology's basic tenants of God,
the world, ethics and society, the theologians themselves, the movement for change within the church
since Vatican II, the questions of violence and

Marxism that have been unjustly attached to the
movement, the criticisms of, and attacks on, liberation
theology from both inside and outside the church.
Good notes and bibliography.

422   "Black Theology and Latin American Liberation Theology." See **918**, pp. 510-15.

Reflections by Paolo Freire, Assmann, Cone and
others. Attempts at dialog between the two religious
traditions in the face of European assertiveness.

The Boffs

423   Boff, Clodovis. *Feet-On-The-Ground Theology. A
Brazilian Journey.* Phillip Berryman, trans.
Maryknoll, NY: Orbis Books, 1987.

The theology of liberation was not born in the
academy or the seminary but on the ground, among
the poor and the oppressed. From these realities, and
from the actual praxis of Christian life in the face of
reality, the open mind and heart derives the categories and the languages to talk about God and God's
relationship to a humanity in need of salvation.
Boff's book is a journal of meetings with remarkable
men and women whose ordinary lives reflect the grace
of creation.

424   —. *Theology and Praxis. Epistemological Foundations.*
Robert R. Barr, trans. Maryknoll, NY: Orbis
Books, 1987.

This is a solid and a hefty work of theology: a
full-blown methodology of doing liberation theology.
After thorough discussions of socio-analytic and

hermeneutic mediations: on its most simplistic level
the meeting of theology and the social sciences, Boff
then goes on to detail the stages of the dialectic of
theory and praxis: the workings of theology and the
theologian amid the contexts of politics, and socio-
economic structures. Exhaustively annotated, with a
remarkable bibliography.

425   —, with Leonardo Boff. *Introducing Liberation
        Theology.* Paul Burns, trans. Maryknoll, NY: Orbis
        Books, 1988.

This short introduction is clearly a work written
after the papal inquisition of Leonardo Boff and the
issuance of the Vatican's *Instruction.* (See **123-124**). It
shows a more tempered, circumspect approach to the
theology that is also genuinely concerned with taking
into account the mystical as well as the prophetic,
the Magisterium as well as the evolution of theology
from the praxis among the poor.

Essential to the Boffs' introduction is the theme
that liberation theology is only a *way* of doing
theology, not a radical new departure. It seeks to
refocus attention on the reality of oppression from a
biblical and evangelical perspective. Chapters deal
with the context of theology in a world of suffering,
the three levels of theology (popular, pastoral, and
professional), the process of liberation theology,
beginning with work among the marginalized, using
various analytical methods, including those of Marxism, but focusing primarily and essentially on the
Bible, then on the social teachings of the church.

Key themes of the theology of liberation include
the practice of liberation as a true sign of faith, the

"preferential option for the poor" against the poten-
tates of the world, the centrality of God's kingdom in
this struggle and of Jesus Christ as its model, and true
liberator, and the continuing presence of the Holy
Spirit in the daily struggle of the oppressed. The
role of Mary as the model and inspiration for much of
the popular devotion to liberation is also stressed.
The church is the sacrament of this liberation, the
"sign and instrument."

Useful sections also include a brief history of
liberation theology and a survey of its influences and
forms around the world. The book is not a work of
apology or an instrument of rebuttal to accusations
against liberation theology but clearly a good-faith
effort to explain current thought and practice in the
context of the church as a whole.

426 —. Salvation and Liberation. *In Search of a Balance
Between Faith and Politics.* Robert R. Barr, trans.
Maryknoll, NY: Orbis Books, 1988.

"Integral liberation" is the definition of this
apology for liberation theology, set in the context of
attacks against the Boffs and other liberation theologians during the pontificate of John Paul II but also in
the aftermath of *Evangelii Nuntiandi* by Paul VI and
of Puebla. The balance between faith and politics is
resolved and restored when the individual Christian
and society as a whole realize the integral connection
between the liberation of the soul and the individual
from sin and that of society at large from the
structures that enshrine sin. They stress that liberation is not the same as political apocalyptic, in
which the individual remains unchanged while
society is dragged through upheaval.

427   —, with George V. Pixley. *The Bible, the Church, and the Poor.* Maryknoll, NY: Orbis Books, 1989.

A close reading of the Hebrew Bible and of the New Testament lays the foundation for this analysis of the church's preferential option for the poor, with special emphasis on the situation in Latin America.

428   Boff, Leonardo. "Christ's Liberation via Oppression. An Attempt at Theological Construction from the Standpoint of Latin America." See **480**, pp. 100-132.

The book of Exodus and Christ's temptations in Luke 4:1-13 serve as the model for the new Christian who rejects both the power and despair of the world in doing God's will.

429   —. *Church, Charism, and Power. Liberation Theology and the Institutional Church.* John W. Diercksmeier, trans. New York: Crossroad, 1985.

This work grows out of the inquisition carried out by Cardinal Ratzinger and his Office of the Congregation of the Faith against Boff in the spring and summer of 1984. While the resulting Vatican document *Instructions* (**123-124**) seemed to endorse liberation theology on its deepest level, the entire process of the inquisition and its expansion to include other theologians – and eventually to demand loyalty oaths from all teachers of theology in Catholic universities – seriously put into question the Vatican's commitment to the new reform ecclesiology of Vatican II.

Boff therefore seems here to meet the central questions of papal, episcopal, theological and lay authority within the church head on and ahead of the issue. Topics discussed include models of authority and pastoral life within the church, the church in the struggle for justice, the rights of the poor, the violation of basic human rights within the structure of the church, converting the power aggrandizement within the current church to service, and the strengths and pathologies of Roman Catholicism as an ecclesiological structure.

The book then goes on to offer some directions for hope and change, including a renewed emphasis on syncretism and ecumenism, the church's need to meet the realities of class in the modern world, the hope born in the base ecclesial communities, the role of the people in framing theology and ecclesiology, and the image of the church not as authoritarian structure but as a sacrament of the work of the Holy Spirit within the world. It is one organized by the charism of its mission and ministry, not by its hierarchies and power structures.

430   —. *Faith on the Edge. Religion and Marginalized Existence.* San Francisco: Harper & Row, 1990.

Not seen.

431   —. *God's Witnesses in the Heart of the World.* Robert Fath, C.M.F., trans. Chicago: Claretian Center for Resources in Spirituality, 1981.

This is a new spirituality for the clerical life from a liberationist point of view. Boff examines every aspect of the religious life, from its symbolic, sacramental, and phenomenological points of view, including its meaning in Catholicism; the experience of God; the three vows of poverty, chastity and obedience; the relationship between the religious and the "secular" lives; the role of prayer and action; and the mission of the clergy to liberate both the individual and society from oppression and sin.

432   —. *Jesus Christ Liberator. A Critical Christology for Our Time.* Patrick Hughes, trans. Maryknoll, NY: Orbis Books, 1987.

This is a Christology – an examination of the nature and role of Jesus Christ – born out of the Latin American experience. Reviews the history of Christology and various schools of interpretation, the hermeneutics of knowing Jesus the Christ, Jesus' understanding of his own ministry, and the implications of the kingdom of God for our situation today. Jesus is also seen as a role model of the creative, imaginative, realistic, and deeply human individual. Boff then meditates on the meanings of Christ's death and resurrection for his followers and believers, and the mythologizing of his life and its cosmic meaning in our lives today. The study concludes with the implications for Christologies from the periphery.

433   —. *Liberating Grace.* John Drury, trans. Maryknoll, NY: Orbis Books, 1987.

This interpretation of grace, ironically, seems to revive the old debate posed between the Renaissance Humanists and the Protestants on the same biblical texts: is grace a substance infused into the world, or is it the result of human action, and the working out of love? Boff's analysis sides with the Humanists – and his own Franciscan forbearers – but he insists that the insights of liberation theology are fully compatible with traditional and orthodox teaching on grace, acts, and salvation. He expands traditional ways of looking at, even of experiencing, grace for the modern world: especially that of the marginalized of Latin America, through and in whose actions and solidarity the spirit works to produce liberation.

434   ___. *The Lord's Prayer. The Prayer of Integral Liberation.* Theodore Morrow, trans. Maryknoll, NY: Orbis Books; Melbourne: Dove Books, 1988.

A close rereading of the text in Matthew with an eye to present realities. Each verse is accompanied by Boff's reflections and his analyses of current experience of human suffering and faith.

435   —.*Passion of Christ, Passion of the World.* Robert R. Barr, trans. Maryknoll, NY: Orbis Books, 1987.

The subtitle reads: "The Acts, Their Interpretation, and Their Meaning Yesterday and Today." This is a book of liberation Christology, for it delves into the problem of Christ's passion, its meaning in divine and human terms, Jesus' own understanding of his passion and death, and interpretations of these events by his early followers and in the Christian tradition. Boff then examines the meaning for modern theology and praxis and offers suggestions for preaching the cross and for the cross as a focus of spirituality.

436   —. *Sacraments of Life. Life of the Sacraments.* John Drury, trans. Washington, DC: Pastoral Press, 1987.

Even in today's technocratic world, the sacraments, and the sense of the sacramental, remain profound realities in our psyches. Boff therefore attempts to reexamine the sacraments as deeply aligned with the most elemental experiences of human life, their symbolism, their roots in Jesus' mission, and their place in the process of liberation.

437   ___. *Trinity and Society*. Paul Burns, trans. Maryknoll, NY: Orbis Books, 1988.

The Trinity is a model for all human society: for it lives and creates through its unity and equality, its diversity and its harmony, in the perfect justice of the workings of its individual persons. After an overview of the question Boff examines the history of interpretation. He then focuses on the doctrine of the Trinity and its meaning for today's culture and society and the role of each person of the Trinity. As with many of his other works and with the growing awareness of all liberation theologians, Boff concludes with a discussion of the role of the Trinity for all creation.

438   ___. *Way of the Cross. Way of Justice*. John Drury, trans. Maryknoll, NY: Orbis Books, 1986.

The way of the cross is the backward-looking focus of theology: the reflection of the historical event of Christ's birth, life, suffering, and death. The way of justice is theology's forward-looking glance: the meaning of Christ's death, resurrection, and our salvation in the context of the present world of suffering. Today Christ's passion is continued whenever any of his followers suffer for justice's sake. The book takes the form of the traditional stations of the cross, each brought to new life by Boff's contextualizations.

439   —. *When Theology Listens to the Poor.* Robert R. Barr, trans. San Francisco: Harper & Row, 1988.

A collection of essays. Topics include the influence of Vatican II, the mission of the church in Latin America, including prophesy, defense of the poor, the reinvention of the church on the grass-roots level; the rights of the poor as the rights of God; the place of the supernatural and of salvation in this process of liberation, or vice-versa; the place of the Eucharist in a world of injustice, the preaching of the cross in a crucified world; and preaching the resurrection in a world obsessed by death.

440   —. with Clodovis Boff. *Liberation Theology. From Dialogue to Confrontation.* San Francisco: Harper & Row, 1986.

This is a review of the young history of liberation theology in the wake of the inquisition of Boff and other leading liberation theologians and the issuance of the Vatican's *Instruction.* The author begin forthrightly by demonstrating the very public and political nature of liberation theology, born as it is in the face of hunger, poverty and desperation; they discuss the experience of a faith that liberates, the nature of their theology as one that reflects on the praxis of liberation. They then insist that liberation theology is only a method of doing theology, not a new theology, and then go on to confront some of the myths that enemies have raised against it: that it is the product of a few intellectuals, that it is reductionist, that is it "Marxist" inspired, and that it is unscientific and a popularizing theology. They then go on to demonstrate the "axes" of this theology: in the nature of God, Christ, Mary, the Church, moral theology, and spirituality.

The Boffs then lay out what they consider the positive achievements of liberation theology and the challenges that lay ahead of it. The second part of the book is a dialog that discusses the *Instruction*, the nature of an "orthodox" liberation theology, the Christian faith that motivates this theology, its agents among the people themselves, the practice of liberation, and an analysis of the Vatican's charges of Marxism. The book concludes with an account of the summons to Rome and the Christian value of resistance to ecclesial pressure.

For a defense along similar lines, see also Segundo, *Theology and the Church* (533).

441   — , with Virgilio Elizondo. *Convergences and Differences.* James Aitlen Gardiner, ed. *Concilium* 199. Edinburgh: T. & T. Clark, 1988.

A collection of essays on Third-World theologies, in Africa, Asia, Latin America, and on U.S. black theology and others that discuss their emergence and their cross-fertilizations. Authors include Engelbert Mveng, Tissa Balasuriya, Julio de Santa Ana, James Cone, Justin Upkong, Pablo Richard, Dorothy Folliard, Hyun-Kyung Chung, Sergio Torres, Samuel Rayan, and Maria Clara Bingemer. Includes bibliographical essays.

442   — , eds. *Option for the Poor. Challenge to the Rich Countries. Concilium* 187. Edinburgh: T. & T. Clark, 1986.

Essays by Santa Ana, John Kavanaugh, Casalis, Rainer Kampling, David Flood, Greinacher, Dussel,

Rayan, and others on the realities of wealth and poverty, the theological meanings of poverty, the poor in Christian tradition, and the irruption of the poor into the consciousness and make-up of the church today.

443   —, eds. *The People of God Amidst the Poor. Concilium* 176, Edinburgh: T. & T. Clark, 1984.

Essays by Molina Oliú, Pablo Richard, Pixley, Alberigo, Dussel, Cardinal Lorscheider, Gutiérrez, Floristan, Boff, Schillebeeckx, and others on the history of the people of God, its emergence in recent councils, in new ecclesial roles, in theological reflection, all with a focus on Latin America.

*

444   Bussmann, Claus. *Who Do You Say? Jesus Christ in Latin American Theology.* Robert R. Barr, trans. Maryknoll, NY: Orbis Books, 1985.

Part 1 examines the theology of liberation as a new way of doing Christian theology, its antecedents, and its basic premises. It then examines critically certain controversial aspects: Marxism, the concept of liberation and salvation, and the relationship between faith and politics.

Part 2 presents the Christologies of leading liberation theologians, including Assmann, Gutiérrez, Galilea, Segundo, Hernandez Pico, Leonardo Boff, Sobrino, Jímenez Límon, Ellacuria, and Pironio. It then examines the notion of the political Jesus, the use of violence, Jesus' death and resurrection, and the kingdom of God as the aim of prophetic criticism and political action.

445   Castillo-Cárdenas, Gonzalo. *Liberation Theology from Below. The Life and Thought of Manual Quintín Lame.* Maryknoll, NY: Orbis Books, 1987.

Manuel Quintin Lame Chantre was a poor Indian of Colombia who lived and died about 200 km from Bogotá. He was an native American leader who fought on behalf of their land rights and dignity with the weapons of the law and the courts. He left behind the manuscript of a work, "The Thoughts of the Indian Educated in the Colombian Forests."

In it Lame describes the nature of the native American in union with the earth, the state of the pre-Colombian Indian spirit; and then delivers a series of discourses on humanity, wisdom, marriage and passion, injustice against the native Americans, spiritual manna, and other topics. They are united under what Lame called "the doctrine and the discipline," a prophetic theology that looks forward to the restoration of the native American life destroyed by the Columban discovery. Jesus, Mary, and the saints all aid in this process of eventual liberation.

Thus the dichotomy between domination and liberation and a reverence for nature and creation are essential themes in his theology. Lame insists on the right and duty to denounce injustice and crimes against the native Americans.

446   CELAM (General Conference of Latin American Bishops). *The Church and the Present-Day Transformation of Latin America in the Light of the Council.* 2 vols. Bogotá: CELAM, 1970; official U.S. edition, Louis M. Colonnese, ed., Washington, DC: United States Catholic Conference, 1970.

These are the documents of Medellin. Volume 1 includes position papers; while volume 2 contains the conclusions, or official documents, of the conference. An excellent source.

447   Cleary, Edward L., O.P., ed. *Path From Puebla. Significant Documents of the Latin American Bishops Since 1979.* Phillip Berryman, trans. Washington, DC: U.S. Catholic Conference, 1989.

An excellent collection of documents, with introductions and outlines, from the Latin American church on renewal and ecumenism, the political order, development and liberation, economic life, critical local issues, including land, refugees and drug addiction and trafficking; and transnational issues, especially war and peace. Documents are culled from nearly every country in the region. This book is essential for every student of liberation theology and its developments in the 1980s.

448   Comblin, José, *Cry of the Oppressed, Cry of Jesus. Meditations on Scripture and Contemporary Struggles.* Maryknoll, NY: Orbis Books, 1988.

The call for liberation can be traced to the roots of the Biblical tradition, in the Hebrew Bible, in the Gospels, as in the reality of Latin America today.

449   —. *The Holy Spirit and Liberation.* Paul Burns, trans. Maryknoll, NY: Orbis Books, 1989.

Like Leonardo Boff (437) Comblin examines the theological nature and role of the Holy Spirit and the meaning of the Christian doctrine for the reality of the oppressed today. The poor and the oppressed have always been the place where the Spirit dwells most particularly. Examines the Holy Spirit as seen in the world, in the church, in individuals, and finally the relationship of the Spirit to the Trinity and to our notion of the workings of divinity.

450   Conway, James. *Marx and Jesus. Liberation Theology in Latin America.* New York: Carlton Press, 1973.

After surveying Marx's critique of religion and its influence on Third-World theology and its methodology, Conway examines the reality of life in Brazil – poverty, oppression, and illiteracy – and then goes on to examine the thought of Comblin, Freire, Assmann, Camara, and Alves in response to these and to the popular religious life of the Brazilian people.

He then examines the theologies of Gutiérrez and Segundo and concludes with sections on praxis in Chile under Allende and a final analysis of liberation theology between praxis and Marx. This book is based on extensive research of the original texts and interviews with all the major theologians discussed. Good bibliography.

451   Cosmao, Vincent. *Changing the World. An Agenda for the Churches.* John Drury, trans. Maryknoll, NY: Orbis Books, 1984.

This is a book on the church's role in the process of "development" for a new world. The book is framed as a series of theses around several central themes: the need for a new economic order that is essential if humanity is to survive; the causes and problems of underdevelopment, seen as the natural outcome of the uneven development of the few at the expense of the many, and the need to conscienticize the oppressed to their condition; the sacralization of inequality through social structures and the creation of "idols;" the church's role in the transformation of the world in liberation, conscientization, the fight for justice, all in drawing on its traditional strengths. These are the Gospels, the praxis of Jesus, the work of the early church for justice.

Cosmao then briefly reviews the "perversion" of Christianity in becoming the civil religion of the West and the need for a critical reading of church history that will free it from this Constantinianism. He goes on to examine the liberative role of realizing the structuralization of sin, the role of liberation, and the role of humanity as steward of the earth. Finally, Cosmao calls on the church to realize the essentiality political role and consequences of its work in transforming the world, the place of God, and the role of theology in accounting for the praxis of the faith.

452   Cox, Harvey. *The Silencing of Leonardo Boff.* Bloomington, IN: Meyer-Stone, 1988.

Retraces the history of Boff's inquisition and silencing and then attempts to draw some conclusions on the ramifications of the current Ratzinger administration for ecumenism, ecclesiology, inculturation, and the traditions of religious liberty, the search for truth and community that the silencing threaten. An excellent bibliography of Boff's and Ratzinger's works, and on works about the inquisition and liberation theology.

453   Cussiánovich, Alejandro. *Religious Life and the Poor.*
        Liberation Theology Perspectives. John Drury, trans.
        Maryknoll, NY: Orbis Books, 1979.

        An attempt to examine the religious life of the
        clergy from the prophetic commitment to the poor and
        oppressed and to attempt to forge a new concept of
        vocation in terms of solidarity. Topics include the
        poor as the starting point of all discussion, various
        historical approaches to religious life, Latin
        American reflection, the political consequences of such
        an option for the poor, and the emerging knowledge of
        the kingdom of God that stems from this life of
        solidarity.

454   Demarest, Bruce. *General Revelation. Historical Views
        and Contemporary Issues.* Grand Rapids, MI:
        Zondervan, 1982.

        An historical survey of epistemology and revela-
        tion from its roots in Augustine, through the
        Protestant formulations of Luther and Calvin, the
        Puritans, the Enlightenment, liberalism, Barth, the
        Reformed Church, the neoliberals, Vatican II
        Catholicism, Third-World theologies, including forms
        of liberation theology (pp. 201-26), and scriptural
        approaches.

455   Dupertius, Atilio René. *Liberation Theology. A Study in
        its Soteriology.* Berrien Springs, MI: Andrews
        University Press, 1987.

        This published dissertation discusses the back-
        ground in Latin America, both historical and theo-
        logical, and the general issue of salvation in history
        and in Exodus. It concludes with remarks on the poor,

the praxis of liberation, and social responsibility.
Excellent, if unannotated, bibliography.

456   Dussel, Enrique. *Ethics and Community*. Robert R.
       Barr, trans. Maryknoll, NY: Orbis Books, 1988.

This is really a handbook of ethics in the classic
tradition of Thomas Aquinas, a glossary of definitions
and postulates that run from the simple definitions of
terms to more complex discussions of structures and
relationships.   Liberation theology is really not a
radical new theology, but a way of talking about God
that derives from new experience that is not Eurocentric. Its therefore requires new nuances and definitions of terms, both biblical and classical, in order to
demonstrate how this theology affects the lives of
the poor who both make it and draw inspiration from
it.

Such terms as love, community, kingdom,
Jerusalem and Babylon, good and evil, idolatry and
sin, poverty, product, work, capital and wealth, body
and flesh, morality and ethics, class, people, and
Christendom lead to discussions of the international
financial system, production for war amid poverty,
class struggle and violence, culture and ecology, the
church's social teaching on all these matters, and the
new contributions of liberation theology.   While the
format of the work is imposing, dividing each
chapter into a series of smaller headings in the
manner of a medieval scholastic text, the discussion is
really quite informal and leisurely as Dussel constantly refers back to his own earlier definitions and
ties discussions solidly to actual experience.

457   —. *Ethics and the Theology of Liberation.* Bernard F. McWilliams, trans. Maryknoll, NY: Orbis Books, 1978.

This is a continuation of Dussel's *History and Theology of Liberation* and of his attempt to examine deeply the theological underpinnings of liberation theology to present it as a genuine, and original, theological movement of Latin America. Topics include theological anthropology, the meaning of the ethical as both a destructive and liberating criticism of existing structures and states of mind, the formation of a theology of politics and a Latin American ecclesiology, stressing the church's prophetic role in society, the role of women in the church, women's alienation, feminism, and the "erotic" (male-female relationship) in Christian thinking. Dussel also addresses the situation of the Christian thinker in Latin America, the role of thought on action and society, a new hermeneutics, and finally a detailed examination of the epistemological status of liberation theology.

458   —. *History and Theology of Liberation. A Latin American Perspective.* Maryknoll, NY: Orbis Books, 1976.

This is a spiritual history of Latin America, the role of the church, the meaning of salvation and liberation, and a presentation of the main tenets of a theology of liberation.

459   —. *Philosophy of Liberation.* Maryknoll, NY: Orbis Books, 1985

Concentrates on the more secular conditions and outcomes of the move toward liberation in Latin

America. The imperialisms of the First and Second Worlds – of the U.S., U.S.S.R. and Europe – in everything from culture to economic and political systems, has left the Third World on the margins of existence. Solutions must therefore recognize these agents and must devise ways of overcoming these diverse forms of oppression.

460   —. "Historical and Philosophical Presuppositions of Latin American Theology." See **479**, pp. 184-212.

Liberation theology grows out of praxis, from the experience of Latin America from Bartolomé de Las Casas **(65-81)** on. While liberation theology must be understood in the context of the universal Catholic church, the voice of that church is not a monolog. Latin American theology is the child of both European and Amerindian cultures, not only of European Christendom. Its tasks are therefore suited to the conditions of Latin America. It must serve to foster independence from authoritarianism and to unmask exploitation, as Christ and Las Casas did.

461   Eagleson, John and Philip Scharper, eds.; John Drury, trans. *Puebla and Beyond*. Maryknoll, NY: Orbis Books, 1980.

See **113**.

462   Ellacuría, Ignacio. *Freedom Made Flesh. The Mission of Christ and His Church*. John Drury, trans. Maryknoll, NY: Orbis Books, 1976.

Ellacuría's words are those of the prophet who reads the signs of his own times and realizes that they speak to him directly and intimately. This is the strength of liberation theology and of its proponents, and this is why it is the most important and irresistible form of theology in the world today, and it explains why soldiers and empires cannot stop the spread of the Gospels that speak the truth. For, like Ellacuría himself, they are written by the world's prophets and martyrs.

Like Christ himself, who lived and died in the real world of political repression and liberation, his church today must take up its mission of liberation, even if this again involves the cross of suffering and death. Christ's salvation is not purely spiritual – he came to save the world, which means flesh and blood as well as spirit. Ellacuría examines the problems of discussing a political ideology of salvation, the political and social elements of Jesus' mission, his relationship to the state and political movements of his time, and then relates these to the situation of the church in Latin America.

Part 3, "Violence and the Cross," examines the problems of aggressiveness and violence, finds their roots in human nature, and examines the choices open to Christians in pacifism (Charles de Foucauld), nonviolence (Martin Luther King) and revolutionary violence (Camilo Torres), and concludes that Christianity is too rich and multifaceted to be restricted to one attitude toward violence. Ellacuría's words carefully avoided passing judgment on any of these forms. His life spoke of choice most elegantly. His death at the hands of El Salvador's military, along with five Jesuit companions and two laywomen, demonstrates the threat that the truth gives to power.

463   Fabella, Virginia, M.M., and Sergio Torres, eds. *Doing Theology in a Divided World*. Maryknoll, NY: Orbis Books, 1985.

A collection of essays from the sixth annual conference of the Ecumenical Association of Third World theologians. Includes work by some of the world's leading liberation theologians, among them Richard, Ruether, Sölle, Wallis, Balasuriya, and Cone.

464   —. *Irruption of the Third World: Challenge to Theology*. Maryknoll, NY: Orbis Books, 1983.

A collection of essays on the need for the theological and ecclesiological renewal that must accompany, and spur, socioeconomic and political renewal in the Third World. Contributors include Pieris, Elizondo, Gutiérrez, and Cone.

465   —, and Mercy Amba Oduyoye, eds. *With Passion and Compassion. Third World Women Doing Theology*. Maryknoll, NY: Orbis Books, 1988. See **214**, pp. 125-90.

Essays by Ivone Gebara, Luz Beatriz Arellano, Nelly Ritchie, Maria Pilar Aquino, Ana Maria Tepedino, and Elsa Tamez.

The context of Latin American women's theology is terrible oppression – economic, social, and – because Latin American is predominantly Christian – political oppression of Christian women. Martyrdom, both in witness to Christianity and in the cause of revolution, is a very real option and reality for these women.

Women are active not only in combatting their own oppression on all these levels but also within the

church and its patriarchal structures. The entire
tradition of the church, from the Bible to the early
history of Latin America, can be seen as a source of
hope for this struggle, as many examples of liberation
exist within this tradition. Yet the source of this
tradition, the Bible itself, must be read with a new
eye, and a "hermeneutic of suspicion" because it was
written by men and then codified by men who sought
to exclude the very real role of women as among Jesus'
chief disciples. The contrast between the Synoptics
and John's Gospel and the actual role of Martha as an
activist leader of the church are examples of this
problem.

466   Ferm, Deane William. *Profiles in Liberation. Thirty-Six
        Portraits of Third World Theologians.* Mystic, CT:
        Twenty-Third Publications, 1988. See **215**.

Theologians from Africa, Asia, and Latin America
are discussed, including their lives, work and
thought. Bibliographies of books and articles, as
well as photographs, are provided for each. An
excellent introduction. Latin American theologians
include Assmann, the Boffs, Míguez Bonino, Cardenal,
Comblin, Dussel, Galilea, Gutiérrez, Libanio, Maduro,
Miranda, Richard, Segundo, Sobrino, and Tamez. See
also **320**.

467   —. *Third World Liberation Theologies. An Introductory
        Survey.* Maryknoll, NY: Orbis Books, 1986. See
        216.

Discusses the various forms of liberation theologies, their resemblances and differences, studies, and
criticisms of this theology. See also **321**.

468 —. *Third World Liberation Theologies. A Reader.* Maryknoll, NY: Orbis Books, 1986. See **217**.

Selections from a host of liberation theologians, including Boff, Gutiérrez, Segundo, Tamez, Galilea, and others. See also **322**.

469 "The Final Document: International Ecumenical Congress of Theology, Feb. 20-March 2, 1980, Sao Paolo, Brazil." See **593**, pp. 231-46.

On the theological and practical life of the basic Christian communities.

470 Galilea, Segundo. *The Beatitudes. To Evangelize as Jesus Did.* Maryknoll, NY: Orbis Books, 1984.

The practical application of the Sermon on the Mount for today's experience.

471 —. *Following Jesus.* Maryknoll, NY: Orbis Books, 1981.

The "imitation of Christ" has long been at the center of orthodox Christian spirituality and activism. To walk in the footsteps of Christ fulfills the biblical call to follow Him. Here Galilea attempts to demonstrate how the modern Christian can follow Christ in his salvific work for the poor and the marginalized.

472 —. *The Future of Our Past. The Spanish Mystics Speak to Contemporary Spirituality.* Notre Dame, IN: Ave Maria Press, 1985.

To speak to the growing awareness of, and need for, a living spirituality growing in the church today Galilea draws on the historical tradition of Latin America, most especially in St. John of the Cross, Teresa of Avila and Ignatius Loyola, all great mystics and reformers who combined inner spirituality with a life of action.

473 —. "Liberation Theology and New Tasks Facing Christians." See **479**, pp. 163-83.

Reviews the accomplishments of the Medellin and Sucre church conferences. Then outlines the tasks that face liberation theology: cultural liberation and conscientization. The new theology must also pursue liberation from violence, both the institutionalized and subversive types. Yet this cannot be overcome by human means, or through violence, but only through the Cross. Christians must shoulder the burden of prophetic proclamation, of denunciation of power and injustice, and the announcement of solidarity with the poor and oppressed, of repentance and reconciliation. "Christian liberation, then, implies reconciliation; hence liberation theology implies a *theology of reconciliation.*"

474 —. *Liberation Theology and the Vatican Document.* Vol. 1: *A General Survey.* Quezon City, Philippines: Claretian Publications, 1988.

An introduction of liberation theology by one of its major proponents as prelude to a reading of the

Instruction on Certain Aspects of the "Theology of Liberation." The reprint of the document is followed by varied analyses written by Jaime Sin, Peter Hebblethwaite, Philip Scharper and *The Tablet.*

475 —. *Spirituality of Hope.* Maryknoll, NY: Orbis Books, 1990.

Hope is to be distinguished from such bourgeois sentiments as optimism, which assumes a sense of mastery and control, and idealism, which lives remote from the suffering of the world and seeks to impose ideologies. Instead, the Christian must live on hope, which is based on a profound faith in God as well as a keen sense of experience, of disappointment and of struggle, and of commitment to and love for individuals and God's creation.

476 —. *The Way of Living Faith. A Spirituality of Liberation.* John W. Diercksmeier, trans. San Francisco, CA: Harper & Row, 1988.

This is an examination of Christian spirituality from the viewpoint of liberation theology. Topics include the identity and sources of Christian spirituality, conversion, the experience of God, the Christian demand of love and mutuality, the love of the poor and of poverty as essential ways, the taking up of the cross, and the spirituality of mission.

477 Garcia, Ismael. *Justice in Latin American Theology of Liberation.* Atlanta, GA: John Knox Press, 1987.

Despite the emphasis of Latin American liberation theologians on the theological interpretation of the realities of oppression and injustice around them,

Garcia contends that they fail to provide a consistent definition of what they mean by "justice." His work is therefore an attempt to analyze this concept in four major theologians and to describe the implications of these meanings for the impact of the theology on economic and political life.

The theologians examined are Assmann, Míguez Bonino, Gutiérrez, and Miranda. While historical consciousness of the development of conditions in Latin American is central to their theological reflections, "liberation" is multidimensional, working on economic and socio-political, historical-utopian, and religious levels.

Final chapters deal with the implications of these ideas on their political and economic outlooks, with practical and realistic outlooks both on the national and international level. Garcia concludes that, despite the claims of critics, the theological outlook is the basis of these thinkers' positions on justice, not vice-versa. Christian motives and forms of discourse are essential, not mere appendices to their thought. Christian faith precedes this commitment to justice, and Christian realization of God's transcendence brings a realistic appreciation of the limitations of human attempts to bring about justice and to create the kingdom of God. Good bibliography.

478   Geffre, Claude, and Gustavo Gutiérrez, eds. *The Mystical and Political Dimension of the Christian Faith. Concilium 96.* New York: Herder & Herder, 1974.

Articles by Galilea, Dussel, Gutiérrez, Leonardo Boff, Comblin, Segundo, Vidales, Muñoz and Míguez Bonino on the role of a prophetic theology. Topics include liberation theology as the meeting ground of politics and contemplation, the domination-liberation dynamic, the Christocentrism of liberation theology, freedom and liberation as theological concepts, and the contradictions between capitalism and socialism. A final section of the book examines popular piety and religious movements in Latin America.

479   Gibellini, Rosino, ed. *Frontiers of Theology in Latin America.* John Drury, trans. Maryknoll, NY: Orbis Books, 1979.

A collection of essays by the region's leading intellectuals, including Boff (**428**), Dussel, Galilea (**473**), Gutiérrez (**488**), Segundo (**530**), and Vidales (**552**).

480   __. *The Liberation Theology Debate.* Maryknoll, NY: Orbis Books, 1987.

This brief but well annotated study examines the impact of the Vatican *Instructions* on the practice and formulation of liberation theology. Topics covered include the origins and method of liberation theology, themes and research topics, the Vatican controversy, including outline analyses of both the *Instruction on Certain Aspects* and the *Instruction on Christian Freedom and Liberation.* Gibellini then provides some commentary by leading liberation theologians.

481   Goizueta, Robert S. *Liberation, Method and Dialogue. Enrique Dussel and North American Theological Discourse.* Atlanta, GA: Scholar's Press, 1988.

This is a rather technical examination of Dussel's contribution. Topics include the emergence of the liberation paradigm, a survey of the history of dialectic from Plato through Hegel to Latin America today; the new "universal" history emerging in Latin America today, the unity of "economies": erotic, pedagogical, political and theological in the analysis of Dussel; and the North American response, concluding in a series of "conversion" to the "other" as "other."

The book includes a survey of the critiques by Novak, McCann, and Roger Vekemans and a discussion of Dussel's and Bernard Lonegran's contributions. Specialized bibliography.

482   Goulet, Denis. *New Moral Order. Studies in Development Ethics and Liberation Theology.* Maryknoll, NY: Orbis Books, 1974.

This book is an attempt to formalize an ethical outlook to the process of "development" in the Third World and is thus a more secular version of the theological investigation undertaken by Enrique Dussel from a historical and theological point of view. Essentially Goulet seeks a rebirth of moral philosophy that will place the vast societal changes and struggle underway in the Third World into an ethical framework: he does so by examining both sociological and ethical thinkers, the church's prophetic role, and the Christian role in turning a faceless process of dialectic and historical development into a human and religious one.

Traces the development of ethical thought among the originators and proponents of liberation theology, including L. J. Lebret, Orlando Fals-Borda, Gonzalo Arroyo and Gustavo Gutiérrez.

Gustavo Gutiérrez

483   Brown, Robert McAfee. *Gustavo Gutiérrez. His Life and
        Work.* Maryknoll, NY: Orbis Books, 1990.

        Sets his biography of Gutiérrez into the context of
        Latin America, the history of liberation theology,
        the Vatican's attacks, the reactions to and interpreta-
        tions of the theology. A careful reading of Gutiérrez'
        work and thought.

484   ——. *Makers of Contemporary Theology. Gustavo
        Gutiérrez.* Atlanta, GA: John Knox Press, 1980.

        Surveys the origins and broad sweep of liberation
        theology, the career and thought of Gutiérrez, the
        emphasis on praxis, his method, and the deeply the-
        ological content of his work. Concludes with a survey
        of the criticisms and the impact of liberation theol-
        ogy on North America. Contains a brief, selected
        bibliography of Gutiérrez' works.

485   Cadorette, Curt. *From the Heart of the People. The
        Theology of Gustavo Gutiérrez.* Oak Park, IL:
        Meyer Stone Books, 1988.

        This is an intellectual analysis of Gutiérrez'
        work. Topics include the socio-economic and political
        background, the cultural and religious world of Peru's
        poor and marginalized, the place of his theology in
        Peruvian thought, the role of Marxism and social
        science in his theology, and a resume of his theology.
        Includes a full bibliography of Gutiérrez' works since
        1970 and a good select bibliography of primary and
        secondary works on liberation theology.

486   Ellis, Marc H., and Otto Maduro, eds. *Expanding the View. Gustavo Gutiérrez and the Future of Liberation Theology.* Maryknoll, NY: Orbis Books, 1990.

These are the papers of a conference at Maryknoll held to celebrate the twentieth anniversary of Medellín and to honor Gutiérrez. Contributors include Schüssler Fiorenza, Pieris, Arthur McGovern, Harvey Cox, Schillebeeckx, Ruether, Penny Lernoux, Leonardo Boff, Johann-Baptist Metz, Gregory Baum, Míguez Bonino, Pablo Richard, McAfee Brown and others.

487   —. *The Future of Liberation Theology. Essays in Honor of Gustavo Gutiérrez.* Maryknoll, NY: Orbis Books, 1989.

This collection is both a gathering of the most important religious writers of the world today and a broad-based meditation on the roots, history, nature and future of liberation theology. Contributors include Arns, Betto, Boff, Brown, Cone, Cox, Lernoux, Metz, Ruether, Schillebeeckx, Schüssler Fiorenza, Sobrino, Tutu, and Wiesel, among many others.

488   Gutiérrez, Gustavo. "Liberation Praxis and Christian Faith." See 479, pp. 1-33.

A basic summation of liberation theology.

489   —. *On Job. God-Talk and the Suffering of the Innocent.* Matthew J. O'Connell, trans. Maryknoll, NY: Orbis Books, 1988.

This is a remarkable work that leaves the reader hoping for commentaries on all the books of the Bible from the perspective of liberation theology. "God talk" is the literal translation of theology, and Gutiérrez' book focuses on how the story of Job is essentially about how his suffering as an innocent brought him to a new revelation about the nature of God and about how humans talk about God.

Job's suffering is undeserved in the traditional context of a theology of retribution and guilt, what the creation spirituality would call fall and redemption in another context: that is, God rewards the good with prosperity and health and punishes the evil with poverty and disease. Rather than admit to any guilt, for he is guiltless in this context, Job protests his innocence and calls for a trial before God. So strong is his conviction that his present reality of oppression and marginalization is undeserved that he stretches the traditional theology of his friends to the breaking point: it can no longer address the reality of the suffering of the innocent.

Job's illumination in the ways of God is gradual, first through a discovery of God's solidarity with the poor and oppressed whose fate he now shares, then of his renewed realization that God has spoken through the prophets, psalms and wisdom literature: that God actually does side with the poor against the mighty who have caused their oppression. Yet this is not enough, for after Job's own insistence that he is innocent even on this score God reveals divinity's true nature to him: humbles him through a series of ironic questions that establishes the priority of God and creation before any human existence, before any human system of good and evil, retribution and reward.

God, Job learns, is the creator first and foremost, the just judge only secondarily, and human concerns are secondary to God's freedom and God's plan for all of creation, not just humanity. The abandonment of egocentrism is a central theme in this reading through liberation theology. Job discovers that his own sufferings are nothing in comparison with the social oppression of the poor as a whole, that only through his embracing his fellow humans can his own suffering make sense, and secondly, only by abandoning anthropocentric preoccupations of God's creation working in ways accessible to human reason can humans accept their own role in creation. In so doing, however, they learn that God has made them co-operators of creation: that is, just as social sin is caused by humans, so too the workings of God's justice can only be accomplished through the cooperation of humans who seek justice. In this sense humans cooperate in the work of creation as a whole: God does not exist to aid human causes and concerns, but humanity exists to implement the divine plan: without human agents God's work, as God has planned it, cannot be fulfilled.

The book ends with a profound contemplation on the joint roles of God's liberating grace, which is essential to Job's salvation as to the world's, and of the works that stem from this gift of God. Gutiérrez also ponders the relationship between prophesy and mysticism in realizing this plan and then in attempting to fulfill it.

490   ___. *The Power of the Poor in History.* Robert R. Barr, trans. Maryknoll, NY: Orbis Books, 1988.

A compilation of eight essays. After examining the biblical roots of liberation theology, Christ's revelation and its proclamation by the poor, Gutiérrez traces the development of theology written by the poor themselves from Medellin, through the 70s to Puebla and beyond. Concludes with reflections on doing theology in the modern world and theology set amid a world of oppression and crisis.

491   —. *A Theology of Liberation*. Caridad Inda and John Eagleson, trans. and eds. Maryknoll, NY: Orbis Books, 1973; Fifteenth Anniversary Edition, 1988.

This is dense, often difficult, but fundamentally important reading for Catholic liberation and nonviolence, not only in Latin America, but around the world. The controversy that surround Gutiérrez' works, the attempt of Cardinal Ratzinger's Holy Office to silence Gutiérrez and Boff, and Pope John Paul II's embrace and eventual vindication of liberation theology have made it the most important theological and *practical* movement in the church today. This book is the key text of that theology.

The church has finally entered an era that calls for a return to earlier Christian traditions: that faith is expressed through charity, that the church must raise a voice of prophesy, and that theology must once again flow from *praxis,* its working in the world, to illuminate the world and become the agent of the world's transformation. The sources of liberation theology are papal documents, such as *Gaudium et Spes* of Vatican II (See 99), Paul VI's *Populorum Progressio* (107), the Medellin Conference, and most importantly, the Bible. Key biblical texts include Galatians 5:1, Luke 4:1-13, and Exodus.

The major characteristics of this theology are the centrality of building the kingdom of God that rejects the old dualism between personal, inner salvation and the institutional action of the church in Constantinian alliance with the powers of the world. Salvation is now seen as integral, that is, the church saves not only souls, but complete persons; it liberates both the oppressed and the oppressors from sin and from the poverty, alienation, exploitation, and oppression that define sin. Its emphasis on change is thus radical and integral, a rejection of older models of change, such as Western-style development, that impose it from the top down, the work of elites either clerical or governmental. Instead, change must come from the poor and the oppressed themselves, first through "conscientization," then through denunciation of sin, and then through the proclamation of liberation.

In this process the structure of the church plays an essential part, for the church must manifest the new society of peace and justice by changing its own life, opting for the poverty of the oppressed, changing its structure to reflect the voice of the humble, rejecting its alliance with power, while defying the threats of the secular state that it is "meddling in politics" when it speaks out for the oppressed. Yet just as Christ refused to hope in the forces of this world or to despair by casting himself down from the temple, the new theology refuses to despair. Neither does it seek utopian solutions to the problems of the world, for these utopias are the works of humans and of ideologies; while the kingdom of God, though implemented by men and women, is really the work of God, and it builds new men and women, not new societies. As such it demands individual conversion, not compulsion or the leadership of enlightened elites.

The church, then, is the visible manifestation of God's kingdom in the world and in history. The church exists not for itself, for its own structures and power, but for the world; it is the self-reflective part of the world. It is thus truly the sacrament of Christ's liberation in history and time. All history, then, is sacred history, the history of salvation, and the growth of God's kingdom is the process of liberation in the world. Only by forging social justice and love, therefore, can the individual and the church know God, and the type of knowledge one has of God through love and action ("orthopraxis") far excels the intellectual knowledge of God through "orthodoxy."

Just as the new theology shifts emphasis from orthodoxy to orthopraxis, so too the sacramental and liturgical life of the church must focus away from individualistic piety and empty cultic worship and to a renewed emphasis on the Eucharist and Christ as the source and symbol of this new solidarity.

Much has been made of the "Marxist" and revolutionary elements of liberation theology. Here Gutiérrez emphasizes that liberation must be the work of love and not of hate, but at the same time he recognizes that the oppressor is the enemy, and that physical poverty and oppression are real evils that must be combatted.

492   —. The Truth Shall Make You Free. Confrontations. Maryknoll, NY: Orbis Books, 1990.

A reflection upon his own work and its impact. It focuses around his call to Rome and his apologia given to the theology faculty of Lyons. In addition, this volume examines Gutiérrez' thinking on the relationships between theology and social science, Christology and ecclesiology, and the essential integralism between the salvation of the soul and of society, between spirit and matter that he has made the hallmarks of liberation theology.

493   —. *We Drink From Our Own Wells. The Spiritual
        Journey of a People.* Matthew J. O'Connell, trans.
        Maryknoll, NY: Orbis Books, 1983.

The working of liberation theology in praxis, in
the lives of the poor in Latin America. Part One discusses the contextual experience of Latin American
liberation, the region's oppression, alienation, and
poverty. Part Two examines forms of Christian spirituality based on biblical paradigms. Part Three
traces the actual developments in contemporary Latin
America, blending theological reflection with the
recollection of events as concrete manifestations of
Christian faith, hope, and love.

494   —, and Richard Shaull. *Liberation and Change.*
        Atlanta, GA: John Knox Press, 1977.

This is a dialog concerning the meaning of North
American revolution on Third-World revolutions and
North America's response to these revolutions.
Gutiérrez holds that liberation theology and Third-
World revolution are in many ways incompatible
with the American revolution, in that they are predominantly concerned with liberating the proletariat
from the middle classes that the North American
revolution made ascendent. In Gutiérrez' thought
freedom means not only liberation from all obstacles
to salvation but also the political consequences of such
freedom, including an endorsement of Latin America's
revolutionary impulse and its confrontation with
North American reaction.
        Shaull takes a similar viewpoint from within
North American society. North American society, he
contends, has become a meaningless dead end: a
society of irrelevant affluence and self-fulfillment in
the face of quickly changing Third-World realities.

American society can be matured, however, not by power from the top but by small groups and communities building a new world. A new *koinonia* rising from the death of the American empire can bring a new vision.

495   Gutiérrez, Juan. *The New Libertarian Gospel. Pitfalls of the Theology of Liberation.* Paul Burns, trans. Chicago: Franciscan Herald Press, 1977.

Today's is a world of stark black and whites, of simple solutions, and of burning desire to have a paradise in this world, since no one believes in the next any more. Liberation theology is the result of this environment: "what a shame that its partial approaches and badly used judgments and methods have distracted the honest intentions of so many...."
This book is a critique, a judgment is more apt, of the theology of Gustavo Gutiérrez, which though it has some merit, "contains...serious defects that should be remedied," although most of his thought is beyond repair. Topics include the theology of liberation, Gustavo Gutiérrez' theology, the classical functions of theology, theology as "historical praxis," and theology as "critical reflection."

*

496   Hennelly, Alfred T. *Liberation Theology. A Documentary History.* Maryknoll, NY: Orbis Books, 1990.

Primary source readings from the 1950s through the 1980s, including the theology's sources in Vatican II, Medellín, and Puebla; criticisms and friendly analyses, the Vatican *Instructions* and the debate over the papal assault on leading liberation theologians.

497   —. *Theologies for a Liberating Church. The New Praxis of Freedom*. Washington, DC: Georgetown University Press, 1989.

Educated in the full flush of Vatican II. Hennelly's aim is to develop a North American liberation theology by paying careful heed to this theology in the Third World. He therefore surveys the origins and development of liberation theology in Latin America, its sociology, content and method, with specific examples in Gutiérrez, Segundo and Sobrino. He then briefly discusses developments in North America before examining the sources for a theology of freedom. Subsequent chapters deal with Paulo Freire as a liberation theologian, with base Christian communities, and the human rights content of the theology. The last chapter examines the Vatican *Instruction* (see **123-124**); while an epilog discusses the structures of sin and grace and other themes of the *Instruction*, which is printed in full as an appendix.

498   —. *Theologies in Conflict. The Challenge of Juan Luis Segundo*. Maryknoll, NY: Orbis Books, 1979.

This is an attempt to encounter liberation theology through a dialog with one of its chief proponents. After introductory materials on official church teaching, new forms of theology, liberation theology and the influence of Gutiérrez, the author discusses some basic tenets of liberation theology: the nature of the Christian, the church, praxis vs. theory, the hermeneutic challenge of liberation theology; the ideological aspects of Christianity in the Bible, in the churches, in eschatology and in its attitudes toward violence; a survey of Christian spirituality and the contribution of the new theology; and the challenge of Marxism.

499 Hinkelammert, Franz. *The Ideological Weapons of Death.* Maryknoll, NY: Orbis Books, 1986.

At its most profound level liberation theology tackles questions about the very nature of God, which is, after all, the meaning of theology. Here the author delves into the most basic Hebrew meaning of idolatry: which is the establishment of fetishes: material goods of the world as ends in themselves, which become the focus of worship, the projections of power. Country, capital, power, status, wealth are all idols that we have erected that obscure the true God of life and that become weapons of death for the world's poor.

500 Kirby, Paeder. *Lessons in Liberation. The Church in Latin America.* Dublin: Dominican Publications, 1981.

Discusses the historical and social situation, the base Christian communities, the role of conscientization, structural supports to organize the poor in their struggle, the role of the theologians in articulating the people's faith, the role of the missionary as servant of popular needs, the bishops as sharing in the suffering of the people. Concludes with a discussion of the hopes raised by the Puebla conference of 1979 and for a new church emerging.

501   Kloppenburg, Bonaventura. *Christian Salvation and Human Temporal Progress.* Paul Burns, trans. Chicago: Franciscan Herald Press, 1979.

Examines the relationship in liberation theology between liberation and salvation; between moral progress and human secular progress through a study of the documents of Vatican II, Medellin, the 1974 Synod of Bishops, and *Evangelii Nuntiandi.* A final chapter surveys non-Catholic thought.

502   —. *The People's Church. A Defense of My Church.* Matthew J. O'Connell, trans. Chicago: Franciscan Herald Press, 1978.

This is an examination of the theological underpining of the program of Christians for Socialism in Latin America. The aim of the book is frankly apologetic: to defend "the church" against those who would "promote an ideological struggle within the church and thereby 'deideologize' and 'reinterpret' the Christian faith, to effect a rereading of the Bible, to liberate the conscience of the masses, to appropriate the liturgy for themselves, and by all these means create a new 'Church of the People.'"

503   —. *Temptations for the Theology of Liberation.* Chicago: Franciscan Herald Press, 1974.

Not seen.

504   Lara-Brand, Jorge. *What Is Liberation Theology?* Atlanta, GA: General Assembly Mission Board, 1980.

Not seen.

505   Lopez Trujillo, Alfonso. *Liberation or Revolution? An Examination of the Priest's Role in the Socioeconomic Class Struggle in Latin America*. Huntington, IN: Our Sunday Visitor, 1977.

The author's subtitle gives away his approach and political outlook: to be involved in the process of liberation theology is to be engaged in the class struggle of the Marxists. Lopez Trujillo's purpose here, however, is more strictly concerned with priests who are members or supporters of the "Christians for Socialism" movement, and who, he claims, have abandoned their sacerdotal role for otherwise commendable goals of social justice and liberation. The assertion that the class struggle must also be waged within the church is additional cause for alarm. While Christian theology may call for the necessary participation in politics, it is not exclusively nor wholly equated with the political process.

The author discusses the urgency – and fashion – of the call to liberation today, the Judeo-Christian religious tradition of liberation, the poor in reality and spirit, the mystery of liberation embodied in the Paschal celebration, Christian eschatology vs. secular utopianism; the divergences between Christian liberation and revolution, including the issue of violence; the dangers of manipulation of the priest's role and trust, of the Gospels, and of theology; and the role of the church as a liberated and liberating community. He concludes with some warning remarks against the politicization of the priesthood. He has been amply rewarded for his loyalty to the Vatican line with a recent promotion to the Roman Curia.

506   Míguez Bonino, José. *Christians and Marxists. The Mutual Challenge to Revolution.* Grand Rapids, MI: W.B. Eerdmans, 1976.

Not seen.

507   —. *Doing Theology in a Revolutionary Situation.* Philadelphia: Fortress Press, 1975.

The book is divided into two parts. The first examines the phenomenon of a new type of Christianity freed from both the colonial and neocolonial Constantinianism that have characterized Latin America and its new links to an integral approach to faith and action.

The second part of the book examines the theological meaning of this movement: a new hermeneutics of action, an examination of the dynamics of Christian love and the problems of poverty, oppression and class; the eschatological element of liberation theology in its quest for a new world and new society; and finally the ecclesiological aspects of this new theology as the people themselves begin to change the meaning of the church and the people of God.

508   —. *Revolutionary Theology Comes of Age.* London: SPCK, 1975.

Not seen.

509   —. *Toward a Christian Political Ethics.* Philadelphia: Fortress Press, 1983.

Discussions include the need for a political ethics in the face of the realities of technocratic rule on the continent; Christian responses to the ethical dilemma of political action, including the issue on nonviolence; the connections between praxis and theory and the influence of sociology and theology; the historical development of Latin American politics from authoritarianism to democracy to the national security state; the meanings of justice in a Christian sense; and the role of hope and power in attaining the kingdom of God.

510 —, ed. *Faces of Jesus. Latin American Christologies.* Maryknoll, NY: Orbis Books, 1984.

Includes essays by Boff, Ellacuria, Galilea, and Vidales, among others. The nature of Jesus Christ interpreted through the eyes of leading Latin American liberation theologians.

511 Miranda, José. *Being and the Messiah. The Message of St. John.* Maryknoll, NY: Orbis Books, 1977.

Not seen.

512 —. *Communism in the Bible.* Robert R. Barr, trans. Maryknoll, NY: Orbis Books, 1982.

"This is a manifesto" that seeks to show, through meticulous scholarship that Marxism – as correctly understood and not associated with any of its historical manifestations – and Christianity are fundamentally the same. Both, for example, stress that the kingdom is to be achieved here on earth, as in an understanding of true Christianity lived in the Acts of the Apostles through a society free of oppression. Both spurned the accumulation of wealth, saw evil as a social problem, and dismissed the profit motive.

Miranda contends that we have misinterpreted Jesus' statements: that the poor will always be with us, that we must render to Caesar, and that his kingdom is not of this world. Instead, the author contends, Jesus' life and message was inherently and explicitly political, and finally that Jesus explicitly approves the use of violence to redress injustice. Jesus approves all the vindictive violence of the Old Testament and himself used physical violence.

513 —. *Marx Against the Marxists.* Maryknoll, NY: Orbis Books, 1980.

A person's Christianity does not hinge solely on his or her beliefs about God, but in actions and attitudes toward the rest of humanity and one's neighbors. Thus Marx's thought was truly Christian at base. In fact, we must learn to deconstruct Marx from his Marxist accretions, to demythologize and to get to the man and his own pure thought.

As Christianity is "solid, unequivocal humanism," Marx must be a Christian. Deeply moral ethics, just like those of Christianity, are the essence of Marx and Engels. Like Jesus Christ, Marx denounces the God mammon; and like primitive Christianity, Marx and Engels seek a community of goods. Marx's hostility to religion and his concept of God are illogical and self-contradictory, however, and cannot be ascribed as a true part of his philosophy.

514 —. *Marx and the Bible. A Critique of the Philosophy of Oppression.* John Eagleson, trans. Maryknoll, NY: Orbis Books, 1974.

The influence of Marx on Catholic social teaching has been clear and irreversible since Pius XI's

Quadragesimo Anno, which accepted most of Marx's analytic categories, while changing some of his wordings. This tradition holds true through to *Progressio Populorum*, despite its conscious attempts to distance itself from Marx. Yet the Marxist influence runs deeper than that. Marx himself belonged to the prophetic tradition of the Bible, and many of his concerns are inherently those of Christian social thought. Miranda's analysis is based on long biblical study in Rome.

Topics include the modern critique of private ownership and its biblical roots, the biblical understanding of God as transcendent of our categories, and as the God of Exodus and liberation. The book concludes with a discussion of Christian faith and dialectic in history, prophetic faith, eschatology and the role of history as a process of liberation.

515   Moser, Antonio, and Bernardino Leers. *Moral Theology. Dead Ends and Alternatives.* Maryknoll, NY: Orbis Books, 1990.

One of the remarkable achievements of liberation theology, and of the Orbis Books' Theology and Liberation Series (545) is that it has reexamined not only the larger role of theology in society and in God's creation, but has also revamped all areas of traditional Christian theology from metaphysics and liturgy, to ecclesiology and ethics. Here the authors trace the development of Catholic moral theology and then use the insights of liberation theology to lay out a new direction for it in the face of obvious injustices and oppressions in the world today. Discussions range from the place of Marxism and capitalism to the nature and role of individual conscience.

516   Muñoz, Ronaldo. *The God of the Christians*. Maryknoll,
       NY: Orbis Books, 1990.

       One of the chief themes of all forms of liberation
       theology is that atheism is no longer a problem in the
       world; but that belief in too many and different gods
       may well be. Today we have erected many false
       idols and worship many gods: power and consumption
       gods, race and nationalistic gods, war and death gods.
       Middle class North Americans seem to have a god
       that comforts them in their affluence, that allows
       them to ignore the suffering of the starving and
       oppressed of the Third World and the justice-working
       of the Christian god. Muñoz therefore sets out to
       investigate what god is revealed by the life and
       work of Jesus Christ and to reexamine the biblical
       texts that reveal that god.

517   Navarez, Jorge. *The Voice of a People in Struggle. The
       Life of Fr. Rafael Maroto*. New York: Circus, 1986.

       Not seen.

518   Nuñez, Emilio Antonio. *Liberation Theology*. Paul E.
       Sywulka, trans. Chicago: Moody Press, 1985.

       Nuñez is an evangelical who was raised in a
       proletarian family of El Salvador and is therefore
       keenly concerned with the process of liberation in
       Latin America. He attempts to examine some key
       questions about the theology: its relationship to
       sociology, its biblical roots, its basic Christianity, its
       very claim to being theological. In certain circles, in
       North America, among Protestants, liberation theol-
       ogy is all the rage now. Despite his unfashionable
       stance, Nuñez insists that liberation theology is still

out of touch with the vast majority of the continent's
people, and in fact, has made little inroad, especially among Protestants. Among Catholics, he
contends, it has descended to the people from intellectuals and higher clergy.

Despite differences of approach and influence,
however, the author does contend that liberation
theology is here to stay in Latin America and will
undergo transformation, for good or bad. He therefore
attempts to highlight the problems of this theology
for pastors and seminarians, while remaining true to
the Bible and to the aspirations of Latin America's
poor.

Topics include the historical and social context in
Latin America; the development of liberation theology; its methodology; its approach to salvation and
liberation, Jesus the liberator, and ecclesiology. It
concludes with a discussion of evangelical theology
and praxis for Latin America. Adequate bibliography.

519   O'Brien and Shannon. *Renewing the Earth.* See **105**,
       pp. 539-79.

Includes an introduction to liberation theology and
the documents of the Medellin Conference on Justice
and Peace, as well as the "Conference's Message to
the Peoples of Latin America." The Medellin Conference was the second general meeting of the
Conference of Latin American Bishops, held in
Medellin, Colombia from August 24 to September 6,
1968. As such it was an official church council, and
its final documents are part of the official teaching of
the Catholic church around the world.

These final documents are the Latin American response to Vatican II and Pope Paul VI's *Populorum
Progressio,* and they form the theological and ecclesio-

logical basis for the church's nonviolent struggle for liberation. Medellin has become the central event for Latin American liberation theologians and is the cornerstone of all later reflection, just as it was the summation of previous practice and theory. These documents are essential to any study of Latin American events and theory in the 1970s and 1980s.

520   O'Connor, James Thomas. *Liberation. Towards a Theology for the Church in the World, According to the Second General Conference of Latin American Bishops at Medellín, 1968.* Rome: Officium Libri Catholici, 1972.

An attempt to clarify the conclusions of the Medellin Conference in line with the church's magisterium going back to Leo XIII. Discusses the various meanings of liberation: from sin, as conversion and as eschatology, the church as the sign of liberation; in overcoming the dichotomies of spirit and matter, of other-worldly and worldly salvation; Christian social ethics and utopianism; and the role of the church as critic. Includes an appendix of Medellin's liberation texts. The bibliography contains source materials, including papal encyclicals and documents of the Latin American churches, books and articles on various aspects of liberation.

521   Pérez Esclarin, Antonio. *Atheism and Liberation.* John Drury, trans. Maryknoll, NY: Orbis Books, 1978.

"Atheism" here means both its twentieth-century meaning of a rejection of traditional notions of God and "atheism" as an attack on idolatry, almost in the ancient Roman sense of the Christians as atheists who rejected their gods and idols. These gods and idols are, for Pérez-Esclarin, the false idols of the capitalist-materialist world in which Christianity is an anemic vegetable: luxury, waste, and arbitrary whimsy of the few to possess and adore material comforts at the expense of those who make these and who lack them.

He begins by surveying the view of twentieth-century humanity in the view of the arts and of psychology: alienated and dehumanized. It is a civilization of idolaters who have no true god. Its idols are, instead, science and the machine, sex, and consumption. Opposed to this is a god of liberation found in Exodus, the prophets and the words and life of Jesus.

The author concludes his book with brief studies of the most prominent exponents of modern atheism: Nietzsche, Feuerbach, Freud, Russell, Marx, Sartre, Camus, and Merleau-Ponty and concludes that these critics of the modern, anemic, Christian God have actually purified our notion of Christianity and brought back to those who heed their words a realization that a life of activism, on behalf of justice and liberation, is the true meaning of the Judeo-Christian message. A fascinating perspective.

522   Peruvian Bishops' Commission for Social Action. *Between Honesty and Hope. Documents from and about the Church in Latin America.* John Drury, trans. Maryknoll, NY: Orbis Books, 1970.

A collection of thirty key documents for the modern church in Latin America, ranging from works of Helder Camara, to the selected Medellin documents. Themes of special prominence include the role of the laity, violence, the reception of *Populorum*

Progressio, and the obligation of the church in over-coming social injustice.

523   Planas, Ricardo. *Liberation Theology. The Political Expression of Religion.* Kansas City, MO: Sheed & Ward, 1986.

An interesting introduction to the subject that emphasizes the political and economic aspects of the theology and its ties to the Latin American situation and Marxist thought.

524   Richard, Pablo. *The Battle of the Gods.* Maryknoll, NY: Orbis Books, 1984.

A collection of essays centered around Richard's themes of idolatries, Christendoms and true religious life.

525   —. *Death of Christendoms, Birth of the Church.* Phillip Berryman, trans. Maryknoll, NY: Orbis Books, 1987.

The subtitle reads "Historical Analysis and Theological Interpretation of the Church in Latin America." Strongly structuralist in historical methodology and moderately deconstructionist in epistemological approach, this is a study of Latin American history through the perspective of ecclesiastical bonds to the political structures (Christendoms) of the continent from 1492 to the present.
Richard views this history as a series of clearly defined periods, actually cycles of Christendom and crisis, culminating in the present crisis of New Christendom that began in the 1960s. He sees a new period coming in which the popular church, which

never entered into an alliance with the secular powers but which maintained the tradition of the early church, will finally come into its own, and the era of Christendoms finally end.

526 —, ed. *The Idols of Death and the God of Life. A Theology.* Barbara E. Campbell and Bonnie Shepard, trans. Maryknoll, NY: Orbis Books, 1983.

One of the most profound insights of liberation theology, a strength that ties it back to the strongest moral strains of the Judeo-Christian tradition, is its use of the prophetic stance against false idols. The idols are the objects of worship of a materialistic, oppressive social and economic system that places profits, control, and process above human needs and aspirations and in the process attempts to topple the God of creation and life from the center of the universe. This is a collection of essays that examine this process in both biblical and socio-political terms and that call for an embrace of the God that gives life and liberation from false idols, sin and the death that they bring.

527 Santa Ana, Julio de. *Good News to the Poor. The Challenge of the Poor in the History of the Church.* Maryknoll, NY: Orbis Books, 1979.

An historical examination of the poor in biblical and Judeo-Christian tradition. Chapters treat the poor and poverty in the Old Testament, in the message of Jesus, in its call to the rich to convert, in the church of the first century, the radical demands of Christian life, the prophets of the church during the

Constantinian era, in the Middle Ages and in our own time.

528   —. *Towards a Church of the Poor. The Work of an Ecumenical Group on the Church.* Geneva: World Council of Churches, 1977; Maryknoll, NY: Orbis Books, 1981.

This is an outcome of the work of the Commission on the Churches' Participation in Development of the World Council of Churches. It reflects on the relationships of the poor to the churches amid the world reality that in the two previous decades the actual condition of the poor had deteriorated rapidly as development more and more benefitted only the upper and upper middle classes in the Third World. Poverty, dependency, marginalization, and oppression are enduring, and worsening, conditions.

Christians, therefore, are forced not only by tradition but also from their very biblical foundations to work in solidarity with the poor, not in charity, but in an attempt to change basic structures. In so doing, however, they not only form new communities, they found new forms of community within the church and begin to change the structure and nature of the churches themselves.

529   Schipani, Daniel S., ed. *Freedom and Discipleship. Liberation Theology in an Anabaptist Perspective.* Maryknoll, NY: Orbis Books, 1989.

A collection of papers that brings together Anabaptist-Mennonite and Latin American Catholic theologians to discuss various elements of liberation theology, including hermeneutics, ecclesiology, Christology, base communities, and work for peace and justice.

Juan Luis Segundo

530   Segundo, Juan Luis, S.J. "Capitalism Versus Socialism: Crux Theologica." See 479, pp. 240-59.

Liberation theology is a whole theology that speaks to the reality of Latin America. This reality is not dominated by the struggle between the U.S. and U.S.S.R. but derives from the plight of the vast majority of its people.

531   —. *Jesus of Nazareth Yesterday and Today.* John Drury, trans. 5 vols. Maryknoll, NY: Orbis Books, 1984-88.

Vol. 1: *Faith and Ideologies.*
Vol. 2: *The Historical Jesus of the Synoptics.*
Vol. 3: *The Humanist Christology of Paul.*
Vol. 4: *The Christ of the Ignatian Exercises.*
Vol. 5: *An Evolutionary Approach to Jesus of Nazareth.*

This immense work is a five-volume attempt to recast Christology in light of the realities of the Third World today. Volume 1 examines the groundwork that must be done in appreciating language, narrative, myth and religious systems: the means and the values imposed upon a set of data to create an interpretation of reality, thus the role and nature of ideology. Segundo delves into the thought of Machovec, Bateson and especially Marx to attempt to extract a modern methodology of analysis that will see past our own ideologies and religious systems.

Theology is, in fact, little more than such a methodology: not stemming from praxis, but praxis itself.

Volume 2 then sets off to trace the quest for the historical Jesus as found in the Synoptic Gospels, focuses in on the parables, and finds a Jesus who seeks to liberate from religion and its narrow confines with the proclamation of the kingdom: effective love that both liberates the individual from sin and society and politics from systems of oppression.

Volume 3 examines Paul's epistles – especially Romans – and their treatment of sin and redemption. Segundo disagrees with most of liberation theology's rejection of Paul as neutral toward the world and sets out to demonstrate that Paul's humanism sets the message of Christ squarely in the context of a very specific political system, on the side of a very specific set of people – the poor and the oppressed – but also teaches us to go beyond the specific forms of oppression, the specific sins of a time and place, to recognize *sin* itself and thus to seek means of liberating ourselves from it that go beyond dead ends.

In Volume 4 Segundo attempts to show how various Christologies *can* bridge the gap between present realities and the historical event of Jesus' life. He chooses Ignatius' *Spiritual Exercises* because it embodies a Christology that is still so influential on the spirituality of Latin America. Finally, volume 5 attempts to trace out how we can develop a new Christology for our time by returning to the sources of Jesus' life in the Gospels, finally putting Jesus and the universe in the contextual meaning of the Cosmic Christ in the recurring realities of birth, death and resurrection, the hope and faith that is kindled by the divine love of the universe.

532   —. *The Liberation of Theology.* John Drury, trans. Maryknoll, NY: Orbis Books, 1988.

One of the essential revelations of Jesus and his life was that God speaks not in systems of thought or law but in the love that humans bear toward one another and that the universe bears toward all creation. Liberation theology, in its various forms, has begun to reawaken this revelation in a way that is irreversible. At the same time, however, a reaction has set in among both ecclesiastical authorities and among members of more traditional schools of academic theology. The effect has been to both demonize liberation theology as a radical, even revolutionary, movement for its very reiteration of church councils from Vatican II to Medellin or to pass it off as unprofessional, naive and transitory.

Segundo thus attempts to follow up the groundbreaking work of Gutiérrez' *A Theology of Liberation,* which proved the serious theological *content* of the theology, with a parallel exposition of its methodology. He therefore discusses the hermeneutics, sociology, politics, and ideological underpinnings of the theology, its connections to popular religion and spirituality, and the problem of elites and change. A fundamental work.

533   —. *Theology and the Church. A Response to Cardinal Ratzinger and a Warning to the Whole Church.* Rev. ed. San Francisco: Harper & Row, 1985.

Like the Boffs in their *Liberation Theology. From Dialogue to Confrontation* (440), Segundo attempts to place Cardinal Ratzinger's *Instruction* (123-124) in context and to respond to the shadow of heresy that Ratzinger has thrown over liberation theology. The

issues that he seeks to address are the influence of
European theology on Latin America, liberation and
secular aims, the hermeneutical approach of liberation theology, and the ecclesiology of the movement,
including the issue of the people of God and the
popular church. He concludes with a warning to the
whole church that Ratzinger's target is not only
liberation theology and all attempts at theological
pluralism within the church, but the entire structure
of the church brought about by Vatican II.
Ratzinger's intent is to elevate the magisterium to an
infallible and unquestionable voice of papal authority and to set the clock back to a centralized papal
monarchy that brooks no dissent. The volume concludes with a reprint of the *Instruction*.

534   —. *A Theology of Artisans of a New Humanity.* 5 vols.
Maryknoll, NY: Orbis Books, 1973-74. Includes:

Vol. 1: *The Community Called Church*
Vol. 2: *Grace and the Human Condition*
Vol. 3: *Our Idea of God*
Vol. 4: *The Sacraments Today*
Vol. 5: *Evolution and Guilt*

This is an attempt to write a complete theology
along liberation lines that addresses itself to all
issues in Christian theology: from ecclesiology (vol.
1), grace, sin and human freedom (vol. 2); our knowledge of God in transcendence and immanence, the role
of prayer, of salvation in time, demythologizing our
concepts of divinity, God's relationship to the world
in Jesus, the politics of the Gospels, and nonviolence
(vol. 3); the sacraments, their meaning and their role
in the church and world today (vol. 4); and the place

of grace, not for the individual but for society, its structures, and for the human species (vol. 5).

535   Tambasco, Anthony J. *The Bible for Ethics. Juan Luis Segundo and First-World Ethics.* Washington, DC: Catholic University of America Press, 1981.

Uses the methodology of Segundo to address two main issues: the relationship of the Bible to Christian ethics; and the relationship of biblical eschatology to morality. Themes in Segundo's theology include his hermeneutic model, social analysis, theology and ideology, his scriptural exegesis, critical appraisal of his Marxist analysis, biblical teaching on the kingdom, the Bible and violence, and his discussion of ideology. The book concludes with the dialog between Segundo and First-World theologians. Good bibliographies arranged by topic, including Segundo's books and articles to date.

*

536   Sobrino, Jon. *Christology at the Crossroads. A Latin American Approach.* John Drury, trans. Maryknoll, NY: Orbis Books, 1978.

Sobrino's attempt here to place traditional views of Christ's nature and mission into the context of Latin American political oppression and liberation were seen as stretching the limits of orthodoxy by making Jesus a model of revolutionary struggle.

254 *Latin America: Theory and Praxis*

537 —. *Jesus in Latin America.* Maryknoll, NY: Orbis
Books, 1987.

This is a collection of articles published between
1978 and 1982. It discusses the basic themes of
Christology, its importance for Latin America, the
meaning of the kingdom of God and the life of the
poor, and the modern imitation of Christ – following
Jesus as discernment – a basic moral theology that
focuses on the poor and outcast, the meaning of Jesus'
resurrection for the "world's crucified," and the
people's faith in Jesus as son of God. This collection
is also an answer to critics' charges that his
Christology at the Crossroads goes beyond orthodox
discourse.

538 —. *Spirituality of Liberation. Toward Political Holiness.*
Robert R. Barr, trans. Maryknoll, NY: Orbis
Books, 1988.

This is a collection of articles published on
spirituality between 1980 and 1984. Though not
specifically on Christian spirituality, it is an examination, in the light of liberation theology, of how
any spirituality must have, and produce, a life of
commitment in the world; and alternatively, of
providing liberation practice with an underlying
spirituality that insures its religious motivation and
outlook. In both directions Sobrino follows the trend
of all liberation theologies in bridging the gap
between inner, private spirituality and social and
political ethics.

Topics include the presuppositions and foundations
of spirituality; the links between a new spirituality
and liberation, the spirituality of liberation theology; and a new form of holiness: "political holiness."

Sobrino then discusses the spirituality of martyrdom and of suffering persecution, and the divine element in the struggle for human rights.

Part 2 of this book then examines Jesus' proclamation and the reign of God, the place of spirituality in evangelization and discipleship, and conflicts within the church.

Part 3 discusses the concrete realities of the martyrdoms of the four North American churchwomen in El Salvador (642-647), the realities and hopes of the poor in Latin America, and the new spirituality that has grown out of the rediscovery of Christ in the region. A final chapter, which is witness to the importance and original vitality of liberation theology, tries to draw some applications for European churches.

539   —. *The True Church of the Poor.* Matthew J. O'Connell, trans. Maryknoll, NY: Orbis Books, 1984.

Bases this call for a liberating theology on his experience among the poor and persecuted in El Salvador. Discusses the differences in theological thought in Europe and Latin America, the promotion of justice as essential to the Gospel message, and the intimate connection between faith, inner spirituality and working for justice. Sobrino stresses how the church of the poor truly reflects the Gospels and constitutes the true church and examines the role of the church of the poor in mediating God's grace to the world, the experience of the church in Latin America, its ramifications within the church itself as a new ecclesiology conflicts with an older, hierarchical one, the theological meaning of persecution and its significance in San Salvador, the role of evangelization, and the all-encompassing nature of a religious life for the Christian in Latin America.

540   —, with Juan Hernández Pico. *Theology of Christian Solidarity.* Phillip Berryman, trans. Maryknoll, NY: Orbis Books, 1985.

It is no accident that the Polish movement for liberation called itself "Solidarity," for within the modern Catholic vocabulary since Vatican II "solidarity" means the form of effective love that turns faith and revelation of divinity into the works of peace and justice As the authors write in their proem, "Solidarity is another name for the kind of love/ that moves feet, hands, hearts,/ material goods, assistance, and sacrifice/ toward the pain, danger, misfortune, disaster, repression or death/ of other persons or a whole people." In his essay Sobrino discusses the theological nature of this solidarity; while Hernández Pico speaks of its praxis in biblical study, work with Archbishop Romero, and in the life of service.

541   Swomley, John M. *Liberation Ethics.* New York: Macmillan, 1972.

The theory and methods of nonviolent change and revolution. The moral conversion of the individual to liberation is necessary before such change can begin. Recent history offers many examples of successful nonviolent change in Latin America. These include the nonviolent revolutions in Chile in July 1931, in Guatemala in 1944, and in El Salvador in 1944. All involved the withdrawal of consent from the dictators by the majority of the people across all classes and professions, often in the face of violent attempts at repression. They are testimony to movements that spring from the grass roots and flow from a Judeo-Christian tradition.

542   —. *The Politics of Liberation.* Elgin, IL: Brethren Press, 1984.

This book attempts to place the work of liberation theologians into a political context. It examines the meaning of political liberation, Judeo-Christian theories of government, and modern forms of political realism and idealism. It also examines the relationship of power and ideology to liberation and the biblical and secular roots of modern liberation.

543   Tamez, Elsa, ed. *Bible of the Oppressed.* Matthew J. O'Connell, trans. Maryknoll, NY: Orbis Books, 1982.

A careful reading of the biblical texts and the meanings of "oppressed" and "oppressors."

544   —, ed. *Through Her Eyes. Women's Theology from Latin America.* Maryknoll, NY: Orbis Books, 1989.

An important collection of essays by leading Latin American feminist theologians discussing such topics as gender, the Trinity, Christology, ecclesiology, spirituality, and the meaning of the kingdom of God.

545   *Theology and Liberation Series.* Maryknoll, NY: Orbis Books.

This editorial undertaking is the English translation of the works of over 100 liberation theologians, historians, and pastoral agents. It originated in the

Franciscan publishing house of Editora Vozes in
Brazil. According to Penny Lernoux (**120**, pp.
113-14), however, it soon became the special target of the
Vatican "Restoration," which forced the resignation
of the publishing house's entire editorial board soon
after Ratzinger's unsuccessful inquisition against
theologian Leonardo Boff. Despite the fact that all
the volumes in the series had received imprimaturs
from the proper church officials, Cardinal Ratzinger
took personal umbrage at the undertaking and blocked
its further publication.

Despite its troubles, the series has been appearing
steadily through Maryknoll and is already of major
importance.

Camilo Torres

546   Broderick, Walter J. *Camilo Torres: A Biography of the
Priest-Guerrillero.* Garden City, NY: Doubleday,
1975.

No collection of works on liberation theology
would be complete without some discussion of Camilo
Torres, the Colombian priest who abandoned the
traditional role of the post-Tridentine cleric to become
a guerilla fighter on behalf of the poor and
marginalized.   He was killed in 1966 in a jungle
skirmish with Colombian army.   While Catholic
conservatives had always pulled out the theory of
the just war to justify any recourse to violence on the
part of states, they cringed in horror at the thought
of church sanction of violence on behalf of the poor or
in the cause of revolution, even though popes as recent
as Paul VI continued to stress the Catholic right of
"just revolution."   In fact, this was one of the
underpinnings of the Nicaraguan revolution.   Torres,

ironically, was killed fighting for his brand of Catholic Christianity in the same year that Cardinal Spellman was in Vietnam blessing canons and ordering soldiers to kill for his.

Even more upsetting for the conservatives was the fact that a lowly priest decided to take such action upon himself, without the official sanction of the alliance of church and state that usually condones violence.

What does Torres and his career have to do with liberation theology? While not a formal theologian, Torres did write, mostly manifestos, in an attempt to rouse the people to fight against oppression. His style of fusing Christ and revolution could be seen as a form of theology in the making from the ground up, based on the realities of the people themselves.

There is no doubt that his specter is raised by every opponent of liberation theology, as if he were representative of the entire range of this movement. Whatever one's uses of Torres, there is no doubt that his life and example pose a fundamental question to all Christians – and all religiously motivated people – who seek social and political change.

This is a biography based on personal observations, documents and interviews, told in a taut, journalistic style, much in keeping with the mood of the late 60s.

547   Garcia, John Alvarez, Christian Restrepo Calle, and Virginia M. O'Grady, eds. *Camilo Torres. His Life and His Message.* Springfield, IL: Templegate Publishers, 1968.

A collection of Torres' writings, with an introduction on the social, political, economic and cultural background of Colombia. Pacifist Dorothy Day provided a lengthy preface.

548   Gerassi, John, ed. *Revolutionary Priest.* June de Cipriano Alcantara, and others, eds. New York: Random House, 1971.

The subtitle reads *The Complete Writings and Messages of Camilo Torres.* A good collection.

549   Guzman, German. *Camilo Torres.* John D. Ring, trans. New York: Sheed & Ward, 1969.

A sympathetic, and first-hand, account of the guerrilla priest by one who writes in the immediate shadow of the man, between present and past.

*

550   Torres, Sergio, and John Eagleson, eds. *Theology in the Americas.* Maryknoll, NY: Orbis Books, 1976.

A collection of essays by the leading theologians in both continents.

551   —, and Virginia Fabella, eds. *The Emergent Gospel. Theology from the Underside of History.* Maryknoll, NY: Orbis Books, 1978.

This collection of essays is divided into four sections: on Africa, Asia, Latin America, and conclusions: the final statement and communique of the Dar es Salaam conference. Contributors include Patrick Masanja, Charles Nyamiti, Kwesi A. Dickson, Manas Buthelezi, Allan Boesak, Carlos Abesamis, S.J., D. S.

Amalorpavadass, Enrique Dussel, and Gustavo
Gutiérrez.

552   Vidales, Raul. "Methodological Issues in Liberation
Theology." See 479, pp. 34-57.

A discussion of liberation theology and its roots in
theory and praxis. Summarizes its historical base
and stresses that faith can only be understood via
action. The basic features of liberation theology
include solidarity with the exploited, a joyous unity
among brothers and sisters, its operation in the midst
of conflict, and a basis in Christian faith that is
above all Christocentric.

553   Winter, Derek. *Hope in Captivity. The Prophetic Church
in Latin America.* London: Epworth, 1977.

See 176.

554   Witvliet, Theo. *A Place in the Sun. An Introduction to
Liberation Theology in the Third World.* John
Bowden, trans. Maryknoll, NY: Orbis Books, 1985.

See 242.

Cuba and the Caribbean

555   Arce Martinez, Sergio. *The Church and Socialism. Reflections from a Cuban Context.* New York: Circus, 1985.

Essays on Christians, the church and revolution, the church mission in a socialist society, evangelization, ecumenism, church renewal, theology and atheism, faith and ideology, Camilo Torres, authentic spirituality, and the creation of a new society. Arce equates Christianity with revolutionary action, and goes so far as to criticize liberation theology for being a form of intellectual enslavement, while he equates Gustavo Gutiérrez' theology as a "theology of oppression" and "dependence."

556   Aristide, Jean-Bertrand. *In the Parish of the Poor. Writings from Haiti.* Maryknoll, NY: Orbis Books, 1990.

In late 1990 Aristide, who had been working quietly – and quite dangerously – among the poor and victimized in Haiti for years, suddenly gained worldwide fame when he was elected president of Haiti, despite the immediate condemnation of the archbishop and papal nuncio and an attempted coup by ex-Duvalier loyalists.

This series of writings is a form of spiritual autobiography of a minister of the people of Haiti; it is also liberation theology being born from the lives of the people themselves.

557   Barrett, Leonard E. *The Rastafarians. The Dreadlocks of Jamaica.* London: Heinemann; Boston: Beacon Press, 1977; rev. ed., Boston: Beacon Press, 1988.

Sees the movement – characterized to many by its dreadlocks, reggae music and "ganja" smoking – as a positive religious force for liberation, with its unity along class divisions, as an answer to the longings of the dispossessed of Jamaica for a spiritual life that meets the realities of their lives. In essence Rastafarianism is a millennial, utopian, messianic sect that divinizes the late Emperor Haile Selassie of Ethiopia as the Black Messiah, the hope of the black oppressed against the oppression of white dominated culture and society. In its more affluent settings Rastafarianism even attracts the white, middle class.

558 Campbell, Horace. *Rasta and Resistance. From Marcus Garvey to Walter Rodney.* Trenton, NJ: Africa World Press, 1987.

A detailed history of the Rastafarian movement and the cultural and religious underpinnings of its push for liberation.

559 Davis, Kortright. *Emancipation Still Comin'. Explorations in Caribbean Emancipatory Theology.* Maryknoll, NY: Orbis Books, 1990.

The history of the Caribbean is one of slavery and colonialism. Its theology therefore addresses the most urgent desires of its people: for liberation. Discusses the roots of Caribbean culture and religion, its theological foundations, the problem of liberating the structures and ministers of the church itself, links to other forms of liberation theology, and liturgical forms of emancipatory expression.

560   Erskine, Noel Leo. *Decolonizing Theology. A Caribbean Perspective.* Maryknoll, NY: Orbis Books, 1981.

Topics include a discussion of the black Caribbean's search for liberation, the historical background of slavery and emancipation in the Caribbean, ties to African-American culture and religion, including black theology, the role of the churches in oppression and liberation, the systematic elements of black theology, revivalism and Rastafarianism, and concluding remarks on a theology of liberation for the Caribbean.

561   Gómez-Treto, Raúl, *The Church and Socialism in Cuba.* Maryknoll, NY: Orbis Books, 1989.

Traces the development of the relationship between the church and government since the revolution. Far from entering a new form of triumphalist alliance, the hierarchy in Cuba seems to be moving toward a social compact that will bring true justice and peace.

562   Hageman, Alice L., and Philip E. Wheaton, eds. *Religion in Cuba Today. A New Church in a New Society.* New York: Association Press, 1971.

This collection of essays include discussions of religion in Cuba, the historical background, theological reflections on the possibility of a Christian religion in a socialist state, and declarations of Cuban church bodies on politics and society. Authors include Serge Arce Martinez, Carlos German Renes, Orlando Contreras, Aldo J. Buntig, and Fidel Castro.

563   Hamid, Idris, ed. *Troubling the Waters.* San Fernando: Trinidad, 1973.

       Not seen.

564   —. *Out of the Depths.* San Fernando: Trinidad, 1973.

       Not seen.

565   Owens, Joseph. *Dread. The Rastafarians of Jamaica.* London: Heinemann's, 1976.

       Examines the religious experience, the adherents, the meaning of "Babylon" in both state and church structures of the West, the role of Haile Selassie as the messianic king, its emphasis on human responsibility and ethics, the power and sanctity of nature, the role of knowledge, i.e., experience, in faith, the role of time and history, and the place of exile on Jamaica and the meaning of Zion: the object of return. Finally, this thoughtful analysis concludes with a discussion of Rastafarian apocalyptism, and the role of persecution in the last days.

Base Christian Communities

566   Azevado, Marcello de Carvalho, S.J. *Basic Ecclesial Communities in Brazil. The Challenge of a New Way of Being Church.* John Drury, trans. Washington, DC: Georgetown University Press, 1987.

       After an introduction to the nature of "BECs," the author examines the origins and formation of base communities in Brazil, their nature as community, ecclesial, and "basic," and problems involved with their understanding. He then compares them to earlier models of community organizing and to the challenge of evangelization in Brazil.

A final section of the book looks at the ecclesiological dimensions of the BECs and the theology of the church as institution, sacrament, herald, servant and community. Excellent bibliography.

567   Barbé, Dominique. *Grace and Power. Base Communities and Nonviolence in Brazil.* Maryknoll, NY: Orbis Books, 1987.

The working theology of liberation in the Brazilian base Christian communities is essentially and fully based upon the Bible and its insights. From its profound Christian roots it then focuses the attention of the poor upon their own salvation, which must involve liberation from social, economic, as well as political oppression. A wide-ranging collection of reflections that center on the saving role of grace in bringing liberation to the poor and oppressed of Brazil.

It begins with Barbé's diary and his recognition of this misery; then discusses the theology of liberation and its impact on the church and on politics; a Trinitarian theology of redemption and liberation; and the role of grace and human power in the struggle for the poor. Barbé also poses a series of questions to the secularist and rationalist tradition of Marxism before describing the life and theology of the base Christian community, the role of the eucharistic ministry there; and the pastoral strategy of the diocese of Sao Paulo. The author concludes with a call for nonviolent social change and the psychological, sociopolitical and theological implications of this nonviolence.

568 —. *A Theology of Conflict.* Maryknoll, NY: Orbis Books, 1989.

Far from condoning violence, the liberation theology of Brazil's base Christian communities is profoundly biblical and Christian in its roots and applications: its form of revolution is nonviolent, and its method is the conscientization of the poor themselves to bring about their own liberation from the structures of oppression. Barbé, like James Douglass who wrote the introduction, Richard Schaull, Gene Sharp and others, is actively working on a theory and a theology of nonviolence as it is applied in the world. From such work will arise a new generation of Christian thought on peace that truly implements its most profound biblical intents.

569 Barreiro, Alvaro. *Basic Ecclesial Communities. The Evangelization of the Poor.* Maryknoll, NY: Orbis Books, 1982.

Combines a solid theological understanding of scripture with first-hand experience as a pastor in a poor outskirt of Rio de Janeiro. Discusses Vatican II and the call to evangelize the poor, the BECs or base ecclesial communities, the poor in the Old Testament and in Jesus' teaching; the liberating education of conscientization; the role of prophetic denunciation, the evangelical role of the BECs in fulfilling Christ's mission and teaching; and the BECs role in turning passive hearers of the Gospels to their active preachers.

570   Bavarel, Michel. *New Communities, New Ministries. The Church Resurgent in Africa, Asia, and Latin America.* Maryknoll, NY: Orbis Books, 1983.

See **206**.

571   Boff, Leonardo. *Ecclesiogenesis. The Base Communities Reinvent the Church.* Robert R. Barr, trans. Maryknoll, NY: Orbis Books, 1986.

This is a popular introduction to the work of the base Christian communities that first introduces the communities, discusses whether they are the church itself or an ecclesial aspect of the church, and then proceeds to the praxis of confronting the realities of oppression and marginalization with the works of liberation. Questions addressed are not only those of society but of ecclesiastical structures themselves, including that of women's role as both laity and clergy.

572   Bruneau, Thomas C. *The Church in Brazil: The Politics of Religion.* Austin: University of Texas Press, 1982.

Examines the 60,000 base Christian communities throughout Brazil. These are the outcome of the church's new approach to evangelization: the work through the people. The communities were begun between 1950 and 1964 and consolidated between 1964 and 1974, despite state repression. While the BECs have not been as successful as hoped in true evangelization, they have presented a real challenge to Brazilian authoritarianism.

573   Cook, Guillermo. *The Expectation of the Poor. Latin American Base Ecclesial Communities in Protestant Perspective.* Maryknoll, NY: Orbis Books, 1985.

The base communities studied are in Brazil.

574   Fragoso, Dom Antonio B. *Face of a Church. A Nascent Church of the People in Crateús, Brazil.* Robert R. Barr, trans. Maryknoll, NY: Orbis Books, 1987.

Crateús is in northeastern Brazil, Fragoso its bishop. This book is a compilation of the thoughts and actions of members of the base ecclesial communities there. It is a day-to-day account of building a church among the poor.

575   Freire, Paolo. *Cultural Action for Freedom.* Cambridge, MA: Harvard Educational Research, 1970.

Freire is universally acknowledged as the educator whose theories and ideals gave rise to the term "conscientization" and the methods of the base Christian communities. This collection presents essays on adult literacy programs as a liberating activity, on conscientization, and on cultural revolution.

576   —. *Education for Critical Consciousness. Education As the Practice of Freedom.* New York: Seabury Press, 1973.

Topics include an examination of a society in transition, closed societies and democratic inexperience, education versus "massification," and education and conscientization.

577   —. *Education, the Practice of Freedom.* London: Writers and Readers Publishing Cooperative, 1976.

Another edition of **575**.

578   —. *Pedagogy of the Oppressed.* Myra Bergman Ramos, trans. New York: Seabury Press, 1970; reprinted New York: Continuum, 1981.

On the process of conscientization. This is the fundamental book that has inspired much of the methods of Latin American liberation theology and the basic Christian communities.

579   —. *The Politics of Education.* Donaldo Macedo, trans. South Hadley, MA: Bergin & Garvey, 1985.

A collection of his essays. Topics include the act of reading and study, adult literacy, peasants and their texts, cultural action for agrarian reform, adult literacy programs as a liberation action, conscientization, political literacy, humanistic education, the church and liberation theology, black theology, and critical pedagogy.

580   —, and Antonio Faundez. *Learning to Question. The Pedagogy of Liberation.* Tony Coates, trans. New York: Crossroad/Continuum, 1989.

Not seen.

581   —, and Ira Shor. *A Pedagogy for Liberation. Dialogues on Transforming Education.* South Hadley, MA: Bergin & Garvey, 1987.

On general issues of liberating education, and then specifically on the issue of whether First-World students need liberating. Social transformation is the end of all liberating education.

582   Gáldamez, Pablo. *Faith of A People. The Life of a Base Christian Community in El Salvador.* Maryknoll, NY: Orbis Books, 1987.

Follows the progress of a base community in El Salvador from concern with ecclesial and sacramental aspects of the religious life, to social and economic, and finally to the revolutionary concerns of the political aspects of the Christian message. Focuses on the individuals in the community themselves, who make this process alive.

583   Juventud Obrero Catolica, eds. *Evangelization and the Working Class. Reflections.* Lima: Y.C.W., Peru, 1975.

Evangelization on behalf of the liberation of the working class, through a revolution brought about by a new gospel and action. Topics include the option for the working class, the project of liberation, the ideological struggle, creating a liberating community, and the formation of a liberating spirituality.

584   Libânio, B. *Spiritual Discernment and Politics. Guidelines for Religious Communities.* Theodore Mowen, trans. Maryknoll, NY: Orbis Books, 1982.

On the role of the ascetics of spiritual discernment: of meditation and prayer, of spirituality in the task of enpowerment, witness, prophesy and seeking the truth and then acting in the world of power and politics. Part 1 discusses the prerequisites for discernment, including the process of purification, generosity and prayer. Part 2 then focuses on the act of discernment, and Part 3 the criteria. Concluding sections deal with the role of faith in unravelling the complexities of political situations.

585   López Vigil, Maria. *Don Lito of El Salvador.* Maryknoll, NY: Orbis Books, 1990.

Don Lito is a lay catechist in a base Christian Community. Journalist López illuminates the daily struggle of the the base communities through a series of interviews. This is theology by and for the poor.

586   Marins, Jose, and team. *Basic Ecclesial Communities. Church from the Roots.* Quezon City, Philippines: Claretian Publications, n.d.

Not seen.

587   Mesters, Carlos. *Defenseless Flower. A New Reading of the Bible.* Maryknoll, NY: Orbis Books, 1990.

The reading is by members of the base communities in Brazil who gain new understanding of the biblical text through the insights of their own experience of poverty and marginalization; and for whom the Bible takes on new importance as a guide to new lives.

588   Perez-Esclarin, Antonio. *Jesus of Gramoven.* Dinah Livingstone, trans. Maryknoll, NY: Orbis Books, 1979.

Gramoven is an impoverished section of Caracas, Venezuela. Here the people of Gramoven follow Jesus during Holy Week in their own Stations of the Cross, a profound meditation on the meaning of Jesus' death and resurrection set amid the suffering of their own life. Implicit in these stations are a critique of the other-worldly spirituality of the ruling class, which would make oppression and poverty purifying penances as preparation for paradise while greed holds sway on earth. A good example of the methodology and the results of base Christian communities making theology from the ground up.

589   Regan, David. *Church for Liberation. A Pastoral Portrait of the Church in Brazil.* Dublin: Dominican Publications, 1987.

Brazil makes up half of South America in both size and population. The Catholic church of Brazil is also the largest in the world. Events and experiments and new forms in Brazil are therefore of great significance for the church and the world as a whole. This book examines the Brazilian church from the viewpoint of its conversion to liberation, its base ecclesial communities, its use of scripture, its option for the poor, its bishops' conference, its pastoral planning, and the spiritual and political dimensions of its message of liberation.

590   Rossa, Alberto, CMF. *Basic Ecclesial Communities. The Stand of Third-Word Bishops: Brazil - Philippines - Mexico.* Quezon City, Philippines: Claretian Publications, n.d..

Not seen.

591   Pastoral Team of Bambamarca. *Vamos Caminando. A Peruvian Catechism.* Maryknoll, NY: Orbis Books, 1985.

      A catechism born out of the needs and experience of villagers of the Peruvian Andes. Liberation theology in the act of being born.

592   Schipani, Daniel S. *Conscientization and Creativity. Paulo Freire and Christian Education.* Lanham, MD: University Press of America, 1984.

      A fresh interpretation of Freire's work that emphasizes his epistemological and theological foundations.

593   Torres, Sergio, and John Eagleson, eds. *The Challenge of Basic Christian Communities.* Maryknoll, NY: Orbis Books, 1981.

      Articles by Torres, Dussel, Gutiérrez, Boff, Sobrino, d'Escoto, and others.

Individual Witness

Dom Helder Camara and Brazil

594   Camara, Helder. *Church and Colonialism. The Betrayal of the Third World.* William McSweeney, trans. London: Sheed & Ward; Denville, NJ: Dimension Books, 1969.

      Camara's discourses on a Christian view of development, the problems of the development model, and proposals for development that directly benefits the people, a middle way between communism and capitalism, the importance of nonviolent direct action, the rise of a new humanism, education for change, and the role of the church in Latin American development.

595   —. *The Conversions of a Bishop: An Interview with José de Broucker.* Hilary Davies, trans. London and Cleveland, OH: Collins, 1979.

A biography of the bishop through a series of interviews in 1975 and 1976. Camara is quite outspoken here about many of the personalities in his life. He offers his thoughts on the struggle of a united people toward liberation, not by guerrilla war or violent revolution but through nonviolence, or "the violence of pacifists," as he prefers to call it. He sharply distinguishes this from "passivism."

596   —. *The Desert Is Fertile.* Dinah Livingstone, trans. Maryknoll, NY: Orbis Books, 1982.

Active nonviolence is a force as strong as nuclear energy. It is the power of love and justice. Camara discusses his half-failure, his six-year attempt to make his Action for Justice and Peace succeed as an organized pressure group. He eventually realized, however, that institutions as such are incapable of bringing about change.

Camara condemns the U.S., U.S.S.R., and E.E.C. for their exploitation and their continued arms race. He rests his hopes on the "Abrahamic minorities" who work in the darkness against all hope to create change.

597   —. *Hoping Against All Hope.* Matthew J. O'Connell, trans. Maryknoll, NY: Orbis Books, 1984.

Camara goes beyond a disgust with poverty, the arms race, waste, materialism, and overspecialization to see hope that this disgust among people will be turned to positive energy to *change*. All these troubles in the world are "signs of God."

This is a theological approach and underpinning to his activist life. It is based heavily on Vatican II, Medellin, and Teilhard de Chardin's teleological approach. Abraham's "hope against all hope" is a model for groups practicing "active nonviolence." These are the "Abrahamic minorities."

598   —. *Into Your Hands, Lord.* Robert R. Barr, trans. Oak Park, IL: Meyer Stone, 1987.

A collection of poems and interpretations of the Gospels.

599   —. *Questions for Living.* José de Broucker, ed. Maryknoll, NY: Orbis Books, 1987.

The journal of a trip to France set as a series of answers to questioners. Addresses such issues as capitalism and communism, materialism, the spirit, prayer and hope. An ad hoc spirituality of liberation.

600   —. *Race Against Time.* Della Couling, trans. London: Sheed & Ward, 1971.

Camara's profound Christianity is the root of his concern for economic and social justice in Brazil. Examines the injustice and oppression of Brazilian society, discusses the need for change, the role of the institutional church, of capitalism and neocolonialism, of the U.S.

Camara calls for a revolution, among the universities and intellectuals especially, and he declares his hopes despite the dehumanizing trends in science and technology. Teilhard de Chardin is an inspiration.

601   —. *Revolution Through Peace.* Ruth Nanada Anshen, ed.; Amparo McLean, trans. New York: Harper & Row, 1971.

The now retired archbishop of Recifé, Brazil, Camara lays out the basic tenets of his revolution: neither capitalism nor communism will work in the Third World to cure the violence of poverty or exploitation, for which the U.S. and the U.S.S.R. are largely responsible both through their own economic exploitation and through the vast amounts they spend on arms while millions starve. Both nations, in fact, put the world in danger of extermination, while the U.S.'s emphasis on communism as the supreme evil of the world ignores the real evils suffered by the poor every day.

What, then, are the solutions to the Third World's problems? Development as practiced by the North American and European technocrats certainly is not. This is change imposed from above for the benefit of oligarchs. Instead, Camara urges a gradual process, first of conscientization among the people, and then once the people have taken their lives into their own hands, a movement for true peace, which is based on justice, truth, charity, and dialog. While violent revolutionaries have attempted to redress the violence of poverty and repression by armed struggle,

Camara refuses to condemn their sacrifices, but he insists that "only love can build. Hate and violence only destroy."

602   —. *Spiral of Violence*. London: Sheed & Ward, 1969.

A description and analysis of violence, repression and counterviolence. Is there a solution? Camara describes his Action for Peace and Justice, its objectives, problems, modes of action, audience, and appeal.

603   —. *A Thousand Reasons for Living*. José de Broucker, ed.; Alan Neame, trans. Philadelphia: Fortress Press, 1981.

Meditations and poems that illustrate Camara's great love of all of creation and underlies his devotion to the struggle for human justice.

604   —. *Through the Gospel with Dom Helder Camara*. Maryknoll, NY: Orbis Books, 1986.

Journalists aim biblical texts rather than questions at the archbishop, whose answers, really a series of meditations, make up the subject of this book.

605   De Broucker, José. *Dom Helder Camara. The Violence of a Peacemaker*. Herma Briffault, trans. Maryknoll, NY: Orbis Books, 1970.

Traces Camara's personality and his daily routine, reviews the poverty and injustice of northeastern Brazil, the church's role in the struggle for justice, and the state's response in repression. Then goes on to analyze Camara's own nonviolence and his

emerging reputation as the Voice of the Third World.
Concludes with a portrait of Camara's life as a
bishop in the Catholic church in Latin America.

606   Hall, Mary. *The Impossible Dream. The Spirituality of
       Dom Helder Camara.* Maryknoll, NY: Orbis Books,
       1980.

       A spiritual biography based on interviews and
       the author's observation of his daily life. Discusses
       his work, the difficulties, and constant reminders of
       the brutal government repression.

607   Hope and Young. *Struggle.* See **190**, pp. 109-44.

       Reviews Camara's life and early rise through the
       hierarchy in alliance with Brazil's political and
       economic establishment, his subsequent conversion fol-
       lowing Vatican II, and his embrace of the cause, and
       life, of the poor and the oppressed. Camara was
       subsequently removed from power and influence,
       banned from appearing in the media, and subjected to
       constant denunciation, harassment, and violent attack
       on his staff and friends.
       Camara rejects both capitalist development and
       communism, both of which empower the elite even
       further and ignore the real needs of individual
       development and liberation. Change must begin with
       the people themselves, through conscientization and
       basic Christian communities. Its impact on society
       must be nonviolent, aimed at converting both the op-
       pressed and oppressor.
       Yet "nonviolence" is too weak a word. Camara
       refuses to condemn the sacrifices of a Che Guevera or
       a Camilo Torres, but he argues that such violence,
       while altruistic, only pits the oppressed against the

oppressed. Still, one cannot condemn the violence of terrorism without first condemning the violence of injustice.

608   Moosbrugger, Bernard. *A Voice of the Third World. Dom Helder Camara.* New York: Paulist Press, 1972.

Often in the bishop's own words, this discusses his road to the bishopric, the poverty, hunger, ignorance and unemployment, the "silent fatalism" of the North. Reviews Camara's appeals for justice and peace in Latin America, the U.S., and Europe, and his hope that international big business can still be made responsible. He retains faith that human institutions – religious, political, economic – can solve problems. His greatest hope rests on youth.

*

609   Casaldáliga, Pedro. *Fire and Ashes to the Wind. Spiritual Anthology.* Quezon City, Philippines: Claretian Publications, 1988.

This is an anthology of poems by the Brazilian bishop that combines themes of social activism and prophesy, traditional Christian devotion and a mystic transcendence into a unity that is truly one of liberation.

610   —. *I Believe in Justice and Hope.* Notre Dame, IN: Fides/Claretian, 1978.

A spiritual manifesto as a kind of autobiography from a life of relative privilege in Spain to the jungle of Brazil, his bishopric, the continuous work on behalf of the poor farmers of the jungle against the *latifundios*, large development companies and government bureaucracies, the military, and against conservatives in his own church. Casaldáliga's faith is held up both by the people around him and by his wide readings of contemporary authors and of scripture. He remains to the heart and root a cleric, and his culture is that of the clergy, for which he asks understanding.

611   —. *In Pursuit of the Kingdom. Writings 1968-1988*
           Maryknoll, NY: Orbis Books, 1990.

A collection of writings on the option for the poor, the church's essential role in defending the rights of native peoples, the connection between inner spirituality and an activist life in the world. Contains the bishop's frank response to the pope on his criticisms of Casaládiga's pastoral methods and his embrace of liberation theology.

612   —. *Mystic of Liberation. A Portrait of Pedro Casaldáliga.*
           Téofilo Cabestrero, ed. Donald D. Walsh, trans.
           Maryknoll, NY: Orbis Books, 1981.

A series of dialogs with Casaldáliga on the bishop's work among the poor and Indians of the Araguaia region of Brazil, the attempts of the military to silence or destroy his work and that of his pastoral team, the concept of a church emerging from the people and the role of conscientization and the formation of community.

Adolfo Perez Esquivel and the Mothers of the Plaza de Mayo

613   "Adolfo Perez Esquivel," *Current Biography Yearbook*. New York: H.H. Wilson, 1981, pp. 321-24.

A good introduction to his life, written after he won the Nobel Peace Prize for 1980, for which he had been nominated by Irish Peace People Mairead Corrigan and Betty Williams. A good supplement to Esquivel's own writing.

614   Agosin, Marjorie. *The Mothers of the Plaza de Mayo*. Trenton, NJ: Red Sea Press, 1990.

Traces the continuing efforts of the Mothers to bring justice out of the Dirty War through the life of one of these women.

615   Esquivel, Adolfo Perez. *Christ in a Poncho*. Charles Antoine ed.; Robert R. Barr, trans. Maryknoll, NY: Orbis Books, 1983, pp. 117-34.

A collection of essays on various aspects of Esquivel's life and work for nonviolent change in Latin America.   Traces his life, organizing efforts, and the events of Argentine history in the 1970s that led to his arrest, imprisonment, and torture under the generals.   Esquivel notes that his major influences have included John the Baptist, Gandhi, Thomas Merton, Francis of Assisi, Ernesto Cardenal, Helder Camara, Lanza del Vasto, the Medellin Conference's declarations on liberation theology, among others. While he is committed to nonviolent change, he rejects "do-gooder" social work aimed at patching the current system and seeks to build a new community from the grass roots up, through such forms as the base Christian communities.

"Nonviolence" is a bad word in Latin America, since for so many it connotes passivity; yet no better word has yet been found. While liberation theology has not yet evolved a complete critique of violence, and liberation reached through armed struggle is not to be condemned, such victory is not efficacious: one cannot cure evil by using it. Instead, one merely replaces one oppressor with another. Nonviolence, instead, must be built on a broad and popular base, it must be the result of people acting in trust and solidarity, whose own nonviolence renders the violence of the oppressor useless. Not even Nicaragua's revolution succeeded through violence, but by the long nonviolent campaign that pushed the Sandinistas into power.

Esquivel rejects both communism and capitalism, and he sees the arms race as linked essentially to the materialism of both the U.S. and U.S.S.R. Therefore the work of the peacemaker must also be to awaken the consciences of those who make, profit from, or remain comfortable with, an arms race that starves the rest of the world.

The collection then goes on to examine several examples of active nonviolence at work in Latin America: the victory of nonviolent strikers and the efforts of Bishop Leonidas Proaño in Peru; the Latin American Charter of nonviolence; and the Mothers of the Plaza de Mayo.

The Mothers are the sisters, daughters, cousins, wives, and mothers of the up to 30,000 men, women, and children who "disappeared" during the "dirty war" waged by Argentina's generals in the years between their coup in 1976 and the restoration of democracy in 1983. They first began in isolation, seeking information about their relatives, but they soon organized to hold weekly protest vigils in Buenos Aires' main square, not only demanding to know what the military had done to the disappeared but demanding justice for all of Argentina's poor and oppressed.

Their original inspiration was nourished by Esquivel's Peace and Justice office. They reject all forms of violence in favor of a gospel form of peacemaking. The Mothers have been willing to suffer accusations of being subversives and communists; they have even been willing to face martyrdom for their witness to the truth that the Argentine generals' defense of "Western Christian Civilization" was a sham. They continue to declare that only through the broad-based, nonviolent methods of the people – boycotts, strikes, noncooperation, civil disobedience, hunger strikes, etc. – can the field be taken from the enemy and his own tools of elitism and violence overthrown.

616   Simpson, John, and Jana Bennett. *The Disappeared and the Mothers of the Plaza: The Story of the 11,000 Argentinians Who Vanished.* New York: St. Martin's, 1985.

This book gives ample credit and fine documentation to the Mothers. It stresses the internal dynamic and initiative of the Mothers themselves. The story of the disappeared, which the authors call the closest thing to Nazi Germany after 1933, is based on hundreds of interviews. The Mothers organized under constant threat, attack, even murder and kidnapping. Their demonstrations were harassed and broken up violently throughout 1978. By 1979 they had almost stopped completely. Finally they decided they had nothing to lose. Their act of courage broke the entire well-laid plan of the generals to commit mass murder via secret means. By 1980 they had turned the tide and had once again begun demonstrating in public.

The authors note the almost total silence of the Argentine hierarchy to the atrocity, except in cases where clergy were the targets. Surprisingly, the role of Esquivel in this drama is ignored almost completely, except for the authors to remark that he also was imprisoned and that he may have invented his story of torture (pp. 281-82).

Bishop Leonidas Proaño

617   Esquivel. *Christ in a Poncho.* See **615**, pp. 71-91.

Recounts the bishop's alliance with the Indians of Toctezinin in Chimborazo province of Ecuador. Together they fight against the corruption of government officials in league with wealthy landowners who seek to end land reform and take the small farmers' lands from them. The small farmers and the diocese's pastoral teams aiding them have faced smear campaigns, accusations of being communist subversives, threats and physical violence from the landlords' thugs, police, and army; but they have rejected all forms of violence as wrong and counter-productive. In a newspaper interview Proaño has called on the inspiration of Bartolomé de Las Casas (See **65** to **81**), the Medellin Conference, and Helder Camara and has declared, "there are only two invincible forces in the twentieth century – the atom bomb, and nonviolence."

Central America

618   Berrigan. Daniel. *Steadfastness of the Saints. A Journal of Peace and War in Central and North America.* Maryknoll, NY: Orbis Books, 1985.

An account of Berrigan's journey from the U.S. via the Plowshares trials and the madness of North American fixation on mass destruction to Central America. In El Salvador he encounters on-going, internal church politics, the refugee camps, the death squads, the Mothers of the Disappeared (yes, even here), theologians and pastors like Jon Sobrino and Medardos Gómez, and all over the base Christian communities, the reservoirs of martyrdom and of hope. A tour through the desolate ruins of the State University, destroyed by the military in a crackdown on student protestors, reveals the spirit of Oscar Romero still alive.

Nicaragua is like day to El Salvador's night. Here Witness for Peace members from North America are welcomed in a country threatened by their own government. Yet here are also signs that the rigors of revolution and of defense are taking their toll: the government's hesitation to grant conscientious objector status, the offensive prevarications of government spokesmen like Ernesto Cardenal, an old friend in whom Berrigan does not hide his disappointment. Yet here too is a thriving Christianity among base Christian communities and the very real threat of the *contras.* Berrigan is also troubled by the conflict between the Nicaraguan state and church and by the dilemma of the priests within the government.

This journal also ranges over his rejection of violence, even that called just by revolution, on this previous exile to Latin America in 1965, on Thomas

Merton, and on the strength and joy his companionship in the Jesuits gives him.

619   Berryman, Phillip. *Inside Central America. The Essential Facts Past and Present on El Salvador, Nicaragua, Honduras, Guatemala, and Costa Rica.* New York: Pantheon, 1986.

A short paperback highlighting the main issues involved in Central America today and providing information on the origins of the conflicts there, the U.S. attempt to confront revolution, U.S. policy and the terms of debate, the actual results of U.S. policy in the region, and the regionalization of the conflict. Also examines the outlook for accommodation and negotiation in the context of U.S. ignorance of the situation there and the wide gap and stalemate between North Americans working for human rights and those obsessed with U.S. national security considerations.

620   —. *The Religious Roots of Rebellion. Christians in Central American Revolutions.* Maryknoll, NY: Orbis Books, 1984.

This is a huge, and very important, work chronicling Christians' activities, violent and nonviolent throughout the region. Essential introduction.

621   Bonpane, Blase. *Guerrillas of Peace. Liberation Theology and the Central American Revolution.* Boston: South End Press, 1985.

This is a personal account, based largely on his diaries, of the radically changing church in Central America from its Constantinian alliance with power to a prophetic force for social justice and change. It broadly surveys the origins of liberation theology, characterizing it as a people's popular movement that is revolutionary. It then traces Bonpane's decision in 1967 to go underground as a priest for the revolution, his eventual dismissal from the Maryknoll order for his commitment, his reflections "within the belly of the beast" in the U.S. The author concludes by dismissing what he considers the vain exercises of traditional theology in favor of a life of committed action.

While Bonpane's motives and actions may be commendable for their revolutionary fervor, this is a book that extolls the personal, the romantic, and the "active" life at the expense of the real theology for the poor being carried out by liberation theologians.

622 Esquivel, Julia. *Threatened with Resurrection.* Elgin, IL: Brethren Press, 1982.

The subtitle reads. *Prayers and Poems from an Exiled Guatemalan.*

623 Kita, Bernice, *What Prize Awaits Us. Letters from Guatemala.* Maryknoll, NY: Orbis Books, 1988.

This is a portrait of the Guatemalan people told through the letters of this Maryknoll missionary, who lived in an Indian village there from 1977 to 1983, during the period of intense persecution of the church and its local communities among the campesinos. One letter of December 1980 sums up the role of various North Americans in the persecution:

"I recently read an article in which an important American business executive said something about liberation theology that sent a chill through me. He said that it was really a Communist tool to lead the people of the Catholic Church in Latin America away from our 'traditional values based on the free enterprise system,' and that the Church needs to be guided back unto the right road."

624   MacEoin, Gary, *Central America*'s *Options. Death or Life.* Kansas City, MO: Sheed & Ward, 1988.

Discusses the historical background of oppression in Central America from colonialism to the present, the civil wars now raging, the role of the U.S. as both armer and ultimate beneficiary of the ruling oligarchies, the role of the Santa Fe Document ridiculing emerging liberation theology and equating it with Marxism, the changing church and the gradual progress of a theology and social ethic of peace and community in the region.

625   McLean, George F., Raul Molina, and Timothy Ready, eds. *Culture, Human Rights and Peace in Central America.* Lanham, MD: University Press of America, 1989.

A collection of essays that includes discussions of the politics, culture, economy, and religious movements of the region. Mario A. Rojas presents "Three Central American Writers of Liberation;" while Eulalio Baltazar writes on "Liberation Philosophy and Theology and Peace in Latin America;" and Brian Johnstone on "Human Rights, Justice and Theology."

626   Richard, Pablo. *The Church Born by the Force of God in Central America.* New York: Circus, 1985.

This is an examination of the Church of the Poor, or the Popular Church then emerging in Central

America. Richard contrasts this model of the church from that of Christendom, one born out of alliances with the powers that be.

Richard focuses on the base ecclesial communities and gives background to the historical roots, the theological foundations, and the historical point achieved in Central America. A brief bibliography, mostly in Spanish.

El Salvador

627   *El Salvador: Background to the Crisis.* Cambridge, MA: Central America Information Office, 1982.

A good, general introduction. Covers the history, the military, the Indians, land and its poverty, urbanization and industrialization, women, the international economy, the Catholic church, human rights, the death squads, agrarian reform, U.S. military and economic aid. The book also provides a chronology, glossaries, and bibliography.

628   Gettleman, Marvin E., Patrick Lacefield, Louis Manache, David Marmelstein, and Ronald Radosh, eds. *El Salvador. Central America in the New Cold War.* New York: Grove Press, 1982.

A collection of essays that provides an excellent introduction to the contemporary political, economic, social, and religious situation in the region.

629   Montgomery, Tommie Sue. *Revolution in El Salvador.* Boulder, CO: Westview, 1982.

An excellent introduction to the economic, social, political, and religious roots of rebellion, and to the progress of that process. The book will demonstrate that the problems of El Salvador and of Central America are native-grown and not the product of East-West superpower conflicts.

630   Sobrino, Jon, Ignacio Ellacuría, and others. *Companions of Jesus. The Jesuit Martyrs of El Salvador.* Maryknoll, NY: Orbis Books, 1990.

Sobrino was a member of the Jesuit community of San Salvador that Salvadoran soldiers massacred, along with their housekeeper and her daughter, in November 1989. Sobrino escaped only because he was out of the country. Among those martyred were noted liberation theologian Ignacio Ellacuría (see **462**), who was also rector of the University of El Salvador. Their crime was to attempt to minister to the needs of the poor and dispossessed in the barrios of El Salvador, to tell them that God had not abandoned them, and to preach to them a gospel of liberation that confirms their dignity as human beings. For this they were branded as communist agitators by the oligarchy and slain at their order.

Sobrino's essay places the martyrs in their context of liberating the oppressed of Latin America, in the context of the martyrdoms of Oscar Romero and the four American churchwomen, and within the context of Christian martyrdom through the ages. The book also includes essays by all six of the slain priests. These writings call on Catholics to examine their role as educated, affluent Christians in a world of growing deprivation.

Oscar Romero

631   Brockman, James R. *The Church Is All of You. Thoughts of Archbishop Oscar Romero.* Minneapolis, MN: Winston Press, 1984.

A collection of short sayings from 1977 to 1980.

632   —. *Romero. A Life.* Maryknoll, NY: Orbis Books, 1990.

This is an expanded and revised version of Brockman's 1983 work. See 633.

633   —. *The Word Remains. A Life of Oscar Romero.* Maryknoll, NY: Orbis Books, 1983.

Oscar Romero was the archbishop of San Salvador in El Salvador. On March 23, 1980 he called on the army of El Salvador to lay down their arms, to stop the brutal repression of their fellow citizens, and to embrace the peace and justice of their religion. The next day he was slain while saying mass by a gunman set on him by the ruling oligarchy. Oscar Romero's life symbolizes the progress of the church in Latin America today.

Raised in the conventional spirituality of the early twentieth century, with its emphasis on internal piety and obedience to authority in alliance with the secular state, Romero rose quickly through his church's hierarchy and became a staunch defender of orthodoxy and political order as the rebellion in El Salvador spread. Soon after his election as archbishop of San Salvador, however, he began to turn away from the government's harsh repression of dissent, its corruption, constant attacks on campesinos and those who would help them, its death squads, tortures, disappearances.

As he saw friends assassinated and unarmed farmers slaughtered, he quickly turned against his former friends in the oligarchy, condemning the violence of repression as well as that of rebellion. He began to forge a new image of the church as the sacrament of salvation that must save both the body and the soul, and embracing the new liberation theology. In the course of this journey Romero gained the support of Pope John Paul II, of Catholic hierarchy and laity around the world, and a nomination for the Nobel Peace Prize for his call for nonviolent revolution against the forces of tyranny.

This is the best account of this martyr to Catholic peacemaking. Brockman bases his account on Romero's own papers, numerous interviews with witnesses to the events described, newspaper accounts, and church documents. He also gives a great deal of attention to Salvadoran church politics, which are as important today to the progress of liberation as the doctrines and actions of the clergy and laity actively making peace in the region.

634   — . *The Violence of Love. The Pastoral Wisdom of Archbishop Oscar Romero*. San Francisco, CA: Harper & Row, 1988.

Sermons, homilies, and writings from March 1977 to March 1980.

635 Erdozaín, Placido. *Archbishop Romero. Martyr of Salvador.* John McFadden and Ruth Warner, trans. Maryknoll, NY: Orbis Books, 1985.

A narrative of events between February 1977 and Romero's assassination in March 1980.

636 Keogh, Dermot. *Romero. El Salvador's Martyr.* Dublin: Dominican Publications, 1981.

Not seen.

637 Lacefield, Patrick. "Oscar Romero: Archbishop of the Poor." See **628**, pp. 198-203.

An interview with the archbishop first published in *Fellowship* in November 1979.

638 Romero, Oscar. *The Church, Political Organization and Violence. The Third Pastoral Letter.* London: CIIR, CAFOD, and Trocaire, 1980.

The text of the letter with introduction.

639 —. *Romero, Martyr for Liberation. The Last Two Homilies of Archbishop Romero of San Salvador.* London: CIIR, 1982.

The texts of his last two homilies with an essay by Sobrino on Romero's martyrdom.

640 —. *Voice of the Voiceless. The Four Pastoral Letters and Other Statements.* I. Martín-Baró and R. Cardenal, eds.; Michael J. Walsh, trans. Maryknoll, NY: Orbis Books, 1985.

Includes his pastoral message to the National Council of Churches, addresses at Georgetown University and at Louvain, and his letter to President Carter on the injustice of conditions in El Salvador. Demonstrates clearly the conversion of this high prelate to the struggle of the poor for their own liberation.

641   Sobrino, Jon, S.J. *Archbishop Romero. Memories and Reflections*. Maryknoll, NY: Orbis Books, 1990.

Since Archbishop Romero was killed more than 50,000 have also been assassinated, most by the government; 5,000 have disappeared, and 15,000 have been killed and wounded in battle. This, as the U.S. and Salvadoran governments boast a return to democracy and peace. More than a half-million have fled the country as kidnapings and murders on both sides, but mostly the government's, continue. Almost 50% of the government budget is for war, wages have not risen since 1980, while prices have risen constantly. Unemployment is 50%. Yet aid from the U.S. totals more than $1 million a day.

This book is both a personal recollection of his friendship with the martyred archbishop and a reflection upon the significance Romero's death has for the individual Christian, and on the influence the man himself has had on the religious and political life of Latin America.

The Woman Martyrs of El Salvador

642   Brett, Donna Whitson, and Edward T. Brett.
       *Murdered in Central America. The Stories of Eleven
       U.S. Missionaries.* Maryknoll, NY: Orbis Books,
       1988.

       The lives and deaths of the martyrs; their repre-
       sentations in art, as in the rotunda of Santo Stefano in
       Rome, most often shocks North Americans into
       discomfort and disbelief that anyone would want to
       dwell on stories of victims. Yet, as comfortable bene-
       ficiaries of the victimization of the less powerful and
       secure, we fail to understand that the tradition of the
       martyrs is not a glorification of suffering and death
       but of the commitments to life and truth that these
       martyrs demonstrate. It is the testimony to a theol-
       ogy that grows from reality: death as well as life,
       defeat as well as victory, the fate of the poor over
       and above that of the wealthy.
          This is a modern martyrology that includes
       Michael Cypher and James Carney in Honduras;
       William Woods, Stanley Rother, John David Troyer,
       James Miller and Frank Xavier Holdenried in
       Guatemala; Dorothy Kazel and Jean Donovan; Ita
       Ford and Maura Clarke in El Salvador. Based on new
       reports, interviews, letters, diaries and other sources.

643   Carrigan, Ana. *Salvador Witness.* New York: Simon &
       Schuster, 1984; Ballantine/Epiphany, 1986.

       A biography of Jean Donovan, one of the
       American Catholic missionary workers raped and
       murdered by the Salvadoran military on the outskirts
       of San Salvador in December 1980. The other three
       were Ita Ford and Maura Clarke, Maryknoll mission-

ary sisters; and Dorothy Kazel, an Ursuline missionary. The biography traces Donovan's conversion from the daughter of North American affluence, to business executive, lay missionary, and martyr for peace and social justice in Central America during the last days of Archbishop Oscar Romero. Called subversives by the government in El Salvador for their protest against repression and genocide and for their aid to the poor and dispossessed, the missionaries were brutally slain precisely because of their Christian witness and work. Their murders were largely ignored by the Reagan administration in the United States until public outrage, the pressure of the Catholic church, the victims' families, and the courageous witness of former U.S. ambassador to El Salvador, Robert White, forced an investigation.

This account is told in a crisp, journalistic style. It is based on extensive interviews with friends, family and acquaintances from all phases of Donovan's life, as well frequent quotations from Donovan's diary and letters.

644   Chapon, Dorothy, *Alleluia Woman. Sister Dorothy Kazel, OSU.* Cleveland, OH: Chapel Publications, 1987.

Not seen.

645   Dear, John, S.J. *Jean Donovan. The Call to Discipleship.* Erie, PA: Pax Christi, 1986.

Dear moves from a brief introduction on El Salvador (5 million citizens, 500,000 refugees within the country, 600,000 abroad, 60,000 killed since 1979, $1.5 million a day spent by the U.S. on military equipment used against the people by their own government), to the monuments to Oscar Romero and to the four American women martyrs on a road outside the capital where they were raped, murdered and hastily buried by the army.

Jean Donovan's story is one of conversion, retracing the choice of the rich young man and deciding to give up all her riches and connections in the U.S. for the path of Christ and martyrdom. This little booklet traces her life with drawings and photographs, first-hand accounts of family and friends both in the U.S. and in El Salvador as a Maryknoll lay missionary. There her life became closely tied to the mission and fate of Archbishop Oscar Romero and all the church workers dedicated to bringing the Gospel to the poor and oppressed. Despite the dangers, and the increasing death threats for her work with poor refugees, or simply for burying the bodies of the dead and mutilated left by the army, Donovan continued to stress her sense of mission and to refuse friends' offers and advice to leave the country.

Jean Donovan and her coworkers – Ita Ford, Maura Clarke, and Dorothy Kazel – are martyrs of our time who accepted God's call. She and her companions have followed Jesus' call to follow him; and their life and death invites others to follow in their steps. Her inner tranquility and outer commitment is the true meaning of peace.

646   Jacobsen, Patricia. "God Came to El Salvador." In Martin Lange and Reinhold Iblacker, eds. *Witnesses of Hope.* William E. Jerman, trans. Maryknoll, NY: Orbis Books, 1981, pp. 141-53.

Sparse, impressionistic, reflective, prayer-like biographies of the slain women missionaries that read like eulogies and that wrench the emotions in the same way.

647   Noone, Judith M., M.M. *The Same Fate As the Poor.* Maryknoll, NY: Maryknoll Sisters Publications, 1985.

This account begins with the grim details of the four church-women's kidnap, rape, and murder by El Salvador's army. It then recounts the story of their lives – professional, solidly middle class and very mainstream – yet touched by a compassion for the worst of the world. Ita Ford's reaction to Oscar Romero's assassination, that "his death will bear fruit," reminds us of the early martyrs. And so it should, for in this book we realize that those of us, mainstream, middle class, comfortable North Americans, who reach out to "share the same fate as the poor," may share it in its truest, most Christ-like sense.

Nicaragua

648   Belli, Humberto. *Breaking Faith. The Sandinista Revolution and its Impact on Freedom and Christian Faith in Nicaragua.* Westchester, IL: Crossway Books, for the Puebla Institute, 1985.

Human rights in the context of oppression, lack of pluralism, free expression, Sandinista lies about their achievements, and an apology for the pope's visit in 1983. Belli contends that the Sandinistas broke the essential link of faith that brought all classes, and Christians and Marxists, together in the revolution.

649 Borge, Tomás. *Christianity and Revolution. Tomás Borge's Theology of Life.* Andrew Reding, ed. & trans. Maryknoll, NY: Orbis Books, 1987.

A collection of the speeches and writings of Borge, who has been outspoken for the need to fuse Marxist and Christian elements. While not always savory or "orthodox" to theologians or proponents of nonviolence, Borge is a thoughtful man involved in changing his country and society, whose essays here are indicative of the entire process and variety of religious thought and its application to liberation.

650 Cabestrero, Téofilo. *Blood of the Innocent. Victims of the Contras' War in Nicaragua.* Robert R. Barr, trans. Maryknoll, NY: Orbis Books, 1985.

This is a powerful collection of first-hand testimony on the death threats, murders, rapes, beatings, kidnapings, tortures, massacres, destruction of property of individuals and cooperatives carried out by President Reagan's "freedom fighters." Victims include Nicaraguans, North Americans, Europeans, men, women, and children. Cabestrero prints his accounts exactly as they were reported to him.

651 —. *Ministers of God, Ministers of the People.* Robert R. Barr, trans. Maryknoll, NY: Orbis Books, 1983.

Detailed, first-person accounts of the Christian's response to the Nicaraguan revolution by some of its best-known leaders, including Ernesto Cardenal, the priest, poet, friend of Thomas Merton and Daniel Berrigan, founder of Solintiname, and Nicaragua's then minister of culture; Fernando Cardenal, S.J., his brother, former Jesuit priest and coordinator of

Nicaragua's successful literacy program; and Miguel d'Escoto, Maryknoll priest and then Nicaragua's foreign minister.

All three men have much in common, most especially their support of the "just revolution" against the Somoza government; their belief that as priests they had something unique to add to Nicaragua's revolutionary government; their subsequent conflict with Pope John Paul II and his command to them to choose either service to the church or service to the government. These are all highly articulate, sensitive, and intelligent people, deeply committed to their Christianity and to the Nicaraguan revolution. While they accept the role of violence in that revolution, they also hope that their presence in it and the influence of many like them will Christianize the revolution. They hope not that the church might rule in alliance with power once again, but that the influence of Christians might truly make the revolution one for the people, imbued with human and religious ideals of the highest order.

652 —. *Revolutionaries for the Gospel.* Philip Berryman, trans. Maryknoll, NY: Orbis Books, 1986.

The subtitle reads, "Testimony of Fifteen Christians in the Nicaraguan Government." This is an important, eye-opening collection that will cause even the most skeptical to wonder. Those interviewed were in high- and middle-level positions in the government: the president of the Supreme Court, comptroller general, minister of education, general secretary of housing, managers of the ports, energy, libraries and archives, judges, and social planners. They are well educated, with more or less solid Christian educations, many at Catholic universities in Central and North America. They are deeply committed to the ideals of Vatican II and its gospel of justice, yet they have almost all accepted the necessity of the revolution, if not of the revolution's violence.

These Christians are aware of the conflict between Christianity and the state on one level, and are careful not to compromise their Christianity for the sake of the revolution. They are also people who believe in civil government, not military dictatorship. They stress that their conflict is not with doctrine, or with the hierarchical church, but with certain bishops and priests.

These are also *practicing* Roman Catholics, some with a traditional orthodoxy, many with a profound spirituality. Biblical citations flow naturally in their conversation, and sections of the Gospels are conscious models for policy. They assert, however, that if Marxist goals are not incompatible with Christian goals and means, they will cooperate fully in the revolution.

653　　Cardenal, Ernesto. *The Gospel in Solintiname.* Donald D. Walsh, trans. 4 vols. Maryknoll, NY: Orbis Books, 1982.

These are are series of commentaries on biblical readings by the peasants of Solintiname, a small archipelago of islands in the Lake of Nicaragua, compiled by Cardenal during his stay in the days before the Nicaraguan revolution made him minister of culture. Cardenal explains that rather than delivering sermons, he would lead his parishioners to readings and discussions in a hall opposite the church after Sunday mass. The insights and interpretations are thus those of the people themselves, forming their own theology based on the Gospels.

The volumes are arranged according to the liturgical calendar of readings. Volume 1 begins with John the Baptist's mission, continues through the infancy narratives, the temptations in the wilderness, the early miracles, parables and sermons, including the beatitudes. Volumes 2 and 3 continue with the parables and further miracles; while volume 4 concentrates mostly on the Last Supper, Passion and Resurrection. A wonderful collection, and probably the best example of theology from the poor.

654 —. *The Psalms of Struggle and Liberation.* Emile G. McAnany, trans. New York: Herder & Herder, 1971.

Not seen.

655 Casaldáliga, Pedro. *Prophets in Combat, The Nicaraguan Journal of Bishop Pedro Casaldáliga.* Phillip Berryman, trans. Oak Park, IL: Meyer-Stone, 1988.

In the words of Leonardo Boff, Casaldáliga "is a sharp observer because he is a mystic." Bishop of a border diocese on the edge of Brazil's rain forest, the author travelled to the borders of Nicaragua to literally be with the marginalized and to observe this border war. This is the record of his "ministry of the border," his mission to Nicaragua on behalf of two dozen Brazilian bishops in an effort to express their solidarity with the people of Nicaragua.

While not formal theology, this record of a people's struggle for dignity and freedom is a theology in-the-making, for it combines the deeply religious awareness of God's role in history with a prophetic style that calls attention to the oppressed and the oppressor. Casaldáliga pulls no punches in laying the blame for the *contra* war and the suffering of innocent Nicaraguans squarely with Ronald Reagan and his administration.

656   Ezcurra, Ana Maria. *Ideological Aggression Against the Sandinista Revolution. The Political Opposition Church in Nicaragua.* Linda Unger and David J. Kalke, eds.; Elice Higginbotham and Bayard Faithful, trans. New York: Circus, 1984.

A prophetic work. Includes chapters in the alignment of the Nicaraguan hierarchy against the Sandinista revolution, the anti-revolutionary work of *La Prensa* and the Institute on Religion and Democracy, the church's social teachings used against the revolution, John Paul II's visit; U.S. policy against Nicaragua, and a chronology of events in church-state relations between December 1983 and July 1984. Appendixes include key documents, messages of John Paul II during his 1983 visit, and analysis.

657   Foroohar, Manzar. *The Catholic Church and Social Change in Nicaragua.* Albany, NY: State University of New York Press, 1989.

SUNY Press at Albany has published several highly professional works on the role of the church in Latin America and the political and social theories of liberation theology. This volume traces the history of the church in the region from colonialism to liberalism, including the Sandino movement; the socio-economic structures in which the church operates; the response of Latin American Catholics to these structures and dynamics, including liberation theology.

The discussion then examines the implementation of liberation theology in Nicaragua, and events leading up to the revolution, the relations between the FSLN and the progressive church, with examples drawn from specific parishes and conflicts. A final chapter discusses the events of the revolution and the hierarchy's attempt to stop it, in league with the U.S. and Nicaraguan bourgeoisie. Well documented. Extensive bibliography.

658   Heyward, Carter, and Anne Gilson, eds. *Revolutionary Forgiveness. Feminist Reflections on Nicaragua.* Maryknoll, NY: Orbis Books, 1987.

This is actually a work by the Amenecida Collective, of thirteen authors. It is a book of liberation theology by North Americans learning from the radical acts of forgiveness of the Nicaraguan people toward their former oppressors and torturers; and it is an attempt to create a theology of life out of one of death. The book deals with the history of U.S.-Nicaraguan relations, the revolution, problems remaining in revolutionary society: including sexism, racism, homophobia, violence and ecclesiatical tensions. Yet these can be overcome by the type of radical forgiveness the authors discuss. Its foundations include a praxis of community, conscientization, the rehabilitation of memory, confessing past faults, repentance, conversion, and solidarity with former victims and victimizers.

659   MacEoin, Gary. *Nicaragua. What They Say...What We Saw*. Kansas City, MO: Sheed & Ward, 1980.

Not seen.

660   Randall, Margaret. *Christians in the Nicaraguan Revolution*. Vancouver: New Star, 1983.

The people whom Randall interviews here, intellectual elite, middle class, poor and semi-literate, are for the most part Christians deeply committed to the revolution in Nicaragua. They all embrace what can be loosely described as the "just-revolution" theory, an outgrowth of the just-war theory; and they still maintain that this revolution must be defended by the gun if their work as Christians is to be maintained. Their language is that of the Crusades, of dying "like Christ, to end the injustices that we have in Nicaragua." They maintain that it is the Gospel that has told them to kill for Christ and the revolution. They emphasize the split between a true church of revolutionaries, who have read and understood the Gospels correctly, and a reactionary hierarchy that continues to distort the words of the Gospel in favor of oligarchs and reactionaries in Nicaragua and in North America.

A true synthesis of Marxism and Christianity can be achieved, they contend. If it cannot, the Nicaraguans interviewed here seem to favor a Christianity that is colored by Marx for the ends of the revolution. Some, in fact, favor a gradual discarding of formal Christianity once either Christian "values" have infused the revolution or once these values prove to be incompatible with it. In the end these Nicaraguans feel that the revolution can only be led by a small committed elite, that most "peasants" are too passive to lead their own revolution, and that it is up to this enlightened elite to pick who will fight, who will kill, and who will die in defense of the revolution. Nonviolence, in the end, is passivity. "Christ was a guerilla fighter."

661 Scharper, Philip, and Sally Scharper, eds. *The Gospel in Art by the Peasants of Solintiname.* Maryknoll, NY: Orbis Books, 1984.

A wonderful visual explanation of the meaning and agents of liberation theology. This series of paintings of Gospel scenes, by members of the base community at Solintiname, gives flesh and blood to the words of the theologians and is the concrete manifestation of the theology that the people themselves have created. A thing of great beauty that reflects the beauty of the revelation enjoyed by the people of Latin America.

* *
*

Chapter 8: *The Liberation of North America*

Bibliographies

662   Bullough, Vern L., W. Dorr Legg, Barrett W. Elcano, and James Kepner, compilers. *An Annotated Bibliography of Homosexuality.* 2 vols. New York: Garland Publishing, 1976.

    An excellent resource. Contains 12,794 items: books and articles, arranged by topic, with indexes of authors and a brief interpretive essay. Religion and ethics are found in items 5081-5575, vol. 1, pp. 331-62.

663   Dickerson, Fay, and Paul D. Petersen, eds. *Liberation Theology, Black Theology, and the Third World. A Select Bibliography from the Files of the ATLA Religion Database.* 4th, rev. ed. Chicago: American Theological Library Association, 1982.

    A huge bibliography, mostly of the journal literature, with listings by subject and author. Unannotated.

664   Dynes, Wayne R. *Homosexuality. A Research Guide.* New York: Garland Publishers, 1987.

    Books and articles, 4858 items with annotations, listed alphabetically by author and arranged by topic. Indexes of subject and personal names. Items on Philosophy and ethics appear on pages 314-32; items on religion on pages 321-54. Religious topics include general, biblical studies, main Christian denominations, gay churches and organizations, gay clergy, the religious backlash, Judaism, and new age spirituality.

665   Evans, James H., and G. E. Gorman, eds. *Black Theology. A Critical Assessment and Annotated Bibliography.* New York: Greenwood Press, 1987.

A very thorough treatment, with articles and books arranged by topic, and then alphabetically by author. It is divided into three main topics: origin and development, liberation, feminism and Marxism, and cultural and global discourse. This bibliography deals with not only African-American theology but also with African, feminist and other liberation topics.

666   Fisher, William H. *Free At Last. A Bibliography of Martin Luther King, Jr.* Metuchen, NJ: Scarecrow Press, 1977.

Works by King, on King, on his life, reviews of books on him. Unnumbered, arranged alphabetically.

667   Fodell, Beverly. *Cesar Chavez and the United Farm Workers. A Selective Bibliography.* Detroit: Wayne State University Press, 1974.

Not seen.

668   *A Gay Bibliography. Eight Bibliographies on Lesbian and Male Homosexuals.* New York: Arno Press, 1975.

Terrible. Photostat-quality, typed pieces grouped together indiscriminately. No index.

669   Hackett, David G. *The New Religions. An Annotated Bibliography.* 3d, rev. ed. Berkeley, CA: Center for the Study of New Religious Movements, 1981.

Some useful information, arranged by topic and author, on black and native American religion, though under the sobriquet "new."

670   Horner, Tom. *Homosexuality and the Judeo-Christian Tradition. An Annotated Bibliography.* ATLA Bibliography Series, no. 5. Metuchen, NJ: Scarecrow Press, 1981.

Books, articles, essays, pamphlets and papers, bibliographies totalling 459 items. Two appendixes of biblical references and periodicals of gay religious organizations. Indexes by subject and author.

671   Johnson, Timothy V. *Malcolm X. A Comprehensive Annotated Bibliography.* New York: Garland Publishing, 1986.

Works by Malcolm X, books and dissertations on him, articles and news reports from the mainstream, African-American, left-wing and African press. Also sections on FBI files, book reviews and indexes.

672   Martin Luther King, Jr. Papers Project, eds. *A Guide to Research on Martin Luther King, Jr. and the Modern Black Freedom Struggle.* Stanford, CA: Stanford University Press, 1989.

Not seen.

673   Martinez, Julio A. *Chicano Scholars and Writers. A Bio-Bibliographical Directory.* Metuchen, NJ: Scarecrow Press, 1979.

Includes material on Virgil P. Elizondo on pages 137-39.

674   Pyatt, Sherman E. *Martin Luther King, Jr. An Annotated Bibliography.* New York: Greenwood Press, 1986.

Books and articles, 1277 items arranged alphabetically by author and subdivided into the following subject categories: King's published works, biographical materials, the Southern Christian Leadership Conference, marches and demonstrations, major awards, FBI and government operations against him, his philosophy, assassination, commemorations, and eulogies. Provides name, subject and title indexes.

675   Raynham, Warner R. *Bibliographies Relating Various Areas of Theological Study to the Black Experience in America.* Boston: Boston Theological Institute, 1973.

Not seen.

676   Richardson, Marilyn. *Black Women and Religion. A Bibliography.* Boston: G.K. Hall, 1980.

Entries cover black American women's religious life in literature, music, art, audio-visual and reference materials, and in autobiography and biography.

677   Tucson Ecumenical Council. *Sanctuary Bibliography.*
        Tucson, AZ: TEC, 1982; rev. ed. 1985

Not seen.

Liberation Theology for the Rich?

678   Anderson, Gerald H., and Thomas F. Stransky, eds.
        Liberation Theologies in North America and Europe.
        Mission Trends 4. New York: Paulist Press, 1979.

Section 2 covers black theology with work by
Wilmore, Cone, the black theology Project, Andrew
Young, and Pannell, among others. Part 3 samples
feminist theology, with essays by Radford Ruether,
Schüssler Fiorenza, Wahlberg, Mollenkott, and
Russell. Part 4 covers Asian American theology, Part
5 native American with work by Vine Deloria, and
Part 6 Hispanic American theology with essays by
Cesar Chavez and Leo Nieto. See also **156.**

679   Armerding, Carl E., ed. *Evangelicals and Liberation.*
        Phillipsburg, NJ: Presbyterian and Reformed,
        1977.

A collection of essays by K. Hamilton, S. C. A.
Knapp, Armerding, H. M. Conn, and C. H. Pinnock on
Gutiérrez, the contributions – negative and positive –
of Latin American liberation theology, and a
liberation theology for North Americans.

680   Bayer, Charles H. *A Guide to Liberation Theology for Middle-Class Congregations.* St. Louis, MO: CBP Press, 1986.

The author points to the fact that if liberation theology is to be valid for the whole church, it must also address the situation of the affluent and middle class of the North and the "captivities" that they suffer. This book is thus intended as an introduction for pastors in order that they may then introduce the problems and questions posed by liberation theology for their own congregations. Bayer attempts to address these issues through the normal functions of the parish: worship, preaching, counseling, liturgy, biblical study, education and social welfare, political involvement and service, stewardship, and evangelism.

He begins by highlighting the captivity of both prisoner and goaler, the contributions of liberation theology and the base communities, the practical work of evangelization, the emptiness of middle-class life, the problem of Marxism and a new biblical hermeneutic, Christian involvement in political action, the problem of violence, liberation of blacks and women, the particular forms of captivity of First-World citizens, and the value of passion as a means of liberation from our materialism, boredom and "prophylactic life." The book concludes with a discussion of liberation theology in its apocalyptic dimension.

681   Brackley, Dean, S.J. *People Power. Together We Can Change Things.* New York: Paulist Press, 1989.

Not seen.

682   Brown, Delwin. *To Set at Liberty. Christian Faith and Human Freedom.* Maryknoll, NY: Orbis Books, 1981.

This book is addressed to the white middle class of North America and attempts to apply the lessons of Latin American liberation theology for it. It discusses freedom as a contemporary issue, as a historical concept, and in the thought of Sartre, Marx and Whitehead. It then goes on to discuss some theological themes of freedom from the viewpoint of liberation theology: God, sin, Christ, and salvation.

683   Brown, Robert McAfee. *Spirituality and Liberation. Overcoming the Great Fallacy.* Philadelphia: Westminster Press, 1988.

Not seen.

684   —. *Theology in a New Key. Responding to Liberation Themes.* Philadelphia, PA: Westminster Press, 1978.

This is an attempt to respond as a North American to the themes of liberation theology, and to ways that make that theology meaningful to North Americans and their own oppressions and alienations.

After reviewing his themes Brown surveys Catholic social teaching of the last century, the progress of the World Council of Churches, and the impact of Latin American developments from Medellin on. He then briefly outlines the major new elements of liberation theology and examines the principle of "hermeneutic suspicion" with which liberation theologians approach the scriptures. He then reviews the various criticisms of this theology.

Brown next embarks on a study of some elements for a North American theology of liberation and presents some models for a church of the future, including faithful remnant and "Abrahamic minority." Contains a brief annotated bibliography.

685   —. *Unexpected News. Reading the Bible with Third World Eyes.* Philadelphia: Westminster Press, 1984.

This is an attempt to interpret key biblical texts from the viewpoint of Third-World peoples and theologies in order to sensitize North Americans to forms of oppression that their own unconscious assumptions may make them party to.

Texts include selections from Exodus, 2 Samuel, Jeremiah, Daniel, Matthew and Luke. Contains a very brief, annotated bibliography.

686   Carmody, John. *Theology for the 1980s.* Philadelphia: Westminster Press, 1980.

Examines the elements that include a theology of ecology and process theology, liberation theology from Latin America, a new theology of personhood, new understandings of the nature of God as "boundary" and a return of Christology to the historical Jesus as a model for contemporary life.

687   Chopp, Rebecca S. *The Praxis of Suffering. An Interpretation of Liberation and Political Theologies.* Maryknoll, NY: Orbis Books, 1986.

Examines the major figures of both theologies, including Gutiérrez, Bonino, Metz, and Moltmann to show the similarities and cultural differences in the theologies while discussing their formal questions.

688   Costa, Ruy O., and Lorine Getz, eds. *In Solidarity. Liberation Theologies in Dialogue.* Maryknoll, NY: Orbis Books, 1990.

Theologians from both North and South America discuss the various forms of liberation theology to which their situations have given rise. Original essays by Costa, Getz, Cone, Ruether, Ellis, Shaull, Cox, Schüssler Fiorenza, and Richard, among others.

689   Damico, Linda H. *The Anarchist Dimension of Liberation Theology.* New York: Peter Lang, 1987.

Goes beyond the links between liberation theology and Marxism to the intellectual roots in anarchy, along a path laid out by José Porforio Miranda. Liberation theology's "emphasis on freedom, justice, and love, its denunciation of political and economic structures of domination, its emphasis on action, and its vision of a future free from all servitudes reveal an indebtedness to anarchism."

690   Donders, Joseph G. *Risen Life. Healing a Broken World.* Maryknoll, NY: Orbis Books, 1990.

Donders applies the lessons of inculturation and liberation theology to a North American audience whose religion is "bourgeois," private, and inner. He offers instead the insights of Luke the physician who seeks to bring Jesus' message of healing and community to an atomized First World, to reunite the life of the spirit with that of society in an integral spirituality that speaks of integral liberation for the individual, the church, and society.

691   Dorr, Donal. *Integral Spirituality. Resources for Community, Peace, Justice, and the Earth.* Maryknoll, NY: Orbis Books, 1990.

The influence of Latin American liberation theology is felt in its translation for a North American mainstream audience, for whom oppression and marginalization are more often read about than felt or lived. Dorr therefore presents a synthesis of new theological directions: both the integration of inner spirituality and moral integrity with the concerns for the poor and oppressed and the fate of creation itself. This new integralism is the meaning of peace, justice, and liberation.

692   —. *Spirituality and Justice.* Maryknoll, NY: Orbis Books, 1985.

Bridges the gap between inner piety and social activism by demonstrating that they must be integrated into a single view of God, the world, and salvation.

693   Dorrien, Gary J. *Reconstructing the Common Good. Theology and Social Order.* Maryknoll, NY: Orbis Books, 1990.

The kingdom of God that liberation theologians speak of is a social order here on earth. What is the nature of that order if it is to be neither capitalist nor communist? An emerging movement, called Christian socialism by its analysts, seems to be the direction of the emerging political and economic praxis. Dorrien here examines the thought of both Latin American liberation theologians, such as Gutiérrez and Míguez-Bonino, along with theologians from the First World, including Tillich, Moltmann, and Ruether. The solutions to specific conditions embedded in this new political theory are not totally conditioned by the socio-economic or cultural structures of a particular time and place but emerge from a longstanding Christian tradition of social teaching and practice.

694   Evans, Alice F., Robert A. Evans, and William Bean Kennedy. *Pedagogies for the Nonpoor*. Maryknoll, NY: Orbis Books, 1987.

Attempts to take the lessons of liberation theology and the methodologies of Paulo Freire and apply them to a North American, comfortable, and educated audience. In keeping with the essential liberation theme that theology must spring from the roots of actual practice and reality, the authors address such issues as world hunger, economic dislocations caused by capital flight and multinational relocations, and parenting for peace and justice.

695   Ferm, Deane W. *Contemporary American Theologies. A Critical Survey*. New York: Seabury Press, 1981.

This includes a survey of Protestant theology from 1900 to 1960; the new secular thought of the 1960s, black theology, South American liberation theology, feminist theology, evangelical, and Roman Catholic trends; and comments on the future of American theology. Examines the development, major tenets and contributions, and the criticisms of these theologies.

696   —. *Contemporary American Theologies II. A Book of Readings.* New York: Seabury Press, 1982.

This is a book of readings from secular, black, liberation, feminist, Evangelical, and Roman Catholic theologies.

697   Furfey, Paul Hanly. *Love and the Urban Ghetto.* Maryknoll, NY: Orbis Books, 1978.

This is a reflection on liberation theology born out of Furfey's own experience of discrimination and marginalization growing up Irish in WASP Boston at the turn of the century. It is also the result of his experience of the Catholic Worker, of meeting Dorothy Day and Peter Maurin, of establishing similar houses in Washington, DC, and then of seeing the impact of liberation theology first-hand in Latin America in the 1970s.

Topics include the paramount importance of Christian love over and above our current bourgeois theology and morality; the structures of social sin; the sin of poverty in death, despair, and marginalization; the contributions of Catholic liberalism and radicalism in North America; and the revolutionary situation in Latin America. Furfey concludes with remarks on the feasibility of forging a theology of liberation that might create a society far more along the lines of the moderate socialisms of Europe than either capitalist or communist paradises.

698   González, Justo L., and Catherine González. *In Accord.*
       Let Us Worship. New York: Friendship Press, 1981.

       A new liturgy that seeks to include the rituals of
       all religious traditions and peoples from the view-
       point of liberation theology.

699   —, ed. *Proclaiming the Acceptable Year.* Valley Forge,
       PA: Judson Press, 1982.

       A collection of sermons by Míguez Bonino,
       Cardinal Arns, Choang-Seng Song, Allan Boesak,
       Winston Lawson, Virgil Elizondo, Roy Sano, James
       Cone, Joan M. Martin, Letty Russell, and Robert
       McAfee Brown on liberation themes.

700   —, and Catherine Gunsalus González. *Liberation
       Preaching. The Pulpit and the Oppressed.*
       Nashville, TN: Abingdon Press, 1980.

       Aimed at the pastoral instruction of a North
       American clergy. Seeks first to define what
       liberation theology really is, then proceeds to
       problems of interpreting scripture according to
       liberation precepts. Also discusses traditional aids in
       biblical interpretation, the development of a libera-
       tion hermeneutic among white male preachers that
       will lead them to ask the right questions from
       scripture. Final chapters deal with the dynamics of
       liberation preaching and the process of liberation
       itself.

701   Green, Susan. *Bread and Puppet. Stories of Struggle and Faith from Central America.* Burlington, VT: Green Valley Film & Art, 1985.

Whether performing on the streets of Brooklyn, NY or in the valleys of rural Vermont, the Bread and Puppet Theater has long combined the political and the religious, the nonviolent with the commitment to liberation in ways that make them a unique North American theological force. Whether portraying the struggle of Oscar Romero and the people of Central America or creating new dramas about greed, exploitation and power, and the faith that the earth itself will protect its own creatures, Bread and Puppet has created a remarkable series of symbols, mythological depictions, and liturgies that are accessible to North Americans of every class, race, and religion. This is an excellent collection of their work.

702   Gundry, Stanley N., and Alan F. Johnson, eds. *Tensions in Contemporary Theology.* 2d ed. Grand Rapids, MI: W.B. Eerdmans, 1983.

Essays by Bernard Ramm, Vernon Grounds, Harold B. Kuhn, Harvie M. Conn and Harold O. J. Brown on European theology, the theology of hope, process theology, recent Catholic forms, and liberation theology.

703   Haight, Roger, S.J. *An Alternative Vision. An Interpretation of Liberation Theology.* New York: Paulist Press, 1985.

This book is an attempt, by a sympathetic observer, to translate and assimilate the insights of Latin American liberation theology for a North

American audience. It also seeks to present a unified picture of this theology in all its features, from a strictly theological point of view, without reference to the world of praxis in politics, economics, or history.

Topics include the origins and nature of liberation theology, its methodology, its discussion of faith; the image of God, its Christology and soteriology, the role of the spirit, sin, grace, salvation and spirituality; the principles of liberation theology for the church and its structures; the role and nature of the sacraments; ministry, spirituality. The book concludes with a discussion, and reprint of, the *Instruction on Certain Aspects of the 'Theology of Liberation.'* (see **123-124**).

704   Haughey, John C., S.J., ed. *The Faith That Does Justice. Examining the Christian Sources of Social Change.* New York: Paulist Press, 1977.

A collection of essays in honor of then Jesuit General Pedro Arrupe. Contributors include Avery Dulles, William Dych, John R. Donahue, William J. Walsh and John P. Langan, Ricard Roach, David Hollenbach and Haughey. David Hollenbach's "A Prophetic Church and the Catholic Sacramental Imagination" reviews various forms of justice theology, including Political and liberation theologies.

705   Herzog, Frederick. *God-Walk. Liberation Shaping Dogmatics.* Maryknoll, NY: Orbis Books, 1988.

When one walks with Jesus in his healing and liberating work, one abandons liberalism – simply talking about an abstract God whom many in North

America assume dead – to God-walk, the practical experience of finding God alive through work and life for justice in the world. Herzog finds his first inspiration in the civil-rights and black theology movements, for it was here that North Americans were first reawakened to the realities of sin and oppression and to the chance of liberation.

Herzog's book is basically a theology primer: reexamining the basic categories of religious doctrine – scripture, authority, creed, Christology, fall and salvation, justification and grace, the sacraments, Christian anthropology and ecclesiology – all from a liberationist experience of struggle. As with all liberation theology, the sacramental and spiritual lives are indistinguishable from the life of action in the world: the human person and role in creation are unified; salvation comes to the individual and to creation in the very same process.

706   —. *Justice Church. The New Function of the Church in North American Christianity.* Maryknoll, NY: Orbis Books, 1980.

This is an attempt to forge a new theology for North Americans without a "hermeneutics of suspicion," and instead to employ a "hermeneutics of volition," that focuses on God's will in attempts to free the bourgeois church from its obsession on control. Topics discussed include the Gospel as a story of praxis, the problem of power in the church, the role of Jesus in teaching vulnerability, especially in the age after Auschwitz, the Bible and Marxism, North American applications of a liberation theology, the call to justice for our churches, and the necessary shift from liberal to liberation theology.

707   —. *Liberation Theology. Liberation in the Light of the Fourth Gospel.* New York: Seabury Press, 1972.

See 35.

708   Hurley, Neil P. *The Reel Revolution. A Film Primer on Liberation.* Maryknoll, NY: Orbis Books, 1978.

Hurley's approach is especially appropriate for a North American theology of liberation, since he treats the heart of the kinetic, high-tech mythology of American life that is the essence of the movies.

Themes for the films examined here fall into the following: peaceful liberation, the charismatic liberator, degrees of consciousness raising, violence and liberation, the anatomy of exploitation, the liberation philosophy of Chaplin, Latin American cinema and human liberation, liberation and the future, and suggestions for film studies on liberation themes.

709   Imboden, Roberta. *From the Cross to the Kingdom. Sartrean Dialectics and Liberation Theology.* San Francisco: Harper & Row, 1987.

This Canadian theologian turns to sociology for the grounding of a structuralist, "materialist" foundation of faith narrative in the same way that Sartre did for existentialism's individualism. She seeks to illumine the themes of personal freedom, commitment, and fidelity as bases for changing the social order through a rejection of Marxist categories and by using Sartre's own concepts of fused group, structures of scarcity, and totalization as a means of interpreting the Gospel narratives of Jesus and the apostles, the collapse of their messianic hopes in the cross, and the new message of the resurrection and mission.

Imboden reminds us that the cross and the kingdom are the two extremes of the Christian message, and both form the basis of a radical critique of twentieth-century society in both its realities of oppression, suffering, and marginalization and its ideal dreams. Much of her inspiration comes from Latin America's base communities and liberation theology. Imboden's work is an attempt to create a First World response. It seeks to contribute to a meaningful praxis for her time and society.

710   Kavanaugh, John Francis. *Following Christ in a Consumer Society. The Spirituality of Cultural Resistance.* Maryknoll, NY: Orbis Books, 1981.

Liberation for North Americans must come in the form of liberation first from our commercial values that negate both community and the individual through materialist consumerism. This is an attempt to apply the Gospel message of the beatitudes with the messages of liberation and solidarity.

711   King, Paul G., Kent Maynard, and David O. Woodyard. *Risking Liberation. Middle Class Powerlessness and Social Heroism.* Atlanta, GA: John Knox, 1988.

This is an attempt to do liberation theology for middle-class Americans that must first attempt to overcome American individualism and their unwillingness to associate themselves with working-class and poor concerns. The book first identifies the American middle class, then examines its structural characteristics, its real powerlessness in the face of corporate wealth, and the inevitability of ideology arising from such relationships. The two final chapters attempt to show how the insights of liberation theology can be applied to the U.S. and the emergence of a new church.

712   King, Paul G., and David O. Woodyard. *The Journey Toward Freedom. Economic Structures and Theological Perspectives.* Rutherford, NJ: Fairleigh Dickinson University Press, 1982.

This book is a collaboration between an economist and a theologian. It is an attempt to both understand liberation theology in its Latin American socio-economic and spiritual contexts and to import a form of liberation theology for a North American audience. Sharing the insights of each scholar, this book also hopes to give the practical edge to the praxis of creating an alternative world out of the vision of theological wisdom and economic knowledge.

The authors discuss a broadening of the liberation agenda; U.S. economic and social institutions; religion in America, including our new "civil religion;" the American economic miracle; the need to bring enough to all; the message of the Gospels; community, freedom, and the reality of the suffering "other;" the need to reorder economic priorities and structures; and some tentative suggestions for a route there.

713   Krass, Alfred C. *Evangelizing Neopagan North America. The Word That Frees.* Scottsdale, PA: Herald Press, 1982.

This is both an evangelically radical and a contextual examination of the process of evangelization

in a society that idolizes power and itself in a schizo-
phrenic and narcissistic way. Mirrors many of the
themes of liberation theology.

714   Lamb, Matthew L. *Solidarity with Victims. Toward a
        Theology of Social Transformation.* New York:
        Crossroad/Continuum, 1982.

Real theology must be take up the preferential
option for the poor and the oppressed that informs
social and political action to transform their condition.

715   Lernoux, Penny. *People of God.* (See **120**).

If liberation theology centers on the self-empower-
ment of the people through a critical reflection on
their own practical experience in the world and how
that experience reveals the working of God in
creation, then the experience of the North American
people, its search for pluralism and democracy in
church structures, and its attempt to implement the
teachings of Vatican II are American forms of
liberation theology.

Lernoux focuses on several aspects of the papal
attempt to squelch many of the most important
elements of American Catholicism in the post-Vatican
II era: greater involvement and voice for the laity,
the role of women in the church and its leadership,
the function of the clergy for service and not rule, a
critical role of the laity's experience in sexual
teachings, the strength and unity of the U.S. bishops'
conference when teaching on peace and justice as the
true province of the church, and the involvement of
local individuals and churches in such struggles as

the Sanctuary Movement where the links between North and Latin American liberation are the most clear.

716   Levi, Werner. *The Catholic Church, the Theologians, Poverty, and Politics.* New York: Praeger, 1989.

A solid introduction and survey. In reviewing this book in the *Catholic Historical Review* (76, 2, April 1990, pp. 323-24) James V. Schall, S.J., a contributor to right-wing critiques of liberation theology (see 820), exults in what can only be characterized as an unseemly manner at the collapse of "Marxism," and feels that his work has therefore been done. His trashing is ample evidence that conservative circles in North America continue to be haunted by any discussion of liberation theology and are all too willing to revive the red-baiting of the McCarthy era against such examples of serious scholarship that seek to explain and understand.

717   Macquarrie, John. *The Faith of the People of God. A Lay Theology.* New York: Charles Scribner's, 1973.

This is an attempt at a theology that matches the reality of the (then) growing role of the laity within the church. It discusses the people of God as the primary theological datum, and theology as the focus of a religious view that encompasses all of life. This "lay theology" is not a simplified, or anticlerical one; it does not grow from a professional theological-clerical class but sees the laity as a full equal in the work of the church and the spirit. The laity is also a people, not a faceless mob or ecclesiastical underclass. Macquarrie's theology is thus fully one of liberation in its insistence on the primacy of praxis and the role of the people of God. He also develops a Christology, theology of sacraments, ministry and mission, prayer, eschatology, and ecclesiology in keeping with this outlook.

718 Mahan, Brian, and L. Dale Richesin, eds. *The Challenge of Liberation Theology. A First-Wold Response.* Maryknoll, NY: Orbis Books, 1981.

A collection of essays that includes Dorothee Sölle, Lee Cormie, James H. Cone, James W. Fowler, Elisabeth Schüssler Fiorenza, Langdon Gilkey, and Schubert M. Ogden.

719 McFadden, Thomas M., ed. *Liberation, Revolution, and Freedom. Theological Perspective.* College Theology Society. New York: Seabury Press, 1975.

Essays by Francis P. Fiorenza, Mary I. Buckley, Elizabeth Bellefontaine, James Cone, T. Richard Shaull, Letty M. Russell, Carl Starkloff, Silvio E. Fittipaldi, Stephen Casey, Leonard Biallas, James Gaffney, Francis J. Reilly and William J. Sullivan on the historical roots and meanings of liberation in the Judeo-Christian tradition, contemporary liberation theologies, including black, feminist, and native American; the question of violence; and criticisms of liberation theology.

720 Merton, Thomas. "Faith and Violence," in *The Nonviolent Alternative.* Revised edition of *Thomas Merton on Peace.* Gordon Zahn, ed. New York: Farrar, Strauss Giroux, 1980, pp. 185-207.

This is a troubled work reflecting Merton's grappling with nonviolence in the late 1960s and his movement toward a "theology of resistance." The modern state is without any justice; it is, in fact, St. Augustine's great band of robbers. Society condemns the isolated, individual violence of criminals while it participates fully in corporate and technological violence in war, and in the violence of poverty. True peace cannot be order alone.

Was Camilo Torres, the Colombian priest turned guerilla, right in his use of force? Is there a valid theology of revolution? Is force to be used if Christianity fails? Merton remains troubled by these questions and calls for the development of a theology of resistance, an activist nonviolence that seeks to bring justice and real peace, while avoiding the moral aggression of self-righteousness.

Merton then turns to contemporary events and declares the Vietnam War an overwhelming atrocity tied to America's suicidal drive to self-destruction. He condemns the draft law as unjust and illegal, as the forced acting out by the young of the manias of their political leaders. In the Civil Rights movement Merton believes that nonviolence may be dead and is not effective. He upbraids white liberals and calls on them simply to act as witnesses, not to attempt to lead the movement. He concludes by praising the "death of God" theology for freeing religion from the restraints of institutionalism and ambiguity. This essay looks forward to several elements of a North American liberation theology.

721		Migliore, Daniel L. *Called to Freedom. Liberation Theology and the Future of Christian Doctrine.* Philadelphia: Westminster Press, 1980.

Examines both the importance and limitations of interpreting the Gospels as the message of freedom. Liberation theology, in the Third World, among people of color and women, is not a fad but a necessary task for the church, as is the reordering of the church's mission toward freedom. Such a realignment is the work of all Christians, not just the clergy. Finally, however, all theologies are inadequate when measured against Christian love and acts of solidarity. Discusses scripture as the liberating word, Jesus as a new type of liberator, the theology of the Trinity in human liberation, a spirituality of liberation, and Christian faith as liberation from the bondage of death.

722		Min, Anselm Kyongsuk. *Dialectic of Salvation. Issues in Theology of Liberation.* Albany, NY: State University of New York Press, 1989.

Min, a philosopher at Belmont Abbey College in North Carolina, offers a thorough examination of the theology of liberation from a Hegelian dialectical point of view and endorses it strongly as a truly contemporary and original form. Thus, his work is less on its theological and ecclesiological nature than on liberation theology as an intellectual system. In this his analysis is ironically more free from polemic and more focused on its central concerns.

Topics include an examination of liberation theology, its roots in philosophy and praxis, and criticisms from such thinkers as Schubert Ogden, Dennis McCann and Charles R. Strain, and from John Paul II and Cardinal Ratzinger. The book also examines the theology's relationship to praxis and hermeneutics, and the dialectic of salvation and liberation that establishes one of the central tensions in the movement. The book concludes with a much-needed examination of the Vatican's own "theology of liberation" that focuses on its theology of sin and salvation, its anthropology, its notions of personal and social sin, and notions of liberation. Good bibliography.

723 Neal, Marie Augusta. *A Socio-Theology of Letting Go. The Role of a First World Church Facing Third World Peoples.* New York: Paulist Press, 1977.

This is an attempt to create a theology of the rich: a theology of liberation that will allow us (relatively) wealthy North Americans to live in solidarity with the peoples of the Third World and that will free us from the oppressions of our own obsessions with power and materialism. This is the process that Neal sums up in the phrase "letting go," and abandoning our own brand of what Robert Bellah termed "civil religion": that legitimization and elevation of our own forms of secular life into a national religion, with its own idols and altars.

In response Neal proposes a new religion of prophesy that will decry our oppressions and our false gods, including our belief that we have a right to 70% of the world's wealth. Neal's final call is for a "theology of relinquishment" that will bring salvation to both rich and poor.

724   Nelson-Pallmeyer, James. *The Politics of Compassion. A Biblical Perspective on World Hunger, the Arms Race, and U.S. Policy in Central America.* Maryknoll, NY: Orbis Books, 1986.

The author's perspective grows from the insights he has gathered in the Third World, through the base Christian communities of Central America and their Bible study classes. He attempts here to apply these insights to a wealthy, powerful North American audience. "Christians in North America, particularly those who are affluent or comfortable," he notes, "will understand the message of Jesus only if we let the poor be our teachers.... We can seriously hope for a world with more justice and less hunger only if we understand history, economics and theology from the vantage point of the poor."

With this as the basis, the author then examines this "call to compassion," the process of liberating theology from its colonial outlook in Latin America, the impact of North American economic interests on the poor in Central America, the biblical basis for stopping the arms race and turning resources toward the cure of hunger and deprivation; and finally avenues for action and hope. The book concludes with a listing of resources: organizations and periodicals that can help.

725   Quigley, Thomas E., ed. *Freedom and Unfreedom in the Americas. Toward a Theology of Liberation.* New York: U.S. Catholic Conference, 1971.

Articles by Goulet, Harvey Cox, Joseph Green, Louis Colonnese, Helen Jaworski, Ruether, James Douglass and others on the conflict between development and liberation, dependence and domination, A Call to Action, powerlessness in contemporary society, Latin American liberation theology, liberation as salvation from sin and oppression, activism and contemplation. Includes an essay on a theology of liberation.

726   Radical Religion Collective, eds. *The Bible and Liberation: A Radical Religion Reader.* Berkeley, CA: Community for Religious Research and Education, 1976.

Not seen.

727   Ramsay, William M. *Four Modern Prophets. Walter Rauschenbusch, Martin Luther King Jr., Gustavo Gutiérrez, Rosemary Radford Ruether.* Atlanta, GA: John Knox Press, 1986.

These include Walter Rauschenbusch and his call for an activist "social Gospel," Martin Luther King, Jr. and his work for justice and liberation; Gustavo Gutiérrez and his theology of liberation, and Rosemary Radford Ruether and her feminist theology. Examines their lives, religious foundations, salient features of their work and thought. Good sketches.

728   Raphael, Pierre. *Inside Rikers Island.* Maryknoll, NY: Orbis Books, 1990.

Rikers is the maximum security prison on an island in the middle of New York City. The author, a former French worker-priest, builds a new "prison theology" from the experience of the inmates as he attempts to build a Christian community there based on the Gospels. This is a clear example of a liberation theology that grows out of the North American experience.

729   Rodes, Robert E. *Law and Liberation.* Notre Dame, IN: University of Notre Dame Press, 1986.

Deeply indebted to Gustavo Gutiérrez and the theology of liberation, Rodes here attempts to apply liberation theology's goals to the North American legal framework. Topics include poverty, trivialization (i.e., the process in North American life in which consumerism and materialism seem to overtake all human values and push them toward the mundane), powerlessness, rootlessness, sex, and violence,
This is a fascinating attempt to create a North American liberation theology, but one that is of its essence North American: it is practical, legal, and concerned with changing the ways in which the wheels of our society turn.

730   Ruether, Rosemary Radford. *Liberation Theology. Human Hope Confronts Christian History and American Power.* New York: Paulist Press, 1972.

This is a collection of essays published in the early 70s on such themes as the origins of liberation theology, celibacy and eschatology, Judaism, Christianity and anti-Semitism, the failure of women's liberation within the church, feminist and ecofeminism, black theology; building a community of liberation; and the limits of a white dominant theology of the left without the insights of the Third World.

731   —. *The Radical Kingdom.* New York: Harper & Row, 1970.

A survey of the theology of revolution. Traces its development from the Puritan Revolution, through the Enlightenment, nineteenth-century utopianism, Christian socialism, and Marxism. In the modern world Ruether discusses crisis theology; secular, death of God, post-Christendom theologies; the theology of hope; and Christian-Marxist dialog. She concludes with the U.S. scene in the 1960s, and the implications for an internalized view of revolution that changes "minds instead" and focuses efforts and hopes on ultimate salvation.

732   Runyon, Theodore, ed. *Sanctification and Liberation. Liberation Theologies in Light of the Wesleyan Tradition.* Oxford Institute on Sanctification and Liberation. Nashville, TN: Abingdon, 1981.

Essays by Runyon, Míguez Bonino, John Kent, Nancy Hardesty, James H. Cone and others on the liberation themes in Wesleyan tradition.

733   Samuel, Vinay, and Chris Sugden, eds. *Sharing Jesus in the Two Thirds World. Evangelical Christologies from the Contexts of Poverty, Powerlessness and Religious Pluralism.* Grand Rapids, MI: W.B. Eerdmans, 1983.

Not seen.

734   Sano, Roy I. *You Can Be Set Free.* Nashville, TN:
       Graded Press, 1977.

       This is a pamphlet designed as an introduction to
       the themes of a liberation theology for comfortable
       North Americans, using biblical stories, analysis of
       American middle-class life; an exposition of the U.S.
       as a world empire, problems of racism and sexism and
       the prison that we have made of our own comfort and
       protection.

735   Shaull, Millard Richard. *Heralds of a New
       Reformation. The Poor of South and North America.*
       Maryknoll, NY: Orbis Books, 1984.

       A liberation theology for the North American
       based on Schaull's work among the poor and margin-
       alized of the continent.

736   Sider, Ronald J. *Rich Christians in An Age of Hunger.*
       Downers Grove, IL: InterVarsity, 1977.

       This is an attempt at a practical, ethical
       Christian way of life to relieve the mass oppression
       and suffering of the world's poor. Discusses the vast
       inequalities of wealth between the rich North, espe-
       cially North Americans, and the world's poor; a
       biblical perspective on poverty and God's identi-
       fication with the poor; economic relations of distribu-
       tion and equality among the Jewish people of the Old
       Testament; the biblical approach to structural evils
       and economic relationships.
           Part 3 then examines some practical steps to put
       Judeo-Christian values into practice. These include a
       graduated tithe, a new life style of conservation,

communal living, anti-consumerism, the house church and the structural changes that these can bring about. This is a practical liberation theology for North Americans that is even more relevant to the world of the 1990s.

737   Snyder, Howard A. *Liberating the Church. The Ecology of Church and Kingdom.* Downers Grove, IL: InterVarsity Press, 1983.

This is a liberation theology for the North American church. The author focuses on the dichotomy between church as institution that perpetuates its own structures and the church as the agency of the kingdom – the sacrament of the world – transforming and bringing the world to the justice God's creation intended for it.

Themes include new models for the church as the instrument of justice; liberation and the kingdom; a new ecclesiology of service; the church as sacrament, community, servant and witness; a church that serves the kingdom in ministry, in liberating its theology, as a new covenant with the creator and as the agent for a new form of life that reflects the Christian values of the kingdom. Final sections deal with the ministerial role of the laity, women, the poor, and pastors as servants.

738   Sölle, Dorothee. *Beyond Mere Dialogue. On Being Christian and Socialist.* Detroit, MI: American Catholics Toward Socialism, 1977.

This booklet takes up three themes: sin and alienation, the cross and class struggle, and resurrection and liberation. Much of her inspiration for this synthesis comes from Latin American theologians, including Segundo and Cardenal, much from Mother Jones. This is a theology of economic life that rejects a capitalistic focus on individual gain in favor of community and wholeness, and thus seeks a North American version of liberation theology.

739   Tabb, William K., ed. *Churches in Struggle. Liberation Theologies and Social Change in North America.* New York: Monthly Review Press, 1986.

This collection of essays is grouped around certain basic themes: theologies of liberation (including the themes of option for the poor, class struggle, black theology, Jewish liberation theology), reclaiming the Christian message in the North American churches, Marxism and religion, theology rooted in the community, and political activism and the mission of the church. Authors include Robert McAfee Brown, Rosemary Radford Ruether, James Cone, Elisabeth Schüssler Fiorenza, Marc H. Ellis, Beverly W. Harrison, Gregory Baum, Norman Gottwald, Phillip Berryman, Cornel West, Donald W. Dayton, Gayraud S. Wilmore, Sheila Collins, and Richard W. Gillett. An excellent collection.

740   Taylor, Mark Kline. *Remembering Esperanza. A Cultural-Political Theology for North American Praxis.* Maryknoll, NY: Orbis Books, 1990.

Combines the author's own experiences as a youth in Guatemala with his reflections on how to apply the insights of liberation theology to a North American audience. The central focus of the oppression visited by, and on, North Americans is their spiritual and intellectual habit of abstraction, which allows both liberal optimism and conservative indifference to the sufferings of both their fellow citizens and the rest of the world. Here Taylor focuses on the particular and the singular to outline a path for our own liberation.

741 *Theology in the Americas.* New York: Theology in the Americas.

742 Vol. 1. *Towards a North American Theology of Liberation.* 1978.

Attempts to forge a new theology that grows out of North America's different social, ethnic, racial, economic and sexual realities, that incorporates North American religious traditions, and exemplifies a communal or collective process. Elements examined include truth and praxis, faith, and ideology. The document also hopes to confront the dominant theological mainstream with new possibilities.

743 Vol. 2. *A First World Response to a Third World Challenge.* 1978.

Includes the Dar es Salaam statement of Third World theologians: their challenge to the First World; and the response from the congregation of the church in Wheaton, Illinois, on the peculiar nature of Christianity in the United States, its strengths and weaknesses, especially concerning the plight of the poor and the poor of the world. This is, at root, a First-World response, on the grass-roots level, to emerging Third-World theologies.

Other volumes include:

744   3. *Theology and the Politics of Appalachian Women.*

745   4. *Black Theology Perspectives. Two Essays.*

746   5. *Latin America and the Puebla Conference.*

747   6. *The Workplace. New York Garment District.*

748   7. *Puebla 1979.*

749   8. *The Familial Economy of God.*

750   9. *In Defense of Native Lands. The Mohawk Nation at War.*

751   —. *Is Liberation Theology for North Americans? The Response of First World Churches to Third World Theologies.* 1978.

A collection of papers. Participants include Sergio Torres, Cone, Vine Deloria, Beverly Harrison, Gutiérrez, McAfee Brown, Ruether, Joe Holland, William Tabb, Robert Handy, Lee Cormie, Kathleen Schultz, Marie Augusta Neal, Edward J. Farrell, M. Douglas Meeks, and Jim Wallis. Themes include the challenges of Latin American, black, native American, Feminist theologies; analyses by sex, class and race, the legacy of the 1960s; and challenges to the U.S. economy; the Western theological tradition; and new alternatives for the church, including prophesy, the role of the poor, and the role of theology amid affluence.

752   Thistlethwaite, Susan Brooks, and Mary Potter Engel, eds. *Lift Every Voice. Constructing Christian Theology from the Underside.* San Francisco: Harper & Row, 1990.

      A sourcebook documenting the varieties of liberation theologies around the world

753   Unger, Linda, and Kathleen Schultz. *Seeds of a Peoples Church. Challenge and Promise from the Underside.* New York: Circus, 1981.

      Articles by Gutiérrez, Arroyo, Ruben Zamora, Cora Ferro, Robert Lopez, Cornel West, Margot Power and others on liberation themes, including the emergence of the poor in history, solidarity with the peoples of South Africa and Central America, work and the human role in God's creation, and building a people's church in North America.

754   U.S. Catholic Conference. *Statement on Central America.* Washington, DC: USCC, 1982.

      The bishops affirm the legacy of Vatican II, Medellin, Puebla, and the theology of liberation. They mourn the martyrdoms of Archbishop Oscar Romero and the four American churchwomen in El Salvador (See **642** to **647**) and confirm the special tie of U.S. Catholics to their brothers and sisters in Central America. The bishops refute U.S. government contentions about communist infiltration in the region and declare that the church there is neither naive nor complacent. The basic threat is from hunger, poverty, and political tyranny.

Base Christian Communities at Home

755   Berrigan, Daniel. *The Mission*. San Francisco: Harper & Row, 1986.

This is the "spin-off" text to the film; and it provides much of the theological background to the events and characters portrayed emblematically there. Much of the point of the film was the need for Christians to entrust the people themselves to become the subjects of their own salvation. Berrigan also reflects on the strengths of the base Christian communities that enable this.

756   Colonnese, Louis M., ed. *Conscientization for Liberation*. Washington, DC: Division for Latin America, United States Catholic Conference, 1971.

A collection of essays by Colonnese, Luis Ambroggio, Rafael Legaria, Cesar Aguiar, Gustavo Gutiérrez, Samuel Ruiz Garcia, Helen C. Volkmener, Paulo Freire, Julio de Santa Ana, Frank Church and others on the North American reception and perception of the changes in the Latin American church.

Topics include the sweeping cultural and political changes in Latin America, Latin American Catholicism and liberation theology, changes since Medellin, North American reactions to liberation theology, American Behaviorism and its "aseptic neutrality," and new North American policy for Latin America.

757   Kinsler, F. Ross, ed. *Ministry By the People. Theological Education by Extension*. Maryknoll, NY: Orbis Books, 1990.

Calls for a reorientation of theological education to outreach programs that empower ordinary laypeople to carry on a Christian ministry in their daily lives. Good contextual theory for base communities in a North American context.

758   McKenna, Megan, "Base Communities in North America." *Pax Christi* 12, 4 (1987): 18-19.

A review and brief analysis.

759   Nottingham, William J. *The Practice and Preaching of Liberation.* St. Louis, MO: CBP Press, 1986.

Jesus is the center and all of Christianity and its preaching. Today that church and preaching must face the fact of the oppression and suffering of millions in the Third World and our own relative prosperity. This is a book devoted to forming a preaching context and text that coveys the message of liberation to the First World.

Topics include the Bible and liberation, Jesus, preaching for conversion, local awareness and global awareness; and a practical guide for liberation preaching, including a selection of lectionary texts.

760   O'Halloran, James. *Living Cells. Developing Small Christian Communities.* Maryknoll, NY: Orbis Books, 1984.

This is a how-to-do-it book for a North American audience interested in experiencing the immediacy of the base Christian community.

761   Schipani, Daniel S. *Religious Education Encounters Liberation*. Birmingham, AL: Religious Education Press, 1988.

Facing the twin facts that there are now more Latin Americans living in the United States than in all of Central America, and that liberation theology has become a leading and well-established school of thought, Schipani seeks to apply the insights of the Latin American experience to the educational problems and realities of North America. The book consists of five chapters based around liberation themes – conscientization, liberation and creativity; prophetic and utopian vision; praxis; faith seeking understanding; and the oppressed and the base community – and then seeks to apply the insights of liberation theology to our own religious educational systems. Pages 6-7 contain an excellent bibliographical essay on liberation theology and religious eduction.

762   Walsh, John J. *Integral Justice. Changing People, Changing Structures*. Maryknoll, NY: Orbis Books, 1990.

A primer to the processes of conscienticizing North Americans to the role of the church in working for justice, first through educating ministers and then through leading parishioners to take on Christian commitments on their own.

763   Wentz, Frederick K. *Getting into the Act. Opening Up Lay Ministry in the Weekday World*. Nashville, TN: Abingdon Press, 1978.

Written in the context of the Carter presidency's call for a new moral equivalent of war in reversing America's role as "greedy Goliath" and in the face of Third World suffering and the energy crisis of the late 1970s. Attempts to take the insights of liberation theology and apply them to the life and actions of North Americans through emphasizing the role of the laity in the mission of the church.

Discusses our notions of liberation and freedom, the church as a liberated minority, the situation of Protestantism in contemporary America, the impact of liberation theology, the need for new, liberated lifestyles in the context of the needs of the world as a whole, and the need to establish what Helder Camara has called "Abrahamic minorities," living in the contemporary desert of North American culture; and more importantly, to unite these to bring about change.

764 Whitehead, Evelyn Eaton, and James D. Whitehead. *The Emerging Laity. Returning Leadership to the Community of Faith.* New York: Doubleday, 1986.

The recent emergence to leadership in the church by its laity is a fact and the context for these reflections on scriptural images of leadership and ministry, communities and power, communities and authority, new forms of leadership, personal and social empowerment, Jesus' witness to the realities of power, the authorization of power through scripture and Christian history, purification of power, the power of the weak and the strong, idolatries and prophesy against power. The basis for a liberating theology of praxis for North Americans.

The Northern Reactionaries

765   Berghoef, Gerard, and Lester DeKoster. *Liberation Theology. The Church's Future Shock – Explanation, Analysis, Critique, Alternative.* Grand Rapids, MI: Christian's Library Press, 1984.

Criticism from the Protestant evangelical view.

766   Bloesch, Donald G. *Faith and Its Counterfeits.* Downers Grove, IL: InterVarsity, 1981.

Not seen.

767   Eppstein, John. *The Cult of Revolution in the Church.* New Rochelle, NY: Arlington House, 1974.

A diatribe on behalf of established powers. While Eppstein regrettably dismisses the violence used by the state against other states as a sad reality of international life, condoned or allowed by Christian theology, and admits that revolution was a prime motive in Puritanism and other periods of the Christian past, he is most uncomfortable with a "theology of revolution" that he sees taking over current theological thought.

He cannot conceive of any revolution that takes place without violence – this book was written before the people's revolutions of the 1980s that overcame Marcos in the Philippines and most of the Communist regimes of Eastern Europe nonviolently – and accuses proponents of such revolution as deceiving themselves.

A theology of revolution is the invention, he contends, of Marxists and Marxist priests and of evolving communist world tactics from the 1950s to the 1970s. Having set up his terms of discussion in this manner, Eppstein concludes that the just-war limits of war, and of revolution, makes it impossible for revolution to be justified in a Christian context.

"However the question be posed, there cannot be any case for the attempt to overthrow the existing political and economic structure – meaning of course, that of states outside the Communist orbit – without regard to the real differences and distinctive circumstances of time and place; and all sweeping generalities break down under honest examination."

768   Ezcurra, Ana Maria. *The Neoconservative Offensive. U.S. Churches and the Ideological Struggle in Latin America.* Elice Higginbotham and Linda Unger, eds. New York: Circus, 1983.

On the general political struggle, and the church's political, not really theological, role in it.

769   —. *The Vatican and the Reagan Administration.* New York: Circus Publications, 1986.

Includes Pablo Richard's essay on the church of the poor in Nicaragua, Wayne Barrett's essay on John Cardinal O'Connor's back-room brand of church and secular politics on behalf of U.S. power and Reagan priorities, the U.S. crisis of confidence, the neoconservative entry into religious debate, their role in anti-Sandinista propaganda, and the Reagan administration and Vatican "confluences" on the ideological struggle in Latin America. Concludes with a reprint of Ratzinger's *Instruction on Certain Aspects* (see **123-124**).

770   Forrester, Duncan. *Theology and Politics*. New York: Basil Blackwell, 1988.

        Not seen.

771   Henry, Carl F. H. *God, Revelation and Authority. God Who Speaks and Shows*. Vol. 4. Waco, TX: Word, 1979.

        Under chapters 22, "New Man and the New Society"; 23, "Marxist Exegesis of the Bible"; and 25, "The Marxist Reconstruction of Man," Henry takes on the political theologies, theologians of hope, liberation theology and other worshippers of false gods. This is a massive work and obviously the result of much thought.

772   Kammer, Charles. *Ethics and Liberation. An Introduction*. Maryknoll, NY: Orbis Books, 1988.

        Approaches traditional Christian ethical teachings from the viewpoint of liberation theology to emphasize that our ethical systems and beliefs must be based on dogma and precepts that derive ultimately from *God* and not from human systems of practical law or convenience. Paradoxically – for traditional systems that is – the author also emphasizes that these ethics must be applied to all of human activity and creation and not simply to the "religious sphere."

773   Kirk, J. Andrew. *Liberation Theology. An Evangelical View from the Third World*. Atlanta, GA: John Knox, 1979.

Examines both the scriptural approach of liberation theology and its contextuality. Topics include
the historical background and origins, basic themes,
and methodology; some leading exponents, including
Gutiérrez, Segundo, Croatto, Miranda, and Assmann.

Kirk then examines these theologians' interpretation of key biblical texts, enters into a critical dialog,
and puts forth an alternative hermeneutic, placing
scripture and revelation, not praxis, as the starting
point, without returning to classic theological
methodology. Select bibliography.

774   —. *Theology Encounters Revolution.* Downers Grove, IL:
       InterVarsity Press, 1980.

Attempts to discover whether a "theology of
revolution," grown quite popular in the 1960s, is a
viable proposition at all. Examines the meanings of
revolution, their historical settings and today, Third
World theological reflections, an examination of
various revolutionary theologies today in Europe
(eastern and western), and North America, black theology and African theology, and liberation theology
in Latin America.

Appendixes examine the role of the World
Council of Churches and of violence. A final chapter
discusses the scriptural bases for revolution.

775   Klenicki, Leon. "The Theology of Liberation. A Latin
       American Jewish Exploration." *American Jewish
       Archives* 35 (April 1983): 27-39.

A negative appraisal.

776   Lefever, Ernest W. *Amsterdam to Nairobi. The World Council of Churches and the Third World.* Washington, DC: Ethics and Public Policy Center, 1979.

This is an exposé of the WCC, which as George Wills characterizes it, "is justly famous for both the intensity and the selectivity of its indignation." The power and importance of Third-World theologies and their threat to the American empire are given due weight in the amount of neo-conservative attention devoted to debunking liberation theology and church activism around the world. The book is no exception.

Here are Lefever and Wills passing judgment on the work of theologians around the world, declaiming categorically about what Christianity is and is not. They do not like the brand proposed by the WCC. Under the heading "The Triumph of liberation Theology: 1969-1979" are grouped campaigns to end racism, the role of violence, the Peoples Republic of China, the Nairobi assembly of 1975, and virulent attacks on the West as represented by transnational corporation and development. Other topics include Marxist links, confusion of ends and means, and true separation of church and state.

777   — . *Nairobi to Vancouver. The World Council of Churches and the World, 1975-87.* Lanham, MD: University Press of America, 1987.

The exposé continues, much like the theological version of "Where in the World Is Carmen Sandiego?" This time Lefever tracks the culprits of the WCC to its activities against NATO's nuclear first-strike policy, its role in Central America and the rise of the "people's church" and the Sandinistas, in Afghanistan, South Africa, East Asia and the Pacific, its criticism of capitalism and accommodation in the Soviet Union. Overall Lefever sees a nefarious double standard that backs revolution all around the world as liberation theology rises in triumph. Lefever's bibliography is curious: it contains books on politics and economics alone, with nothing of theology or religion.

778   McCann, Dennis. *Christian Realism and Liberation Theology. Practical Theologies in Creative Conflict.* Maryknoll, NY: Orbis Books, 1981.

This critique of theology that stems from experience and suffering is decidedly in the tradition of Niebuhr's "Christian realism." That "realism," both cozily academic and reactionary at this date, here exposes its discomfort and dislike of realities of a different sort. It is basically suspicious of the role of basic Christian communities and of individual Christians taking action that can be characterized as "political."

McCann asserts that the Christian must leave the problems of the world to political solutions worked out by secular agents. Briefly reviews the leading liberation theologians, asserting that Gutiérrez, for example, has stretched Medellin's option for the poor as a full endorsement of his position, that Segundo rejects "pacifism" as contributing to the status quo and calls for a liberating violence whose religious basis is illusionary, and that Segundo says the manipulation of the masses by a revolutionary elite dedicated to liberation is justified, and that he believes "the end justifies the means."

779   McElevaney, William K. *Good News is Bad News is Good News.* Maryknoll, NY: Orbis Books, 1980.

Critique of liberation theology and its biblical readings from the viewpoint of a comfortable, middle-class American.

780   McGovern, Arthur F. *Liberation Theology and Its Critics. Towards an Assessment.* Maryknoll, NY: Orbis Books, 1990.

Here is an attempt to move beyond ideology and to assess both liberation theology and northern reactions with fairness. Focuses on the most disputed aspects of the theology for a North American, capitalist-bred audience: the relationship between a theology and a [different] economic system, that is, in American theologians' attempts to use Marxist socio-economic methods of analysis to define the base of experience for their peoples and God's working in the world.
Reviews the history of the theological movement and of its major critics and attackers, as well as the on-the-ground praxis of this theology among base Christian communities.

781   —. *Marxism. An American Christian Perspective.* Maryknoll, NY: Orbis Books, 1980.

Part 1 offers a thorough examination of Marx the man, his background, historical context and thought, Marxism since Marx, and the Church's reactions, ranging from the anathemas of papal encyclicals to the church councils of the 1970s. Part 2 traces the impact of Marxism on Christian social thought and action, including the critique of capitalism in the Third World and a survey of liberation theology on pages 172-209. This part concludes with a section on the Chilean experience in the 1970s. Part 3 discusses objections to Marxism in key areas, such as its atheism and materialism, notions of property, class struggle and violence. The book concludes with personal reflections on the situation in the U.S.

782 Nash, Ronald H., ed. *Liberation Theology.* Milford, MI: Mott Media, 1984; Grand Rapids, MI: W.B. Eerdmans, 1988.

This collection of all white men aims its considerable prowess at liberation theology in its Latin American form. Presents essays by Harold O. J. Brown, Michael Novak, Nash, James V. Schall, S.J., Clark H. Pinnock, Edward Norman, Robert C. Walton, Carl F. H. Henry, Dale Vree, and Richard John Neuhaus.

Nash sums up the theme of this hostile collection thus: "liberation theology in view in this book is the movement among Latin American Catholics and Protestants that seeks radical changes in the political and economic institutions of that region along Marxist lines. But of course Europe also has its stock of Christian theologians who believe that a hybrid social theology resulting from a cross between Christianity and Marxism is both desirable and necessary. And as a growing number of North American theologians translate their theoretical displeasure and distrust of capitalism into action, the language and literature of liberation theology becomes increasingly more prominent."

783   —. *Social Justice and the Christian Church.* Milford, MI: Mott Media, 1983.

Not seen.

784   Nessan, Craig L. *Orthopraxis or Heresy? The North American Theological Response to Latin American Liberation Theology.* Atlanta, GA: Scholar's Press, 1989.

This is an excellent survey of the Northern reaction. First examines Latin American liberation theology as a formal theology and in its context of poverty and oppression. Part 2 then examines some of the key responses from North America, including those of Shaull, Cone, Herzog, McAfee Brown, Radford Ruether, Sider, Wallis, and Krass, and the theology in the Americas group. It then samples certain criticisms, both from sympathetic and unsympathetic writers. The latter include Novak and Benne, Sanders and McCann, Neuhaus and Braaten, Wagner, Henry, Bloesch; and Migliore, Hodgson, Cobb, Delwin Brown and Ogden.

Part 3 then analyzes the theological "impasse" at present, the issues of the polarization, including Marxist analysis, the defense of democratic capitalism and Christian realism and other critiques, and the limitations of Latin American liberation theology. These include its philosophical basis, its methodology, its anthropology, and concept of liberation. The author concludes with a survey of the strengths of the theology, including its roots in Christian tradition, its understanding of Latin America, and the insufficiency of traditional academic theology. Excellent bibliography.

785   Neuhaus, Richard John. *The Catholic Moment.* San
        Francisco: Harper & Row, 1990.

        A Lutheran theologian converted to high
        Catholicism, Neuhaus sees the "Catholic Moment" as
        the bright light being shed by John Paul II's and
        Cardinal Ratzinger's attack on liberation theology
        and its alleged attempt to equate political liberation
        with salvation. Yet he sees a chastened version as a
        sign of renewed vigor for the church.

786   Norman, Edward. *Christianity and the World Order.*
        New York: Oxford University Press, 1979.

        Describes the change in Christianity in the
        preceding two decades through "politicization," so
        that its thrust is no longer on metaphysics or internal
        spirituality, but on social and political change. In
        doing so the churches have lost their moral and
        religious influence, tagging along with the definitions
        of world problems created by secular thinkers and
        institutions. Examines the process of a political
        Christianity, the change of the clergy, the new
        imperialism caused by this politicization, and the
        social discredit this has caused. The author concludes
        with a call to regain the "indwelling Christ" of the
        spirit that transcends the cause of the moment.

787   Novak, Michael. *Freedom with Justice. Catholic Social
        Thought and Liberal Institutions.* San Francisco:
        Harper & Row, 1984.

        A thoughtful, if ideologically rightist, survey of
        Catholic social thought, beginning with definitions,
        moving on to various categories, including economic

life, various utopianisms, and the U.S. bishops and new definitions of social and economic sin. Novak then reviews the development of Catholic social thought from 1848 to 1982, concluding with what he terms John Paul II's "Creation Theology," which is actually his theology of work as an alternative to liberation theology. Part 3 outlines some directions of future Catholic social thought.

788   —. *Liberation South, Liberation North.* Washington, DC: American Enterprise Institute, 1981.

Essays by Segundo, Ralph Lerner, Joseph Ramos, Sergio Molina, Sebastian Piñera, and Roger W. Fontaine on the capitalist-socialist conflict, the Anglo-American model, Gustavo Gutiérrez' theology, poverty and reform in Latin America, and the paths toward liberation.

789   —. *The Spirit of Democratic Capitalism.* New York: Simon & Schuster, 1982, esp. pp. 272-314.

Much of the criticisms of the Latin American liberation theologians of capitalist development are based on a faulty understanding of economics and the role of international capital. While dependency certainly has its shortcomings, this is not the fault of the wealthy industrialized nations, which have managed to provide a good life for the overwhelming majority of their peoples. The structural problems of Latin America are very much the result of their own cultural heritage and history of development. The models of democratic capitalism developed by the industrialized world are still valid tools for helping all the world's impoverished peoples.

790   —. *Will It Liberate? Questions About Liberation
       Theology.* New York: Paulist Press, 1986.

Probably the most important and well argued of
the Northern reactionaries, Novak is open-minded,
even handed, and truly concerned with the issues of
liberation, if not with theological salvation. Both
North and South America have their own brands of
liberation theology, he contends: in the South it is
found in books, in the North in institutions, the basic
freedoms of our lives, our ability to overcome the
oppressions of poverty, class, race; to forge a new life
and be the masters of our own destinies.

Novak is not being blind to the theological issues
of liberation theology, nor to the very real contributions of that theology to illuminating the structures of
oppression in Latin America. He clearly recognizes
the fact that fundamental structures must be altered
in Latin America before the freedoms that the Latin
Americans crave, and that North Americans (or the
white, male, and prosperous ones) enjoy. It is the
means of achieving this in which he differs from his
colleagues in the South.

Novak contends that in the intellectual circles of
both South and North it is fashionable to bash the
North American system, and those precise elements
that make for stable, sustained economic, social and
political freedom; and that now the time has come to
defend the basic truths of Americanism and our own
brand of "liberation theology."

While one cannot fault this approach for its
intent, one wonders whether Novak has not taken to
heart much of the criticisms of the liberation
theologians of precisely the kind of "civil religion"
that he preaches, and whether he does not ignore the

very different contexts of the two forms of liberation – and the intrinsic nature of the liberation -- that the Latin and North Americans discuss. For Novak a material freedom seems to be the liberation he holds high, while at the same time condemning what he contends is Latin America's flirtation with materialistic forms of progress, most importantly Marxism.

While he sees much to admire, the final question he puts to the Latin Americans is itself the essence of North American materialistic pragmatism: "will it liberate?" i.e., don't give me theory: what is the bottom line? He faults the theologians for not having the socio-economic vision of economists or political scientists. At the same time, much of Novak's and his colleagues' strongest argument in the attack on liberation theology comes when they condemn American theologians, North or South, whenever they *do* discuss anything *but* theology.

Novak is even-handed in his respect for the Latin American theologians and admits openly that neither liberation nor liberalism will bring about the kingdom of God, but that both are essays that must be debated, but openly and with the view that the North has created the material conditions for true liberation. While open to the future proof of a socialism that the Latin Americans prophesy, Novak clings to tested results. In the end Novak's theology is a political theology of the North American status quo, whose reality is not as bright as he contends, nor as dark as he contends Latin American critics make it. Ultimately one wonders whether he and the Latin American theologians are really talking on two separate planes of reality, about two very separate series of questions and problems.

Topics discussed in detail include the Latin American attack on the North, the ultimate efficacy of their social model, the chief tenets of their attack, the pope and liberation theology, "creation theology" (that is, the papal counter theology of work), Latin American statistical profiles, basic concepts of liberation theology (Novak's choice, the historian-ethicist Dussel as his model over a careful reading of Gutiérrez, Segundo, or Boff, is problematic), the meaning of dependency and the poor, interpretations of "socialism" by Cubans, Latin American intellectuals, Segundo, Gutiérrez and political thinkers; the workings of socialism in Latin America, a liberal North American "constitution" (or catechism), and an analysis of Ratzinger's *Instruction*. Novak includes a series of appendixes: anecdotes on the progress of freedom in Latin America.

791 —, ed. *Capitalism and Socialism. A Theological Inquiry.* Washington, DC: American Enterprise Institute, 1979.

While the subtitle reads "A Theological Inquiry," none of the participants – Irving Kristol, Seymour Martin Lipset, Peter Berger, Novak, Ben Wattenberg, or Penn Kemble – are particularly known for their theological work. This is, instead, an early manifesto of the neo-cons. The basic message is that theologians and clergy should stick to "religion" and leave "politics" to ideologs, such as the authors included here. They might have heeded their own advice and left theology to the theologians.

792   —. *Liberation Theology and the Liberal Society.*
        Washington, DC: American Enterprise Institute,
        1987.

        A collection of addresses devoted to the dialog
        between Latin American and North American forms of
        liberation and liberalism.   Contributors include
        Novak, William P. Glase, Hugo Assmann, George
        Weigal, Peter Berger, Arthur McGovern, Arturo
        Fontaine, Mark Alcoff, and others on democracy and
        the debt crisis in Latin America, underdevelopment,
        dependency theory, the systematics of liberation the-
        ologians, and the effects on economic growth of Latin
        American political systems.

793   Ogden, Schubert M. *Faith and Freedom. Toward a
        Theology of Liberation.* Nashville, TN: Abingdon
        Press, 1979.

        This is an attempt to meet the challenge of
        liberation theology by an analysis of what Ogden
        considers the four major failings of these theologies.
        These are: that they are not theology but witness or
        ideology; that they are anthropocentric, dealing with
        God's meaning for us, and not the true nature of God;
        that they confuse secular liberation with theological
        salvation; and that they too narrowly focus on one
        form of bondage: of race, sex, economy, etc., without
        taking into account the entire experience and meaning
        of true religious emancipation.

794   Rand Corporation. *Latin American Institutional
        Development. The Changing Catholic Church.
        (Memorandum RM-6136-DOS).* Luigi Einaudi,
        Richard Maullin, Alfred Sepan, and Michael

Fleet, eds. Santa Monica, CA: Rand Corporation, 1969.

Examines the new move in the church of Latin America to separate itself from the state in order to avoid identification with the status quo and to exercise its "prophetic mission" to criticize living conditions and government programs that do not meet moral criteria for social justice.

795   *Rockefeller Report on the Americas.* Chicago: Quadrangle Books, 1969.

The emerging left and the religious left are among the chief threats to "development" in the region. Both need careful monitoring and control.

796   Schall, James V., S.J. ed. *Liberation Theology in Latin America.* San Francisco: Ignatius Press, 1982.

Schall immediately links liberation theology to secret arms caches, Molotov cocktails, friends of Fidel Castro, Camilo Torres hiding out in the jungle. He runs with his themes from there. In Latin America political problems are still mistaken for religious ones; Marxism has got its insidious hold on complacent intellectuals; while good old Uncle Sam is unjustly blamed for every failing of that region and society.

Though it is sometimes hard to discern his true feelings and beliefs under his breezy *Time* magazine tone, to Schall, liberation theology is born out of a Latin inferiority complex: a desire to change good old Catholicism because it is blamed for too much of the region's backwardness. What is their solution to plop

Latin America onto world center stage? Liberation theology, a perfect blend of South American flavor with Germanic terminology, dedicated to rewriting all the "major elements and themes of Christianity." Marx's hold on the thinkers there will surely bring about a neo-Constantinianism as action supersedes thought and familiar biblical phrases are used over and over again for partisan purposes.

Schall follows this introduction with a discussion of where such theologies lead. After a breezy discourse on heresy in Christian history we are treated to a parade of no-longer à la mode theologies, including existentialism, the "death of God," the secular city, small is beautiful, and "self-styled theologies of hope." The whole trendy crowd is dismissed before we come to the latest fashion statement, a blend of Fidel, political and revolutionary theology and the ilk. Need one go on?

Schall then invites his friends to lend a bash; the "theological" cast includes Jeanne Kirkpatrick, editorials in *Civiltà Cattolica*, Michael Novak, Roger Heckel, and John Paul II in ample doses. Of the thousands of books and articles written by and about liberation theologians, Schall includes a bibliography of fifteen items, rather skewed to lead the reader to the polemical side.

797   Wagner, C. Peter. *Latin American Theology. Radical or Evangelical?* Grand Rapids, MI: W.B. Eerdmans, 1970.

Not seen.

The Sanctuary Movement

798   Bau, Ignatius. *This Ground Is Holy. Christian Sanctuary and Central American Refugees.* New York: Paulist Press, 1985.

This is a thorough and excellent examination of the issue of sanctuary. Topics include the development of the Sanctuary Movement, U.S. immigration law on refugees and its history, the federal prosecutions of sanctuary workers, and the legal implications of the movement itself. Bau then examines the ancient tradition of sanctuary in Judeo-Christian and Greco-Roman history, and the law of sanctuary in England from the Anglo-Saxon to Renaissance periods. He next studies the practice in U.S. history from the colonial era, through the underground railroad of the Civil War era to the Vietnam War period. A final chapter discusses the theological nature of the Sanctuary movement and its place within liberation theology.

Excellent bibliographies on the history of sanctuary, legal articles on the Sanctuary Movement and cases, *New York Times* reports and other related topics.

799   Chicago Religious Task Force on Central America. *Sanctuary. A Justice Ministry.* Chicago: Chicago Religious Task Force on Central America, 1983.

Not seen.

800   Corbett, Jim. *The Sanctuary Church*. Wallingford, PA:
       Pendle Hill, 1986.

       This pamphlet is less about the movement than
       about the theological and historical traditions of
       sanctuary and then about the conflict between the
       post-Constantinian church and the U.S. legal system.

801   Crittenden, Ann, *Sanctuary. A Story of American
       Conscience and the Law in Collision*. New York:
       Weidenfeld & Nicolson, 1988.

       A well annotated and indexed account of the
       movement, the undercover operation, arrest, trial and
       convictions.

802   Davidson, Miriam, *Convictions of the Heart. Jim Corbett
       and the Sanctuary Movement*. Tucson, AZ:
       University of Arizona Press, 1988.

       A dramatically told story of the Quaker witness
       of the Corbetts in their work for the Sanctuary
       movement, the trials and convictions of the Sanctuary
       workers, and the spread of the movement as a
       practice of solidarity with the oppressed of Central
       America.

803   Golden, Renny, and Michael McConnell. *Sanctuary:
       The New Underground Railroad*. Chicago: Guild
       Books; Maryknoll, NY: Orbis Books, 1986.

       The best introduction and survey available.

804   Lernoux, Penny. *People of God.* (See **120**).

Pages 258-79 give a concise summary of the movement and a discussion of its broader significance in the context of liberation and in the struggle to implement the call of Vatican II for Catholics to involve their religious commitments to the world at large.

805   Loder, Ted. *No One But Us. Personal Reflections on Public Sanctuary.* San Diego, CA: Lura Media, 1986.

On the decision of the First United Methodist Church of Germantown, PA to offer Sanctuary.

806   MacEoin, Gary, ed. *Sanctuary. A Resource Guide for Understanding and Participating in the Central American Refugees' Struggle.* San Francisco: Harper & Row, 1985.

Originally a project of the Tucson Ecumenical Council, this is a collection of essays grouped around certain themes: historical precedent and overview; the theological basis and biblical perspectives; the situation in Central America; ethical, legal and human-rights issues; the words of the refugees themselves; and the challenge to the North American conscience that the movement entails. Contributors include Elie Wiesel, MacEoin, Davie Napier, Elsa Tamez, Robert McAfee Brown, Richard Shaull, Renny Golden, Yvonne Dilling, Marshall Meyer, Marta Benavides, Jim Wallis, Jim Corbett and others.

807   McDaniel, Judith. *Sanctuary. A Journey.* Ithaca, NY: Firebrand Books, 1987.

This is a very personal collection of poetry, brief reminiscences, and essays that reflect the author's experience as a Witness for Peace and hostage of the Contras in Nicaragua, in the Seneca Peace Camp, and in work with the Sanctuary Movement. It brings these all together into the single reality of peace and human liberation.

808   *The Sanctuary Movement.* Oakland, CA: Data Center, 1985.

Not seen.

809   Simpson, Dick, and Clinton Stockwell. *The Struggle for Peace, Justice, Sanctuary.* Chicago: Institute on the Church in Urban-Industrial Society, 1985.

Not seen.

810   Tomsho, Robert. *The American Sanctuary Movement.* Austin, TX: Texas Monthly Press, 1987.

A survey of the movement that includes accounts of individual flight, the response of the Reagan administration, the crackdown on the movement, the informants, and the State Department's double standards.

First Americans: Native American and Hispanic Theology

811   Acuña, Rodolfo. *Occupied America. The Chicano's Struggle Toward Liberation.* 3d ed. San Francisco: Harper & Row, 1988.

A history from earliest times to the present. Good background, with bibliography.

812   Allen, Paula Gunn. *The Sacred Hoop. Recovering the Feminine in American Indian Traditions.* Boston: Beacon Press, 1986.

Topics include regaining lost gynocratic heritage, women realizing their own strength through their spiritual traditions, remythologizing as a means toward self-definition, recapturing the heart and soul of American Indian literature, ceremony, and the spiritual foundations of native American poetry.

A final section deals with the political and social struggle of native American women, recasting the history of the white conquest and of the Indian tradition, academic interpretations, the lesbian in American Indian culture and spirituality. Contains a good select bibliography by topic.

813   Arroyo, Antonio M., ed. *Prophets Denied Honor. An Anthology on the Hispanic Church in the United States.* Maryknoll, NY: Orbis Books, 1980.

This is a large collection of texts on Hispanic Christians in the U.S. and in Latin America. It includes texts on the historical development, on Mexican and Puerto-Rican intellectual traditions, on the formation of a Hispanic church, and the meanings of liberation for the Hispanic church. Authors include Virgilio Elizondo, Octavio Paz, Clara Lair, Baltasar Carrero, Cesar Chavez, Piri Thomas, Patricio Flores, Juan Hurtado, Ada Maria Isasi Diaz, and others. Excellent bibliography.

814   Brant, Beth. *A Gathering of Spirit. Writing and Art by North American Indian Women.* Rockland, ME: Sinister Wisdom, 1984.

See Carson (**991**), item 245.

815   Day, Mark. *Forty Acres. Cesar Chavez and the Farm Workers.* New York: Praeger, 1971.

A review of the movement and of its personalities.

816   Deloria, Vine. *God Is Red.* New York: Grosset & Dunlop, 1973; Dell, 1983.

Traces the native American movement in the U.S., then traces their religion on a number of themes: time and space, creation, history, death, human personality, the group, the impact of Christianity and contemporary American culture, tribal religions, the aboriginal world and Christianity, and Indian religion today. Throughout Deloria stresses that native American religion is a foundation for self-identity, and the liberation of all native Americans since the sacred is interwoven inextricably with the fabric of everyday life.

817   Elizondo, Virgilio. *Christianity and Culture. A n Introduction to Pastoral Theology and Ministry for the Bicultural Community.* Huntington, IN: Sunday Visitor, 1975.

This is a theology for the Chicano community of North America. It surveys the changes of the modern world: mechanization, urbanization, secularization, democratization, economic enslavement. It then reviews the development of the Catholic church and the role of Vatican II. Elizondo next examines pastoral theology in light of the council; the biblical tradition in both Old and New Testaments; and the meaning of mission in the bicultural community. This book provides much of the theological background for a base Christian movement in North America.

818   —. *The Future Is Mestizo. Life Where Culture Meets.* Oak Park, IL: Meyer Stone Books, 1988.

A liberationist interpretation of the Mexican American experience: from disruption, alienation and marginalization in a society of the mainstream, toward a recognition of the strengths of their own culture, and thus toward an encounter with North American culture on equal terms. The result of this enpowerment and activism is the realization of a new fellowship both on the part of the "mainstream" and on the part of those formerly excluded. "Universal Mestizaje" is the result, a recognition of the common power of people to confront structures of domination and empty technologies and to create a new culture that recognizes diversity and difference and in so doing creates a newly liberated society, not imperial or dominating, and a new stage in human evolution.

819   —. *Galilean Journey. The Mexican-American Promise.* Maryknoll, NY: Orbis Books, 1983.

The Chicanos of the Southwest, while seen as a marginalized minority amid the boom of the sun belt, have actually impressed the culture of both the region and the entire nation with a profound sense of the unity of the religious and the secular life. This enpowerment of rootedness and of identity has given them the strength to begin to wage the struggle for political and economic enpowerment that will enrich not only their own culture but that of the entire nation, of which they remind us, they are among the very first.

820   Guerrero, Andrés Gonzales. *A Chicano Theology.* Maryknoll, NY: Orbis Books, 1987.

Discusses the key elements of a Mexican-American theological experience and understanding, including the role of the Virgin Mary in spirituality and in understanding the role of the divine in human affairs.

821   Hall, Douglas John. *Lighten Our Darkness. Toward an Indigenous Theology of the Cross.* Philadelphia: Westminster Press, 1976.

Not seen.

822   Hoffman, Pat; foreword by Cesar Chavez. *Ministry of the Dispossessed.* Los Angeles, CA: Wallace Press, 1987.

Not seen.

823   Jenkins, J. Craig. *The Politics of Insurgency. The Farm Worker Movement in the 1960s.* New York: Columbia University Press, 1985.

A political history of the movement. Excellent bibliography.

824   Levy, Jacques E. *Cesar Chavez. Autobiography of La Causa.* New York: W.W. Norton, 1975.

A biography of the man and the United Farm Workers to 1975. Throughout whenever Chavez does reflect on the struggle and its nature, he is explicit about its fundamentally Christian outlook to justice.

825   Matthiessen, Peter. *Sal Si Puedes. Cesar Chavez and the New American Revolution.* New York: Random House, 1970.

A personal, firsthand account of the United Farm Workers and of Cesar Chavez under the attack of the Nixon administration.

826   Rendon, Armando B. *Chicano Manifesto. The History and Aspirations of the Second Largest Minority in America.* New York: Macmillan, 1971.

Not seen.

827   Sandoval, Moises. *On the Move. A History of the Hispanic Church in North America.* Maryknoll, NY: Orbis Books, 1990.

The Commission on Church History of Latin America is undertaking a history of every church in Latin America on the eve of the 500th anniversary of Columbus' voyage. This is the first volume of that series. Traces the origins and development of the Hispanic church and culture in North America and illustrates its growth from a subdued, marginalized, and ignored "minority" element to a new force that is awakening to its own heritage, power, and theological identity. This is an excellent introduction to

"Chicano theology" and necessary background to understanding the dynamics of this North American variety of liberation theology.

828   Starkloff, Carl F. *The People of the Center. American Indian Religion and Christianity.* New York: Seabury Press, 1974.

A good introduction to the fundamental convergences and many of the differences between the native American and Christian perceptions of the universe, humanity, and one's ethical and spiritual place in it.

829   Theology in the Americas. *Position Paper of the Native American Project. Detroit II.* Detroit, MI: Theology in the Americas, 1980.

Topics include the identity of native peoples and Christianity perceived through native American eyes. Central to these are the dichotomy between native American reverence for the earth as divine and European practice. Inherent in this dichotomy is the stark contrast between Christian belief and Christians' practice and structures.

A part of the sad past of Christian European and native American confrontation has been structures — schools, church, government, economic and social — that have attempted to eradicate the unique identity of the native Americans and their belief systems, on creation, the earth and humanity's relationship to it, which are now finally coming into their own and winning converts from Christianity.

Black Theology

830   Barrett, Leonard E. *Soul-Force. African Heritage in Afro-American Religion.* Garden City, NY: Doubleday-Anchor, 1974.

See Evans (665), item 335.

831   Braxton, Edward K. *The Wisdom Community.* New York: Paulist Press, 1980.

Not seen.

832   Brown, Hubert L. *Black and Mennonite. A Search for Identity.* Scottsdale, PA: Herald Press, 1976.

Discusses both the ironic place of an African-American in a staunch bastion of European Christianity and the role of that African-American to recall the Mennonite tradition back to its rejection of hierarchy, its claim to the equality of all humans; and the author's call for the whites to abandon their own ghetto to move in the world of blacks as blacks must move in the world of whites. Also discusses black theology and Anabaptism. Brief bibliography on black theology.

833   Bruce, Calvin E., and William R. Jones, eds. *Black Theology II. Essays on the Formation and Outreach of Contemporary Black Theology.* Lewisburg, PA: Bucknell University Press, 1978.

See Evans (665), item 018.

834   Cannon, Kate G. *Black Womanist Ethics.* Atlanta, GA:
        Scholar's Press, 1988.

        "Womanist" is a term adopted by many black
        women writers to make a clear distinction with
        "feminist," which many of them view as the class
        expression of white, upper-middle professionals who
        really do not understand many aspects of oppression.
        Seeks to show how black women, who suffer the
        triple oppression of sex and race, as well as of eco-
        nomic oppression, can create a moral order based on
        their practical experience, not on a priori rules set by
        a white, male society and religious tradition.
        Examines the historical situation of black women,
        their rise from slavery to creating themselves as
        their own moral agents in the modern world. The
        author also examines black women's literature as a
        source for this moral agency, using the life of Zora
        Neale Hurston as an example; and interprets the
        theology of Howard Thurman and Martin Luther
        King, Jr. as foundations for a black theology of libera-
        tion. Includes a good bibliography.

835   Cleage, Albert B., Jr. *Black Christian Nationalism.*
        New Directions for the Black Church. New York:
        William Morrow, 1972.

        See Evans (665), item

836   —. *The Black Messiah.* New York: Sheed & Ward,
        1969.

        See Evans (665), item 032.

837   Cone, Cecil Wayne. *The Identity Crisis in Black*
        Theology. Nashville, TN: Abingdon Press, 1975.

See Evans (665), item 035.

James H. Cone

838   Cone, James H., "Black Theology and African Theology. Considerations for Dialogue, Critique, and Integration." See **918**, pp. 463-76.

The basis of both theologies is the liberation theme in Exodus and the New Testament theme of Christ as liberator found in Galatians 5:1.

839   —. *Black Theology and Black Power.* 20th Anniversary ed. San Francisco: Harper & Row, 1989.

See Evans (665), item 071.

840   —. *A Black Theology of Liberation.* Philadelphia: Lippincott, 1970; 2d ed., Maryknoll, NY: Orbis Books, 1986; 20th Anniversary ed., Maryknoll, NY: Orbis Books, 1990.

As the theology of liberation was developing in Latin America, North American black theologians led by James Cone began to develop a parallel methodology and insight into the position of blacks in the U.S. Written in the spirit of the black power movement, which saw the radical empowerment of blacks as the only way to their salvation on an equal footing with the dominant society and its methods of oppression, Cone's work casts a critical eye on white Christianity. It questions the entire notion of a "white" God and instead calls for a theology of blackness. God is the God of liberation: the God of Exodus, the God of the prophets who liberates his people from slavery: not a God of missionaries who teach meekness and the acceptance of one's lot.

Cone's epistemological break with traditional white, and academic, theology was based upon the experience of the black people: dehumanization, oppression and marginalization. So long as oppression and marginalization is directed against blacks, God is a black. So long as Jesus is the suffering God, he suffers in the black ghettos, so long as he sides with the powerless, speaking of him is black theology.

Cone has been criticized widely for being too tied to the original European roots of the academic theology that he here attacks, and for not sufficiently taking into account the history of the black church in America as the cradle of black liberation and black culture for preserving the African roots of much of black American spirituality. Yet his analysis was revolutionary and laid the foundation for a truly genuine North American theology of liberation.

841   — . *For My People. Black Theology and the Black Church.* Maryknoll, NY: Orbis Books, 1984.

Black theology was often criticized for the same shortcomings that many perceived in the black power movement, the replacement of one power elite with another at the expense of other marginalized groups: most especially women. In this book Cone surveys the history of black theology and addresses the need for black theologians to speak to all the oppressed and marginalized – including women, the poor of whatever race, and those of the Third World – with an equal voice and compassion. His work thus demonstrates the tendency among all theologies of liberation to seek out the common ground and to recognize the will toward power and domination in all of us. See Evans **(665)**, item 357.

842   —. *God of the Oppressed.* New York: Seabury Press, 1975.

See Evans **(665)**, item 056.

843   —. *My Soul Looks Back.* Nashville: Abingdon, 1982.

An intellectual autobiography.

844   —. *Speaking the Truth. Ecumenism, Liberation and Black Theology.* Grand Rapids, MI: W.B. Eerdmans, 1986.

A collection of essays written between 1975 and 1985 on two major themes: black theology as a theology of liberation; and black theology and its impact on the black church. Cone discusses Christian theology as an expression of God's liberation of the poor, black worship as an expression of this process, faith and praxis, relations with the American Catholic church, and the issue of violence.

In Part 2 Cone surveys the history of black religious thought, the nature of the church, worship, and the role of ecumenism in the liberation struggle. He concludes with a perspective on the situation in South Africa.

*

845   Cronon, Edmund D. *Black Moses.* Madison WI:
         University of Wisconsin Press, 1964.

         The figure of Moses as the liberator who leads
         his people out of captivity in Egypt is central to all
         liberation theologies; and it has been central to black
         religious consciousness in the New World from the
         start. An important formulation of the underpinnings
         of black theology.

846   Dodson, Jualynne, ed. *Papers Presented to the Tenth
         Anniversary Convocation of the Black Theology
         Project.* New York: Black Theology Project, 1988.

         Collected essays by leading black theologians on
         the state of black theology now, its changes over the
         last two decades and the challenges still faced.

847   Dubois, W. E. B. *The Souls of Black Folk.* Reprint ed.
         New York: Dodd, Mead, 1967; New York: Penguin
         Books, 1989.

         Dubois' work, first published in 1903, had a
         profound impact. For the first time a black thinker
         spoke about the black in North America as the
         master of his or her own fate: the subject of history
         who could make a contribution to American life and
         whose experience of life affected his or her experi-
         ence of God.

848   Evans, Anthony Tyrone. *Black Theology and the Black
         Experience. A Biblical Analysis of Black Theology.*
         Dallas, TX: Black Evangelical Enterprise, 1977.

         Not seen.

849   Felder, Cain Hope. *Troubling Biblical Waters. Race, Class, and Family.* Maryknoll, NY: Orbis Books, 1989.

        Not seen.

850   Gardiner, James J., and J. Deotis Roberts, Sr. *Quest for a Black Theology.* Philadelphia: Pilgrim Press, 1971.

        See Evans (665), item 199.

851   Harrison, Bob, and Jim Montgomery. *When God Was Black.* Grand Rapids, MI: Zondervan, 1971.

        Not seen.

852   Healey, Joseph G. *The Fifth Gospel. The Experience of Black Christian Values.* Maryknoll, NY: Orbis Books, 1981.

        The praxis of missionary work in Tanzania opened new insights into the meaning of the Gospels upon a return to pastoral work in Detroit. Bridges the gap between black American and African theologies.

853   Hodgson, Peter Craft. *Children of Freedom. Black Liberation in Christian Perspective.* Philadelphia: Fortress Press, 1974.

        See Evans (665), item 108.

854   —. *New Birth of Freedom. A Theology of Bondage and Liberation.* Philadelphia: Fortress Press, 1976.

This is a fascinating look at all the forms of freedom and liberation, of bondage and oppression from religious, social, economic, psychiatric, points of view. Topics include the vision of freedom in America, various forms of freedom, theological meanings of freedom; forms of bondage, sin and oppression; the role of Christ as liberator, the gospel of liberation; and the dialectics of freedom in history. The author concludes with a examination of the symbolism of freedom in our understanding of faith, love, life, and hope.

855   Hopkins, Dwight N. *Black Theology USA and South Africa. Politics, Culture, and Liberation.* Maryknoll, NY: Orbis Books, 1990.

        See **268**.

856   Jackson, Giovanna R. *Afro-American Religion and Church and Race Relations.* Bloomington, IN: Indiana University Libraries, 1969.

        Not seen.

857   Johnson, Joseph A. *Proclamation Theology.* Shreveport, LA: Fourth Episcopal District Press, 1977.

        See Evans (**665**), item 177.

858   Jones, Major J. *Black Awareness. A Theology of Hope.* Nashville, TN: Abingdon Press, 1971.

        See Evans (**665**), item 123.

859   —. *Christian Ethics for Black Theology.* Nashville, TN: Abingdon Press, 1974.

See Evans (**665**), item 122.

860   — . *The Color of God. The Concept of God in Afro-American Thought.* Macon, GA: Mercer, 1987.

This is an attempt to explore the rich insights that black theology can give to Christianity as a whole. Topics include a historical study of black theology, its African roots, hermeneutics of an African-American theology, theodicy and God's moral character, Jesus Christ and the humanity of God, and God's continuing presence among us.

861   Jones, William A. *God in the Ghetto.* Elgin, IL: Progressive National Baptist Publishing House, 1979.

Not seen.

862   Jones, William R. *Is God a White Racist? A Preamble to Black Theology.* Garden City, NY: Anchor Books, 1973.

See Evans (**665**), item 128.

863   Jordan, Robert L. *Black Theology Exposed.* New York: Vantage Press, 1982.

Not seen.

864   Jordan, Theodus J. *The Contributions of Black Theology to Contemporary Thought.* New York: Vantage, 1988.

Not seen.

Martin Luther King, Jr.

865   Ansbro, John J. *Martin Luther King, Jr. The Making of a Mind.* Maryknoll, NY: Orbis Books, 1982.

A good intellectual biography that has, however, been criticized for focusing too much on the *intellectual* influences on King from formal theology and not enough on the contextuality of his experience as a preacher and leader of the black church itself. It is from this experience that his spirituality of hope emerges.

866   King, Martin Luther, Jr. *The Measure of A Man.* Philadelphia: Fortress Press, 1988.

See Fisher (**666**), page 4.

867   —. *Stride Toward Freedom. The Montgomery Story.* New York: Harper & Row, 1958.

See Fisher (**666**), page 4.

868   —. *Strength to Love.* New York: Harper & Row, 1963.

See Fisher (**666**), page 4.

869   —. *A Testament of Hope. The Essential Writings of Martin Luther King, Jr.* James Melvin Washington, ed. San Francisco: Harper & Row, 1986.

An excellent and large collection of his writings from 1956 until his death in 1968. These are grouped into five parts. Part 1 includes philosophy, including religious nonviolence, social integration, and black nationalism. Part 2 contains famous sermons and pub-

lic addresses; 3, historic essays; 4, interviews; and 5, books, including the texts of *Stride Toward Freedom; The Strength to Love; Why We Can't Wait; Where Do We Go From Here;* and *The Trumpet of Conscience.*
Includes a good index and excellent bibliography of works by MLK, and book and articles on him.

870   —. *The Trumpet of Conscience.* New York: Harper & Row, 1968; 2d ed., 1989.

Five talks originally broadcast over the Canadian Broadcasting Corporation in November and December 1967 as the Massey Lectures. Topics include nonviolence and opposition to the Vietnam War; conscience raising among youth, and a Christmas sermon on peace.

871   —. *We Shall Live in Peace. The Teachings of Martin Luther King, Jr.* Deloria Harrison, ed. New York: Hawthorn Books, 1968.

See Fisher (**666**), page 19.

872   —. *Where Do We Go From Here? Chaos or Community?* New York: Harper & Row, 1967.

See Fisher (**666**), pages 4-5.

873   —. *Why We Can't Wait.* New York: Harper & Row, 1964.

See Fisher (**666**), page 5.

874   —. *The Words of Martin Luther King, Jr.* Coretta Scott King, ed. New York: Newmarket Press, 1983.

A series of brief selections grouped under the topics of the community of man, racism, civil rights, justice and freedom, faith and religion, nonviolence, and peace. Also includes the texts of the "I've Been to the Mountaintop," and "I Have a Dream" speeches.

875   Lincoln, C. Eric, ed. *Martin Luther King Jr., A Profile.* New York: Hill & Wang, 1970.

A collection of essays on the impact, message and meaning of MLK. Contains articles by David Halberstam, Louis Lomas, and others.

876   Oates, Stephen B. *Let the Trumpet Sound. The Life of Martin Luther King.* San Francisco: Harper & Row, 1982.

Considered by many to be one of the best biographies available.

877   Smith, Kenneth L., and Ira G. Zepp. Jr. *Search for the Beloved Community. The Thinking of Martin Luther King Jr.* Valley Forge, PA: Judson Press, 1974.

See Fisher (**666**), page 60.

*

878   Lecky, Robert S, and H. Elliott Wright, eds. *Black Manifesto. Religion, Racism and Reparations.* New York: Sheed & Ward, 1969.

Essays by the editors, James Forman, William Stringfellow, Robert S. Browne, James Lawson, Harvey Cox, Stephen C. Rose, Dick Gregory on black power, black political theology, the demand for reparations, nonviolence, the role of the churches.

Appendixes contain the text of the Black Manifesto of April 1969 calling on white Americans to pay reparations to African-Americans for the two hundred years of slavery that they subjected them to, and addresses and declarations by black and white churches and papers.

879   Lincoln, C. Eric. *The Black Experience in Religion.* Garden City, NY: Anchor Books, 1974.

See Evans (**665**), item 139.

880   —. *The Black Muslims in America.* Boston: Beacon Press, 1961.

We often forget that many of the West African blacks brought forcibly to the New World were already Moslems when they lived in Africa. This is an important contribution not only to this cultural and religious inheritance but also for the work of the black Muslims in setting the stage for black liberation and black theology.

881   Lucas, Lawrence. *Black Priest/White Church.* New York: Random House, 1970.

Uses his own experience to speak of the white, middle-class values of the contemporary Catholic church in North America, the necessity for the church to come to grips with the diversity within its own numbers, and of white Catholics to face some of the prejudices and myths that populate their own psyches.

Lucas also speaks of his own difficult position in a church that remains steadfastly racist, or patronizing of African-Americans at best. Rather than leave, or adjust, he has decided to stay in the church and ministry and to fight.

Malcolm X

882   Goldman, Peter. *The Death and Life of Malcolm X.* New York: Harper & Row, 1973.

    See Johnson (**671**), item 2-10.

883   Malcolm X. *The Autobiography of Malcolm X.* New York: Grove Press, 1965.

    Along with Martin Luther King, Jr., Malcolm X must be regarded as the second pillar of black theology. In his evolving thought on the need for black liberation through black nationalism and in his espousal of force as a last resort to liberate blacks from non-being at the hands of white oppression, Malcolm X called for a new theology that would make a black consciousness and a black God central to black experience. Enpowerment is the essential prerequisite to human dignity, and his life and words spoke to this need on a personal and political level.

884   —. *By Any Means Necessary. Speeches, Interviews and a Letter by Malcolm X.* George Breitman, ed. New York: Pathfinder Press, 1971.

    See Johnson (**671**), item 1-2.

885 ——. *The End of White World Supremacy.* New York: Seaver, 1971.

See Johnson (**671**), item 1-3.

886 ——. *Malcolm X Speaks.* George Breitman, ed. New York: Grove Press, 1966.

See Johnson (**671**), item 1-5.

887 ——. *Malcolm X Talks to Young People.* New York: Pathfinder, 1982.

See Johnson (**671**), item 1-6.

888 ——. *Two Speeches by Malcolm X.* New York: Pathfinder, 1972.

See Johnson (**671**), item 1-8.

*

889 Massie, Proscilla, ed. *Black Faith and Black Solidarity.* New York: Friendship Press, 1983.

See Evans (**665**), item 408.

890 Mosley, William. *What Color Was Jesus?* Chicago: African American Images, 1987.

Not seen.

891   Moyd, Olin P. *Redemption in Black Theology.* Valley
           Forge, PA: Judson Press, 1979.

           "Redemption" means both liberation and confed-
           eration, as it is at the root of a black theology that
           Euro-Americans have ignored and that Latin
           American liberation theology does not fully address.
           After examining the realities of blacks in the U.S.,
           Moyd then lays out the distinctive expression and
           ideas of redemption in black theology, its nature as
           kerygmatic, apologetic and eristic: a theology that
           sees a new chosen people in covenant with God and in
           community.

892   Newman, Richard. *Black Power and Black Religion.*
           Essays and Reviews. West Cornwall, CT: Locust
           Hill Press, 1987.

           Essays on black power, black Religion, and
           reviews of books on topics that include the U.S. and
           Africa. Pages 159-60 includes "Some Recent Bibliog-
           raphic Resources for Black Religion."

893   Oglesby, Enoch Hammond. *Ethics and Theology from*
           the Other Side. Sounds of Moral Struggle.
           Washington, DC: University Press of America,
           1979.

           Examines the ethical element of a black theology.
           Topics include an examination of the black church's
           moral tradition, the ethical meaning of black theol-
           ogy on Christianity as a whole, an examination of
           the black power movement and its theological
           counterparts, the role of Martin Luther King in
           developing a liberation ethic, and the path toward a

black Christian social ethic. Includes a selected bibliography.

894   Paris, Peter J. *The Social Teachings of the Black Churches.* Philadelphia: Fortress Press, 1985.

See Evans (665), item 170.

895   Pero, Albert, and Ambrose Moyo, eds. *Theology and the Black Experience. The Lutheran Heritage Interpreted by African and African-American Theologians.* Minneapolis, MN: Augsburg, 1988.

See **235.**

James Deotis Roberts

896   Roberts, James Deotis. *A Black Political Theology.* Philadelphia: Westminster Press, 1974.

See Evans (665), item 191.

897   —. *Black Theology in Dialogue.* Philadelphia: Westminster Press, 1987.

This dialog derives from the black experience in both Third and First Worlds and from the insights of metaphysics, moral philosophy, history of religion, behavioral science, and biblical interpretation. Topics include the contextualization of theology, African roots of black theology, African-American dialog, the dialog between Jesus and his church, the holy spirit and liberation, love as a costly grace, justice, power in Christian ethics (especially in the context of a right-wing Christian backlash), the role of faith in confronting collective evil, and our role as co-creators and co-laborers.

Roberts concludes with two examples of dialog: with minjung theology in Korea, and with Judaism, and with some thoughts on the future of black theology.

898 —. *Black Theology Today. Liberation and Contextualization.* New York: E. Mellen Press, 1983.

See Evans (665), item 177.

899 —. *Liberation and Reconciliation. A Black Theology.* Philadelphia: Westminster Press, 1971.

See Evans (665), item 198.

900 —. *Roots of a Black Future. Family and Church.* Philadelphia: Westminster Press, 1980.

See Evans (665), item 183.

901 —. *A Theological Commentary on the Sullivan Principles.* Philadelphia: International Council for Equality of Opportunity, 1980.

Not seen.

902 —, and James J. Gardiner, eds. *Quest for a Black Theology.* Philadelphia: Pilgrim Press, 1971.

See Evans (665), item 199.

*

903 Sally, Columbus, and Ronald Behm, eds. *What Color Is Your God? Black Consciousness and Christian Faith.* Secaucus, NJ: Citadel Press, 1988.

Not seen.

904 Shannon, David T. *Black Witness to the Apostolic Faith.* Grand Rapids, MI: W.B. Eerdmans, 1988.

Articles by the editors, Jeffrey Gros, Thomas Hoyt, Jr., J. Deotis Roberts and others on various aspects of the black experience of Christianly and liberation. Also contains ecumenical documents on the black experience and racism.

905 Skinner, Tom. *How Black Is the Gospel?* Philadelphia: Lippincott, 1970.

See Evans (665), item 214.

906 Smith, Shelton H. *In His Image, But.... Racism in Southern Religion, 1780-1910.* Durham, NC: Duke University Press, 1972.

On the development of a white theology of racism. Traces its origins, underpinnings, the failure of the anti-slavery movement through the end of the Civil War, the theology of slavery, and "Christian" ideologies that reinforce racism. Good background for the development of black theology.

907 Thibodeaux, Mary Roger. *A Black Nun Looks at Black Power.* New York: Sheed & Ward, 1972.

Not seen.

908 Thurman, Howard. *Jesus and the Disinherited.* Richmond, IN: Friends United Press, 1981.

Attempts to face the question of why Christianity is incapable of dealing with the problems of racism, hate, and economic oppression not only in society at large but also within the American church itself. Thurman examines a Jesus who speaks to those "with their backs against the wall," that is, the vast majority of the poor, displaced, and disinherited of the world.

Jesus was a spokesman of the powerless and the disinherited, a prophet of spiritual survival and eventual triumph against the brutal subjection of Israel to Roman rule.

Thurman then examines some of the theological implications of the life of the oppressed: fear, deception, hate; but then also of a love that can overcome these, as Jesus overcame his own enemies with a new ethic. Thurman's work, first published in 1949, is a landmark in the development of a black theology of liberation.

909 Trayman, Warner R. *Christian Faith in Black and White. A Primer in Theology from the Black Perspective.* Wakefield, MA: Parameter Press, 1973.

Not seen.

910 Washington, Joseph R. *Black Religion. The Negro and Christianity in the United States* Boston: Beacon Press, 1964; rev. ed. Lanham, MD: University Press of America, 1984.

See Evans (665), item 236.

911 — . *Black Sects and Cults.* Garden City, NY: Doubleday, 1972.

Black theology and black religion are more than a mere black version of European Christianity. They derive also from the still very strong influences of African religion as they came over with the slaves and were modified in the context of the New World. This study is a very useful reminder of these origins and their meaning for spirituality and thought in black theology.

912 — . *The Politics of God. The Future of Black Churches.* Boston: Beacon Press, 1970.

See Evans (**665**), item 235.

913 West, Cornel. *Prophesy Deliverance! An Afro-American Revolutionary Christianity.* Philadelphia, PA: Westminster Press, 1982.

See Evans (**665**), item 326.

914 — . *Prophetic Fragments.* Grand Rapids, MI: W.B. Eerdmans, 1988.

This is a collection of essays on diverse topics, including Martin Luther King, Jr., the black church and socialist politics, South Africa, religion and culture (Part 2), and on religion and contemporary theology (Part 3). In Part 3 essays and book reviews touch on Juan Luis Segundo, Elisabeth Schüssler Fiorenza, Sharon D. Welsh, among other topics.

915   Wilmore, Gayraud S. *Black and Presbyterian. The Heritage and the Hope.* Philadelphia: Westminster Press, 1983.

See Evans (665), item 251.

916   — . *Black Religion and Black Radicalism. An Interpretation of the Religious History of Afro-American People.* Maryknoll, NY: Orbis Books, 1983.

This is a history of the religious life of the African-American people from their roots in Africa to present-day America. Excellent background. See Evans (665), item 249.

917   — . *Last Things First.* Philadelphia: Westminster Press, 1982.

See Evans (665), item 254.

918   — , and James H. Cone, eds. *Black Theology. A Documentary History 1966-1979.* Maryknoll, NY: Orbis Books, 1979.

A collection of essays and documents, including 255, and 838. See Evans (665), item 256.

919   Witvliet, Theo. *The Way of the Black Messiah. The Hermeneutical Challenge of Black Theology as a Theology of Liberation.* John Bowden, trans. London: SCM; Oak Park, IL: Meyer Stone Books, 1987.

This is an excellent introduction to the history, nature, central tenants, and controversies of black theology, even more so in that Witvliet is a Dutch liberation theologian who observes the U.S. scene from afar and is thus able to analyze and criticize from a more objective point of view. On the other hand, his discussion does tend to make the same mistake that he criticizes some of the black theologians themselves for: in some points of discussion he relies very heavily upon older categories and figures of traditional European theology, such as Barth, for many insights and parallels, thus making his work more academic than public in its discourse.

Despite these criticisms, however, this is an excellent book in that it approaches black theology as a true liberation theology and does so from the viewpoint of liberation theology itself: the historical development and context, the process and nature of liberation, and the nature of the ideology of the theology and of its critics. The author's primary focus is on the overall context and practice that have influenced and formed the theology. At the same time, Witvliet also acknowledges that certain individuals must be singled out for their major influence. Among these are Martin Luther King, Jr., Malcolm X, and James Cone.

His discussion of historical roots is excellent, delving into the nature of slavery in the U.S., African religious life, black Christianity, black nationalism, the civil rights movement, black power and black ecclesial politics. Excellent annotations that contain a superlative bibliography.

920 Young, Josiah U. *Black and African Theologies. Siblings or Distant Cousins?* Maryknoll, NY: Orbis Books, 1986.

A comparative study of the liberative emphasis of black American theology and of the indigenization movement in African theology. See **243**.

Amerasians

921 Sano, Roy I., ed. *Amerasian Theology of Liberation. A Reader.* Oakland, CA: Asian Center for Theologies and Strategies, 1973.

A collection of readings demonstrating the variety and maturity of Asian-Americans' thought on their own identity, both materially and spiritually, in North America.

922 —, ed. *The Theologies of Asian Americans and Pacific Peoples. A Reader.* Oakland, CA: Asian Center for Theologies and Strategies, 1976.

This is a collection of about forty-five reprints of articles by Sano, Violet Masuda, Donna Dong, Hyung-Chan Kim, David Hirano and others on various aspects of Asian-American religious life in the U.S.

Creation Theology

923 Barnette, Henlee H. *The Church and the Ecological Crisis.* Grand Rapids, MI: W.B. Eerdmans, 1972.

Examines the issue of the "ecology crisis," its causes, elements of an ecological ethics, strategies for survival, and attempts to develop a theology for ecology. Such a theology focuses on God as creator, on the place of creation as God's realm of cosmic redemption, and on the church's role for conscienticizing the people to the sacredness of nature.

924   Berry, Thomas. *Dream of the Earth.* San Francisco, CA: Sierra Club, 1988.

Thomas Berry has long been in the forefront of a new spiritual appreciation of the earth, and conversely, of a new earth-centered spirituality that takes its roots in the Judeo-Christian tradition but that in many ways grows beyond it. This is one of Berry's most mature reflections upon the place of humanity in creation. Berry's "twelve principles" for a new earth spirituality infuse the chapters.

925   —. *Riverdale Papers on the Earth Community.* New York: Riverdale Center for Religious Research, 1989.

Essays written between 1970 and 1988 on the ecological age, classical Western spirituality and the U.S. experience, the spirituality of the earth, and twelve principles for a new ecological spirituality

926   Birch, Charles, William R. Eakin, and Jay B. McDaniel, eds. *Liberating Life. Contemporary Approaches to Ecological Theology.* Maryknoll, NY: Orbis Books, 1990.

Essays by Ernesto Cardenal, Lois K. Daly, Jong-Sun Noh, Thomas Berry, John F. Haught, Sallie McFague and others present the parameters of a liberating ethic for ecology that seeks to free all of God's creation from forms of exploitation and oppression. This is a form of theology that shares much in common with liberation theology, for it dethrones "man" from the center of the universe and replaces God and God's creation there. Humanity thus takes its rightful place among the works of creation that respects the freedom of all its parts.

927   Birch, Charles, and John B. Cobb, Jr. *The Liberation of Life. From the Cell to the Community.* New York: Cambridge University Press, 1981.

This is a far-reaching and deep-thinking reflection on a theology and ethics of natural creation. Topics include ecologies from the molecular, to the cell, to population levels, evolution, models of life on earth, the relationship between the human and natural worlds, an ethic of life, a theology of life and creation, ethical issues in human manipulation of nature, an ethic for a just and sustainable ecological order, including reflection on economic development, its models, its political manifestations, and its urban, rural, and ecofeminist perspectives.

928   Carmody, John. *Ecology and Religion. Toward a New Christian Theology of Nature.* New York: Paulist Press, 1983.

Reviews the recent impact of ecological issues on theological discourse and enumerates these from natural science, technology and economics, and politics and ethics. Part 2 of the book attempts to work up a Christian theology of nature from biblical, traditional, systematic, ethical and spiritual sources. Contains an annotated bibliography of works on ecology and attitudes.

929   Cobb, John B. *Is It Too Late? A Theology of Ecology.*
        Beverly Hills, CA: Bruce, 1972.

        Cobb was prophetic in his call for a new
        spirituality that would address the issues of both
        survival and spiritual meaning on a planet too long
        ignored and exploited and of a humanity that held
        itself above the natural.

930   Fox, Matthew. *The Coming of the Cosmic Christ. The
        Healing of Mother Earth and the Birth of a Global
        Renaissance.* San Francisco: Harper & Row, 1988.

        The creation theology that Matthew Fox pro-
        pounds here, and for which he has earned the ire of
        the Vatican, has been described as a form of libera-
        tion theology for North Americans. Indeed, it is.
        This theology speaks of freeing consumer-oriented,
        patriarchal, bored, rationalistic and materialistic
        Western culture from the bonds of the spiritual crisis
        of our time: the very destruction of God's creation
        that is embodied in Mother Earth.
        Creation theology calls on all of us to recognize
        the mystic and the creator in all of us: the Cosmic
        Christ that with God continues the work of creation,
        thus freeing our imaginations and our spirits to
        acknowledge what is most fundamental to our natures:
        the creating, mothering, nurturing forces of life.
        Yet, like Latin American liberation theology,
        creation theology is not about individual men and
        women; it is not anthropocentric, as Fox reiterates. It
        is, instead, about the liberation and continuing perfec-
        tion of God's creation, in which all creatures,
        including humans, play a role. Salvation comes not
        through individual practices in outworn liturgical set-
        tings; not from fall-redemption theologies but from a

theology that seeks to save the entire world, both
human societies and the natural world, from destruction.   Salvation, as for Gutiérrez, and as for Oscar
Romero comes not to the individualistic ascetic
athlete but to society as a whole: all are saved or
none are saved, Fox stresses.

"The idea of private salvation is utterly obso-
lete," Fox contends.   There can be no such thing as
internal salvation and spirit if the world outside, be
it the community, the political unit, indeed the world
itself, is doomed to damnation.   Fox thus rejects the
worn-out dualisms of an Augustinian, Newtonian cosmology and looks forward to an integrated humanity.

The key to liberating the world and all its
creatures, including humanity, is the empowerment of
realizing and then unifying ourselves to the powers of
creation, both within ourselves and in the cosmos at
large: this is the meaning of the coming of the Cosmic
Christ.

931   —. *Original Blessing. A Primer in Creation Spirituality.*
Santa Fe, NM: Bear & Co., 1983.

Less concerned with the Christological aspects of
creation spirituality – the cosmic nature of a Christ
figure – than with the work of the first person of the
Trinity and the call that all the world's religions
make on individuals to continue God's original work
of creation in their lives and work.   The experience of
reading and appreciating Fox's work is truly a liberating one, for his basic message is that creation and
all of God's creatures are good, that the gifts of life,
body, human love and passion, the urge to create are
all goods that must be recaptured by the world's
religions if creation is to survive.   This is a call to
empowerment on its most fundamental level: that of

individual responsibility and dignity, a celebration of diversity, simplicity, and vulnerability. Like all true theologies of liberation, Fox's work emphasizes that only through suffering and pain, through grappling with the emptiness, marginality, and loss that true human experience encompasses can we cope with our own true powers as cocreators.

932 —. *A Spirituality Named Compassion.* Minneapolis, MN: Winston Press, 1979; San Francisco: Harper & Row, 1990.

Compassion is a celebration of our connection to others, it is a work of justice and mercy, a public, not a narcissistic, private spirituality; it rejects asceticism in preference to passion and welcomes the contribution of the intellect and of human reason. It is a way of life that brings together the spirit and material, self- and other-love.

Fox discusses the role of compassion in human sexuality, psychologies of competition, dualism, of letting go and forgiveness, creativity, the role of compassion in our science and view on the universe; in our economic life and relations, in our politics; and in the place of our society in the global village as a whole.

933 Hart, John. *The Spirit of the Earth.* New York: Paulist Press, 1984.

Addresses such issues as environmental devastation, economic decline, poverty and hunger in the midst of plenty through a new consciousness of the theological meaning of the earth. He bases his reflections on the biblical injunctions to preserve the land as a work of creation (Lev. 25:23; Ps. 24:1; Mt.

25:31-46), the Christian tradition of Francis of Assisi, and the religious life of the native American. Hart focuses on the destruction of the American heartland and offers a theology that will help redress it.

Examines America's overworked, exploited and exhausted lands, the economic displacement this has and will cause, and religious alternatives: the Goddess, the earth as God's creation, and humanity as co-creators, the Hebrew Sabbatical year and Jubilee; our role as pilgrims on the earth; the American populist tradition; and the American Catholic tradition, from papal documents to the Catholic Worker, to episcopal statements. He concludes with sections on land reform and a sense of the spirit of the earth.

934   Lilburne, Geoffrey R. *A Sense of Place. A Christian Theology of the Land.* Nashville, TN: Abingdon Press, 1989.

While the immediate needs to "clean up the environment" are pressing, such measures will only be stop-gap unless humans, especially those of the West most responsible for impending environmental disaster, also clean up their souls. Given the clear-cut concern for the earth inherent in the Hebrew scriptures, it is disconcerting for the Christian, whose tradition may be largely responsible for the desecration of the earth, that the Christian scriptures seem completely to bypass this concern with creation.

Lilburne argues, however, that the Christian, and Westerner, cannot abandon this Christian inheritance, but must, in fact, come face to face with it. The process may be painful but can also bear great fruit, because a return to the understanding of the Cosmic Christ through Jesus, who is God's manifestation on earth, may help resolve these contradictions. Thus

Christ's redemptive work was also literally one of "reconciling the world to God."

Lilburne takes his experience in Australia and his debt to the Australian aborigines and their religious understanding of creation to derive a new theology of the land.

935 Lonergan, Anne, and Caroline Richards, eds. *Thomas Berry and the New Cosmology*. Mystic, CT: Twenty-Third Publications, 1987.

Essays by Berry, Lonergan, Richards, Donald Senior, Gregory Baum, Margaret Brennan, James Farris, Stephen G. Dunn, and Brian Swimme on the issues of human life in the world, a creation theology as a new basis for religious unity, biblical perspectives, the call to action, the alienating role of patriarchy in our tradition, the meaning of redemption in terms of a new earth theology, the call for a new ethic, cosmology and science, and Berry's twelve principles that see the created universe as the primary manifestation of divinity and the universe itself as a psychic and physical being.

936 McDonagh, Sean. *The Greening of the Church*. Maryknoll, NY: Orbis Books, 1990.

In the face of Third-World development that actually leads to the further impoverishment and marginalization of its peoples, the church must take up a new stance of stewardship that sees the eco-system as part of the overall divine plan of salvation and humanity as part of that cosmic system. McDonagh thus takes the insights of liberation, growing from the experience of the people of the

Philippines and combines them with an integral approach to salvation.

937   —. *To Care for the Earth.*

The European title of the above.

938   McFague, Sallie. *Models of God. Theology for an Ecological, Nuclear Age.* Philadelphia: Fortress Press, 1987.

Part 1 discusses the new realities of the nuclear and ecological age, theological responses, metaphors and models of divinity and its relationship to the world, the "Christian paradigm," and models of God: monarchial, the world as God's body, and God as mother, lover, friend.

Part 2 discusses at length some models of God for the new age: as mother; in agape, creation and justice; as lover in eros, saving and healing; and as friend in *philia,* sustaining love and companionship.

939   McGinnis, James. *Journey Into Compassion. A Spirituality for the Long Haul.* Bloomington, IN: Meyer Stone, 1989.

This concise handbook combines the experience of oppression and marginalization, the lessons of liberation theology and peacemaking and combines them with a vision of a renewed earth to form a spirituality for the peacemaker and the new mystic. In this it is essentially a work of liberation theology, for it erases the distinction between inner spirituality and external action: making the salvation of the earth and the attainment of paradise one and the same, combining deep spirituality with broad avenues for action, liturgy with resistance. It is a positive sign of the emergence of a new theology that can appeal directly to the consciousness and lives of North Americans.

940   Moltmann, Jürgen. *God in Creation. A New Theology of Creation and the Spirit of God. The Gilford Lectures, 1984-1985.*

This is a thorough working out of an "ecological doctrine of creation," which realigns our theology of creation from knowledge of God to that of God's creation in nature. Topics include God's role and meaning in creation, the ecological crisis and modern theories of alienation, our knowledge of creation, the agent (God), time, space of creation, the nature of heaven and earth, the role of evolution, humanity as God's image in creation, the primacy of embodiment, the meaning of Sabbath as the feast of creation, and symbols of the created world from the world's religious and mythological heritage.

941   Murphy, Charles M. *At Home on Earth. Foundations for a Catholic Ethic of the Environment.* New York: Crossroad/Continuum, 1989.

Outlines a Catholic moral theology of human relations with the environment and an interpretation of church teaching on the subject. Murphy emphasizes one of the key themes of liberation theology: that salvation does not mean flight from the world, but the salvation of God's creation itself. Based on both biblical and Catholic tradition, as well as on modern ecological insights.

942   Sölle, Dorothee, with Shirley A. Cloyes. *To Work and to Love. A Theology of Creation.* Philadelphia: Fortress Press, 1984.

This is a praise of the goodness of God's creation, an acceptance of the world and its imperfections, and a detailed explication of the human role of co-creation through work, creativity, sexuality, and solidarity. Sölle examines work in its biblical sense as punishment for the first sin in paradise, in its Marxist sense as a process of alienation from one's own self and means of creativity, as self-expression, as a means of social relatedness, and as a reconciliation with nature and creation.

She then turns to the creativity of human sexuality and studies it also in terms of alienation, both in a biblical sense and as alienation experienced in a capitalist-materialist society, an expression of exploitation, power and cynical distrust; "love" as a consumer item and drive, the roles of male and female as creator and consumer. Opposed to this is the role of ecstasy and trust, of mutuality, of wholeness and solidarity in our most physical selves, as well as our economic, material lives. An excellent series of reflections.

943   Starhawk. *Dreaming the Dark: Magic, Sex and Politics.* Boston: Beacon Press, 1988.

See **1049**.

944   Swan, James A. *Sacred Places. How the Living Earth Seeks Our Friendship.* Santa Fe, NM: Bear & Co., 1990.

Recounts the realities of the sacred places of the world, with particular emphasis on North America: native American sites that have become recognized for their spiritual power. Swan then surveys the problems faced by the sites in the face of rapid development; lays out a new paradigm for respecting the earth as sacred; and offers suggestions for visits to such sites. Very brief bibliography.

945   Winter, Gibson. *Liberating Creation.* New York: Crossroad, 1981.

The Western tradition of an essentially good creation has been distorted by the West's equally deep-rooted drive toward technological mastery that seeks to subjugate what is seen as a neutral or hostile world to human ends. Winter, like Fox, looks toward the artistic and creative imagination to begin the process of liberation from destructive nihilism, toward healing, and toward a renewed life of justice and peacemaking.

Gay/Lesbian Theology

946   Archdiocese of San Francisco. Task Force on Gay/Lesbian Issues. *Homosexuality and Social Justice.* San Francisco: Archdiocescan Commission on Social Justice, 1982.

A landmark in Christian theology of homosexuality, albeit a cautious one. Accepts as valid the gay and lesbian experience of Christianity and addresses issues of violence, the Latino community, language and church teaching, the family and issues of child rearing, gay and lesbian spiritual life and ministry, gays and lesbians in religious life, sexual

disenfranchisement, and the church's role to educate
for justice. The report concludes with recommendations for implementation.

947   Boyd, Malcolm. *Take Off the Masks.* Garden City, NY:
       Doubleday, 1978.

A personal and spiritual autobiography of the
well-known priest and writer who declared his gayness in 1977 and the conflicts between his open
avowal of peace, justice, women's, Jewish, black and
other causes and his fear of speaking for himself and
other gays.
Boyd also reflects on the churches' refusal to
embrace the twenty million gay men and women who
are Christian; and makes some tentative remarks, in
chapter 5, on a theology of gayness.

948   Bucher, Glenn A., ed. *Straight/White/Male.* Philadel-
       phia: Fortress Press, 1976.

This is a series of essays on the liberation of
women, homosexuals, blacks and the dominant
straight, white, male society that oppresses them
and itself. Includes essays by Bucher, Benjamin D.
Berry, Patricia R. Hill, Patricia N. Dutcher, and
Charles E. Linder.

949   Burton, Jack Robert. *Our Common Humanity. The Need
       for Tenderness and Realism in Discussing Sexuality.*
       London: Gay Christian Movement, 1980.

A speech delivered shortly after the report of the
Anglican church on homosexuality. Burton notes that
the report left so much ambiguity that it was still
possible for churchmen to deny the existence of

homosexuality or to speak of "cures." Instead, the
author calls on Christians to accept the reality of
homosexuality and to construct a Christian theology
for it.

950   Coleman, Peter Everard. *Gay Christians. A Moral
       Dilemma.* Philadelphia: Trinity Press Inter-
       national; London: SCM, 1989.

       A good introduction to the facts and controversies.
       Examines the issue of gays within the traditional
       Christian church; linguistic, medical, psychological,
       spiritual and other aspects of homosexuality; biblical
       texts and traditions of homosexuality; Christian
       attitudes from St. Paul to the 1950s; recent develop-
       ments, including the gay movement within the
       churches in the 1960s, Catholic teachings, church
       reports on homosexuality in the 1970s; and the state
       of flux in attitudes brought about in the 1980s. A
       final section deals with arguments for and against
       changing church attitudes to, and the status of, homo-
       sexuals. A brief bibliography arranged by topic.

951   Downing, Christine. *Myths and Mysteries of Same-Sex
       Love.* New York: Continuum, 1989.

       Examines the myths of homosexuality and les-
       bianism in Freud and Jung, and then the mysteries
       related by classical mythology. Concludes with an
       epilogue on sexuality and AIDS, love and death. A
       lengthy and thoughtful analysis.

952   Edwards, George R. *Gay/Lesbian Liberation. A Biblical Perspective.* New York: Pilgrim Press, 1984.

Edwards, a biblical scholar, seeks to model a conscious theology of gay liberation, within the over-all context of liberation theology. He does so by first setting the context and matching the material poverty of Latin Americans with the sexual imma-turity and constructions of more affluent North Americans. Edwards contends that discrimination against homosexuals has marginalized even middle-class Americans. He then delves into the relatively few biblical texts that have been used as the religious basis of homophobia over the millennia.

In a theological sense, Edwards seeks to forge a "transgenital awareness" of the personhood of the gay or lesbian, or the heterosexual man or woman, that is not confined to a definition based upon the use and application of one's sexual organs; to convey a theology that stresses the agape of social community and activism above the narrower eroticism of hetero- or homo-sexuality.

Topics discussed include gay/lesbian liberation within contemporary theology; an examination of the historical attitudes toward "sodomy" ("homosexu-ality" is a late nineteenth-century term); biblical attitudes toward sodomy based on very close and scholarly readings of the original texts; a gay/lesbian theology based on the New Testament; and an ethical-biblical perspective on homosexual love. Includes a good bibliography.

953   Fortunato, J. *AIDS. The Spiritual Dilemma.* San Francisco: Harper & Row, 1987.

This book is an attempt at a spiritual response to the plague of AIDS that goes beyond the medical, legal, therapeutic and other approaches and sees the disease, and those afflicted by it – which, Fortunato reminds us, is all of us – as a profoundly spiritual problem that asks the deepest questions about human life and love, about the nature of God and human suffering. The author also confronts some sorry truths about Christian responses: a fear of embodiment and sexuality that is deep-rooted in its tradition; the overstress on God's masculinity and thus on the sacred nature of the division between male and female, animus and anima within each human being, and the forms of compassion and love that Christians are thus allowed, or forced, to express. It also confronts us with one of the deepest mysteries of religious life that has tormented us since the book of Job: how can God allow such senseless suffering?

Like many of the mystics in the late medieval and counter-reformation church, Fortunato brings us to the realization that we can reach heaven, and God, through a deep meditation on human suffering, and on the suffering God in Christ, and that the best theology is one securely based on the context of human existence. Another praiseworthy element of this work is Fortunato's refusal to allow theological truth to be the monopoly of the clergy and to stress both his deep faith and his orthodox Christianity. An excellent work.

954   —. *Embracing the Exile. The Healing Journey of Gay Christians.* New York: Seabury Press, 1982.

Reflections on the therapeutic process for gay Christians that affirms gay sexuality as a God-given gift. The theme of exile is one that is of particular importance for a theology of liberation; for it focuses our attention on full human beings who have been marginalized and who are now in the process of recovering their humanity and freeing themselves from deadly stereotype and hatreds. Bibliography.

955   Gearhart, Sally, and William R. Johnson, eds. *Loving Women/Loving Men. Gay Liberation and the Church.* San Francisco: Glide Publications, 1974.

Not seen.

956   Grahn, Judy. *Another Mother Tongue. Gay Words, Gay Worlds.* Boston: Beacon Press, 1984.

On gay spirituality and its roots; the understanding of shamanism as a form of gay spirituality. See Carson (**991**), item 273.

957   Gramick, Jeannine, ed. *Homosexuality and the Catholic Church.* Chicago: Thomas More, 1983.

Essays by Brian McNaught, Ann Borden, Gramick, Barbara Zanotti, Robert Nugent, Theresa Kane, Cornelius Hubbuch, Charles Curran, and Kenneth McGuire on both sociological and ecclesial perspectives. Topics include personal reflections, new sociological theory on homosexuality, the structural evils of male domination and heterosexism, homosexuality and the celibate religious life, civil rights within the church, moral theology and homosexuality, and changing attitudes.

958   —. *Homosexuality in the Priesthood and in the Religious Life.* New York: Crossroad, 1989.

Sixteen first-hand accounts of homosexuals within the church introduced by essays on the religious, theological, ministerial, and institutional experience of homosexuality within the orders of the clergy that focus on the issue of homosexuality as a paradigm for far larger issues: patriarchy and hierarchialism. Overall a vivid testimony to the growing voice of the disenfranchised and marginalized both in the church and in society.

959   —, and Pat Furfey, eds. *The Vatican and Homosexuality.* New York: Crossroad, 1988.

The subtitle reads, "Reactions to the 'Letter to the Bishops of the Catholic Church on the Pastoral Care of Homosexual Persons.'"
After an excellent introduction to the topic of Catholic teaching on homosexuality in the United States since the 1960s and a synopsis of the arguments presented below, the editors reprint the Vatican letter (pp. 1-12). The essays are grouped into three sections: analyses and critiques of the document; pastoral and personal responses; and debate and developments for the future. Contributors include Archbishop John R. Quinn of San Francisco, William H. Shannon, Dan Grippo, Nugent, Mary Segers, Gramick, Carolyn Osiek, Peter Hebblethwaite, Margaret Traxler, Sarah M. Sherman, Mary Jo Weaver, André Guindon and others.

960   Hannigan, J. P. *Homosexuality. The Test Case for Christian Sexual Ethics.* New York: Paulist Press, 1988.

Not seen.

961   Hasnaby, Richard, ed. *Homosexuality and Religion.*
        New York & London: Harrington Park Press, 1989.

        A collection of essays that points toward some
        fundamentals for a theology of homosexuality. Con-
        tributors include Nugent and Gramick, Yoel H. Kahn,
        Aaron Cooper, George R. Edwards, E. Ann Matter,
        Gary David Comstock, Clare B. Fischer, Michael J.
        Garazini and John A. Struzzo on such issues as the
        religious traditions, gay/lesbian movements, funda-
        mentalist homophobia, homosexuality in Christian
        spiritual tradition, gay and lesbian religious leaders,
        and pastoral theology.   Several articles include
        excellent bibliographies.

962   Hoagland, Sarah Lucia. *Lesbian Ethics. Toward New
        Value.* Palo Alto, CA: Institute of Lesbian Studies,
        1988.

        Topics include definitions of terms, separating
        from heterosexuality, female agency, power and
        paternalism, integration of reasoning and emotion,
        moral agency and interacting, and moral revolution in
        the struggle for justice, duty, caring, and integrity.

963   Johnston, Maury. *Gays Under Grace.* Nashville, TN:
        Winston-Derek Publications, 1983.

        The subtitle reads, "A Gay Christian's Response
        to the Moral Majority." Under the pressure of attacks
        from the Falwellian right, Johnston attempts to
        answer prejudice and stereotype with a carefully out-
        lined essay in gay theology. Topics include the pre-
        sent religiously based attack, Hebrew history and
        homosexuals, the New Testament and Paul, and a gay
        sexual ethic.

The author discusses the Christian call to holiness, sin, sex and scripture, relationship, a biblical approach to balanced sexuality, and the call of Christ to transcendence.

964   Kroll, Una. *What the Church Should Be Saying to Homosexuals.* London: Gay Christian Movement, 1979.

Not seen.

965   Lanphear, Roger G. *Gay Spirituality.* San Diego, CA: Unified Publications, 1990.

Discusses sexuality, human relations, reconciliation, and the threat of AIDS.

966   Macourt, Malcolm, ed. *Towards a Theology of Gay Liberation.* London: SCM, 1977.

A collection of essays by Macourt, David Blamires, Rictor Norton, James Martin, Jim Cotter, Norman Pittinger, Giles Hibbert, and Michael Keeling on recent Christian perspectives, a framework of debate for creating a gay theology, biblical roots of homophobia, the gay challenge to traditional sexual roles, the meaning of being human, gay liberation and Christian liberation, and a Christian basis of gay relations. An excellent collection on the topic.

967   McNeill, John J. *The Church and the Homosexual.* 3d ed. Boston: Beacon Press, 1988.

This is a classic in the field and still a fundamental resource. McNeill, who ministered to gay congregations and individuals for many years, was ousted from the Jesuits in 1987 for his opinions. Topics include a review of moral theology on homosexuality, in which McNeill takes issue with Charles Curran's apparently unconscious homophobic views; the scriptural bases of homophobia, which actually boil down to three texts: the Sodom story of Genesis 19:4-11, in which the righteous Lot offers his virgin daughters up for rape; the grisly story of the gang rape and murder of the Levite's wife by the men of Gibeah told in Judges 19:1-21:25, also given up willingly by the husband to avoid his own rape; and Paul's comments in Romans 1:26. The two former stress the violation of the customs of hospitality, the last excoriates the pagan customs of temple prostitutes and fertility cults. McNeill then discusses the tradition of attitudes toward homosexuality, historical anthropologies, and modern scientific data.

After these excellent background pieces, McNeill then goes on to build a theology of homosexuality, citing the very positive contributions of gay and lesbian people to the human community, and highlighting the service of these people in the caring, nurturing and healing arts, emphasizing that gayness offers human society a clear-cut model for compassion and nonviolent relationships. In his last chapters he then discusses the failure of the church to meet the pastoral needs of the gay/lesbian community and calls for the churches to make positive action to reach out to the homosexual on behalf of justice.

968   —. *Taking a Chance on God. Liberating Theology for Gays, Lesbians, and Their Lovers, Families and Friends.* Boston: Beacon Press, 1988.

This is an attempt to develop a spirituality based on the unique experience of gays and lesbians. Topics include the context of Christian upbringing and attitudes; the challenge of gay atheism; pathological and healthy religious modes; a mature gay and lesbian spirituality; fear, anger, guilt, shame and self-hate in the approach to God; trust, thanksgiving and reconciliation; gay virtues in hospitality and compassion, including some debunking of homophobic biblical myths; celebrating life, corporality, sexuality; the role of Mary in the gay and lesbian community; and the reality of death, especially in the context of the AIDS epidemic.

In this section McNeill deals with the spirituality of death, time, judgment and mourning. He concludes with discussions of a spiritual community for gays and lesbians as a liberating one and on a liberation spirituality.

969   Nugent, Robert, ed. *A Challenge to Love. Gay and Lesbian Catholics in the Church.* New York: Crossroad, 1983.

Articles by Gramick, Gregory Baum, John McNeill, Michael Guinan, Margaret A. Farley, Matthew Fox, M. Basil Pennington, Marguerite Kropinak and others on societal, biblical, theological, pastoral, and vocational perspectives on the issue of homosexuality. The collection aims to demonstrate that a gay perspective has much to contribute to building a more humane society and toward furthering our understanding of human nature and divinity. Bibliography of books and key church documents.

970   —, and Jeannine Gramick, eds. *A Time to Speak.* Mt. Rainier, MD: New Ways Ministry, 1982.

Not seen.

971   —, Jeannine Gramick, and Thomas Oddo. *Homosexual Catholics. A Primer for Discussion.* Washington, DC: Dignity, 1982.

Not seen.

972   Oberholtzer, W. Dwight, ed. *Is Gay Good? Ethics, Theology, and Homosexuality.* Philadelphia: Westminster Press, 1971.

Essays by Oberholtzer, John von Rohr, Carl F. H. Henry, Troy Perry, Henry J. M. Nouwen, Del Martin and Phyllis Lyon, and others on legal, religious, ethical, and personal aspects of homosexuality. Thomas Maurer and Martin and Lyon attempt a theology of gayness and lesbianism. William Parker provides an excellent bibliography.

973   Perry, Troy D, with Charles L. Lucas. *The Lord Is My Shepherd and He Knows I'm Gay.* Los Angeles, CA: Nash Publishing, 1972.

This is an autobiography of a gay minister that describes his life and work, his homosexuality, the gay community, gay militancy, and attempts a practical theology of gayness in the re-experience of God as a marginalized person who has felt deep anguish.

974 Pittinger, N. *A Time for Consent. A Christian's Approach to Homosexuality.* 3d ed. London: SCM, 1976.

Discusses the present situation, the theological meanings of humanity and sin, the homosexual "condition" and "act," various homosexual organizations, the morality of homosexual acts, the biblical foundations and changing attitudes, issues of fidelity and permanence in homosexual relations, and a homosexual ethic. A final chapter deals with the issue of homosexual love in a Christian context.

975 Ratzinger, Joseph Cardinal. *Letter to the Bishops of the Catholic Church on the Pastoral Care of Homosexual Persons.* Vatican City: Congregation of the Doctrine of the Faith, 1986.

Ratzinger immediately limits his letter to the Catholic moral teaching (2), and reemphasizes the teachings of the *Declaration...on Questions Concerning Sexual Ethics,* of 1975, in which a distinction is made between a homosexual "condition or tendency" and homosexual "actions" (3). He then condemns the "overly benign interpretation" given the homosexual condition by scholars and theologians and reemphasizes what he considers its evil nature. Genesis 19:1-11 and Leviticus 18:22 and 20:13, with their condemnations, are still the guiding texts (6). Paul, in 1 Cor. 6:9 and Rom. 1:18-32, reiterates these.

Choosing someone of the same sex, the cardinal writes, annuls the creator's plan for sexuality and is thus a "moral disorder." In the church today, however, there is a large lobby pushing for an acceptance of this disorder, and ministers must take care not to be be misled by this point of view (8).

Like the good witch hunter that he is, Ratzinger goes right to the heart of the theological issue: the homosexual pressure groups are by and large not good or practicing Catholics, they seek to manipulate issues, well-meaning people, and the "softness" of civil laws. (9)   In this document the cardinal thus shows the same penchant that he displays in his other letters: an appeal to the unchangeable nature of traditional (rigid) readings of scripture and then a launching into what is nakedly political diatribe, name calling and innuendos of ill-will and evil intentions. The cardinal goes so far as to claim that no one should be surprised if violent reactions against homosexuals increase (10)!

Having thus opened the door to hate and demagoguery against homosexuals, and having issued his own naked threats of the church sanctioning violence against them, Ratzinger takes the rest of the letter to advise homosexuals on ways to mend their sinful lives (12), to pastors on ways of helping the homosexual back to the right path (13), to bishops to avoid any programs or groups seeking to change church teaching (14-15), ironically stressing through all this that homosexuals are indeed human beings not defined by their sexuality (16).   He then exhorts bishops to spread the word to all the faithful in strict adherence to the capitalized "Magisterium."

Finally, the cardinal comes to the point of his letter: the official marginalization of the homosexual community: "all support should be withdrawn from any organization which seeks to undermine the teaching of the church, which is ambiguous about it, or which neglects it entirely" (17).   This include use of church facilities (including schools and colleges), and special services, while the bishops will "defend and promote family life."

What pretends to be a theological letter is thus nothing else but an exercise in administrative fiat: theological and moral issues of the greatest concern to all Catholics, Christians, and religious people are reduced to the level of power politics and control of real estate.

976   Scanzoni, Letha, and Virginia Ramey Mollenkott. *Is the Homosexual My Neighbor? Another Christian View.* San Francisco: Harper & Row, 1978.

The question, of course, is rhetorical. This book is a call for Christian love of neighbor that examines the theological, sociological, scientific, cultural and ethical meaning of homosexuality in Christian history and today. The authors use biblical analogies to see the homosexual as the Samaritan of our time and examine the biblical passages supposedly condemning homosexuality to arrive at a new understanding. They conclude with a proposal for a new homosexual Christian ethic. Contains an annotated bibliography of books on homosexuality and religion.

977   U.S. Catholic Conference. *To Live in Christ Jesus.* Washington, DC: USCC, 1976.

Contains one section on the Catholic theology of homosexuality, outlining protections under civil law and special pastoral care.

978   Walker, Mitch, and friends. *Visionary Love. A Spirit Book of Gay Mythology and Trans-Mutational Faerie.* San Francisco: Treeroots Press, 1980.

See Carson (991), item 683.

979 Williams, Harry Abbot. *The Gay Christian Movement and the Education of Public Opinion*. London: Gay Christian Movement, 1979.

A brief address concerning the issues of injustice, but also of exploitation and obsession, and the need to educate public opinion by living a just life.

980 Wolf, James G., ed. *Gay Priests*. New York: Harper & Row, 1989.

Essays by Wolf, R. Edwards, T. Thompson, R. Roberts, and K. Lawrence on gay priests' lives, experiences, fears and hopes. Includes an excellent annotated bibliography of books and articles on gay theology.

981 Woods, Richard. *Another Kind of Love. Homosexuality and Spirituality*. New York: Doubleday/Image, 1978.

Deals with the religious mystery of homosexuality, the contexts of life in a gay and straight world, gay life within the church, gay spirituality, activism, and joy. Good, brief bibliography.

982 Zanotti, Barbara, ed. *A Faith of One's Own. Explorations by Catholic Lesbians*. Freedom, CA: Crossing Press, 1986.

Essays by Karen Doherty, Joy Christi Przestwor, Jayne Young, Mary Moran, Maggie Redding, Gloria Anzaldua, Fulana de Tal, Margaret Cruikshank, and others on a lesbian theology, on coming out in the church, on the struggle for freedom, on resistance, and on new forms of spirituality that go beyond the confines of Catholic teaching.

Zanotti brings a collection together that both demonstrates the contribution of lesbians to dismantling the patriarchal and misogynist institutions and attitudes of the church and that seeks to locate Catholicism less in adherence to an institution than in a deep image on the soul. Other themes include the devastating effects of Catholic political involvement against women's control of their own bodies and status in society, the notion of authority and where it resides, of community and women's culture.

The Bishops' Economic Pastoral

983   Berryman, Phillip. *Our Unfinished Business. The U.S. Catholic Bishops' Letters on Peace and the Economy.* New York: Pantheon, 1989.

This is an excellent survey of the current status of American Catholic teaching and streams of thought on war, peace, social and economic justice that takes its cue from both bishops' pastorals, *The Challenge of Peace* and *Economic Justice for All.* It clearly and succinctly sums up liberal, radical and conservative arguments on these issues, including insightful reviews of the major thinkers on these issues.

984   Ellison, Marvin Mahan. *The Center Cannot Hold. The Search for a Global Economy of Justice.* Washington, DC: University Press of America, 1983.

Surveys the development debate in the social scientific literature; then within the ecumenical church movement, including a selection on the Catholic church and the debate between development and liberation. Part 2 then discusses some examples, including Latin American liberation theology. The book concludes with an examination of the meaning of the debate for Christian ethics.

985   Hug, James E. *Christian Faith and the U.S. Economy.* Kansas City, MO: Leaven Press, 1985.

A reflection on the bishops' pastoral letter on the U.S. economy. Hug uses the Vatican *Instruction* on liberation theology (**123-124**) to emphasize its positive statements and to show how these challenge current U.S. economic thought and institutions. He also addresses the relationship between Christian faith and politics and analyzes the bishops' theological methods in coming to their conclusions.

986   National Conference of Catholic Bishops. *Economic Justice for All. Pastoral Letter on Catholic Social Teaching and the U.S. Economy.* Washington, DC: National Conference of Catholic Bishops, 1986.

Topics include a survey of the U.S. economy, the urgent problems facing Americans, and the need for a moral vision (chapter 1); a Christian vision of economic life (2); selected economic policy issues (3); and the positive recommendations of the bishops, including a new partnership among business, government, and nations; and the positive role that religious people and bodies, including the Catholic church, must play in the world today.

While solidly within the framework and tradition of Roman Catholic social teaching, the document – and the comment period that went into its creation – were among the most controversial actions ever undertaken by the U.S. bishops. The neoconservatives allied with the Reagan administration mustered witness after witness, and even issued their own report to counter the perceived bombshell that the bishops' letter would generate. Many of the same opponents of liberation theology (765-797) reappeared here, for they rightly perceived that the U.S. bishops were attempting to apply the very same Vatican II spirit and social teachings that had helped create liberation theology in Latin America.

987   Vallely, Paul. *Bad Samaritans. First World Ethics and Third World Debt.* Maryknoll, NY: Orbis Books, 1990.

Discusses both the workings of the international economic order, in which the Third World remains the economic dependent of the First; the need for individual conversion, change of life and social activism to bring about a more just order both here and around the world.

*   *

*

Chapter 9: *Feminist Theology*

Bibliographies

988   Ballou, Patricia K. *Women. A Bibliography of Bibliographies.* 2d ed. Boston: G.K. Hall, 1986.

Bibliographies for women and religion are treated on pages 93-98.

989   Bass, Dorothy C., and Sandra Hughes Boyd. *Women in American Religious History. An Annotated Bibliography and Guide to Sources.* Boston: G.K. Hall, 1986.

Books and articles, 568 items, divided into topic by general works, including feminist studies; Protestantism, historically and by denomination; Roman Catholicism; Judaism; African-American religion, native Americans; utopianism. Indexed by name.

990   Cantor, Aviva. *The Jewish Woman: 1900-1980.* Fresh Meadows, NY: Biblio Press, 1982.

Books, articles, and chapters.

991   Carson, Anne. *Feminist Spirituality and the Feminine Divine. An Annotated Bibliography.* Freedom, CA: Crossing Press, 1986.

Books and articles, 739 items, arranged alphabetically. Subject index. An excellent guide.

992   Choquette, Diane. *The Goddess Walks Among Us. Feminist Spirituality in Thought and Action. A*

Select Bibliography. Berkeley, CA: Graduate Theological Union Library, 1981.

A checklist on the library's extensive holdings in the field. Books and articles are arranged here by topic and then alphabetically by author. Some brief annotation. Includes reference sources, the Goddess in history and myth, new rituals, theory and research, and periodicals.

993   Farians, Elizabeth. *Selected Bibliography on Women and Religion, 1965-72.* Washington, DC: NOW, 1973.

Typescript, on books, articles, bibliographies, films, packets, reports, newsletters, organizations, and whole issues. Not annotated.

994   Fischer, Clare Benedicks. *Breaking Through. A Bibliography of Women and Religion.* Berkeley, CA: Graduate Theological Union Library, 1980.

Judeo-Christian, feminist and nonfeminist sources. Arranged by topic, then alphabetically by author. Not annotated.

995   Frazer, Ruth F. *Women and Religion. A Bibliography Selected from the ATLA Religion Database.* 3d, rev. ed. Chicago: American Theological Library Association Religion Indexes, 1983.

Articles, divided into subject and author sections, and alphabetically within each. Sections on feminist theology (119-21), the Goddess (pp. 134-37), lesbianism (p. 187), Catholic and Jewish women (pp. 379-81), women's theology (pp. 384-92).

996 Hamelsdorf, Ora, and Sandra Adelsberg. *Jewish Women and Jewish Law*. Fresh Meadows, NY: Biblio Press, 1982.

Fifty items in English.

997 *Heresies*.

Volume 2, 1 (1982): 132-34 contains over 100 books on the great Goddess.

998 Kendall, Patricia A. *Women and the Priesthood. A Selected and Annotated Bibliography*. Philadelphia: Episcopal Diocese, 1976.

Books and articles, study papers and tape cassettes. Alphabetical by author. Annotated.

999 King, Margot. *A Bibliography on Women and the Church*. Saskatoon, SASK: Shannon Library, 1975.

Materials from 1970 to 1974 arranged by language. 1,000 entries.

1000 Leonard, Harriet Virginia. *Women in the Bible. A Bibliography*. Durham, NC: Leonard, 1977.

Arranged by books in all languages, in English, French, German, in other languages, with Duke University call numbers. Not annotated.

1001   Loeb, Catherine. *Women's Studies. A Recommended Core Bibliography, 1980-1985.* Littleton, CO: Libraries Unlimited, 1987.

Items on religion are presented on pages 331-44.

1002   Richardson, Marilyn. *Black Women and Religion. A Bibliography.* Boston: G.K. Hall, 1980.

Annotated, 867 items, books and articles arranged by author. Subtitles include black women in literature, music, reference materials, autobiography and biography. General index.

1003   Ruud, Inger Marie. *Women and Judaism. A Select Annotated Bibliography.* New York: Garland Publishing, 1988.

Books and articles, 842 items, arranged alphabetically by author, with topographical, subject, and author indexes.

1004   Walker, Barbara G. *The Women's Encyclopedia of Myths and Secrets.* New York: Harper & Row, 1983.

An excellent source; articles contain bibliographical references. Excellent bibliography on the Goddess. See also Carson (991), item 682.

1005   *The Woman in the Church. International Bibliography.* 2 vols. Strasbourg: Cedric, 1975-1982.

Arranged alphabetically by author. Books, pamphlets, articles. A general index, and indexes by language.

Women and the Goddess

1006   Adler, Margot. *Drawing Down the Moon. Witches, Druids, Goddess Worshippers and Other Pagans in America Today.* Boston: Beacon Press, 1981.

    A fundamental work on the lost tradition and reemergence of the Goddess among feminists and those seeking a spirituality more in harmony with the earth. See Carson (991), item 5.

1007   Bachofen, J. J. *Myth, Religion, and Mother Right.* Princeton, NJ: Princeton University Press, 1967.

    Basic research on the women-guided culture and mythology of the stone age that strongly suggests that the role of the earth and of its divinity was seen in feminine terms, and that these terms, the language of metaphor and myth have since been lost to linear, patriarchal forms of talking about divinity.

1008   Budapest, Zsuzsanna E. *The Feminist Book of Lights and Shadows.* Los Angeles: Luna Press, 1976.

    Not seen.

1009   —. *The Holy Book of Women's Mysteries.* Los Angeles: Luna Press, 1979. Reissued, 2 vols. Oakland, CA: SBA Coven, 1986.

    See Carson (991), item 91.

1010   Cady, Susan, Marian Ronan, and Hal Taussig. *Sophia.*
        The Future of Feminist Spirituality. San Francisco:
        Harper & Row, 1986.

        A survey of the nature and role of Sophia in
        wisdom literature. Topics include Sophia's place in
        feminist spirituality, in the Hebrew and Christian
        scriptures, in the postbiblical era, in socio-historical
        context of the wisdom tradition, and Sophia's role in
        the future of feminist spirituality. Well annotated.

1011   —. *Wisdom's Feast. Sophia in Study and Celebration.*
        San Francisco: Harper & Row, 1990.

        Sophia, the Greek word for Wisdom, is the
        symbolic language used to describe the preexistent
        creative force of divinity that continues to guide
        creatures and creation: it is the Sophia spoken of in
        the wisdom literature of the Hebrew Bible, the Word
        in John's theology of the Logos. In classical mythol-
        ogy *Sophia* is also the attribute of Athena, the
        ungenerated wisdom of Zeus, born of nothing and
        preexisting with God.

1012   Campbell, Joseph. *The Masks of God.* 4 vols. New
        York: Penguin Books, 1988.

        Vol. 1: *Primitive Mythology,* pp. 299-354 et passim.

        The religion of the cave-dwellers of Europe, and
        of Africa and central Asia, were bound together in the
        worship of the image of the Goddess who gave both
        life and death: the regenerative image of the earth,
        its bounty and the gifts of the hunt. For the earliest
        humans God was a woman.

Vol. 2: *Oriental Mythology.*

"Oriental" here means the mythological systems of the "nuclear Middle East," originating in Mesopotamia, which Campbell takes as the originator of almost all current world mythological systems, via diffusion of peoples and archetypes. Intrinsic to these Oriental mythological systems is the predominance of celestial cults that either displace or transfigure the preexisting cults of the earth, associated with the Goddess.

Campbell's loyalties are clearly with the latter, as they survived in the various cults of Goddesses in India, in Egypt, and in the Celtic and Greco-Roman myths of the classical and pre-classical periods.

Vol. 3: *Occidental Mythology,* pp. 3-93 et passim.

Campbell demonstrates clearly how the mythology of the pre-heroic age, that of the original planter societies, was one of the nurturing, yet also death-dealing, Goddess. The societies built upon this mythological world found their fullest expression in the life-loving, and apparently non-violent society of the Minoans and Anatolians before the arrival of the Indo-European and Near Eastern sky gods, including Zeus and Yahweh, and their lusts for power and domination over the older female principals. Good background.

Vol. 4: *Creative Mythology.*

Focuses on the legend of Tristan and Isolde, and of the related historical lives of Abelard and Heloise as paradigms of the modern age's liberation from the bondage of old religious systems. Heloise's frank, and heroic, embrace of her love for Abelard is a keystone in the recognition of the erotic. In the modern world these mythological archetypes and profound truths have been spelled out again in the fictions of Joyce and Mann.

1013   Christ, Carol P. *Laughter of Aphrodite. Reflections on a Journey to the Goddess.* San Francisco: Harper & Row, 1989.

The journey is that of the author: from the patriarchies and dominations of Christianity with its religious equation of sinfulness and earned salvation, to that of the Goddess and its embrace of creation, life, and a deep spirituality that integrates spiritual, physical, and emotional spheres.

1014   —, and Judith Plaskow, eds. *Weaving the Visions. New Patterns in Feminist Spirituality.* San Francisco: Harper & Row, 1989.

An important, and excellent, collection of essays on women's religious heritage in Jewish and pre-Christian religious systems; on the feminine divine, sexism and religious language, varieties of feminist theology, and feminist theology's commitment to social transformation.

Contributors include the editors, E. Schüssler Fiorenza, Gimbutas, Spretnak, Alice Walker, Nelle Morton, McFague, Ruether, Delores S. Williams, Mary Daly, B. W. Harrison, Naomi Goldenberg, Carter Heyward, Thistlewaite, Starhawk, Sharon Welch, and others.

In a remarkable preface the editors confess their growing distance since editing *Womanspirit Rising,* (see **1015**) as Christ has moved more toward the

Goddess and Plaskow toward the reform of the Jewish tradition.

1015   —. *Womanspirit Rising: A Feminist Reader in Religion.* San Francisco: Harper & Row, 1979.

This is a classic collection of essays by some of the leading feminist theologians and theorists. Topics range from the relevance of traditional theology to women's experience and needs, the rereading and rewriting of biblical history and dogma, the contextual situation of women changing the reception of their own religious traditions, and directions for the creation of a new tradition in women's spirituality that resurrects the Goddess from obscurity.

The editors' introductory essay is an excellent survey of the issues and research.

1016   Condren, Mary. *The Serpent and the Goddess. Women, Religion, and Power in Celtic Ireland.* San Francisco: Harper & Row, 1990.

The original religion of prehistoric Ireland was that of the Goddess of life and death, which was supplanted first in Celtic times and then definitely with the conversion to Christianity. The life and death of the Goddess reflects the decline of matriarchy both in Ireland and in the rest of Western culture. This book analyzes the implications of this shift, the possibilities for a resurgence of a feminist theology, and the problems that such a resurgence face within the Catholic church and society at large.

1017   Craighead, Meinrad. *The Mother's Song. Images of God the Mother.* New York: Paulist Press, 1986.

A wonderful collection of forty paintings. Images include water, egg, cycle, mother and daughter, dreaming, rain, storyteller, hallower, changing woman, earth, weaver, moon tree, wisdom, maze, death, night, vessel, healer, journey, and woman as seasons.

1018   Davis, Elizabeth Gould. *The First Sex.* New York: Putnam, 1971.

While criticized for its lack of scholarly rigor and its clear-cut point of view, this remains a fundamental account of the age of matriarchy that gave birth to the first civilizations in the Near East.

1019   Dexter, Miriam Robbins. *Whence the Goddess.* Elmsford, NY: Pergamon Press, 1990.

A survey of the mythological and archetypal powers of the great goddesses of the Near East, Egypt, the Mediterranean, and Europe. These include Isis, Athena, Shakti, Artemis, Hera, and Hecate. These goddesses reveal the divine feminine as enabling, strengthening, nurturing, and as the virgin, matron, and crone.

1020   Downing, Christine. *The Goddess. Mythological Images of the Feminine.* New York: Crossroad/Continuum, 1984.

Analyzes the meaning of the Goddess in Greek mythology to draw important conclusions on the nature of the feminine in divinity. See Carson (**991**), item 176.

1021 Eisler, Riane. *The Chalice and the Blade. Our History, Our Future.* San Francisco: Harper & Row, 1990.

Relying on such insightful researchers as Marija Gimbutas (see **1024**), the author traces the shift from egalitarian, matrifocal, nonviolent cultures and religion to the violent, patriarchal, and hierarchical societies of the early historical period. Paralleling this is the shift from the cults of the earth-Goddess and her nurturing cycles of birth, life and death, to those of the sky-gods – Zeus, Jupiter, Wotan or Yahweh, and their violent, wrathful, and vengeful ways.

1022 Forfreedom, Ann, and Julie Ann, eds. *Book of the Goddess.* Sacramento, CA: Temple of the Goddess Within, 1980.

Not seen.

1023 Gadon, Elinor W. *The Once and Future Goddess. A Symbol for Our Time.* San Francisco: Harper & Row, 1990.

Uses the visual arts to trace the nature and extent of the Goddess cult in prehistoric and ancient cultures, its demise, and reemergence in modern times as a paradigm of feminist theology and liberation. The work of such modern artists as Louise Bourgeois, Meinrad Craighead, and Judy Chicago demonstrates the archetypal continuity of woman's images.

1024   Gimbutas, Marija. *The Language of the Goddess.*
        Unearthing the Hidden Symbols of Western
        Civilization. San Francisco: Harper & Row, 1990.

Gimbutas is one of the leading archaeologists of
Europe and the United States, and her work over the
years has built up a coherent and to many, convincing,
view of culture in Europe before the arrival of the
Indo-Europeans. Her presentation of the artifacts and
art of this civilization has also provided a
generation of feminist artists with a working vocabulary and syntax.

Gimbutas contends that from c.7000 BCE to c.3500
BCE this pan-European culture was agriculturally
based, egalitarian in structure, nonviolent, and dedicated to the earth Goddess of recurring fertility, life
and death. With the arrival of the Indo-Europeans
the archaeological record shows the first appearance
of weaponry, fortifications, and patriarchal social
hierarchies, all based around a cult of violent
sacrifice to vengeful and aggressive warrior gods of
the sky. This overthrow of the old Goddess is still
reflected in the mythologies of Classical Greece and
Rome and reveals to us a literary and religious
counterpart to the archaeological record. Excellent
background and data for the nature and role of the
Goddess in both prehistoric and contemporary
religion.

1025   Goldenberg, Naomi. *Changing of the Gods. Feminism*
        and the End of Traditional Religions. Boston: Beacon
        Press, 1979.

See Carson (991), item 269.

1026　—. *The End of God. Important Directions for a Feminist Critique of Religion in the Works of Sigmund Freud and Carl Jung*. Ottawa: University of Ottawa Press, 1982.

See Ruud (**1003**), item 270.

1027　Graves, Robert. *The White Goddess*. New York: Farrar Strauss Giroux, 1966.

Graves' text is a "historical grammar of poetic myth" and a profound influence on modern poetry and on our appreciation for the myths of the Goddess. At the same time the mythology that Graves sets out to codify so clearly is that of the Goddess in all her manifestations.

1028　Haddon, Genia Pauli. *Body Metaphors. Releasing God-Feminine in Us All*. New York: Crossroad, 1988.

Not seen.

1029　Harding, M. Esther. *Women's Mysteries. Ancient and Modern*. New York: Bantam Books, 1973; New York: Harper & Row, 1976.

First published in 1931 and a fundamental work. See Carson (**991**), item 286.

1030　*Heresies. The Great Goddess Issue*. Revised ed., 1982.

A collection of essays by Merlin Stone, Carol Christ, Lucy Lippard, and others.

1031   Ide, Arthur Frederick. *Woman in History*. Mesquite, TX: Ide House.

This series of over 100 volumes, either the dozen or so written by Ide or by others, traces the female role in religion and divinity from prehistoric to modern times.

1032   Iglehart (Austen), Hallie. *The Heart of the Goddess*. Berkeley, CA: Wingbow Press, 1990.

The subtitle reads "Art, myth and meditations of the world's sacred feminine." The author examines both ancient and contemporary manifestations of the Goddess.

1033   Keith, W. Holman. *Divinity as the Eternal Feminine*. New York: Pageant Press, 1960.

On a neopagan revival of feminist values.

1034   Kinsley, David R. *The Goddess' Mirror. Visions of the Divine from East and West*. Albany, NY: State University of New York Press, 1989.

A survey of Goddess religion in East and West. Goddesses discussed include Durga, Kuan-yin, Laksmi, Amaterasu and Sita from Asia; and Inanna, Athena, Isis, Aphrodite and Mary from the Middle East and West. Well annotated, with excellent bibliography. A good introduction, especially for classroom use.

1035   Lantero, Erminie Huntress. *Feminine Aspects of Divinity*. Wallingford, PA: Pendle Hill, 1973.

See Carson (991), item 380.

1036   Luke, Helen. *Woman: Earth and Spirit. The Feminine in
        Symbol and Myth.* New York: Crossroad, 1981.

        Luke insists on the fundamental differences, both
        physical and psychic, between men and women, and
        warns that women who attempt to emphasize either
        the masculine or the androgynous do so at their great
        peril. This book is therefore an attempt to nourish
        the liberating forces of the feminine within woman.
        She examines various goddesses and images: of
        the dawn, the hearth, mother and daughter mys-
        teries, the mature women (straw and gold), related-
        ness (money images), and woman as avenger. See
        Carson (991), item 409.

1037   Neumann, Erich. *The Great Mother. An Analysis of the
        Archetype.* Princeton, NJ: Princeton University
        Press, 1963.

        A classic work of Jungian interpretation. See also
        Carson (991), item 475.

1038   Noble, Vicki. *Motherpeace. A Way to the Goddess
        Through Myth, Art and Tarot.* San Francisco:
        Harper & Row, 1982.

        This is an attempt to bring together the
        matriarchal consciousness that addresses the concerns
        of liberation, social justice, and peace through a
        meditation on the Goddess. Noble approaches the
        subject intuitively and through symbol, using a fasci-
        nating, newly created Tarot by her and Karen Vogel
        that expresses the wisdom of the female divine. This
        is in a tradition that stretches from the woman's cave
        art of the stone age through to Judy Chicago's *Dinner
        Party.* These are the sources of strength and hope

that will help wage the struggle for these goals. Good bibliography.

1039   Ochshom, Judith. *The Female Experience and the Nature of the Divine.* Bloomington, IN: University of Indiana Press, 1981.

See Carson **(991)**, item 492.

1040   Olson, Carl, ed. *The Book of the Goddess. Past and Present. An Introduction to Her Religion.* New York: Crossroad/Continuum, 1983.

Essays on feminist religion and the Goddess from many religious traditions. Gathers together the mythological data on the female goddesses from around the world as a handbook for the student. Good background. See also Carson **(991)**, item 499.

1041   Perera, Sylvia. *Descent to the Goddess: A Way of Initiation for Women.* Toronto: Inner City Books, 1981.

See Carson **(991)**, item 516.

1042   Preston, James J., ed. *Mother Worship. Theme and Variations.* Chapel Hill, NC: University of North Carolina Press, 1982.

Essays by Ena Campbell, Moss and Cappannari, Tullio Tentori, Joanna Hubbs, Jacob Pandian, Pauline Kolenda, P. F. McKean, Daniel F. McCall and others on the Goddess in the New World, in the European Madonna, the great Goddess in South Asia, and the divine feminine in Southeast Asia and Africa. Each article contains a good bibliography.

1043   Rae, Eleanor, and Bernice Marie-Daly. *Created in Her
        Image. Models of the Feminine Divine.* New York:
        Crossroad, 1990.

        Addressing the nature of the Holy Spirit in
        Christian theology has led the authors to investigate
        the feminine nature of divinity, our use and misuse of
        theological language, and the symbolic nature of
        religion.
        Discusses the nature of the Spirit as the feminine
        divine, insights of feminist and Jungian psychology to
        understanding this feminine divine, the Goddess and
        the destruction of "matristic" societies, androgyny as
        a model of gender relations within human society and
        within the Trinity, the personal conversion necessi-
        tated by the discovery of the feminine divine within
        our religious tradition and consciousness, and histor-
        ical examples of women mystics from the Middle
        Ages.
        The book concludes with a historical review of
        matricentric, patriarchal, ecofeminist, and feminist
        models leading to an "omnicentric" age.

1044   Rush, Anne Kent. *Moon, Moon.* New York: Random
        House; Berkeley, CA: Moon Publications, 1976.

        See Carson (**991**), item 592.

1045   *Signs.*

        This journal was started in 1975 for feminist
        scholarship and has become one of its major resources.

1046 Sjöö, Monica. *The Ancient Religion of the Great Cosmic Mother of All*. Barbara Mor, ed. Trondheim, Norway: Rainbow Press, 1981.

See Carson (**991**), item 625.

1047 —. *The Great Cosmic Mother. Rediscovering the Religion of the Earth*. San Francisco: Harper & Row, 1987.

This is a remarkable work of historical synthesis and feminist theory and theology. Topics include the role of women as creators; women's early religion, cosmology, mythology, and cults; the woman culture and religion of the neolithic, its myths, rites and sites; and the impact of patriarchal culture and religion. The final chapters of this hefty book survey the status of women and their religion in the modern world and the need to recapture the meaning and spirituality of the mother Goddess in order to heal us all. Excellent and extensive bibliography and notes.

1048 Spretnak, Charlene. *Lost Goddesses of Early Greece. A Collection of Pre-Hellenic Myths*. Boston: Beacon Press, 1984.

See Carson (**991**), item 635.

1049 Starhawk. *Dreaming the Dark: Magic, Sex and Politics*. Boston: Beacon Press, 1988.

It is no mistake that Matthew Fox (**930-932**) was silenced by the Vatican for refusing to fire this woman from the Oakland, CA institute where they both taught. Starhawk is a witch, that is, she is a practitioner of the ancient religion of the Goddess, the spirit of the earth that gives life and death to all of us on the planet, that teaches and nurtures and regulates all forms of existence. In this she is an adherent to a religion that antedates the patriarchies of the religions of the book and that survived the transformation of human society from one that respected the cycles and gifts of the earth to one that used the earth and its bounty as a mechanism: to be exploited and dominated. In this the earth shares the fate of women, children, people of color, and all the marginalized and alienated from the dominant centers of power.

While not all adherents of such neo-paganism or of new age spirituality are equally politically committed to new forms and structures of economic, political and spiritual life, Starhawk clearly demonstrates the essential link between the enpowerment of the individual, the couple, the group and the society and the issues of justice, healing, and peace on a global scale. Radical feminism thus arises from the same wellspring as a rejection of patriarchal ways of perceiving divinity both in the world and in ourselves, as the impetus to create new societies and groups within the dominant one, and thus to plant new seeds of hope in the darkness of a death-centered culture and politics. A unique contribution to all forms of liberation, peace and justice.

1050   —. *The Spiral Dance. A Rebirth of the Ancient Religion of the Great Goddess.* San Francisco: Harper & Row, 1979.

See Carson (**991**), item 640.

1051   Stone, Merlin. *When God Was a Woman*. New York: Dial Press, 1976.

        See Carson (991), item 646.

1052   —, as ed. *Ancient Mirrors of Womanhood. Our Goddess and Heroine Heritage*. 2 vols. New York: New Sibylline Books, 1979.

        See Carson (991), item 644.

1053   Tucker, Janice. *Way of the Rainbow Warrioress. A Practical Handbook of Wisdom*. Parker, CO: El Rancho, 1989.

        Not seen.

1054   *Unique.*

        This journal publishes articles on the Goddess and feminist theology regularly.

1055   Walker, Barbara G. *The Crone. Women of Age, Wisdom and Power*. San Francisco: Harper & Row, 1988.

        New trends in women's spirituality have begun to reject the oppressive Judeo-Christian tradition and have instead turned to small groups of study, ritual and worship devoted to the prepatriarchal Goddess. This movement is private, home-centered, and thus invisible to the media and to a male-dominated church and society.
        Yet this also poses problems, because without true material power women will remain exploited, no matter how spiritually free they feel among them-

selves. Walker advocates a new feminist approach to logic, ordering, and power that will not abandon but replace the current system. The greatest power that women possess is, of course, their power to love – but also to destroy – and this can be preserved and directed through an understanding of ancient archetypes embedded in pre-Judeo-Christian religion.

All these tendencies are summed and personified in the Crone – the venerable earth Goddess – neither virgin nor mother but powerful women, often feared and misinterpreted by male authorities as the marginalized witch, but never tampered with, and never controlled.

1056   —. *The Skeptical Feminist. Discovering the Virgin, Mother, and Crone.* San Francisco: Harper & Row, 1987.

Walker believes in a feminism that is morally, spiritually and materially preferable and better in itself than patriarchal systems. Females of all species are better able to nurture the young, are more intelligent, quicker, and more common-sensical. These are the elements of a skeptical feminism toward male ideologies.

Feminist skepticism strikes most deeply at male society in its understanding of divinity and the disastrous results of patriarchal theology. Here the cult of the Goddess brings the greatest challenge, since it fully reinterprets patriarchal attitudes toward the virgin, mother, and crone that Judeo-Christian traditions have perverted.

1057   —. *The Women's Dictionary of Symbols and Sacred Objects*. San Francisco: Harper & Row, 1988.

Divided by topic into motifs, sacred objects, secular-sacred objects, rituals, deities' signs, supernaturals, zodiacs, body parts, nature, animals, birds, insects, flowers, plants, trees, fruit and foods, minerals, stones and shells. Good bibliography.

1058   —. *Women's Rituals. A Sourcebook*. San Francisco: Harper & Row, 1990.

Rituals of equipment and objects, techniques, physical rituals, mental rituals, rituals of play, guided meditations, celebrating women's forgotten history, and seasonal rituals. Silence, invocation, planets, dancing, flowers, dolls, stones and cards, masks, banners, nakedness, the earth, "thealogy," healing, baptisms and rites of passage are among the rituals clearly and even-handedly described.

1059   Whitmont, Edward. *Return of the Goddess. Recovering the Feminine Aspects of the Soul.* New York: Crossroad/Continuum, 1982.

See Carson (**991**), item 700.

1060   *WomanSpirit.*

A journal that publishes regularly on the Goddess.

Biblical Reinterpretation

1061   Arthur, Rose Horman. *The Wisdom Goddess. Feminine Motifs in Eight Nag Hammadi Documents.* Lanham, MD: University Press of America, 1984.

See Carson (**991**), item 28.

1062   Bal, Mieke. *Death and Dissymmetry. The Politics of Coherence in the Book of Judges.* Chicago: University of Chicago Press, 1988.

The book of Judges is a man's book par excellence. It celebrates death in all its forms, most especially the murder of the weak and innocent. War, rape, murder, dismemberment are its delight. But Judges presents a frightening dissymmetry of death: women who kill men are politically motivated: liberation of their people is the motive; while men who kill women kill innocent young daughters. As in her other work Bal uses both biblical scholarship and the newer semiotics of deconstruction to unravel the mysteries of this text and to unravel its gender-bound violence.

Themes include the coherence of politics and politics of coherence: construction and deconstruction in Judges; the themes of virginity and its destruction; sacrifice and the violence of the father; the language of the woman's body as a challenge to patriarchy; the home and unhomeliness; and the displaced mother. Excellent bibliography.

1063   —. *Lethal Love. Feminist Literary Readings of Biblical Love Stories.* Bloomington, IN: University of Indiana Press, 1987.

This is a radical deconstruction of certain texts and biblical personages according to a feminist hermeneutic. Bal approaches the Bible, however, as a believer only in the primacy of the post-modern interpreter of texts: it is morally neutral, neither "feminist resource nor sexist manifesto."

Bal thus delivers a series of reinterpretations of Eve, Ruth, Tamar, Delilah, and Bathsheba that stress only the value of differences of interpretation, in most cases away from misogynist traditions, to be sure.

Forms, frames, narratology, text, symmetry, power, the interpreter as the focus of interpretation.

1064 — . *Murder and Difference. Gender, Genre, and Scholarship on Sisera's Death.* Matthew Gumpert, trans. Bloomington & Indianapolis, IN: Indiana University Press, 1988.

Discusses the central text of Jael's murder of Sisera in her tent in Judges 4 and 5. Yet, as biblical scholars have long emphasized, the two texts are very different, and tell remarkably different stories. Bal's work examines these differences, contending that Deborah's song of Judges 5 reflects not slight textual variations, but profound differences of outlook and context; they speak in very different "codes."

These codes can be historical, theological, anthropological, and literary, according to the discipline examining a text. They can also be transdisciplinary: by themes or gender.

1065 Carmody, Denise Lardner. *Biblical Woman. Feminist Reflections on Scriptural Texts.* New York: Crossroad/Continuum, 1988.

The texts are careful readings of twenty-four passages in both Hebrew Bible and New Testament that analyze the place and religious role of women in the Bible and that reflect on the status of women today. See also **2**.

1066   Collins, Adela Yarbro. *Feminist Perspectives in Biblical Scholarship.* Chico, CA: Scholars Press, 1985.

Not seen.

1067   Evans, Mary J. *Woman in the Bible.* Exeter: Paternoster, 1983.

Examines the essential texts in both Hebrew and Christian scriptures. Good bibliography on the general question of the portrayal of women in the Bible.

1068   Faricy, Robert, S.J. *The Lord's Dealing. The Primacy of the Feminine in Christian Spirituality.* New York: Paulist Press, 1988.

Examines the conflict between the primacy of the feminine in Christian religion and the reality of women's oppression and the suppression of the feminine in our culture and lives. The author contends that only by restoring the feminine will Western culture recover from its various ills.

Faricy takes insights from Jungian psychology and the life and teaching of Jesus to analyze various topics. These include the dualisms and alienations of our lives expressed in the personal and natural world, man and women, person and human nature; the mutuality of God and creation as expressed through the nature of Jesus in the thought of Jung and Teilhard de Chardin; "the eternal feminine" in Teilhard's thought and its manifestations in the cult of Mary; Jung's insistence on quaternity, rather than trinitarian thought; and the cosmos as the body of Christ.

One comes away from Faricy's book with a sense of good intentions, solid Catholic theology, and the continuing cooptation of the divine female by the male theologian, churchman, and analyst.

1069   Fiorenza, Elisabeth Schüssler. *Bread Not Stone. The Challenge of Feminist Biblical Interpretation.* Boston: Beacon Press, 1985.

Not seen.

1070   —. *Foundational Theology. Jesus and the Church.* New York: Crossroad/Continuum, 1984.

A feminist perspective on the origins of the church.

1071   —. *In Memory of Her. A Feminist Theological Reconstruction of Christian Origins.* New York: Crossroad, 1983.

This is one of the essential texts of women's theology: for it breaks ground in the reinterpretation of women's role in the foundation of the church and its orders that rejects the patriarchal rewriting of early Christian history and stresses the benefits of remaining within a tradition that can be made whole by such a revision.

1072   Fisher, Kathleen. *Woman at the Well. Feminist Perspectives on Spiritual Direction.* New York: Paulist Press, 1988.

This gathers the insights of feminist therapists, psychologists and theologians to derive a new feminist spirituality. It also derives from new readings of familiar biblical texts: of the images of women giving birth, yeast becoming bread, and the cosmic womb of Christ.

Topics include feminist contexts for spiritual direction, new models of holiness, and the image of the woman at the well, feminist approaches to theology, Jesus and women, new forms of prayer based on scripture; feminist insights into the process of discernment; the issues of women and power, which are the key for salvation and liberation; and the reinterpretation of power away from dominance to mutuality. The author also discusses the spiritual consequences and context of violence against women; nonviolence, passivity, and strength; anger, its origins and uses; forgiveness; and the spiritual meanings of motherhood, daughterhood and the implications for reclaiming a women's tradition.

1073   Gottwald, Norman K., ed. *The Bible and Liberation: Political and Social Hermeneutics.* Maryknoll, NY: Orbis Books, 1983.

See 6. Contains essays by Schüssler Fiorenza and Schottroff.

1074   Grassi, Carolyn M., and Joseph A. Grassi. *Mary Magdalene and the Women in Jesus' Life.* Kansas City, MO: Sheed & Ward, 1986.

A careful textual and historical study of the relationship between Jesus and Mary Magdalene and the other women of the Jesus movement; provides valuable insights into the historical roots of women's increasing leadership role in the church and in society today.

1075   Grassi, Joseph. *Hidden Heroes of the Gospels. Female Counterparts of Jesus.* Collegeville, MN: Liturgical Press, 1989.

"Hidden" means both hidden from history but more appropriately here hidden as all the Gospels were hidden, sacred texts gradually unfolded during the celebration of the eucharistic mystery and drama. Analyzes the audience, themes, and dramatic discourse of each Gospel. The Marys, Jairus' daughter, the woman with the hemorrhage, Peter's mother-in-law, the Canaanite woman, the women at the cross are examined in a socio-political framework.

1076   Greeley, Andrew M. *The Mary Myth. On the Femininity of God.* New York: Seabury Press, 1977.

A discussion of the nature of divinity and of woman's nature – both male and female – as revealed through Mary. Topics include a reemergence of the figure of Mary, the religious meaning of experience, material life, symbols, language, and sacraments; the androgyny of God; and images of Mary as mother of God, eternal virgin, both life symbols, and as *sponsa* (the sexual mate), and pietà, the mother that receives us back into death. Overall a delicate, and enlightened, treatment of the divine feminine.

1077   Heine, Susanne. *Women and Early Christianity. A Reappraisal.* John Bowden, trans. Philadelphia: Fortress Press, 1988.

A review of feminist biblical scholarship. Heine first introduces feminist hermeneutics, its critics and opponents, then examines basic biblical themes before focusing on the life, crucifixion, and resurrection of Jesus.

Heine maintains that feminist scholars have made a substantial contribution, but also sees that they have brought their own distortions into the argument.

Heine attempts to both deepen, and demythologize, feminist understandings of many biblical passages as a corrective to what she sees as undue polarization along gender allegiances, the compounding of "negative theories" out of women's exploitation, hurt and anger, which see Christianity, maleness, or church as essentially negative values. Heine also attempts to define what historical research can and cannot achieve in the pursuit of truth or ideology. Her work, however, is not one of retrenchment or reaction, but is committed to realistic goals and expectations of a continuing struggle for liberation, equality, and then alliance between the sexes.

1078   Laffer, Alice L. *An Introduction to the Old Testament. A Feminist Perspective.* Philadelphia: Fortress Press, 1988.

This is an excellent volume. Examines the Pentateuch, Deuteronomy, the prophets, and the Wisdom literature from a feminist perspective. Each section includes an introduction to both historical and literary considerations; issues that feminist interpretation address, including patriarchy, hierarchy, language, women as chattel, stereotyping in role and sexuality, men's and women's history; and the presentation of key texts. Each section ends with conclusions and recommended readings of books and articles.

1079   Meyers, Carol. *Discovering Eve. Ancient Israelite Women in Context.* New York: Oxford University Press, 1988.

A reconstruction of Eve shorn of misogynist interpretations and false traditions associated with her, and by implication, with all women. Through this focus Meyers hopes to point to all the women of ancient Israel who were written invisible in the Bible and Jewish tradition, and to see the lot of all women through a new appreciation of biblical archetypes. In this quest both feminist biblical scholarship and modern "materialist" readings are used.

Topics include Eve as the symbol of women, the problem of patriarchy, the highland environment of ancient Israel, which sets the context of the Eve story and that of women in ancient Israel, the Genesis paradigms of Genesis, the family household of ancient Israel, female roles and gender relationships.

1080   Mollenkott, Virginia Ramey, *The Divine Feminine. The Biblical Imagery of God as Female.* New York: Crossroad/Continuum, 1984.

A comprehensive study of the subject.

1081   —. *Godding. Human Responsibility and the Bible.* New York: Crossroad, 1987.

Biblically based theologizing on issues of war, racism, and sexism.

1082   —. *Women, Men, and the Bible.* New York: Crossroad/Continuum, 1988.

This is a a careful textual study analyzing what
the scriptural tradition has to say about relationships between the sexes and their relationship to
God. It is intended as a straightforward introduction
to notions of feminism and mutuality as based in the
Judeo-Christian tradition. Topics include the Christian way of relating, the question of God's masculinity, freedom from stereotypes, the contradictions
within the Pauline corpus, learning how to interpret
the Bible accurately, and biblical doctrines and
human equality.

1083   Moltmann-Wendel, Elisabeth. *A Land Flowing with
        Milk and Honey. Perspectives on Feminist Theology.*
        New York: Crossroad/Continuum, 1988.

This is both an excellent introduction and a careful analysis of many essential issues in feminist
theology. They include the process of women's self-
discovery as the context, the formal structures of a
critical feminist theology, and new forms of a
feminist Christology.

Topics include changing images of women in
partnership, work, and sexuality; new analyses of
patriarchy; the history and role of the Goddess in
history and today; feminist theology as a liberation
theology; feminist biblical interpretation; God as
mother; and suppressed Goddess and mother traditions within Christianity itself.

Moltmann-Wendel concludes with discussions of a
new Jesus written by and for women; the theological
role of mutuality in women's thought; self-love; patriarchal and matriarchal forms of love, including the
insights of the "Sophia" literature; and new models
for women from pagan to biblical and contemporary
examples.

1084   —. *The Women Around Jesus.* New York: Crossroad/ Continuum, 1989.

Uses textual analysis, art and church history to bring to the fore the role of women in the Jesus movement and in the formation of the early church. See **10**.

1085   Patai, Raphael. *The Hebrew Goddess.* New York: Avon Books, 1978.

See Carson (**991**), item 513.

1086   Ruether, Rosemary Radford. *To Change the World. Christology and Cultural Criticism.* New York: Crossroad, 1981.

Breaks with such recent Christologies as Küng's and Schillebeeckx' to reinterpret Christ's messianic message in light of feminist perspectives on liberation.

1087   Russell, Letty, ed. *Feminist Interpretation of the Bible.* Philadelphia: Westminster Press, 1985.

Essays by Zikmund, Cannon, Farley, Sakenfeld, Ringe, Exum, Setel, Thistlethwaite, Radford Reuther, Schüssler Fiorenza, Russell and Trible on critical consciousness, examples of feminist interpretation, and feminist critical principles.

1088   —. *The Liberating Word. A Guide to Nonsexist Interpretation of the Bible.* Philadelphia: Westminster Press, 1976.

Essays by Russell, Ringe, Schüssler Fiorenza, and Dewey on language, hermeneutics, biblical authority, interpreting patriarchal traditions, images of women as prophets and religious leaders, the church and changing language.

1089   Scanzoni, Letha, and Nancy Hardesty. *All We're Meant to Be. A Biblical Approach to Women's Liberation.* Waco, TX: Word Books, 1974.

Jesus' message was one of liberation, and his message was especially meaningful for women, who responded gladly to his call to discipleship. This book is an attempt to show that Christian tradition is one of equality between men and women, both in the religious understanding of personhood and in sexuality, as well as in outlook on the world and work.

Topics include the male/female polarity, the biblical background, Jesus and the women around him, and the role of women in the hierarchical church. Final chapters deal with women in the modern world: issues of reproduction, single women, the church and women, and women defined on their own terms apart from men and marriage.

1090   Schaberg, Jane. *The Illegitimacy of Jesus. A Feminist Theological Interpretation of the Infancy Narratives.* San Francisco: Harper & Row, 1987.

See **13**.

1091   Schaupp, Joan. *Woman. Image of the Holy Spirit.* Denville, NJ: Dimension Books, 1975.

See Carson (**991**), item 600.

1092   Schneiders, Sandra M. *Women and the Word. The
        Gender of God in the New Testament and the
        Spirituality of Women.* Mahwah, NJ: Paulist Press,
        1986.

        Judeo-Christian tradition has never assigned
        gender to God, even in discussing the Trinity; these
        names are only significant of relations. In fact, the
        Vatican's 1977 letter excluding women from the
        priesthood may be heretical for its insistence on the
        theological maleness of Jesus.
        This book is an attempt to lay bare the false
        assumptions of the masculinity of God as reveled
        through the Hebrew scriptures and through Jesus in
        Christian scripture.
        Schneiders contends that Jesus' life, personality,
        and teachings were a radical challenge to patriarchy
        and current definitions of masculinity.

1093   Sheres, Ita. *Dinah's Rebellion. A Biblical Parable for
        Our Time.* New York: Crossroad/Continuum, 1990.

        Not seen.

1094   Stagg, Evelyn, and Frank Stagg. *Woman in the World
        of Jesus.* Philadelphia: Westminster Press, 1978.

        Discusses women in the world of Jesus, in Jewish,
        Greek and Roman society; the relationship that Jesus
        had with women; women in the early church. The
        authors contend that there is a solid basis for women
        in the ministry; and they call for openness against
        rigid structures.

1095   Stanton, Elizabeth Cady. *The Women's Bible.* New
        York: European Publishing, 1895.

Stanton's contribution to the field of feminist theology has been long recognized in feminist thought. Her Bible contains many radical rereadings of essential texts, including that of the priority of Adam's creation.

1096   Stendahl, Krister. *The Bible and the Role of Women. A Case Study in Hermeneutics.* Emilie T. Sander, trans. Philadelphia: Fortress Press, 1966.

On whatever grounds – on the biblical exegesis of the key texts, on the biblical views of male and female, and on the obvious grounds of the "emancipation" of women – it is clear that if Christians believe God created man and women equal, women ought to be ministers.

1097   Thompsett, Frederica H. *Christian Feminist Perspectives on History, Theology and the Bible.* Cincinnati, OH: Forward Movement, 1986.

This brief pamphlet succinctly examines the various forms of writing women's history and concludes that the most valuable is that written from the point of view of women, their experiences and values, and their own definitions. She then examines reading the Bible from a woman's perspective; and she concludes with reflections on reforming theology to empower individuals and to change institutions.

1098   Tolbert, Mary Ann. *The Bible and Feminist Hermeneutics.* Decatur, GA: Scholar's Press, 1983.

Not seen.

1099 Trible, Phyllis. *Texts of Terror. Literary Feminist Readings of Biblical Narratives.* Philadelphia: Fortress Press, 1984.

The author uses literary critical tools to uncover the classic "victims" of texts traditionally unconcerned with them to bring out the people themselves, in marked contrast to the interest of the "ruling class" that had so objectified them.

Trible presents the texts with only the briefest introductions to the stories, but with excellent analysis and critical documentation, of "Hagar, the slave used, abused, and rejected [Gen. 16:1-16; 21:9-21]; Tamar, the princess raped and discarded [2 Sam. 13:1-22]; an unnamed women, the concubine raped, murdered, and dismembered [Judges 19:1-30]; and the daughter of Jephthah, a virgin slain and sacrificed [Judges 11:29-40]."

1100 Weems, Renita J. *Just a Sister Away. A Womanist Vision of Women's Relationships in the Bible.* San Diego, CA: Lura Media, 1988.

A study of biblical women, including Hagar and Sarah, Naomi and Ruth, Martha and Mary, Jephthah's daughter and the mourning women, Miriam, the women in the Jesus movement, Vashti and Esther, Elizabeth and Mary, and Lot's wife and her daughters. Written in a nonscholarly manner, with appropriate questions following each section. Brief, but useful, bibliography.

1101 Whalberg, Rachel Conrad. *Jesus According to a Woman.* New York: Paulist Press, 1975.

Treats various biblical stories in which Jesus related to women. Stresses his openness to women and his stance of equality toward them. Jesus chose women for the ministry, and a women (Mary Magdalene) was the first to receive the good news of the Resurrection.

1102   —. *Jesus and the Freed Women.* New York: Paulist Press, 1978.

Over the centuries, the author contends, the church has retreated from Jesus' openness and equal treatment of women. This book therefore attempts to focus on some of the worst stereotypes that deny liberation and to present others that foster it. Includes discussions on Jesus and the freed woman, Cana, Jesus and his use of the imagery of birth and the model of the woman's body as an image of rebirth that shows his closeness to the world of women, the image of the foot washer and servanthood, Jesus' use of the mother hen image, and the story of the assertive woman who obtains justice by her perseverance.

Women and the Churches

1103   Armstrong, Karen. *The Gospel According to Woman. Christianity's Creation of the Sex War in the West.* London: Elm Tree Books, 1986.

A non-narrative history of the shift in Christian attitudes to woman from Jesus' "good news" to the misogynist tradition so firmly embedded in the structured church since the third century. Armstrong takes the celibate tradition in the West and its dichotomy between body and spirit as the core and root of the inferior status of women, whom the West sees as essentially "sexual beings." From this basic identification of woman as sexual and of sexuality as evil came the tradition of Eve the temptress, of the powerful woman as the witch; and the Christian religious ideals of virgin, martyr, and mystic: models of independent woman, fully the equals of men, yet that today continue to shackle women to dead myths from past social ages.

In these chapters on historical models Armstrong offers many valuable insights into the ambiguous and double-edged archetypes of the woman expressed in Christian history: models of courage and independence yet also of dangerous pursuits for many of today's women who need fresh models and ways of expressing their spirit and spirituality that go beyond Protestantism's "wife and mother" options and the Catholic masochisms of "holy anorexia."

1104   Ashe, Kaye. *Today's Women. Tomorrow's Church.* Chicago: Thomas More Press, 1983.

Attempts to deal with the issues of women in the Catholic church and the crux of the issue: can there be such a thing as "Christian feminism"? Ashe believes that there can be, but only if deeply informed by the leading feminist theory and strongly committed to a struggle against the phallotocracy of the church through women's ordination, women's conferences within the church, and a process of conversion. Bibliography.

1105   Bantley Doeley, Sarah, ed. *Women's Liberation and the Church. The New Demand for Freedom in the Life of the Christian Church.* New York: Association Press, 1970.

See Bass and Boyd (**989**), item 61.

1106 Brown, Joanne Carlson, and Carole R. Bohn. *Christianity, Patriarchy and Abuse. A Feminist Critique.* New York: Pilgrim Press, 1989.

Not seen.

1107 Byrne, Lavinia. *Women Before God.* London: SPCK, 1988.

Reflections on the place of women as individuals, women, and members of the church and religious orders.

1108 Campbell-Jones, Suzanne. *In Habit. A Study of Working Nuns.* New York: Pantheon, 1978.

See Loeb (**1001**), item 936.

1109 Carmody, Denise Lardner. *Feminism and Christianity. A Two-Way Reflection.* Nashville, TN: Abingdon Press, 1982.

Carmody seeks the centrist ground of a "Christian feminism," both of which are alternatives to the materialistic dead end of North American culture, but also seeks to demonstrate that feminist theory can inform all traditional fields – from theology to psychology to sociology to ecology – with a new sense of the divine.

Topics include new study of the feminine divine through the Goddess, a new Christocentrism, new insights into selfhood through feminist and Christian thought, feminist and Christian social theory, and feminist and Christian theologies of nature.

1110   Carr, Anne E. *Transforming Grace. Christian Tradition and Women's Experience.* San Francisco: Harper & Row, 1988.

Addresses the issue of Christian feminism and concludes that there is nothing contradictory in the term. In fact, Carr sees feminism and Christianity as deeply united in the truth of their visions.

Topics include coming of age in the church, the women's movement and its challenge to the churches, ordination of women in history, theology and ethics, feminist theory and feminist theology, women's experience and theological anthropology, feminist reflections on God, feminism and Christology, Christ, Mary and the Church, and Christian feminist spirituality. Excellent bibliography.

1111   Chittister, Joan, O.S.B. *Job's Daughters. Women and Power.* New York: Paulist Press, 1990.

Not seen.

1112   —. *Winds of Change. Women Challenge Church.* Kansas City, MO: Sheed & Ward, 1986.

Collected essays on issues of peace, justice, and liberation with an emphasis on the religious and spiritual context of Catholicism.

1113   —. *Women, Ministry and the Church.* New York: Paulist Press, 1983.

On the role of women in the pastoral mission of the church, new forms of language to express new realities and aspirations, religious life, ministry and secularism, post-conciliar spirituality among Benedictine women, renewal in the Catholic church, women as witnesses for peace, the role of holy disobedience, and new forms of leadership.

1114 Curb, Rosemary, and Nancy Manahan, eds. *Lesbian Nuns. Breaking Silence.* Tallahassee, FL: Naiad Press, 1985.

See Loeb (**1001**), item 939.

1115 Daly, Mary. *The Church and the Second Sex.* New York: Harper & Row, 1968.

Essential reading. On the inherent misogyny of the Christian church in its traditions of thought, language, ritual, organization, and action. This is a classic work, and one in which Daly rejects the association of Christianity and feminism as incompatible. See also Carson (**991**), item 153.

1116 Donovan, Mary Ann. *Sisterhood As Power. Women Religious as Catalysts of the Future.* New York: Crossroad/Continuum, 1989.

The role of women religious in bringing about institutional change.

1117 Dowell, Susan, and Linda Hurcombe. *Dispossessed Daughters of Eve. Faith and Feminism.* London: SPCK, 1987.

Examines the inherent contradictions and tensions of "Christian feminism." The authors discuss their own and many other women's alienation from a church that rejects their equal role. Discusses the historical developments of feminism in society and church, a reexamination of the Bible and its social and political message so distorted by neoconservatives and fundamentalists, the feminist assault on Christian traditions (they reject "radical" positions in favor of homosexuality and abortion), a maturing feminist theology, the contradictions of a Constantinian Christendom, a new feminist covenant with the earth, and a commitment to struggle that will bypass any attempts to get a "fair deal" from male structures.

1118 Dunfee, Susan N. *Beyond Servanthood. Christianity and the Liberation of Women.* Washington, DC: University Press of America, 1989.

This is a profound meditation on the challenge posed by Mary Daly's rejection of Christianity as an essentially patriarchal manifestation of male religion, and thus incompatible with women's lives and religion: women and Christianity have as much in common as a healthy woman and cancer.

Dunfee therefore begins with her own experience of Christianity, which she says has been informed by the feminist movement to take full cognizance of sexism, patriarchal authoritarianism, and resistance to change. But like Ruether, Schüssler Fiorenza, Moltmann-Wendall and others, she sees the possibility of a "Christian feminism" that will not so much accommodate women to Christian male structures as find the liberating seeds within Christianity to empower women to find their own liberation.

Discusses the liberating aspects of Christianity, the thought of leading Christian feminist theologians, the liberating potential of Christian symbols of service and altruism, which Dunfee concludes is little. Service and altruism may, in fact, disguise bondage and self-negation, and are therefore fraught with great danger for women. She therefore turns to the works of D. D. Williams, Niebuhr, and Tillich on altruistic love and mutuality and then goes on to examine the nature of the freedom created by this love.

She concludes with the insights of Sölle, Bultmann, Delwin Brown, and Jürgen Moltmann that the Christian community was formed as one of mutuality and service between friends, thus attempting to find at the roots of Christianity the remedies for Christianity's two millennia participation in the enslavement of women. Brief bibliography.

1119   Eigo, Francis A., ed. *A Discipleship of Equals. Towards a Christian Feminist Spirituality.* Villanova, PA: Villanova University Press, 1988.

Not seen.

1120   Elizondo, Virgilio, and Norbert Greinacher, eds. *Women in a Men's Church. Concilium* 134. New York: Seabury Press, 1980.

Topics include the historical development of a "men's church," the situation today, the masculinity of God and the role of women in both Old and New Testament, and the role of feminist theology as a liberation theology and in the emancipation of women. Includes essays by Ida Raming, Nadine Foley, Elizabeth Carroll, Rosemary Haughton, Maria Agaledo and others.

1121   Ermath, Margaret S. *Adam's Fractured Rib. Observa-*
        tions on Women in the Church. Philadelphia:
        Fortress Press, 1970.

        See Bass and Boyd (989), item 268.

1122   Ferraro, Barbara, and Patricia Hussey, with Jane
        O'Reilly. *No Turning Back. Two Nuns Battle with*
        the Vatican Over Women's Right to Choose. New
        York: Poseidon Press, 1990.

        A narrative of the nuns' struggle over freedom of
        conscience, speech, obedience, women's rights, and the
        new wave of oppression within the Catholic church.

1123   Fiorenza, Elisabeth Schüssler, and Mary Collins, eds.
        Women, Invisible in Theology and Church.
        Concilium 182. Edinburgh: T. & T. Clark, 1985.

        Essays by Schüssler Fiorenza, Mary Collins, Marie
        Zimmerman, Margaret Brennan, Marjorie Proctor-
        Smith, Adriana Valerioi, Kari Vogt, Mary Hunt,
        Marga Bührig, Isis Muller, and Mary Boys on church
        structures, ecclesial discourse in church history,
        anthropology, theology, ecumenism, and ritual itself
        that make women invisible, and the role of theology
        education in this process. Mary Boys also discusses
        the role of women in changing the process.

1124   Fitzpatrick, Ruth M., ed. *Liberating Liturgies.* Fairfax,
        VA: Women's Ordination Conference, 1989.

        A series of liturgies that stress the bipolarity of
        divinity and give voice to feminist insights in lan-
        guage, symbol, ceremony, and structure.

1125   Franklin, Margaret Ann. *The Force of the Feminine. Women, Men and the Church.* Boston: Allen & Unwin, 1986.

Essays by Franklin, Eileen Jones, Eileen Byrne, Barbara Thiering, Kevin Giles, Leo Hay, Marlene Cohen, Marie Tulip, Veronica Brady and others on women and the church, the church's role in perpetuating sexual stereotypes, the ordination of women in the Bible and the Catholic church, psychological analysis of the objections to women's ordination, institutional sexism, sexist theological language, feminization of religious structures through religious orders, and the fundamentally feminine element of Christian life.

1126   —, and Ruth Sturmey Jones, eds. *Opening the Cage. Stories of Church and Gender.* Boston: Allen & Unwin, 1987.

A collection of personal stories by men and women of major Christian denominations of Australia that reflect the struggle to change church structures and values toward sexuality, gender, and equality within Christianity. Contributors include L. and D. Balfour, Julia Perry, Pat Bundock, Merle Goldsmith, Kath McPhillips, Shirley Randell, Marie Tulip and others.

1127   Furlong, Monica, ed. *Feminine in the Church.* London: SPCK, 1984.

Essays by Furlong, Rowan Williams, Eric Doyle, Janet Morley, Jane Williams, Ann Hoad, Henriette Santer and others on women in the ministry, the ordination of women in Roman Catholicism, the "maleness" of Christ, Jesus and women, the image of

Mary, sexual stereotypes in church and society, and views of hierarchy and the fall.

1128	—, ed. *Mirror to the Church. Reflections on Sexism.* London: SPCK, 1988.

Articles by Furlong, A. Peberdy, J. Morley, R. McCurry, E. Storkey, U. Kroll, J. Robson and others on ritual and power, sex and sexuality in the church, the family as a creative sacrament, femininity and the Holy Spirit, and other topics.

1129	—. *Shrinking and Changing.* Faringdon, OX: David Blamires, 1981.

Not seen.

1130	Grant, Jacquelyn. *White Women's Christ and Black Women's Jesus. Feminist Christology and Womanist Response.* Atlanta, GA: Scholar's Press, 1989.

In recent years an open debate has emerged in feminist and feminist theological circles over the disparity between the socio-economic, and thus the theological, contexts of white, middle-class intellectuals and black intellectuals and activists; between "Christ" theologies still permeated with subtle and unquestioned triumphalism of class, education, and background and "Jesus" theologies born out of true oppression and struggle. This book attempts to highlight some of the contradictions in a feminist theology that often speaks of oppression and the need for liberation with very little solidarity between the classes and races.

1131   Gundry, Patricia. *Neither Slave Nor Free. Helping Women Answer the Call to Church Leadership.* San Francisco: Harper & Row, 1987.

From the realization that women, as equally as men, *are* the church, comes the decision that one need not plead for admission into the ministry, that one can be a minister through the power of one's own Christian calling and unique gifts. Rather than continue to knock at closed church doors, women should form new, relevant ministries of their own, abandoning structures in favor of functions that nurture life and spirit. This book is a guide to that process.

1132   —. *Woman, Be Free!* Grand Rapids, MI: Zondervan, 1977.

Discusses the status of women as second-class citizens in the church, the nature of women in Christian religious tradition; Christian stereotypes that keep woman in a domestic, subservient role; the biblical texts that have been used to bolster this; and positive biblical role models for women in every walk of life.

1133   Hageman, Alice L., ed. *Sexist Religion and Women in the Church. No More Silence.* New York: Association Press, 1974.

See Bass and Boyd (989), item 65.

1134   Hagen, June Steffensen, ed. *Gender Matters. Women's Studies for the Christian Community.* Grand Rapids, MI: Academe Books, 1990.

Not seen.

1135   Heinzelmann, Gertrud, ed. *We Won't Keep Silent Any Longer! Women Speak Out on Vatican Council II.* Zurich: Interfeminas, 1965.

Not seen.

1136   Heschel, Susannah, ed. *On Being a Jewish Feminist. A Reader.* New York: Schocken Books, 1983.

See Carson (**991**), item 304; Loeb (**1001**), item 952; and Ruud (**1003**), item 336.

1137   Kirk, Martha Ann, CCVI. *Celebrations of Biblical Women's Stories. Tears, Milk and Honey.* Kansas City, MO: Sheed & Ward, 1989.

Recent feminist exegesis has now made possible liturgies of liberation based upon a clearer understanding of the role of women in biblical history and revelation. Includes the liturgies and music.

1138   Koltun, Elizabeth, ed. *The Jewish Woman. New Perspectives.* New York: Schocken Press, 1976.

Essays by Judith Plaskow, Carol Christ, Rachel Adler, Arlene Agus, Deborah Weissman, Blu Greenberg, Phyllis Trible, Mary Gendler, and others on Jewish feminism, women's liberation and a theology of liberation, rituals and the Jewish year, women in Jewish law, historical models, Jewish women today, and women in Jewish religious literature: the Bible, Rabbinic tradition, Vashti. Includes a bibliography arranged by topic.

1139   Lack, Roslyn. *Women and Judaism. Myth, History and Struggle.* Garden City, NY: Doubleday, 1980.

See Carson (**991**), item 375; Ruud (**1003**), item 433.

1140　Loades, Ann. *Searching for Lost Coins. Explorations in Christianity and Feminism.* Allison Park, PA: Pickwick Publications, 1988.

Begins with the assumption that while "Christian feminism" may be a contradiction in terms, Christianity may still offer some keys to renewing a sense of human community that can bring together gender. Discusses the possibility of reform in a patriarchal society, rediscovering the feminine in Christian tradition, the "morbid over-identification with Christ as suffering victim," and with the long religious tradition of woman as co-sufferer and masochistic mate of Jesus crucified; new voices for women in the Christian community; and new language and images of God as female. Good bibliography.

1141　Maitland, Sara. *A Map of the New Country. Women and Christianity.* London & Boston: Routledge & Kegan Paul, 1983.

This is consciously not a book of theology but an attempt to bridge the gaps between feminism and Christianity and to describe the blend.
Discusses origins of Christian feminism, the women's movement, communities of faith, women's ordination, women in church bureaucracies, new language, liturgy and spirituality.

1142　Marriage, Alwyn. *Life-Giving Spirit. Responding to the Feminine in God.* London: SPCK, 1989.

Attempts to resolve the conflict between a patriarchal and sexist theology and church and the new insights and demands of feminist theology by side-stepping the issue of inclusive language and by reviving the importance of the Holy Spirit as the divine feminine.

1143 Martin, Faith McBurney. *Call Me Blessed. The Emerging Christian Woman.* Grand Rapids, MI: W.B. Eerdmans, 1988.

Reexamines many of the key passages of scripture that have been underpinnings of patriarchal authority. Rather than rejecting the Bible, Martin sees that a correct rereading of these texts can provide new insights that will liberate women from many stereotypical roles in society and church and to the reconciliation of women and men.

Topics include new awareness of women's rights and voice within the church, Christian feminism, the traditions of biblical and church history, the male in authority, violence and oppression against women; the liberating role of Jesus, a theology that will account for true differences in men and women, if indeed there are such in nature; God in male and female image; women in authority; Paul on women; and new concepts of fatherhood, the language of God and humanity, and the new children of God.

1144 Mayeski, Marie Ann. *Women. Models of Liberation.* Kansas City, MO: Sheed & Ward, 1988.

An anthology of original source readings on the history and contributions of eight women in the life of the church with critical introductions to the historical context and meaning of the text itself. Includes, among others, Perpetua, Heloise, Julian of Norwich, Teresa of Avila, and Caryll Houselander.

1145   Mollenkott, Virginia Ramey. *Women of Faith in Dialogue.* New York: Crossroad/Continuum, 1987.

Sponsored by the American Jewish Committee, this ecumenical collection reflects the meeting of Protestant, Catholic, Jewish and Moslem women on common issues of concern within their respective institutional churches and on the nature of women's spirituality and religious life.

1146   Moltmann-Wendel, Elisabeth. *Liberty, Equality, Sisterhood. On the Emancipation of Women in Church and Society.* Ruth Gritsch, trans. Philadelphia: Fortress Press, 1978.

Published lectures on women in the New Testament and ancient world; women's coming of age intellectually, politically, economically, socially, and sexually; the gradual assertiveness of women to their own dignity; the emancipation of women in the church, and in society.

1147   Morley, Janet. *All Desires Known. Prayers Uniting Faith and Feminism.* Wilton, CT: Morehouse-Barlow, 1988.

A collection of liturgical prayers for each season from a feminist point of view. The texts and their style are compellingly direct and elegant.

1148   Osiek, Carolyn, R.S.C.J. *Beyond Anger. On Being a Feminist in the Church.* New York: Paulist Press, 1986.

This is a book written in full awareness of the approaching crisis within the Catholic church over the role of women, both within and outside religious orders. It is aimed at those, who despite insult, exploitation, arrogance, and complete lack of concern from the male authorities of their church, have decided to remain dutiful daughters. This causes much pain, suffering, and anger; and Osiek seeks to address much of this in both herself and her companions, those who remain loyal, no matter what, and those who thus, and from their backgrounds and ways of thought, are within the "majority culture" of Roman Catholicism.

Discusses raised consciousness, ways of adopting and adapting to the grim reality that that consciousness must confront, deciding to "choose life," adopting a theology of the cross to bear this "redemptive suffering," and a practical spirituality of survival.

One wonders whether this hybrid of "Christian feminism," if considered apart from its obviously brave commitment, would not be seen as masochistic and traditionally "feminine" if viewed in a secular relationship of persons or power.

1149   Papa, Mary Bader. *Christian Feminism. Completing the Subtotal Woman.* Chicago: Fides/Claretian, 1981.

Examines sexism within Christian tradition and church and offers some tentative solutions. Issues include that of justice for women, sexism, women in struggle not only against male structures but internally – in women's internalized hatred of their bodies – in many women's contempt and fear of feminism, in religious sanction of these attitudes, the importance of the women's movement and of women taking ministry onto themselves, the surprising willingness of men to cooperate in women's struggles – even while many women oppose them – mutuality, and an agenda for equality.

1150 Parvey, Constance F., ed. *The Community of Women and Men in the Church. The Sheffield Report.* Geneva: World Council of Churches, 1983.

Issues of theology, liturgy, institutional power, and authority.

1151 Pro Mundi Vita. *Women, the Women's Movement, and the Future of the Church.* Brussels: Pro Mundi Vita, 1975.

Not seen.

1152 Ranke-Heinemann, Uta. *Eunuchs for the Kingdom of Heaven. The Catholic Church and Sexuality.* Peter Heinegg, trans. New York: Doubleday, 1990.

This book is about more than Catholic attitudes about sex. It is an indictment of the patriarchal structure of the Roman Catholic church and its methodological and consistent contempt for women within its structures and congregations. The book is a treasure-trove of the rightfully discarded: a long litany of misogynist statements from respected Catholic and early Christian theologians on the inferiority, irrationality and sinfulness of women. The core of the book, however, is her focus on the celibate male elite that has gathered all the religious and physical power of Christianity into its own hands and perpetrated the myth of celibacy's superiority to married life and sexuality. Even more dangerous – and absurd – however, is this professedly celibate male's presumption to speak with any authority upon sexuality and its moral or physical regulation.

While the book has been criticized for its over-emphasis on misogyny and one-sided attack on the church's disdain for sexuality, the author *has* been fired from her professorship in the history of religion at the University of Essen, Germany for questioning the "virgin birth." Meanwhile, Doubleday, long *the* mainstay of Catholic religious publishing, has been condemned by John Cardinal O'Connor of New York for publishing this book, of which he claims to have read only the dust jacket.

1153 Riley, Maria, O.P. *Transforming Feminism*. Kansas City, MO: Sheed & Ward, 1989

Examines recent Catholic social teaching from a feminist perspective and finds that church dogma ignores many of the needs and insights of women. Calls for a new formulation of church teaching that will incorporate feminist insights in order to achieve true liberation for both church and society as a whole.

1154 Ruether, Rosemary Radford. *Mary. The Feminine Face of the Church*. Philadelphia: Westminster Press, 1977.

See Carson (991), item 583.

1155 —. *Women-Church. The Theology and Practice of Feminist Liturgical Communities*. San Francisco, CA: Harper & Row, 1988.

While Latin American liberation theology focuses on a return to the traditions of evangelical Christianity, with a renewed emphasis on Christology and a "reform" direction; feminist theology seeks to go beyond the patriarchal forms of biblical religion, to reincorporate the Goddess into worship, and to form communities of faith and worship – as well as action – among women.

These rituals and communities are the focus of this book. It discusses the historical and theological foundations for liberating communities, the exodus from patriarchy, new understanding of the symbols of baptism and eucharist, and new liturgical forms that reflect and follow the woman's life cycle, women's crises and healing, but that in themselves only point to developing liturgies, not laid-in-stone doxologies.

Good bibliography for feminist liturgies. The introduction is an excellent essay on feminist spirituality, liturgy, and theology.

1156   Schneider, Susan Weidman. *Jewish and Female. Choices and Changes in Our Lives Today.* New York: Simon & Schuster, 1985.

See Loeb (**1001**), item 971; Ruud (**1003**), item 680.

1157   Smith, Jackie M, ed. *Women, Faith and Economic Justice.* Philadelphia: Westminster Press, 1985.

Examines the economic forces that shape women's lives and work, the biblical attitudes of the Jesus movement to economics, a new consciousness for peace and economic justice, the need for women to work for change. Includes a list of resources for women's working groups, organizations, audiovisuals, legislative information, and further reading.

1158   Swidler, Arlene. *Sistercelebrations. Nine Worship Experiences.* Philadelphia: Fortress Press, 1974.

See Carson (**991**), item 649.

1159   —. *Woman in a Man's Church. From Role to Person.* New York: Paulist Press, 1972.

The author hopes to clear the air of preconceived answers – and questions – about the role and nature of women that have been defined and enforced for millennia by men. Instead, she hopes that her book will be an essay in freeing women to ask their own questions, perhaps to eventually defining their own answers.

1160   Turner, Rita Crowley. *The Mary Dimension.* London: Sheed & Ward, 1985.

Examines the women's movement, male sexism and patriarchy, the Catholic church as the strongest and longest-surviving enemy of women's freedom, and the issue of feminism and Christianity.

Turner concludes that despite two millennia of misogyny from male church leaders, women can find in the Bible and in the life of Jesus a way to freedom. Jesus was the champion of women, but his message of mutuality was distorted by late antique misogynist outlooks.

She then turns to the figure of Mary and shreds away centuries of using her as the model of the domesticated, and docile, women. Mary, instead, should emerge as the queen, as a model of women's strength. She then examines the contradictory – and to Protestants and feminists repulsive – doctrine of Mary as Virgin-Mother, as a remote and unattainable embodiment of good. Yet here Turner can find both positive, and very natural models for women's nurturing and relational roles – if we bear in mind that women will not be restricted to these alone. Thus Mary, "the woman and the symbol, could point the way out of the present impasse that feminism has led us into."

1161 Von Wartenberg-Potter, Bärbel. *We Will Not Hang Our Harps On the Willows. Global Sisterhood and God's Song.* Fred Kaan, trans. Oak Park, IL: Meyer Stone Books, 1988.

A series of reflections on the existential roots of women's spirituality, their role in the churches, their place in biblical traditions, all supplemented and founded on the first-hand experiences of individual women around the world.

1162 Weaver, Mary T. *New Catholic Women. The Contemporary Challenge to Traditional Religious Authority.* San Francisco: Harper & Row, 1985.

This is an excellent survey of issues concerning Catholic women in the context of John Paul II's attempts at restoration and attacks on the post-Vatican II church. Topics include the historical development of American Catholic women; the immigrant church and the maturing of American Catholicism away from old authoritarian molds; the impact of feminism on religious women; the feminist goals of ordination, power within the church and self-defined status as equals; of women-church; Catholic feminist theology, including the influence of Judith Christ and Starhawk; and an analysis of the work of Anne Carr, Elisabeth Schüssler Fiorenza, Rosemary

Radford Ruether and Mary Daly; and Catholic feminist spirituality.

1163　Weber, Christin Lore. *Blessings. A WomanChrist Reflection on the Beatitudes.* San Francisco: Harper & Row, 1990.

Expands upon the insights of *WomanChrist* (**1164**) to analyze the destructive dualisms of patriarchal religion. "WomanChrist" contains all the inherent contradiction in Christianity for a woman: for God is revealed on one level as a man; and yet Paul (1 Cor. 1:25) and the Christian tradition itself makes very clear the association between Jesus and divine Sophia: the feminine face of God. This book is about the wrenching pain of these polarities and the attempt of feminist theologians to heal the rift to wholeness.

Here Weber examines the mystery and contradictions of the Beatitudes and demonstrates how they are a song to the possibility that life and creation can be made whole again.

1164　— . *WomanChrist. A New Vision of Feminine Spirituality.* San Francisco: Harper & Row, 1987.

An attempt to redefine a Christianity that can be hospitable to women by linking the archetypal, and deeply personal, experiences of a woman's life and body to the images and language of God expressed in Christianity. Ultimately this is an attempt to coopt the traditional imagery for feminist uses.

1165　Weidman, Judith L., ed. *Christian Feminism. Visions of a New Humanity.* San Francisco: Harper & Row, 1984.

Essays by Weidman, Ruether, Schüssler Fiorenza, Brock, Russell, Nannette Roberts, Clare Fischer, B. Wildung Harrison, and Constance Parvey on feminist theology and spirituality, feminist biblical interpretation, feminist Christology, women and ministry, women in work, life style, sexuality and mutuality, and women's tradition and memory.

1166   Wilson-Kastner, Patricia. *Faith, Feminism, and the Christ.* Philadelphia: Fortress Press, 1983.

Not seen.

1167   Zanotti, Barbara. *A Faith of One's Own. Explorations by Catholic Lesbians.* Freedom, CA: Crossing Press, 1986.

See **982.**

Women as Priests

1168   Carmody, Denise Lardner. *The Double Cross. Ordination, Abortion, and Catholic Feminism.* New York: Crossroad/Continuum, 1986.

The two crosses for Catholic feminists are the ordination of women and the issue of abortion. Carmody seeks to chart a middle ground between radicals on both issues that will fully acknowledge the deeply religious foundations of equality and reverence for life.

In today's world and climate of official church oppression of dissent and of open discussion, however, Carmody's call for a faithful "Catholic feminism" may strike many readers as oxymoronic as the traditional sobriquet of "Catholic intellectual." The debate remains defined by the men at the top, receiving the grace and making the rules.

1169 Coriden, James, ed. *Sexism and Church Law. Equal Rights and Affirmative Action.* New York: Paulist Press, 1977.

This is a collection of essays written around the publication of the the Vatican statement on the ordination of women in 1976 (appendix 2). It includes essays by Katherine Meagher, Hamilton Hess, Francine Cardman, Nadine Foley, Edward J. Kilmartin, and others on women and orders, women in the ministry of the early church, the tradition and hermeneutics of ordination, participation of women in the full life of the church, and women in Vatican documents.

1170 Gryson, Roger. *The Ministry of Women in the Early Church.* Jean Laporte and Mary Louise Hall, trans. Collegeville, MN: Liturgical Press, 1976.

Examines his themes through the sources: Old and New Testament, second-century texts, third-century writers, Alexandrian Fathers, the *Didascalia*, Greek canonical texts of the fourth to sixth centuries, other Greek documents, Ambrosiater and Pelagius, and Latin canonical sources from the fourth to the sixth century. Good bibliography for women in the ministry.

1171 Hayter, Mary. *The New Eve in Christ. The Use and Abuse of the Bible in the Debate About Women in the Church.* London: SPCK; Grand Rapids, MI: W.B. Eerdmans, 1987.

Focuses less on the biblical texts pro or con women's ordination but on the use of the Bible as a bolster for this debate. Hayter eschews the polemics of both the fundamentalist right and of post-Christian feminists who see the Bible as either a patriarchal text for little patriarchs or one for misogynists that clearly excludes women. Hayter, instead, seeks to carefully examine the key texts in Genesis 1-3 and 1 Corinthians to demonstrate that the Judeo-Christian tradition may, in fact, be one of unfolding liberation. While the Bible may be the word of God, it is not the last, but the "seminal," word.

1172   Ide, Arthur Frederick. *Woman As Priest, Bishop and Laity in the Early Catholic Church to 440 A.D.* Mesquite, TX: Ide House, 1984.

Reviews the historical background, the role of women in the Roman world, in Apostolic thought, in the early church, and the controversy over reference to women ministers in Romans 16, the ordination of women, male collaboration against women, women and sexuality in early Christianity.

1173   Jewett, Paul King. *The Ordination of Women. An Essay on the Office of Christian Ministry.* Grand Rapids, MI: W.B. Eerdmans, 1980.

See Loeb (1001), item 957.

1174   Lang, Judith. *Ministers of Grace. Women in the Early Church.* Middlegreen, Slough: St. Paul Publications, 1989.

Traces the role of women's ministry but focuses on the lower orders of deacons, widows, and virgins, avoiding the call to ordination of women as priests.

1175   LaPorte, Jean. *The Role of Women in Early Christianity.* New York & Toronto: Edwin Mellen Press, 1982.

Uses texts to illuminate the various areas of women's role, including martyrdom, in conjugal life, in contemplative life; as prophets, widows, virgins and deacons; and women as symbol in various writers: vice and virtues, mother, Sophia, and the Blessed Virgin Mary.

1176   Rhodes, Lynn N. *Co-Creating. A Feminist Vision of Ministry.* Philadelphia: Westminster Press, 1987.

Drawing on the theological work of Letty M. Russell, Beverly Wildung Harrison, and Rosemary Radford Ruether; and on the experience and wisdom of many women clerics and pastoral workers, Rhodes attempts to outline a new feminist ministry.

Issues discussed include authority, the meaning of salvation, mission, vocation, and the meanings of friendship and solidarity.

1177   Swidler, Arlene, and Leonard Swidler, eds. *Women Priests. A Catholic Commentary on the Vatican Declaration.* New York: Paulist Press, 1977.

This is a large collection of essays and commentaries around the Vatican's 1977 *Declaration on the*

Question of the Admission of Women to the Ministerial Priesthood, which is reprinted here on pages 37-49.

Contributors include the Swidlers, Carroll Stuhlmueller, M. Nadine Foley, Elizabeth Carroll, Carolyn Osiek, E. Schüssler Fiorenza, Thomas P. Rausch, Adela Yarbro Collins, Robert Karris, Anne Carr, R. Radford Ruether, Mary Ellen Sheehan, Pauline Turner and Bernard Cooke, Sidney Callahan and many others.

Issues include the historical testimony, sacramental implications, the meaning of apostleship, scholastic doctrine, the image of Christ, and contemporary events.

1178   Van der Meer, Haye, S.J. *Women Priests in the Catholic Church? A Theological-Historical Investigation.* Arlene and Leonard Swidler, trans. Philadelphia: Temple University Press, 1973.

Examines the evidence of scripture, the church fathers, the church's magisterium, and theological speculation, to conclude that God created humanity, in both male and female, in fullness. To deny any office based on gender is to deny the humanity of that person and to negate God's creative action.

1179   Wijngaards, J. N. M. *Did Christ Rule Out Women Priests?* Great Wakening, Essex: McCrimmons, 1986.

The answer is no; but since his first edition in 1977 the author has come to the revelation that the issue of human rights for women has a full theological significance that the Vatican's intransigence to dialogue cannot dismiss.

1180   Witherington, Ben. *Women in the Ministry of Jesus.*
         New York: Cambridge University Press, 1984.

         The subtitle reads, "a study of Jesus' attitudes to
         women and their roles as reflected in his earthly
         life." Jesus certainly forged new ground for his con-
         temporaries in his attitudes toward women, his
         acceptance of their important roles, his contacts with
         them, and their voice in his movement.
         The author examines women and their roles in
         Palestine, in Jesus' teaching, in his ministry, and in
         his actions. His new attitude of equality was con-
         tinued into the early church. Bibliography divided
         by chapter.

Third-World Feminist Theology

1181   Cho Wha Soon, *Let the Weak Be Strong. A Woman's
         Struggle for Justice.* Lee Sun Ai and Ahn Sang Nim,
         eds. Oak Park, IL: Meyer Stone Books, 1988.

         Follows the struggle of Korea's women factory
         workers, their exploitation and oppression, their
         movement of resistance, and the feminist theology of
         liberation that is emerging from it.

1182   Chung, Hyun Kyung. *Struggle to Be the Sun Again.
         Introducing Asian Women's Theology.* Maryknoll,
         NY: Orbis Books, 1990.

         See **311.**

1183   Eck, Diana L., and Devaki Jain, eds. *Speaking of Faith.
         Global Perspectives on Women, Religion and Social
         Change.* Philadelphia: New Society, 1987.

Twenty-six essays, including work by Carol Gilligan, Sisela Bok, Nawal el Saadawi, Judith Plaskow, Jean Zaru, all aiming to bring a feminist foundation to religious life.

1184   Fabella, Virginia, M.M., and Mercy Amba Oduyoye, eds. *With Passion and Compassion. Third World Women Doing Theology.* Maryknoll, NY: Orbis Books, 1988.

These are the published papers of an ecumenical conference of the Women's Commission of the Ecumenical Association of Third World Theologians held in Oaxtepec, Mexico in December 1989. Contributions are gathered under the headings Africa, Asia, and Latin America but are bound together by certain very clear concerns and methods.

"Women doing theology" is a new term describing a new situation: women theologians themselves discussing and working through their lives and relationship to the Christian tradition between the two poles of "contextuality" and Jesus Christ. The experience of real and individual women, and men – their status of oppression – is the starting point for these discussions. The focus of their religious hope and faith and courage is Jesus' own ministry both as a historical and theological reality and as a point of critique of current church structures that simply maintain the oppressive systems of colonialism and of indigenous Third-World religious and social structures. A true but "suspicious" reading of the Bible, focusing on the Jesus community, but aware that the existing canonical collection was written and codified by men, can be a truly liberating experience for Third-World women, and the men who are also caught up in a system of oppressor and oppressed.

A true reading of the Bible will reveal that Jesus gave women a central role as disciples, in revealing his divinity and his resurrection, and in the earliest ministry of announcing the good word and in spreading it. Passion is the erotic involvement in the struggle for liberation, and compassion the liberating experience for both the oppressed and the oppressor. See also **214**.

1185   —, and Sun Ai Lee Park, eds. *We Dare to Dream. Doing Theology as Asian Women.* Maryknoll, NY: Orbis Books, 1990.

Asian women theologians examine some of the fundamental Christian themes and theological categories: Christology, ecclesiology, and biblical studies from their feminist perspective.

1186   Gebara, Ivone, and Maria Clara Bingemer. *Mary. Mother of God, Mother of the Poor.* Maryknoll, NY: Orbis Books, 1990.

This appreciation of Mary by two Brazilian theologians takes its starting point from the practice of the poor in Latin America and the steadfast devotion to the Virgin among the continent's poor, especially women. Rather than dismiss this as a throwback to an outmoded and internalizing spirituality, the authors argue that Mary's place in scripture must be radically reinterpreted away from patriarchal models and recast to fit modern appreciations of the Goddess, of the role of women in the church and in society, and in the light of a careful reading of both Hebrew Bible and Gospels for the meaning of her birth and life. They then trace the role of Mary in Latin America since the conquest and colonial times and draw some conclusions for her as a central figure in the struggle for liberation both within the church and within society.

1187   Heyward, Carter, and Anne Gilson, eds. *Revolutionary Forgiveness. Feminist Reflections on Nicaragua.* Maryknoll, NY: Orbis Books, 1987.

Thirteen North Americans share their experiences of Nicaragua, its revolution, and the attempts there to forge a new, liberated society. As women their support of revolution is tempered by a recognition that old forms of oppression – patriarchy, sexism, disregard for the young, old and infirm – must still be part of a truly revolutionary agenda. See also **658**.

1188   Isasi-Díaz, Ada Maria. *Hispanic Women, Prophetic Voice in the Church. Toward a Hispanic Women's Liberation Theology.* San Francisco: Harper & Row, 1988.

Not seen.

1189   Katoppo, Marianne. *Compassionate and Free. An Asian Woman's Theology.* Maryknoll, NY: Orbis Books, 1986.

Freedom comes with the removal of male domination and the newer imperialisms of European culture and religious forms. Asian women must assert their own identities and differences in socio-economic as well as religious and cultural spheres.

1190   National Conference of Asian Women Theologians.
        *An Ocean with Many Shores. Asian Women Making
        Connections in Theology and Ministry.* Warwick,
        NY: AWT, 1986.

        A progress report and bibliography.

1191   Oduyoye, Mercy Amba. *Hearing and Knowing.
        Theological Reflections on Christianity in Africa.*
        Maryknoll, NY: Orbis Books, 1986.

        African theology, its major themes, and women's
        liberation.

1192   O'Neill, Maura. *Women Speaking, Women Listening.
        Women in Interreligious Dialogue.* Maryknoll, NY:
        Orbis Books, 1990.

        The problems of discussing gender in a theological
        context when the dialog is intercultural and inter-
        religious. Topics include religious pluralism, theories
        of person, epistemology, value, and communication;
        the universality of feminism; the question of reli-
        gion's ability to liberate; and forms of dialog: inter-
        national, interreligious, between men and women.

1193   Pobee, John S., and Barbel von Wartenberg-Potter, eds.
        *New Eyes for Reading. Biblical and Theological
        Reflections by Women from the Third World.*
        Geneva: World Council of Churches, 1986.

        Critiques of existing structures in church and
        society and reflections for change from a feminist per-
        spective, from Africa, Asia, and Latin America on the
        Bible, church, and society.

1194   Russell, Letty M., Kwok Pui-lan, Ada Maria Isasi-
        Díaz, and Kate G. Cannon, eds. *Inheriting Our
        Mothers' Gardens. Feminist Theology in Third-
        World Perspective.* Philadelphia: Westminster
        Press, 1988.

        Essays by the editors, Mercy Amba Oduyoye,
        Chung Hyun Kyung, Joann Nash Eakin, Marta
        Benavides on women's political struggles and identity
        in Africa, Asia and Latin America; cherishing tradi-
        tions after immigration; innovation in issues of race,
        class, gender, and the tradition handed down through
        women to other women. Annotated bibliography on
        pages 165-81.

1195   Tamez, Elsa, ed. *Against Machismo.* John Eagleson,
        transl. Oak Park, IL: Meyer Stone Books, 1987.

        This is a series of interviews with leading *male*
        liberation theologians that elicits from them, often
        for the first time formally, a liberationist perspective
        on the realities of oppression for women in church and
        society. Tamez' perspective is that there can be no
        genuine liberation if all people are not included in
        both the struggle, in the perspective, and in the form-
        ing of the theology. Interviewees include Segundo,
        Boff, Dussel, Boff, Betto, Richard, and Vidales,
        among others.

1196   —. *Through Her Eyes. Women's Theology from Latin
        America.*

        See **544.**

1197   Wartenberg-Potter, Bärbel von, ed. *By Our Lives.*
        Stories of Women, Today and in the Bible. Geneva:
        World Council of Churches, 1985.

        A Third-World perspective on reading biblical
        texts.

1198   Webster, John C. B., and Ellen Low Webster, eds. *The*
        Church and Women in the Third World.
        Philadelphia: Westminster Press, 1985.

        An international group of authors discusses Chris-
        tian images of women, the role of women in the
        church, and the church's role on changing the position
        of women in the Third World.

1199   Women's Concerns Unit. *Reading the Bible As Asian*
        Women. Singapore: Christian Conference of Asia,
        1986.

        Biblical studies and reflections on poverty, justice,
        and freedom.

Feminist Theology in the First World

1200   Andolsen, Barbara Hilkert, Christine E. Gudorf, and
        Mary D. Pellauer, eds. *Women's Consciousness,*
        Women's Conscience. A Reader in Feminist Ethics.
        San Francisco: Harper & Row, 1987.

        Essays, mainly on ethics, from a feminist
        perspective. Includes articles by Schüssler Fiorenza
        ("Discipleship and Patriarchy: Early Christian Ethos
        and Christian Ethics in a Feminist Theological
        Perspective"), Starhawk ("Ethics and Justice in God-

dess Religion"), and Margaret A. Ferley ("Feminist Theology and Bioethics").

1201   Avis, Paul D. *Eros and the Sacred*. London: SPCK, 1989.

A self-consciously male attempt to examine the androgynous "eros" of the divine: the spark of creativity and life that is inherent in divinity and in humanity as images of God, and which women have been denied through Christian tradition.

Avis sees the progress of women toward full equality of status within the church as the only hope for this last bastion of sexism, patriarchy and hierarchical domination in Western society.

Examines the feminist challenge to Christianity, patriarchy, sex and gender, androgyny, an androgynous Christology, patriarchal images of God, the church as a therapeutic community where the "erotic" (the life-giving) is dominant, sacred and profane sexuality in the Old and New Testaments, eros and a theology of embodiment, God's eros, the ethical and profoundly human nature of eros – with the exception of homosexuality – which Avis takes great pains to distance himself from.

1202   Bennett, Anne M. *From Woman Pain to WomanVision. Writings in Feminist Theology*. Mary E. Hunt, ed. Philadelphia: Fortress Press, 1989.

A posthumous collection of essays by this noted feminist theologian. Topics include theological implications of the women's movement; feminist criticism of traditional theology; women's hidden heritage; feminist approaches to scripture; the connection between feminist theology, peace, and liberation; and the need for mutuality in personal and public life. Contains a bibliography of her writings.

1203   Bianchi, Eugene C., and Rosemary Radford Ruether. *From Machismo to Mutuality. Essays on Sexism and Women-Man Liberation.* New York: Paulist Press, 1976.

A collection of essays by the two authors on the historical experience of sexism in Western tradition, on the experience of growing up male, images of woman in industrial society, and institutionalized male violence. They also discuss the process of healing and wholeness in a sexuality that removes the old polarities between body and spirit; mutuality, women's liberation from forms of sexism, and of men away from machismo to mutuality.

Ruether also gives concluding remarks on the work that remains to be done.

1204   Boff, Leonardo, O.F.M. *The Maternal Face of God. The Feminine and its Religious Expressions.* Robert R. Barr and John W. Diercksmeier, trans. San Francisco: Harper & Row, 1987.

Boff's approach is tentative and in full recognition of the problems inherent in attempting to cast Christianity in light of feminist revelations of the past decades. His task is to interpret Mary as the reflection of divinity and to analyze the feminine in all its religious aspects.

Part 1 discusses the principles of Mariology; Part 2, the epistemological, psychological, philosophical and theological approaches to the feminine; Part 3, the historical evidence for Miriam of Nazareth; 4, the Catholic theology of Mary, her immaculate conception, virginity, human and divine motherhood, her assumption, and role as queen.

Boff then examines Mary's role as "woman of liberation" and model of the oppressed. Part 5 then ventures into the area of myth, archetype and symbol for some implications and future developments of our understanding and interpretation of Mary.

1205 Brock, Rita Nakashima. *Journeys By Heart. A Christology of Erotic Power.* New York: Crossroad, 1989.

The erotic is central to the human religious experience, for it is the very act of creation by which we participate in the work of divinity. This is a feminist reinterpretation of Christ, his mission, and the erotic power that the Gospels portray as the feminist hermeneutic of love and redemption.

Christology, however, has long been a stumbling block of feminist theology: the male cradled by the male trinity. Brock therefore sets out to examine the patriarchal ideologies of human and divine love: in everything from the male nature of the Father to the exclusive obsession of the churches on Jesus' maleness as his chief distinguishing human characteristic, thus making the male normative.

Brock then examines the traditional model of salvation – life through death – and finds it senseless from a feminist and women's point of view: life derives from life and life force.

Examining the Holy Ghost, she calls up the dualistic tendencies in Christianity that see the body, and the female, as corrupt and polluted. She then discusses the forces of feminist theology that can liberate the Gospels, most especially of liberating Jesus from the "unholy trinity." She sees him again as a broken and "brokenhearted" male in Mark's Gospel who represents both the male and female of the divine and the male's inability to come face to face with the divine father and with the oppressive and destructive forces of patriarchy.

Here "heart," the erotic or the power for intimacy, becomes the central image of understanding Jesus. Yet this heart is not a naive hopefulness, but a full recognition of the power of violence to destroy. Yet it is also a clear-headed, and hearted, option for love. This understanding derives equally from the new feminist spirituality, the tradition of the Goddess, and from Asian sensibilities.

1206   Bruns, J. Edgar. *God As Woman. Woman As God.* New York: Paulist Press, 1973.

See Carson (**991**), item 85.

1207   Cannon, Katie G. *Black Womanist Ethics.* Atlanta, GA: Scholar's Press, 1988.

See **834**.

1208   Carmody, Denise Lardner. *Seizing the Apple. A Feminist Spirituality of Personal Growth.* New York: Crossroad, 1984.

Not seen.

1209   Casey, Juliana M. *Where Is God Now? Nuclear Terror, Feminism and the Search for God.* Kansas City, MO: Sheed & Ward, 1987.

Combines a scriptural and feminist theology with an activist approach to peacemaking to derive a theology for a nuclear age, for reconciliation and conversion.

1210   Chopp, Rebecca S. *The Power to Speak. Feminism, Language, God.* New York: Crossroad, 1989.

This is an attempt to examine and redefine both the language and the politics of discourse about and by women, specifically, theological discourse. Topics include the place of modern Protestant theologies and the Word's loss of power in them; the discourses of feminist theologies; the place of woman's "otherness" as a positive value in the church and world; the role of proclamation as a theology and in relation to the Scriptures; the hermeneutics of "restlessness," taking the contexts of both reader and text as a dynamic dialog; and the hermeneutics of "marginality." The author discusses building a new ecclesia; and the place of Christian witness within the world.

1211   Christ, Carol P. *Diving Deep and Surfacing. Women Writers on Spiritual Quest.* 2d ed. Boston, MA: Beacon Press, 1986.

Uses the writings of five women: Kate Chopin, Margaret Atwood, Doris Lessing, Adrienne Rich, and Ntozake Shange, to demonstrate that women's own revelations of power and spirit are adequate to replace worn-out forms of patriarchal religious texts. In this quest not only the individual but the society as a whole is renewed and made whole by the courage to reach out and to touch.

1212   Clanton, Jann Aldredge. *In Whose Image? God and Gender.* New York: Crossroad, 1990.

Not seen.

1213　Clark, Elizabeth, and Herbert Richardson, eds. *Women and Religion. A Feminist Sourcebook of Christian Thought.* New York: Harper & Row, 1977.

This is a survey of religious thought *about* women, not by women. Julian of Norwich, Elizabeth Cady Stanton and Mary Daly are the exceptions.

1214　Collins, Sheila. *A Different Heaven and Earth. A Feminist Perspective on Religion.* Valley Forge, PA: Judson Press, 1974.

See Carson (991), item 129.

1215　Condren, Mary, ed. *For the Banished Children of Eve. An Introduction to Feminist Theology.* Bristol, England: SCM, 1976.

Not seen.

1216　Conn, Joann Wolski. *Spirituality and Personal Maturity.* New York: Paulist Press, 1989.

Not seen.

1217　—. *Women's Spirituality. Resources for Christian Development.* New York: Paulist Press, 1986.

This is an excellent collection of essays on the issues of women's spirituality, psychological and religious development, and forming a new vision of Christian spirituality. It contains readings from Catherine of Siena, Teresa of Avila, John of the

Cross, Ignatius Loyola, and essays by Conn, Sandra Schneiders, Anne Carr, Carol Gilligan, Jean Baker Miller, Luise Eichenbaum and Susie Orbach, Naomi Goldenberg, Elisabeth Tetlow, Rosemary Haughton, Elisabeth Schüssler Fiorenza, and others.

1218 Cornwall Collective. *Your Daughters Shall Prophesy. Feminist Alternatives in Theological Education.* New York: Pilgrim Press, 1980.

Topics discussed include feminist understanding of theological education, learning and communities of learning, racism, marginality and alternative structures, power and institutional change. Appendixes include case histories of women's programs at major theological seminaries in the United States.

1219 Cypser, Cora E. *Taking Off the Patriarchal Glasses.* New York: Vantage, 1987.

The "patriarchal glasses" are the hermeneutics of a male-dominated church and society that have misread God's essential message in the Bible. This book discusses feminist interpretation of key biblical texts, reinterpretations of the theology of others, and questions about the male authorship of books in the Hebrew and Christian scriptures. The latter include the woman author of the Jahwist texts, and possible female authorship of the Gospels. Cypser also discusses the role of women in the Bible: from Zipporah and her role in the Exodus, and the women in the Jesus movement and in the early church.

Mary Daly

1220   Daly, Mary. *Beyond God the Father. Toward a Philosophy of Women's Liberation.* Boston: Beacon Press, 1974.

So much of Daly's discourse and categories have become central to feminist theory and the critique of established orthodoxies that the reader must pause to realize the originality and the wide impact of this book.

The goal of feminist theology and philosophy is "diarchy": the true androgyny that comes about when male and female realize the commonality of their human nature and the complexity of their psychic makeup. This does not mean that feminist theology sets out to replace a male god with a female god who acts in the same authoritarian and life-denying way: the Goddess, whom Daly calls upon religiously motivated men and women to recapture, is one aspect of the divinity within each of us, but one that more truly reflects the nature of divinity: the process of becoming human that must proceed within each of us.

Patriarchy – the imposed order of male, violent, authoritarian human structures and their divine projections upon a Yahweh or God the father – produces nothing but negation: power in the hands of a male elite, and nothingness in the majority of the world's population: the women who either accept or have been forced to accept a psychology and spiritual vision defined by males and their structures. In this sense sexism is more than a "parallel oppression" to racism, nationalism, class structures, and capitalism; for it underlies the ontological grounding of us all and shows itself through other forms of oppression.

Daly's work is truly in the forefront of liberation theology. Her discussions touch on all the categories of what was later to emerge as a full theology: born out of the context of oppression, its focus on action as the basis of theology, or "God-talk," the image of a god who liberates from oppressive structures, the need for conscientization among the oppressed, the responsibility for liberation by the oppressed themselves and not from even well-intended do-gooders, the pinpointing of various idolatries, be they patriarchal authority or Jesus himself, that have replaced God in discourse and life.

One point of discussion that Daly emphasizes here is the unique nature of sexism, often criticizing peace and justice and black theology for their continued sexism. This is a point that has opened many eyes to the various forms of oppression that do exist but also one that has resulted in a dialog that has begun to form a "ecumenism of the margins." The influence of class and race have also begun to enter strongly into later discussions.

1221   —. *Gyn/Ecology: The Metaethics of Radical Feminism.* Boston: Beacon Press, 1978.

See Carson (991), item 156.

1222   —. *Pure Lust: Elemental Feminist Philosophy.* Boston: Beacon Press, 1984.

As opposed to phallic lust, this is lust of the double-axed labryses, "that which is most intimate and most ultimate, for depth and transcendence, for recalling original wholeness" in a decade and a world grown mad with the ravings and rapes of the "fathers, sons and holy ghosts," the demons of aggression and obsession that beset the earth.

In contrast, women must take up "wanderlust," that is moving away from the fixed points of dead structures and definitions in church, state, language, and human relationships. Much of this can be accomplished through an understanding of the metaphor of the Goddess, the force that will overcome patriarchy and death, that will bring women back to connection with the elemental forces of the universe.

Daly not only outlines a fundamental feminist philosophy, but she does so with a new feminist lexicology, which she provides as she proceeds, to replace old patriarchal meanings of terms long associated with the sexual stereotyping of women, with a new liberating sense. Her style as well takes on a new intuitiveness and multi-dimensional logic. Theology and philosophy, literature, anthropology, and etymology all provide food for thought and for new definitions.

Solidarity, shared memory, new consciousness, contextuality, metamorphoses are among the liberation themes of this remarkable work.

*

1223   Dematrakopoulos, Stephanie A. *Listening to Our Bodies. The Rebirth of Feminine Wisdom.* Boston: Beacon Press, 1982.

See Carson (**991**), item 165.

1224   Diamond, Irene, and Lee Quincy, eds. *Feminism and Foucault: Reflections on Resistance.* Boston, MA: Northeastern University Press, 1989.

Includes the essay by Sharon Welch, "The Truth of Liberation Theology: Particulars of a Relative Sublime."

1225   Dunne, Carrin. *Behold Woman. A Jungian Approach to Feminist Theology.* Wilmette, IL: Chiron Publications, 1988.

The title is, of course, the feminization of the "ecce homo" of Christ's passion and is meant as a parallel to the passion of women in a society that denies them their own soul: substituting the stereotype of inferior man for the archetype of the female.

Beginning with the insights of her own dreaming subconscious, Dunne examines linguistics, comparative mythology from East and West and from native American tradition, including biblical creation stories, to conclude that the Western Christian insistence on the triad must give way to Jung's more complete four to include the figure of the woman.

1226   Engelsman, Joan Chamberlain. *The Feminine Dimension of the Divine.* Philadelphia, PA: Westminster, 1979.

See Carson (991), item 201.

1227   Fiorenza, Elisabeth Schüssler. *Bread Not Stone.* Boston: Beacon Press, 1983.

This book attempts to create a feminist biblical hermeneutics, first from their own experience, then to develop a "hermeneutics of suspicion" against the layers of patriarchal interpretation, then in terms of political struggle, which is the natural context and result of this hermeneutic as right-wing, patriarchal interpretations of religion and society rise again.

The key to such an approach is the "women-church" that will restore women to their role as actors, away from the margins, exploitation, and alienation. "Relinquishment" for men and self-affirmation for women are keys to this new feminist theology. The experiences not only of women but of women in struggle against patriarchy are the foundations of the women-church. The Bible, those texts that support this process, are the basis for transformation. It is a "structuring prototype," rather than a timeless archetype.

Topics include the definition of the women-church; biblical interpretation as the basis for a community of faith; feminist hermeneutics of scripture and liberation theology; feminist analysis of patriarchy. In an excellent section on historians and historiography, the author discusses regaining the feminist past through a sound understanding of the nature of historical discourse, its "objectivity," its audience and goals, thus cannot be "value-free" but must speak by and for a community.

Such insights apply not only to historical writing but to biblical scholarship, where self-awareness is a duty, as the theologian and scholar attempt to unravel their own relationships to God and the "facts" of revelation as they unravel the texts themselves. In this feminist context this points to the need to abandon an "objective" view of biblical revelation and to instead realize its context and meaning as deriving from a social group, time, and place: revelation as the result of changing process, not eternal verity.

This book is deliberately technical in a theological sense, since Schüssler Fiorenza opposes feminist anti-intellectualism as an abandonment of a vital source of power.

1228 Garcia, Jo, and Sara Maitland, eds. *Walking on the Water.* London: Virago, 1985.

Essays and art on feminist spirituality. See Carson **(991)**, item 239.

1229 Giles, Mary E., ed. *The Feminist Mystic and Other Essays on Women and Spirituality.* New York: Crossroad, 1982.

A collection of essays exploring the role of historical women mystics for new women's spirituality. Includes essays by Meinrad Craighead, Margaret Miles, Dorothy H. Donnelly, Wendy Wright, and Kathryn Hohlwein. See Carson **(991)**, item 253.

1230 Goodison, Lucy. *Moving Heaven and Earth. Sexuality, Spirituality and Social Change.* Toronto: The Women's Press, 1990.

Using the study of symbolism and imagery, and historical precedent, such as that of Cretan civilization, the author argues that recent, patriarchal systems have imposed a series of debilitating dualities: spirit/matter, male/female, white/black, active/passive, superior/inferior that must be overcome if an integral view of human nature, human activity, and society is to be restored. An emphasis on the feminine nature of the divine is essential to this process.

1231   Gross, Rita, ed. *Beyond Anthrocentrism*. Missoula, MT: Scholar's Press, 1976.

See Carson (991), item 281.

1232   Grey, Mary. *Redeeming the Dream. Feminism, Redemption and Christian Tradition*. London: SPCK, 1989.

A feminist approach to the Christian doctrine of redemption. Discusses the spiritual need to retouch roots and sources, to rekindle links to the primal reality, new hermeneutics, insights drawn from nature, the path to renewal both in traditional spirituality and new feminist forms, a critique of traditional patriarchal views of redemption, and new "right relations" as a key to redemption and its theology.

1233   Haddad, Yvonne Yazbeck, and Ellison Banks Findly, eds. *Women, Religion and Social Change*. Albany, NY: SUNY Press, 1985.

The elements within all great religious traditions that support the struggle for justice and liberation.

1234   Haddon, Genia Pauli. *Body Metaphors. Releasing the God-Feminine in All of Us*. New York: Crossroad, 1988.

Drawing insights on male-female differences from various disciplines, the author calls for a rethinking of theological categories about divinity that affect all aspects of faith from ethics to liturgy.

1235 Hammett, Jenny Yates. *Woman's Transformations. A Psychological Theology.* New York: Edwin Mellen, 1982.

Topics include the use of metaphor when we talk about God, the female-male dichotomy in creation, sin and the image of the feminine, feminine transformation and Christian salvation, the Goddess as symbol of feminine consciousness, Sophia, the place of the dream and the image symbol, psychic transformation, and the use of myth and symbolic language to embody divinity.

1236 Hampson, Daphne. *Theology and Feminism.* Oxford and Cambridge, MA: Basil Blackwell, 1990.

Hampson, and her work, reflect the shift of many feminists from the struggle for equality within the structure of the church to a "post-Christian" feminist theology. She believes that Christianity and feminism are incompatible; and that the Christian myth is untrue both in its image of God and of woman.

The need remains, however, to find a way of talking about God that fits the Western spiritual and cultural tradition. This book attempts to do this by analyzing the nature of Christianity, the "post-Christian" position, the limits of Christology, feminism and Christ; the concretion of God found in biblical religion, and the need to break free from its bonds, a feminist anthropology and feminist theology of sin, salvation, creation, angst, death, and eternal life (all classic elements of a liberation theology). She concludes with sections on the need for a new theology, and a new image of God. Good, select, bibliography by topic. An important milestone in the path to a new Western theology of liberation.

1237 Harris, Maria. *Dance of the Spirit. The Seven Steps of Women's Spirituality.* New York: Bantam Books, 1989.

Not seen.

1238 Heine, Susanne. *Matriarchs, Goddesses and Images of God. A Critique of Feminist Theology.* Philadelphia: Fortress Press, 1989.

A feminist committed to the issues confronting women in their struggle for liberation, Heine, nevertheless, believes that intellectual self-criticism is a path to self-awareness and therefore to greater flexibility and strength. Part of this criticism must be aimed at feminist theology and its admitted achievements, but also its failings to really change structures and attitudes profoundly, aside from a fashionable and skin-deep acceptance of slogans and causes of the moment.

Heine's purpose is therefore to carefully, and logically, critique (mostly German) feminist theologies of God as mother, the Goddess, matriarchy and androgyny, Jesa Christa (the feminine Jesus as manifestation of the feminine divine), and the entire question of feminine hermeneutics. She does so through a use of "systematics," which she realizes is a word fraught with theological dangers but which is, nevertheless, necessary if feminist thought is to free itself from self-deceiving ideologies, assertions, moral imperatives, and cliché.

1239 —. *Christianity and the Goddesses. Systematic Criticism of a Feminist Theology.* London: SCM, 1988.

The same as above.

1240 Heyward, (Isabel) Carter. *Our Passion for Justice. Images of Power, Sexuality and Liberation.* New York: Pilgrim Press, 1984.

See Loeb (1001), item 953.

1241 —. *The Redemption of God: A Theology of Mutual Redemption.* Lanham, MD: University Press of America, 1982.

Not seen.

1242 —. *Speaking of Christ. A Lesbian Feminist Voice.* Ellen C. Davis, ed. New York: Pilgrim Press, 1989.

Not seen.

1243 —. *Touching Our Strength. The Erotic as Power and the Love of God.* San Francisco: Harper & Row, 1990.

Women's spirituality, as embodied by the women Western mystics, has always carried with it an integralist message and form: that God is felt and loved intimately and physically in both divine revelation and in forms of discourse. For women mystics the erotic has always been part and parcel to religious language. Male spirituality, especially in the monastic tradition, has tended to emphasize dualities: the fleeing of the body and the unity of the soul with God as if the mind (the soul) has finally been freed from the evil of the body. Male eroticism, at the same time, has often been tied to the will to power and domination, removed from love.

A growing number of theologians, from the liberation theologians of Latin America to the creation theologians of North America, have begun

asserting the essential unity of life, the artificiality
and Manichaeism of the body-mind dichotomy, and
the essential goodness of the body and bodily
experience. Thus erotic love, which is the love of
God's creative power, is the fitting expression of
religious love: the Song of Songs aptly used the sexual
union of true lovers to describe human relationship
with divinity. At the same time, human sexual love
in and of itself reaches to the intimate core of the
other person, ennobles and empowers both partners,
and opens the human to experience the creative force
of God.

1244   Hunt, Mary E. *Making Connections. Feminist Liberation
        Theology and Spirituality.* Kansas City, KS:
        National Catholic Reporter (Credence Cassettes),
        1985.

        See Carson (**991**), item 316.

1245   Hurcombe, Linda, ed. *Sex and God. Some Varieties of
        Women's Religious Experience.* New York:
        Routledge and Kegan Paul, 1987.

        Poetry and prose selections from Hurcombe,
        Starhawk, Aileen La Tourette, Mary E. Hunt,
        Hannah Ward, C.S.F., Polly Blue, Elaine Willis,
        Leonie Caldecott, Mykel Johnson, Susan Dowell,
        Ruether, Sheila Briggs, and Susan Griffin. Topics
        include the Goddess, a women's activism that com-
        bines the erotic with the political, and the personal,
        celibacy, body theology, feminist theology, asceti-
        cism, birthing, and feminist monogamy.

1246   Iglehart, Hallie. *Womanspirit. A Guide to Women's
        Wisdom.* San Francisco: Harper & Row, 1983.

See Carson (**991**), item 320; Loeb (**1001**), item 955.

1247 *Journal of Feminist Studies in Religion.*

Launched in 1986, this is edited by Judith Plaskow and Elisabeth Schüssler Fiorenza. Semiannual.

1248 *Journal of Women and Religion.*

Its first issue was in 1981. Biennial.

1249 Kalven, Janet, and Mary Buckley, eds. *Women's Spirit Bonding.* New York: Pilgrim Press, 1984.

Addresses and essays from the Grailville, Ohio Center on women and poverty, women and nature, racism, pluralism and bonding, women and literature, war and peace, lesbianism and homophobia, the varieties of religious tradition, and envisioning an alternative future. The three dozen contributors are among the most prominent feminist thinkers and writers today.

1250 King, Ursula. *Women and Spirituality. Voices of Protest and Promise.* Houndmills, England: Macmillan, 1989.

Examines the role of feminism and its ties with traditional spirituality in ways that transform both. Begins with the realities of women's oppression and anger, then surveys women in religious tradition, in theological language, in institutions and in religious experience. King then examines the meaning of women's experience: physical, intellectual, social, and spiritual before discussing the tradition of women's own spiritual history. She uses the cult of the Goddess in the past and its meaning for today and discusses the meaning of androgyny as a religious concept.

In final chapters the author marks out the path of a new feminist theology, the controversies within theological contexts and within the life of the churches; concluding with the prophetic role of women in the redefinition of power, of peace, nonviolence, and reverence for the earth. Contains both an excellent bibliography and a guide for further reading arranged by topic.

1251   Massey, Marilyn Chapin. *Feminine Soul. The Fate of An Ideal.* Boston: Beacon Press, 1985.

See Loeb (**1001**), item 961.

1252   Merchant, Carolyn. *The Death of Nature. Women, Ecology and the Scientific Revolution.* San Francisco: Harper & Row, 1980.

This is a fundamental feminist text and a great influence of interpretations of women's spirituality. Merchant's central point is that the scientific revolution and the rationalism of the Enlightenment have alienated us from our psychic connection to the feminine in both nature and ourselves. It has objectified nature as a great machine, annihilating its image and reality as a living and nurturing organism. At the same time this male rationalism has subjected the feminine, and women, in our culture as inferior, largely out of a profound fear of female power and sexuality. See also Carson (**991**), item 440.

1253 Miles, Margaret Ruth. *Carnal Knowing. Female Nakedness and Religious Meaning in the Christian West.* Boston: Beacon Press, 1989.

Not seen.

1254 Mollenkott, Virginia Ramey. *The Naming of God.* Granit Falls, WA: Marvel, 1982.

An audio cassette on language and image for divinity.

1255 —, and Catherine Barry. *Views from the Intersection. Poems and Meditations.* New York: Crossroad/Continuum, 1984.

Poems by Barry, a Catholic; and essays by Mollenkott, the Protestant evangelical.

1256 Morton, Nelle. *The Journey Is Home.* Boston: Beacon Press, 1986.

The subtitle reads, "The Distinguished Feminist Theologian Traces the Development of Her Personal and Theoretical Vision." This is a spiritual autobiography that follows a journey over ten years through the essays collected here. Topics include women's activism, new forms of feminist language to match new realities, a whole theology that speaks of women's experience, preaching, the meaning of "spirit," new forms of education, the new image of the woman's body and the work of Emily Culpepper, Adrienne Rich, Mary Daly, and Judy Chicago, the metaphor of the Goddess, and unfinished business and new issues.

1257   Mud Flower Collective. *God's Fierce Whimsy. Christian Feminism and Theological Education.* New York: Pilgrim Press, 1985.

Leading feminist theologians and educators contend with the problems of seminary education, structures, and possibilities for engendering social justice. Bibliography.

1258   O'Brien, Theresa K., ed. *The Spiral Path. Essays and Interviews on Women's Spirituality.* St. Paul, MN: Yes International, 1988.

Essays by Sivananda Radha, Dorothy Hale, Chandra Patel, Anne Lamb, Qahiri Qalbi, Brooke Medicine Eagle, Keiju Okada, Tessa Bielecki, Erminie Huntress Lantero, Mary E. Giles, Lynn Gottlieb and others on feminist spirituality from all religious traditions.

1259   Ochs, Carol. *Behind the Sex of God.* Boston: Beacon Press, 1977.

The subtitle reads, "Toward a New Consciousness. Transcending Matriarchy and Patriarchy." See Carson (**991**), item 490.

1260   —. *Women and Spirituality.* Totowa, NJ: Rowman & Allanheld, 1983.

See Carson (**991**), item 491.

1261   Plaskow, Judith. *Sex, Sin and Grace. Women's Experience and the Theologies of Reinhold Niebuhr and Paul Tillich.* Washington, DC: University Press of America, 1980.

Essentially her 1975 Yale dissertation. Topics include women's experience, the theology of Reinhold Niebuhr, that of Paul Tillich, and concluding remarks on theology and women's experience.

Plaskow discusses the impacts of cultural myth and reality on women's experience, life within patriarchy, the essential concern with men's identity in traditional theologies, such as that of Niebuhr (despite his positive concerns for justice and for women's situations), the contributions of Tillich's theology of sin, estrangement, and the development of self.

Plaskow concludes that while traditional theology may be useful in understanding the women's experience, the identification of human with male experience remains problematical. Instead, she attempts a women's theology from her own experience as a white, middle-class Westerner.

1262   —. *Standing Again At Sinai. Judaism from a Feminist Perspective.* San Francisco: Harper & Row, 1990.

As women take their place in the writing and shaping of theology, our views of God and revelation begin to reflect this neglected insight. Plaskow surveys the field of Jewish theology and tradition to demonstrate how concepts of community, God, creation, sexuality, social justice, peace, and Judaism are being reshaped by women.

1263   —, and Joan Arnold Romero. *Women and Religion.* Rev. ed. Missoula, MT: AAR and Scholar's Press, 1974.

See Carson (991), item 530.

1264   Rabuzzi, Kathryn Allen. *The Sacred and the Feminine.*
Toward a Theology of Housework. New York:
Seabury Press, 1982.

As a liberation theology that derives from the
context of people's lives, this work addresses itself to
the reality of most women the world over, and to
many men as well: that of domestic life, devoid of all
its mythology yet infused with so many cultural
values that it is difficult to separate it out from the
very ground of being.

It is a theology of the every day, and an attempt
to outline the immanence of divinity in it. This is not
the divine as feminine, or vice-versa, but the divine
for a world of women that while largely replaced by
work and other activities among the upper middle
classes in North America and Europe, still strongly
shapes most lives for women there. More than that,
it is an attempt to explain how daily life is infused
with a mystic element of divinity.

Rabuzzi is a clear-cut feminist who does not
recommend an acceptance of exploitative relationships or roles but attempts to underscore the inherent
dignity of many women's lives. It is this consciousness
that will make them the subjects of their lives, not
the objects of someone else's. She examines the theology of the home: as sacred space, symbol, and myth;
of housework as ritual enactment, of its cosmic nature,
and of the analogous role as caretaker for creation.
Finally, she examines the theological implications of
women's traditional roles including the patient
woman, waiting – Penelope or Griselda – the role of
fact and imagination in shaping male views of women
in narrative, and the mystical possibilities of transcendence.

Rosemary Radford Ruether

1265   Ruether, Rosemary Radford. *Disputed Questions on Being a Christian*. Maryknoll, NY: Orbis Books, 1989.

These questions include those of faith and modern consciousness, Jewish-Christian relations, politics and religion, including liberation theology, and feminism in religion and in the Catholic church.

1266   —. *Liberation Theology. Human Hope Confronts Christian History and American Power*. New York: Paulist Press, 1972.

See **730**.

1267   —. *New Woman/New Earth. Sexist Ideologies and Human Liberation*. New York: Seabury Press, 1975.

See Carson (**991**), item 584.

1268   —. *Sexism and God Talk. Toward a Feminist Theology*. London: SCM, Boston: Beacon Press, 1983.

See Carson (**991**), item 587.

1269   —, ed. *Religion and Sexism. Images of Women in Jewish and Christian Traditions*. New York: Simon & Schuster, 1974.

See Ruud (**1003**), item 656.

1270   —, ed. *Womanguides. Readings Toward a Feminist Theology.* Boston: Beacon Press, 1985.

        See Carson (991), item 590.

1271   —, and Rosemary Skinner Keller, eds. *Women and Religion in America.* 3 vols. San Francisco: Harper & Row, 1990.

        This is the basic and fundamental sourcebook for women religious thought in the U.S. As such it is important background for feminist theology.

1272   —, and Eleanor McLaughlin, eds., *Women of Spirit. Female Leadership in the Jewish and Christian Traditions.* New York: Simon & Schuster, 1979.

        This is an excellent collection of essays that traces the history of women in the Judeo-Christian tradition from biblical times through the Middle Ages, Reformation, and American history to the present.
        Authors include the editors, Elisabeth Schüssler Fiorenza, Ruth P. Liebowitz, Elaine C. Huber, Catherine F. Smith, Barbara Brown Zikmund, Nancy Hardesty, Lucille Sider Dayton and Donald W. Dayton, Mary Ewens, O.P., Dorothy C. Bass, V. L. Brereton and C. R. Klein, E. M. Umansky, and Norene Carter.

1273   Snyder, Mary Hembrow. *The Christology of Rosemary Radford Ruether. A Critical Introduction.* Mystic, CT: Twenty-Third Publications, 1988.

        This is a book born out of the author's experience of deep pain: the death of relatives, illness, the martyrdom of the four American churchwomen in El Salvador, the death of her mother, her departure from a religious order, her experience of Christian feminists in Peru. Her readings of Rosemary Radford Ruether, and that theologian's understanding of suffering in its socio-political context, led to this book.

Topics include a review of Ruether's life, her intellectual foundations, and the elements of her Christology; the contributions of liberation theology in its Latin American, ecological, and feminist forms; as well as alternative Christologies.

Concluding chapters deal with Ruether's work in ecumenism and her Christology in terms of the Third World, women, ecology, and tradition. She concludes with some implications of this Christology. Includes a complete chronological bibliography of Ruether's works up to 1987.

Letty M. Russell

1274   Russell, Letty M. *The Future of Partnership.* Philadelphia: Westminster Press, 1979.

While the term "partnership" is used so much as to be a meaningless cliché, often disguising exploitation and gross inequality, Russell takes it to mean commitment to responsibility, vulnerability, equality and trust; common struggle that transcends the defining limits of the partners; and contextuality, a dynamic process that also goes beyond the immediate partnership. Thus it is "a new focus of relationship in which there is continuing commitment and common struggle in interaction with a wider community context." In this her theology is at the core of feminist thought: mutuality as opposed to hierarchy, love over authority.

Russell discusses partnership in relation to God, the human role in creation, divine history and Christian community, human sexuality, church structures and communities, Christian eschatology, new forms and definitions of ministry, liberation communities, and a revolution of consciousness in our thinking about present and future community.

1275　—. *Growth in Partnership*. Philadelphia: Westminster Press, 1981.

Not seen.

1276　—. *Household of Freedom. Authority in Feminist Theology*. Philadelphia: Westminster Press, 1987.

On the essential problem of authority in the Reformed tradition and for feminist theology today, the need to change from paradigms of domination to those of partnership, shifts already underway in liberation, feminist and creation theology, the power of words in constructing our images of the world, ourselves, and our relationships, and the need for a new theology that will speak of God in terms of "Sophia," the Goddess," and "housekeeper" from the wisdom literature, and family rather than father ruler, the authority of those at the bottom, the shift from forms of kingdom to household in discussing Jesus' life and his retention of power even in weakness, and means through which the church can be mended to more reflect the household of mutuality rather than the kingdom of power.

1277　—. *Human Liberation in a Feminist Perspective. A Theology*. Philadelphia, PA: Westminster Press, 1974.

Russell rejects any attempt to develop a "feminine theology," that is, one that sees differences between masculine and feminine tendencies or attributes, and instead one that seeks liberation for women as women and as equal human beings. This is the root direction of feminist theology.

In this sense it is a theology of liberation; and like all theologies of liberation, it can also trace its formal roots to the theologies of hope and political theologies. Yet it is also written out of women's particular experience of oppression. In this it not only reexamines the traditional categories of theology but seeks new ground and expresses itself in a new language that leaves patriarchal forms, and assumptions and aspirations, behind.

Themes discussed include the realities of oppression and the process of liberation; the elements of a theology of liberation; reinterpreting tradition, language and history; the issues of salvation vs. liberation, conscientization, and conversion; new definitions of humanity and the female; and new forms of ecclesiology that must match new realities and aspirations.

*

1278   Schmidt, Alvin J. *Veiled and Silenced. How Culture Shaped Sexist Theology.* Macon, GA: Mercer University Press, 1989.

Not seen.

1279   Smith, Christine M. *Weaving the Sermon. Preaching in a Feminist Perspective.* Louisville, KY: John Knox, 1989.

Not seen.

Dorothee Sölle

1280   Sölle, Dorothee. *Choosing Life.* London: SCM; Philadelphia: Fortress Press, 1981.

A series of lectures first delivered in Argentina in 1979 that focus on our lives from the viewpoint of the victim, as was Jesus. The context for these, however, is our affluent First-World lives of luxury and cynicism to suffering and death. Instead, she opts for the message of Deut. 30.19ff, to "chose life" through adherence to a religious way of life away from consumerism, violence, oppression, the structures of sin and estrangement.

Sölle speaks of taking up the cross of solidarity, compassion and liberation, but most of all of abandoning an idolization of Christ the risen and instead sharing in that resurrection with him: making that event not a once-in-history salvation for our complacency but understanding its true meaning: each of us must share with Christ and change dead lives for life.

1281   —. *Of War and Love.* Rita and Robert Kimber, trans. Maryknoll, NY: Orbis Books, 1983.

Essays and poems on peacemaking, human rights, the draft, Ita Ford, native Americans, El Salvador and other topics.

1282   —. *Revolutionary Patience.* Rita and Robert Kimber, trans. Maryknoll, NY: Orbis Books, 1977.

This is a collection of poems on Jesus, woman's liberation, peace and war, the poor and oppressed, Christians and leftists, of hope and fulfillment.

1283   —. *The Strength of the Weak. Toward a Christian Feminist Identity.* Robert Kimber and Rita Kimber, trans. Philadelphia: Westminster Press, 1984.

Sölle takes as her context the godless post-war world that ironically clings to bourgeois correctness and the promises of materialist utopias. Such an empty vision oppresses both men and women, but in recent years there have been signs of hope, not the least of which is the emergence of liberation theology.

Combining the insights of a socio-political critique, Christian mysticism, and feminism, Sölle points to the strengths of a feminist theology to free both women and men and to open us to compassion and self-revelation amid a world that fears rebellion and liberation.

*

1284   Spretnak, Charlene, ed. *The Politics of Women's Spirituality.* New York: Doubleday Image, 1982.

The subtitle reads: "Essays on the Rise of Spiritual Power Within the Women's Movement." Includes essays by Starhawk, and others. See Carson **(991)**, item 636.

1285   Thistlethwaite, Susan Brooks. *Sex, Race, and God.*
       Christian Feminism in Black and White. New York:
       Crossroad, 1989.

This is a fascinating attempt by a white feminist
to reject all the props of her race and class when
talking of oppression and liberation. It is an attempt
to strip away the masks of intellectualizing discourse
and theology when discussing the role of women and
their place – in solidarity with and in domination
over women of the Third World and of the marginalized Fourth World.

Liberalism, the author contends, is the ideology
behind a racist feminism: a feminism that allows
women to attend conferences on oppression while black
and Hispanic maids take care of home. She therefore
concentrates on the experience of black women for
insights into a liberating theology that is based on
experience. At the same time she is painfully aware
that any critique of feminist theology will be used as
a weapon against feminism and women's struggles.

From a foundation in the thought and lives of
black women, she then goes on to discuss the role of
anger; the historical place of slavery in white feminism in issues of race, sex and class; and of solidarity
in the face of the liberal myth of the "individual."
Thistlethwaite then discusses some points of
divergence between black and white feminist theology, and one of convergence: violence against women.

The author also stresses that this was a book of
self-discovery, of unmasking her own immigrant, oppressed and working-class roots that the pursuit of
American "middle-class" life had obliterated.
Though she provides here a rich stock for self-
criticism – and handles for others to beat feminists
with – her work is a good example of feminist theol-

ogy that seeks to strike at the roots of meaning and existence.

1286 Trible, Phyllis. *God and the Rhetoric of Sexuality.* Philadelphia: Fortress Press, 1978.

See Ruud (1003), item 767.

1287 Vorster, W. S., ed. *Sexism and Feminism in Theological Perspective.* Pretoria, SA: University of South Africa, 1984.

Essays by C. Landman, F. Edwards, D. M. Ackermann, L. Q. Baqwa, S. Viljoen, L. C. Gerdes, with responses, on feminist theology, God from a feminist perspective, the role of women in the church, and women in South African society.

1288 Welch, Sharon D. *Communities of Resistance and Solidarity. A Feminist Theology of Liberation.* Maryknoll, NY: Orbis Books, 1985.

This is an attempt to outline the connections between feminist theology and other forms of "liberating" theologies, including liberation theology and black theology. It is written forthrightly from the author's ambiguous perspective of being both "oppressed" and "oppressor." The book is written from a "liberal" Protestant perspective that has come to see the dead end of this tradition in accounting for both the doubts of faith and the injustices of life.

Nihilism/relativism and oppression are the two poles of doing Welch's theology. Foucault's deconstructionism is the primary inspiration for her methodology; and, in fact, Foucault is quoted or dis-

cussed on nearly every page of this book, while the
Bible is hardly mentioned. This comes as no surprise
since, unlike the liberation theologians whom she
quotes (Gutiérrez, Sobrino, Cone) she dismisses any
theology that seeks to legitimize itself through
adherence to the Bible or the Christian tradition, in
fact, criticizing these theologians for doing so.

Part and parcel of this is the book's emphasis not
on the suffering, the poor, the experience of real
women as subjects of their own destiny but on the
thought of other theologians, psychologists, and social scientists. In fact, this book's emphasis upon the
discourse of reason, of truth, of knowledge rejects the
irrational, the transcendent, the primordial and the
eternal.

At the same time, Welch's emphasis on this
social-scientific and rational discourse lies at the
heart of the liberal Protestant tradition and not at
all at that of the black or Third-World theologians
she seeks to discuss here. Welch's emphasis on
liberation theology as a matter of "episteme" seems
to miss the point. Her assertion that "Christianity
has often been either repressive or quiescent" restates
the basic Lutheran position of Niebuhr and the will
to power of Nietzsche and seems to ignore the long
history of the struggle for liberation and justice that
is one of the hallmarks of the early, medieval and
early-modern churches. Latin American theologians
readily acknowledge this and draw hope and
inspiration from it as evidence of God working within
history; but Welch's liberal tradition may have over-
looked or have been ignorant of the historical value
of tradition because of its inherent categories of
historicized periods of decline and righteous reform
essential to the Protestant psyche.

1289   —. *A Feminist Ethic of Risk.* Philadelphia: Fortress
        Press, 1989.

This book grows out of Welch's concern with the
nuclear arms race and the threat that it poses to the
world and creation.   Above and beyond that, however, her analysis offers an exploration of the evil
effects of good intentions, of an ethic of control that
has brought the world to the verge of necrophilic
idolatry of death.

She counterpoises, instead, an ethic of risk that
draws on the insights of African-American women
who have created an ethic of resistance that is based
not only on critical analysis but on an awareness of
divine immanence found in the very active involvement with changing the world.   In this reflective
activism Welch finds a source of hope for the white,
middle-class, and affluent North American reduced to
despair by an ethic of tight control, of ever present
annihilation, and of complacency.

Chapters include narratives of healing and transformation, the ethic of control, memory and account-
ability, the heritage of persistence, imagination and
solidarity, the healing power of love, the ideology of
cultured despair, an ethic of solidarity and difference, and a theology of resistance and hope.

1290   Winter, Miriam Therese. *Woman Prayer. Woman
        Song. Resources for Ritual.* Oak Park, IL: Meyer
        Stone Books, 1987.

A series of prayers, songs, liturgies that are
divided into the rituals of: creation, liberation, and
transformation.   This collection seeks to uncover
women's connections to their past and their role in the

church both as reflections of the divine feminine and as agents of change

1291   —. *WomanWord. A Feminist Lectionary and Psalter. Woman of the New Testament.* New York: Crossroad/Continuum, 1990.

Not seen.

1292   *WomanSpirit.*

The first of the magazines devoted to feminist spirituality.

1293   Wren, Brian. *What Language Shall I Borrow? God-Talk in Worship. A Male Response to Feminist Theology.* New York: Crossroad/Continuum, 1989.

Really a male's appreciation of the work of Ruether, McFague and other feminist theologians to the issues of theology ("God-talk") and the patriarchal forms in which this talk goes on in everything from formal theology to liturgy. Wren maintains that the names and metaphors we use to describe God can evolve to meet the new insights brought by feminist theology while they continue to enrich the religious tradition.

Wren himself is a hymn writer whose work focuses on the lives of the marginalized and the oppressed; and he publishes many of his new versions that speak of the need of liberation and that talk of God without sexist language.

1294   Young, Pamela Dickey. *Feminist Theology. Christian Theology. In Search of Method.* Minneapolis, MN: Fortress Press, 1990.

Not seen.

1295 Zola, Elemire. *The Androgyne.* New York: Crossroad, 1989.

The mythological, artistic and historical roots of our gender-alienated forms of spirituality and the revolutions brought about by seeking a more androgynous definition of humanity and divinity.

* *
*

Index of Titles

537

Index of Authors and Editors

Typesetting and Design of This
Book Was Completed on
January 18, 1991
at Italica Press,
New York,
NY
*